INVISIBLE LOVE

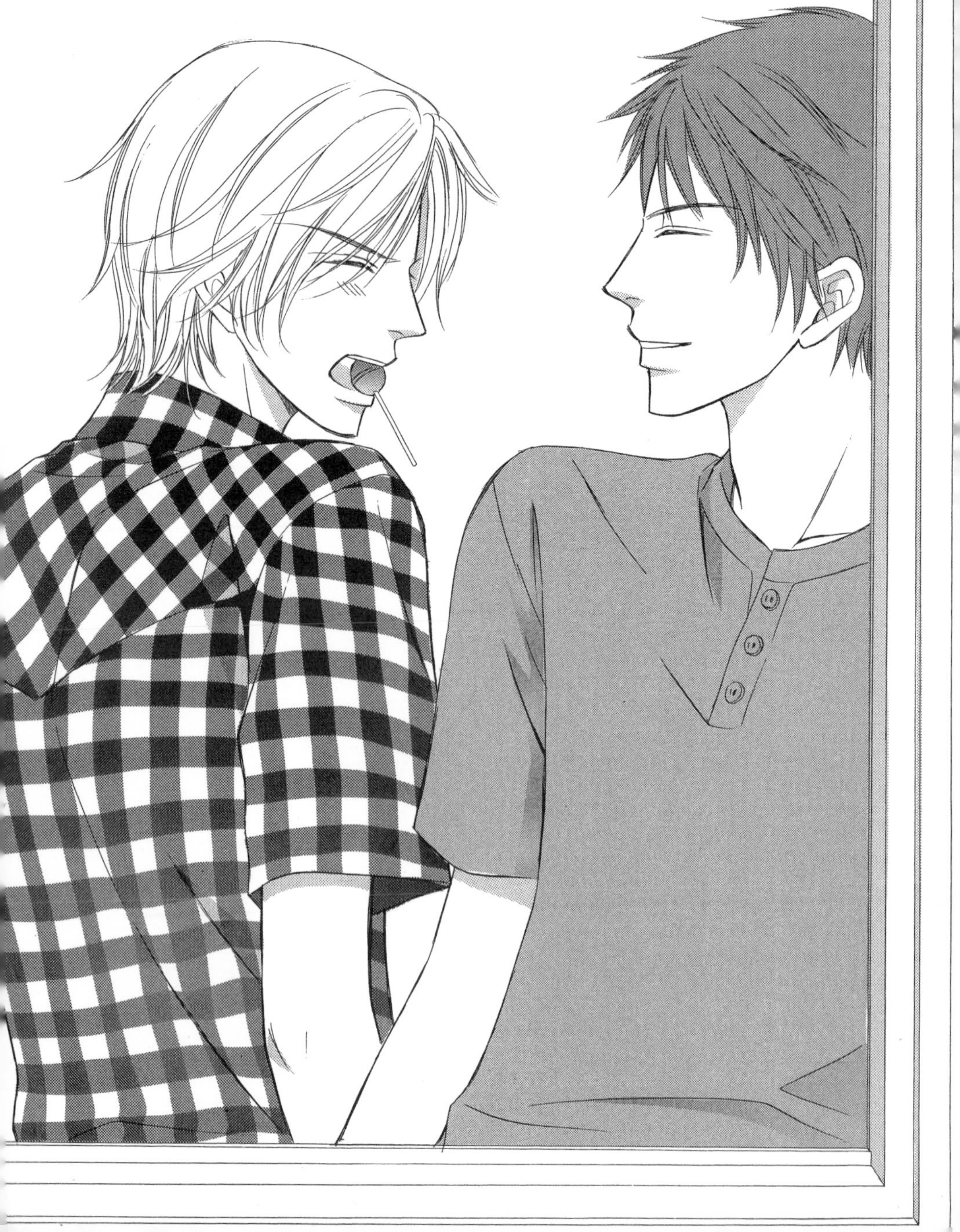

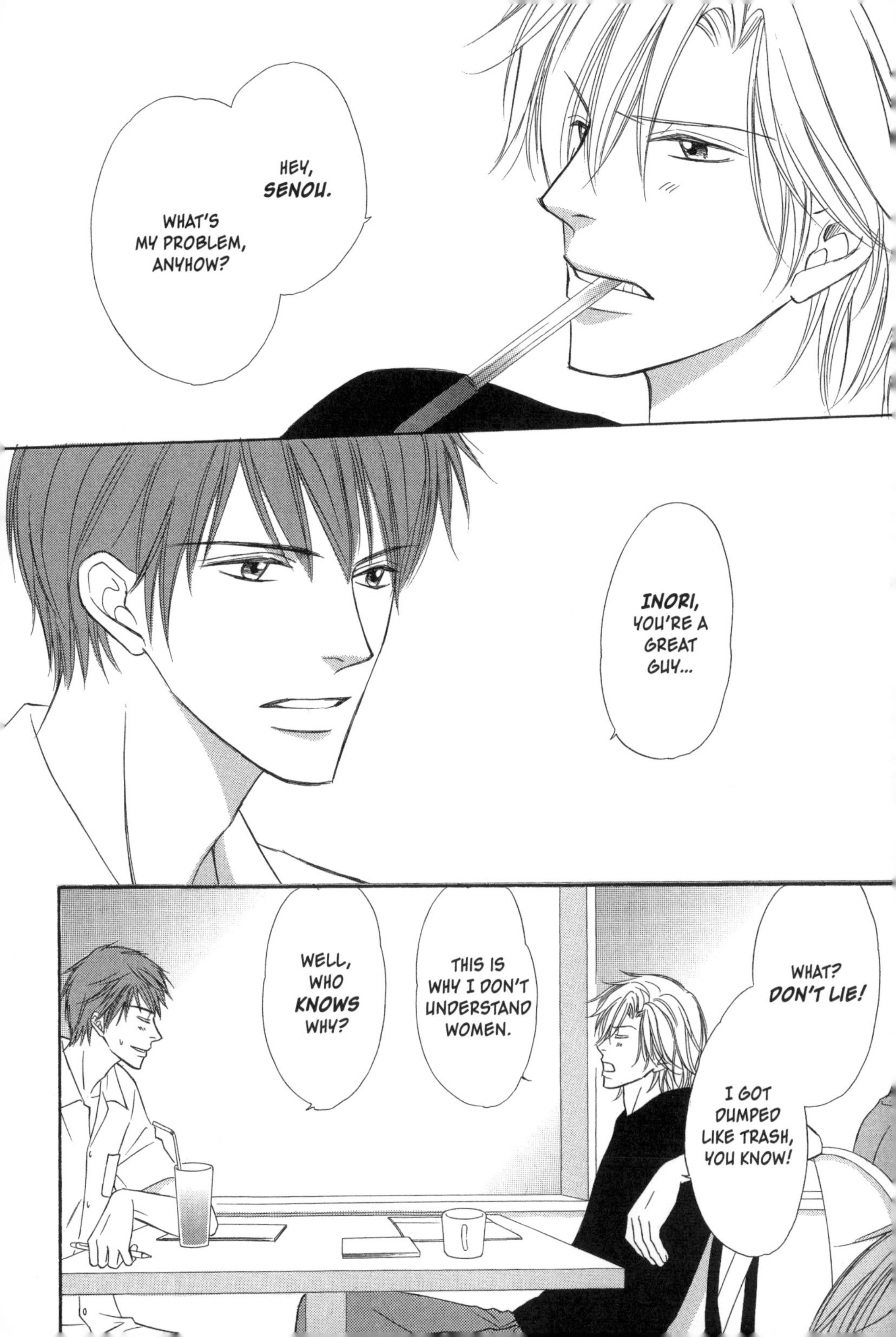
HEY, SENOU.
WHAT'S MY PROBLEM, ANYHOW?
INORI, YOU'RE A GREAT GUY...
WHAT? DON'T LIE!
I GOT DUMPED LIKE TRASH, YOU KNOW!
THIS IS WHY I DON'T UNDERSTAND WOMEN.
WELL, WHO KNOWS WHY?

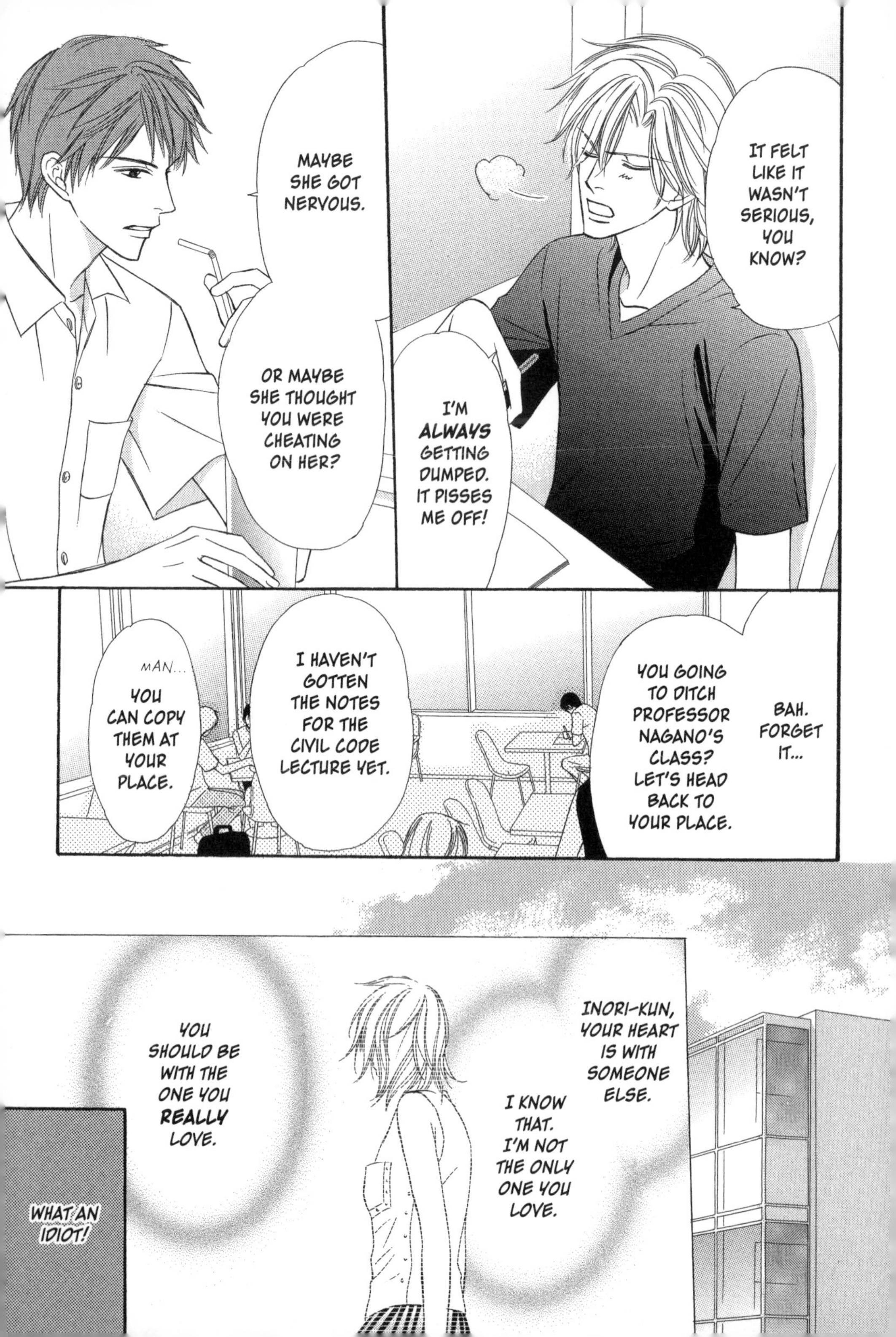
IT FELT LIKE IT WASN'T SERIOUS, YOU KNOW?
I'M ALWAYS GETTING DUMPED. IT PISSES ME OFF!
MAYBE SHE GOT NERVOUS.
OR MAYBE SHE THOUGHT YOU WERE CHEATING ON HER?
BAH. FORGET IT...
YOU GOING TO DITCH PROFESSOR NAGANO'S CLASS? LET'S HEAD BACK TO YOUR PLACE.
I HAVEN'T GOTTEN THE NOTES FOR THE CIVIL CODE LECTURE YET.
MAN... YOU CAN COPY THEM AT YOUR PLACE.
INORI-KUN, YOUR HEART IS WITH SOMEONE ELSE.
I KNOW THAT. I'M NOT THE ONLY ONE YOU LOVE.
YOU SHOULD BE WITH THE ONE YOU REALLY LOVE.
WHAT AN IDIOT!

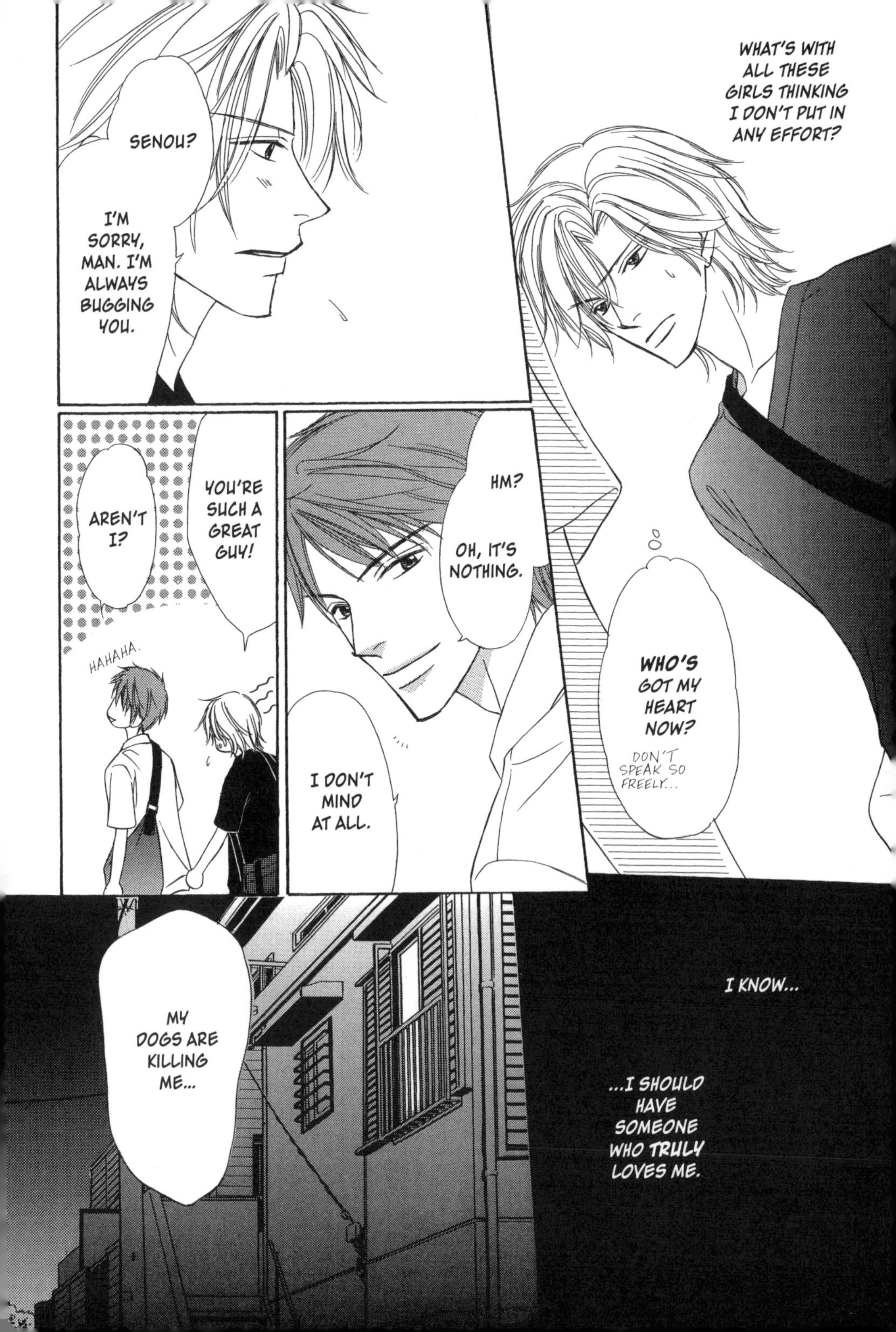
WHAT'S WITH ALL THESE GIRLS THINKING I DON'T PUT IN ANY EFFORT?
WHO'S GOT MY HEART NOW?
DON'T SPEAK SO FREELY...
SENOU?
I'M SORRY, MAN. I'M ALWAYS BUGGING YOU.
HM?
OH, IT'S NOTHING.
I DON'T MIND AT ALL.
YOU'RE SUCH A GREAT GUY!
AREN'T I?
HAHAHA.
I KNOW...
...I SHOULD HAVE SOMEONE WHO TRULY LOVES ME.
MY DOGS ARE KILLING ME...

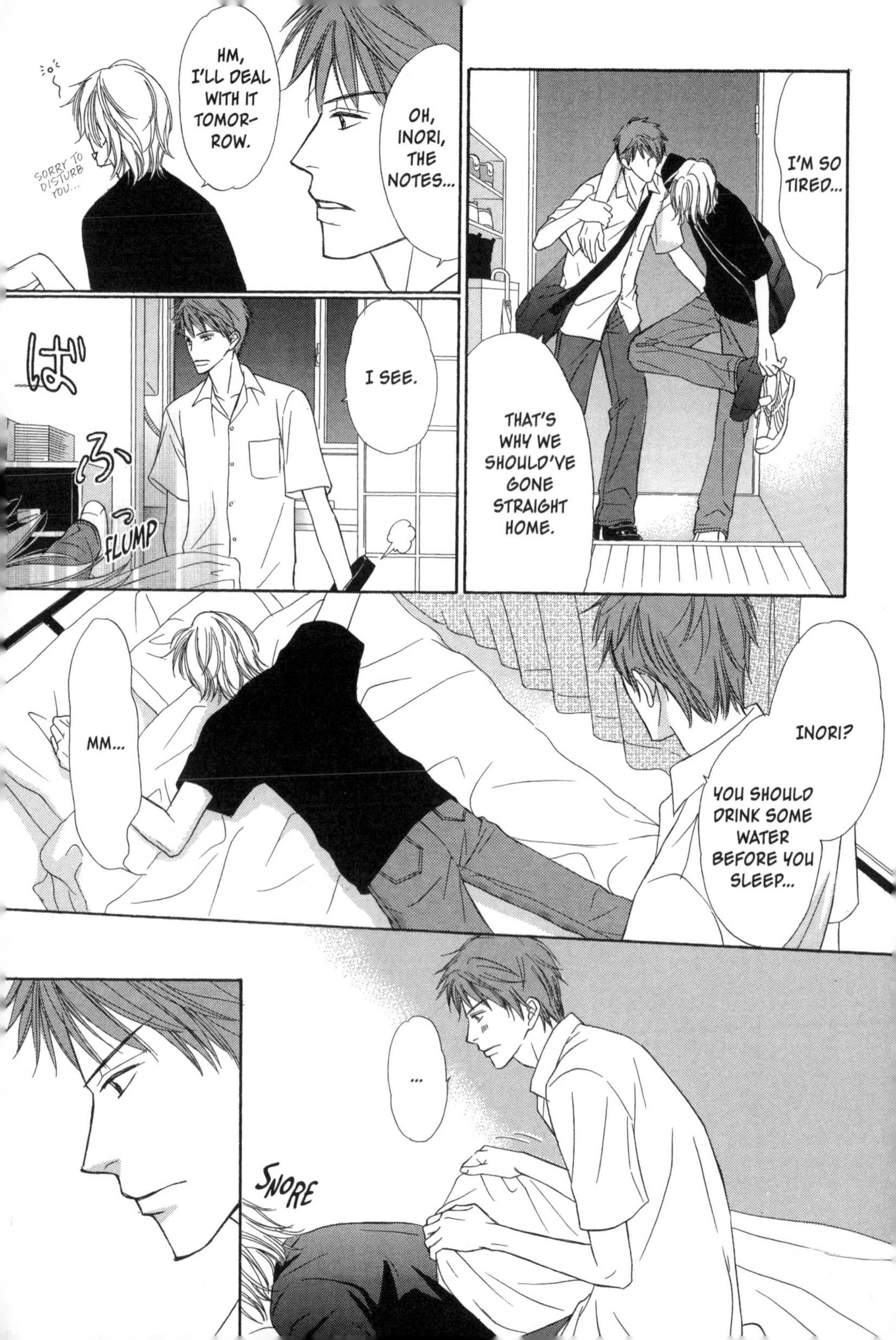
I'M SO TIRED...
THAT'S WHY WE SHOULD'VE GONE STRAIGHT HOME.
OH, INORI, THE NOTES...
HM, I'LL DEAL WITH IT TOMORROW.
SORRY TO DISTURB YOU...
I SEE.
ばふっ
FLUMP
INORI?
YOU SHOULD DRINK SOME WATER BEFORE YOU SLEEP...
MM...
...
SNORE

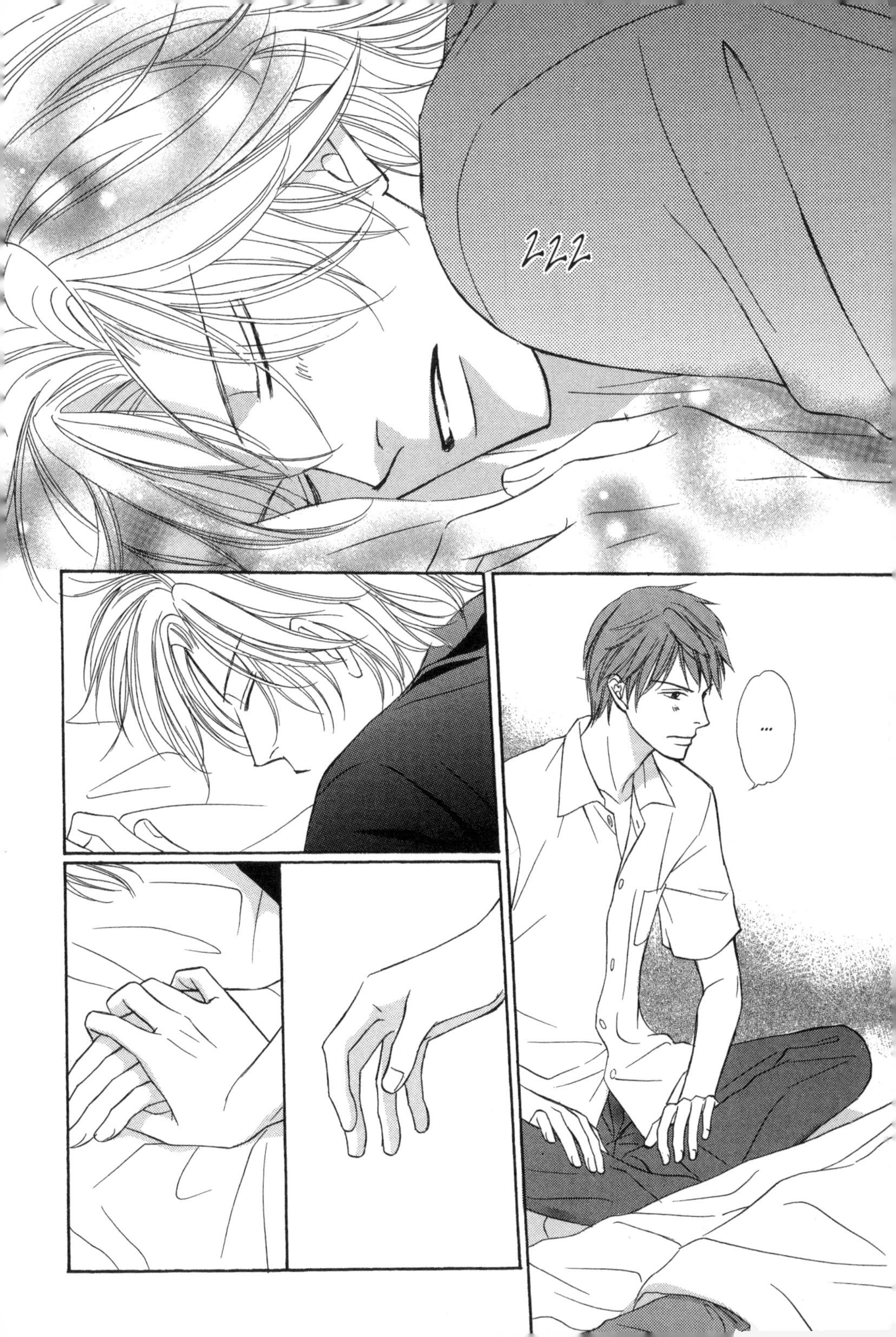
zzz
...

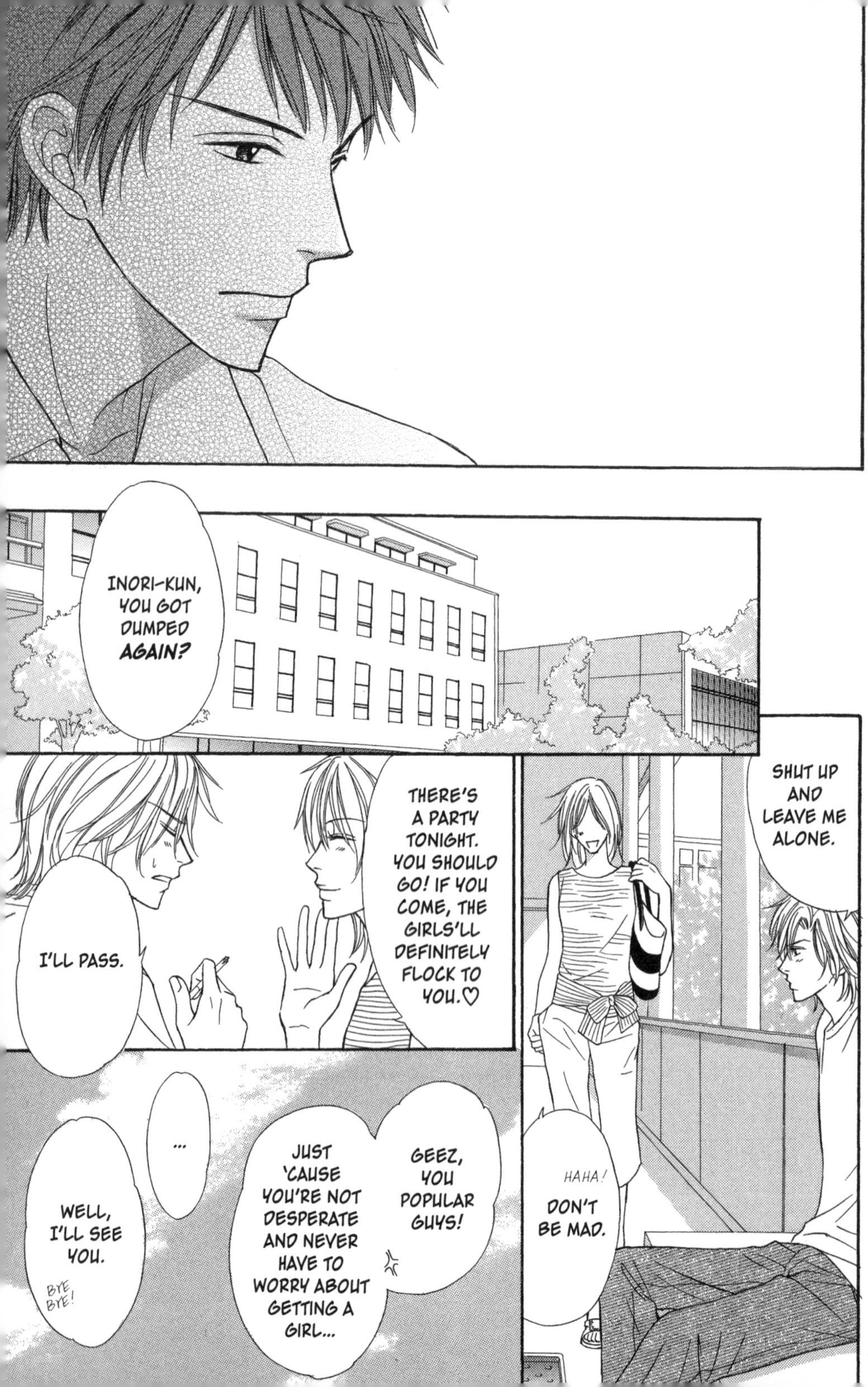
INORI-KUN, YOU GOT DUMPED AGAIN?
SHUT UP AND LEAVE ME ALONE.
HAHA!
DON'T BE MAD.
THERE'S A PARTY TONIGHT. YOU SHOULD GO! IF YOU COME, THE GIRLS'LL DEFINITELY FLOCK TO YOU.♡
I'LL PASS.
GEEZ, YOU POPULAR GUYS!
JUST 'CAUSE YOU'RE NOT DESPERATE AND NEVER HAVE TO WORRY ABOUT GETTING A GIRL...
...
WELL, I'LL SEE YOU.
BYE BYE!

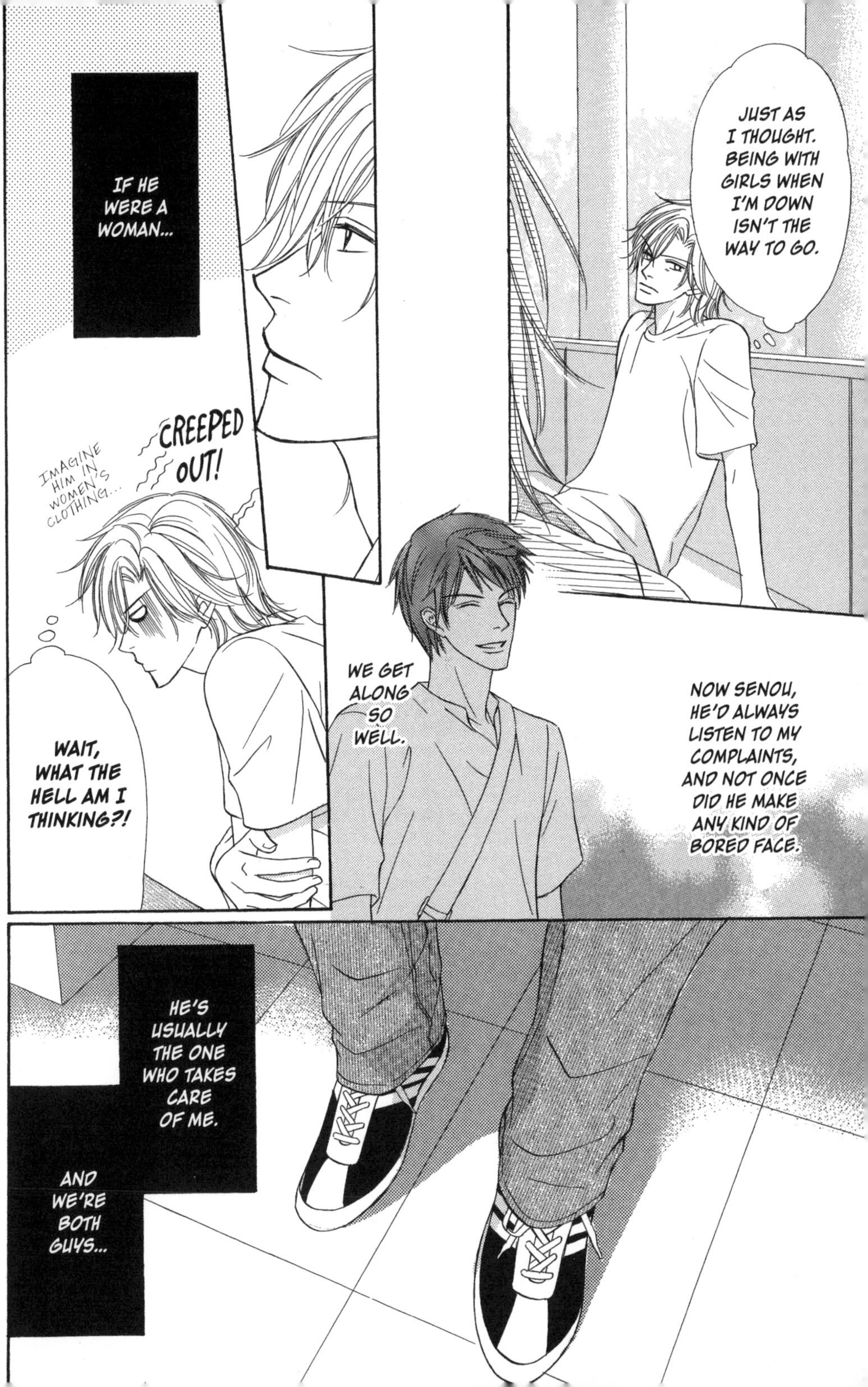
JUST AS I THOUGHT. BEING WITH GIRLS WHEN I'M DOWN ISN'T THE WAY TO GO.
NOW SENOU, HE'D ALWAYS LISTEN TO MY COMPLAINTS, AND NOT ONCE DID HE MAKE ANY KIND OF BORED FACE.
WE GET ALONG SO WELL.
IF HE WERE A WOMAN...
CREEPED OUT!
IMAGINE HIM IN WOMEN'S CLOTHING...
WAIT, WHAT THE HELL AM I THINKING?!
HE'S USUALLY THE ONE WHO TAKES CARE OF ME.
AND WE'RE BOTH GUYS...

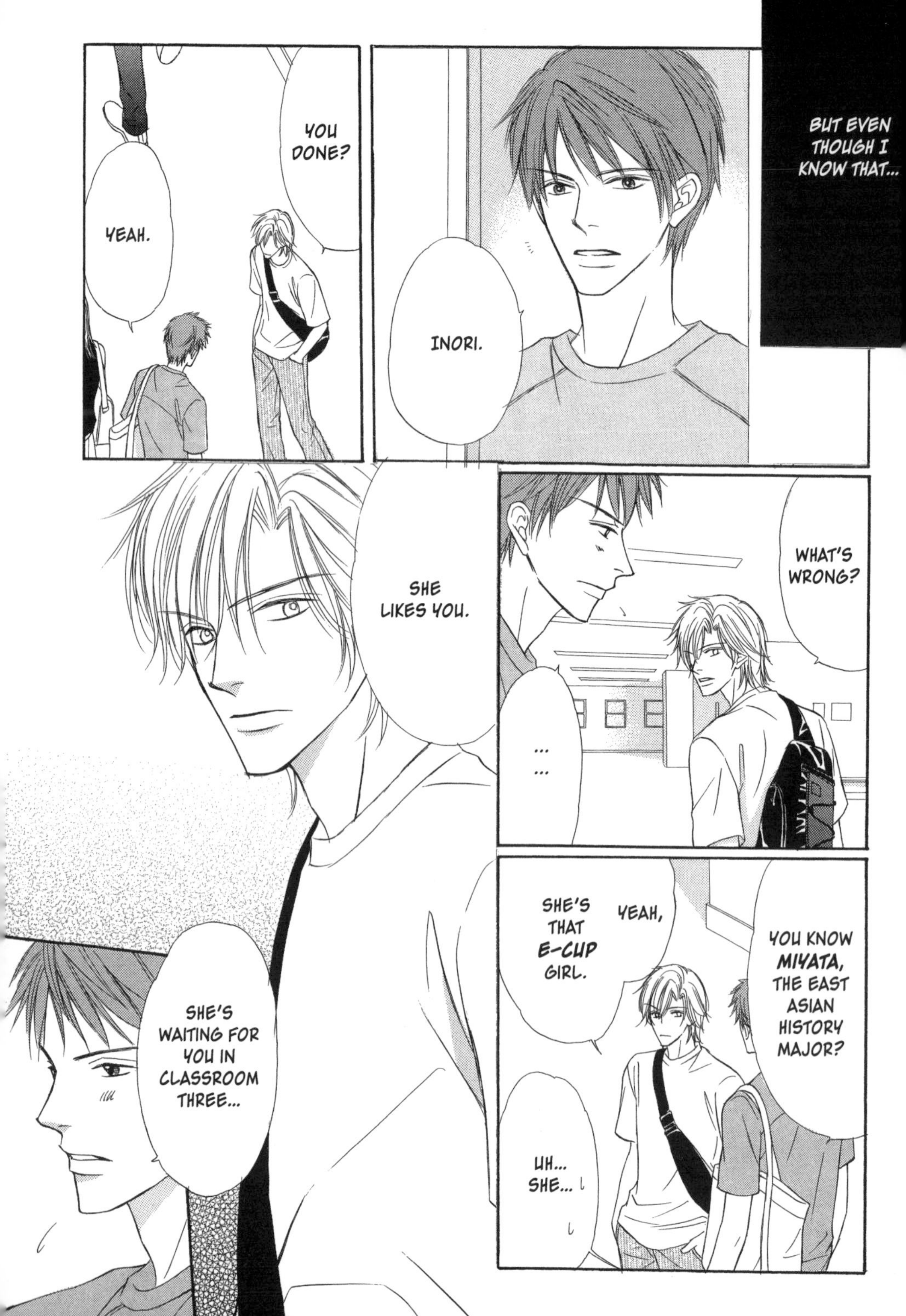
BUT EVEN THOUGH I KNOW THAT...
INORI.
YOU DONE?
YEAH.
WHAT'S WRONG?
... ...
YOU KNOW MIYATA, THE EAST ASIAN HISTORY MAJOR?
YEAH,
SHE'S THAT E-CUP GIRL.
UH... SHE...
SHE LIKES YOU.
SHE'S WAITING FOR YOU IN CLASSROOM THREE...

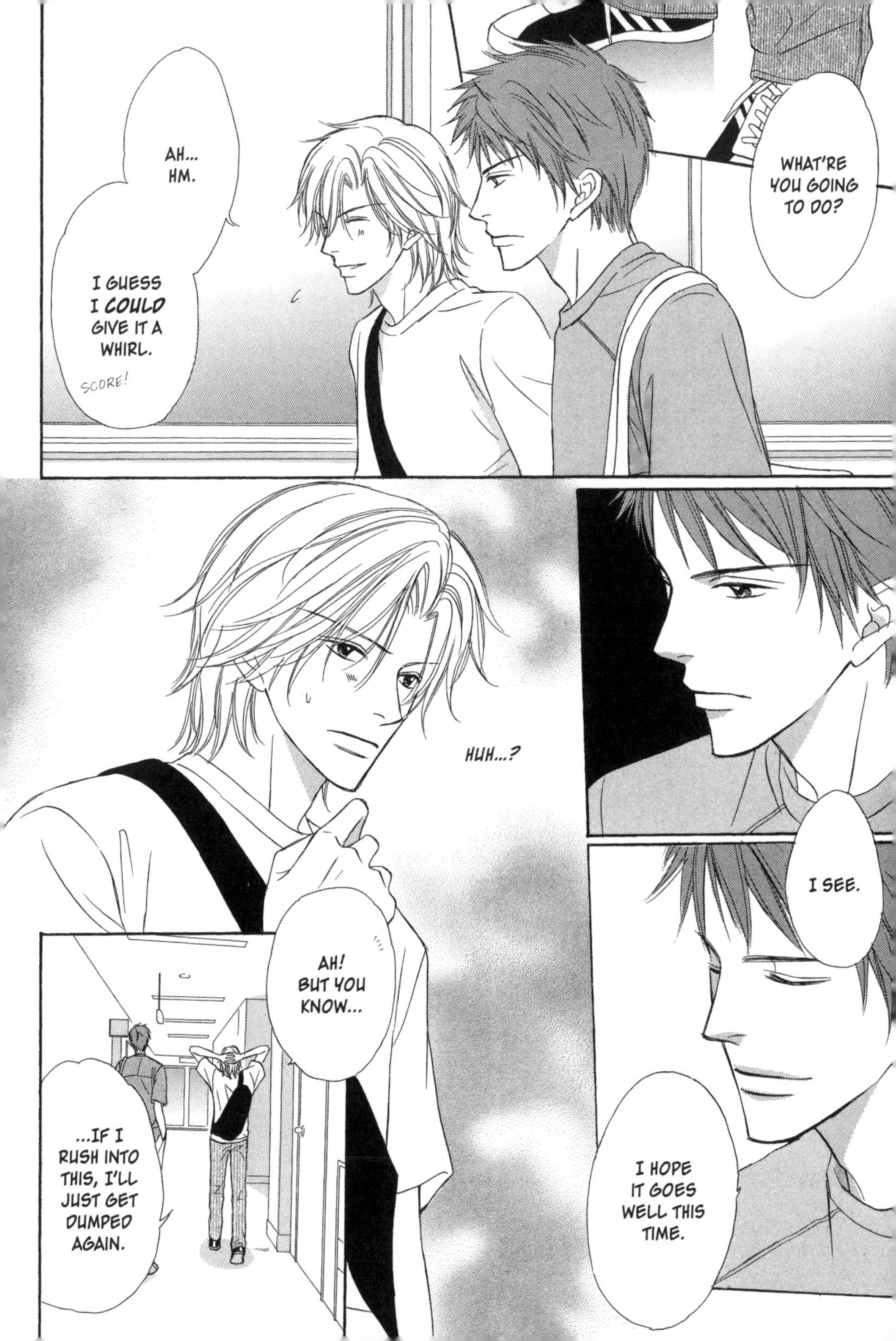
WHAT'RE YOU GOING TO DO?
AH... HM.
I GUESS I **COULD** GIVE IT A WHIRL.
SCORE!
HUH...?
I SEE.
I HOPE IT GOES WELL THIS TIME.
AH! BUT YOU KNOW...
...IF I RUSH INTO THIS, I'LL JUST GET DUMPED AGAIN.

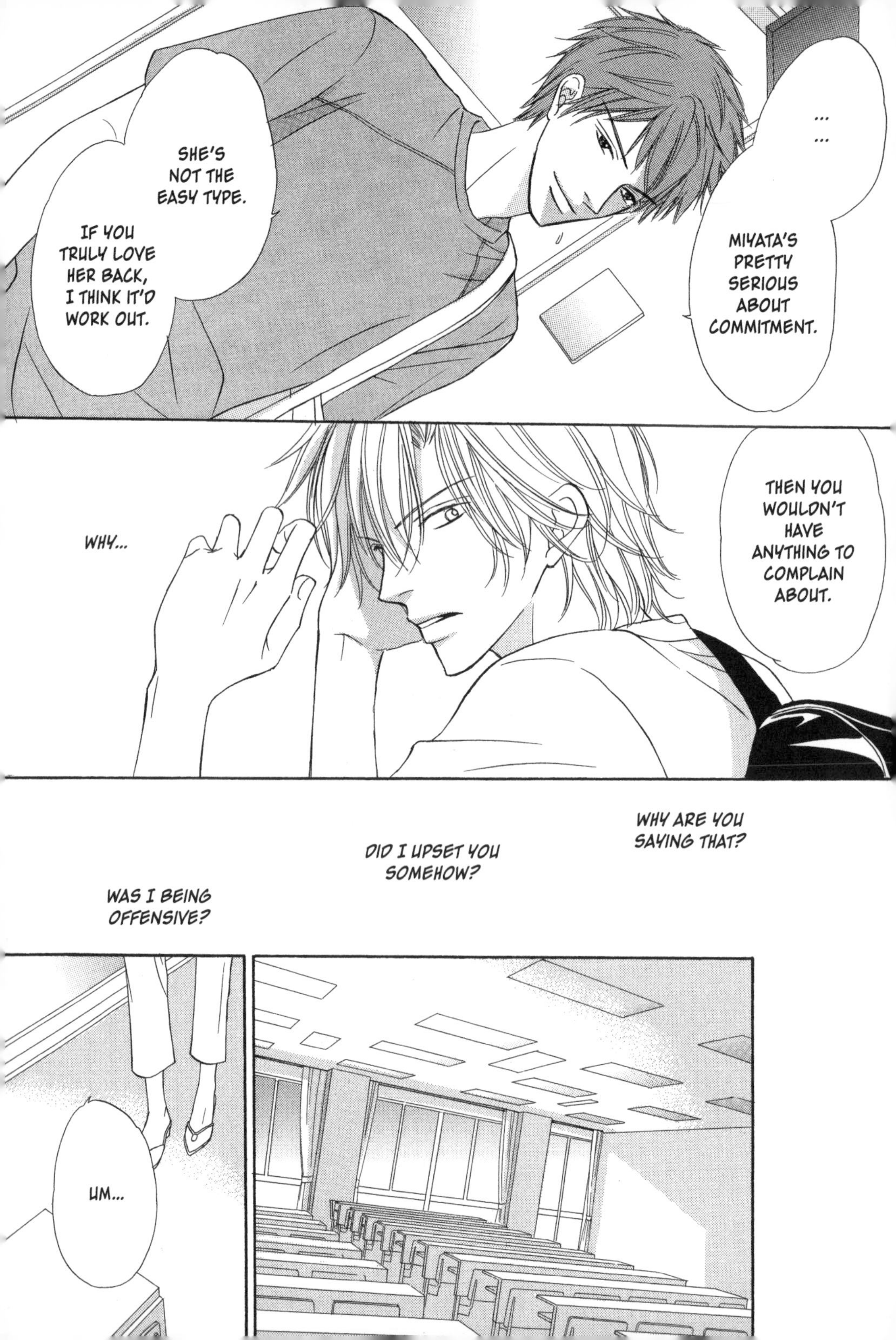
……
MIYATA'S PRETTY SERIOUS ABOUT COMMITMENT.
SHE'S NOT THE EASY TYPE.
IF YOU TRULY LOVE HER BACK, I THINK IT'D WORK OUT.
THEN YOU WOULDN'T HAVE ANYTHING TO COMPLAIN ABOUT.
WHY...
WHY ARE YOU SAYING THAT?
DID I UPSET YOU SOMEHOW?
WAS I BEING OFFENSIVE?
UM...

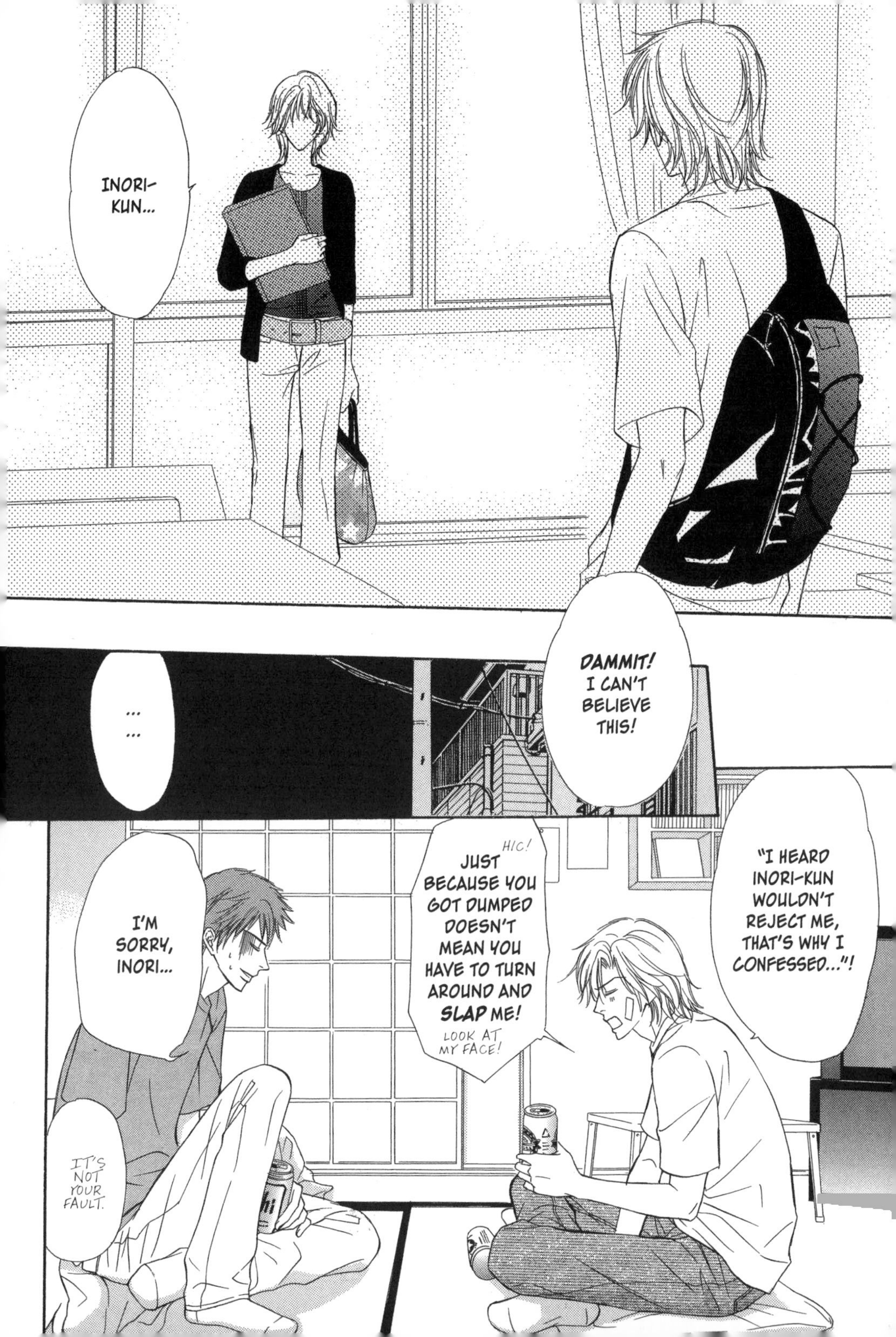
INORI-KUN...
DAMMIT! I CAN'T BELIEVE THIS!
... ...
"I HEARD INORI-KUN WOULDN'T REJECT ME, THAT'S WHY I CONFESSED..."!
HIC!
JUST BECAUSE YOU GOT DUMPED DOESN'T MEAN YOU HAVE TO TURN AROUND AND SLAP ME!
LOOK AT MY FACE!
I'M SORRY, INORI...
IT'S NOT YOUR FAULT.

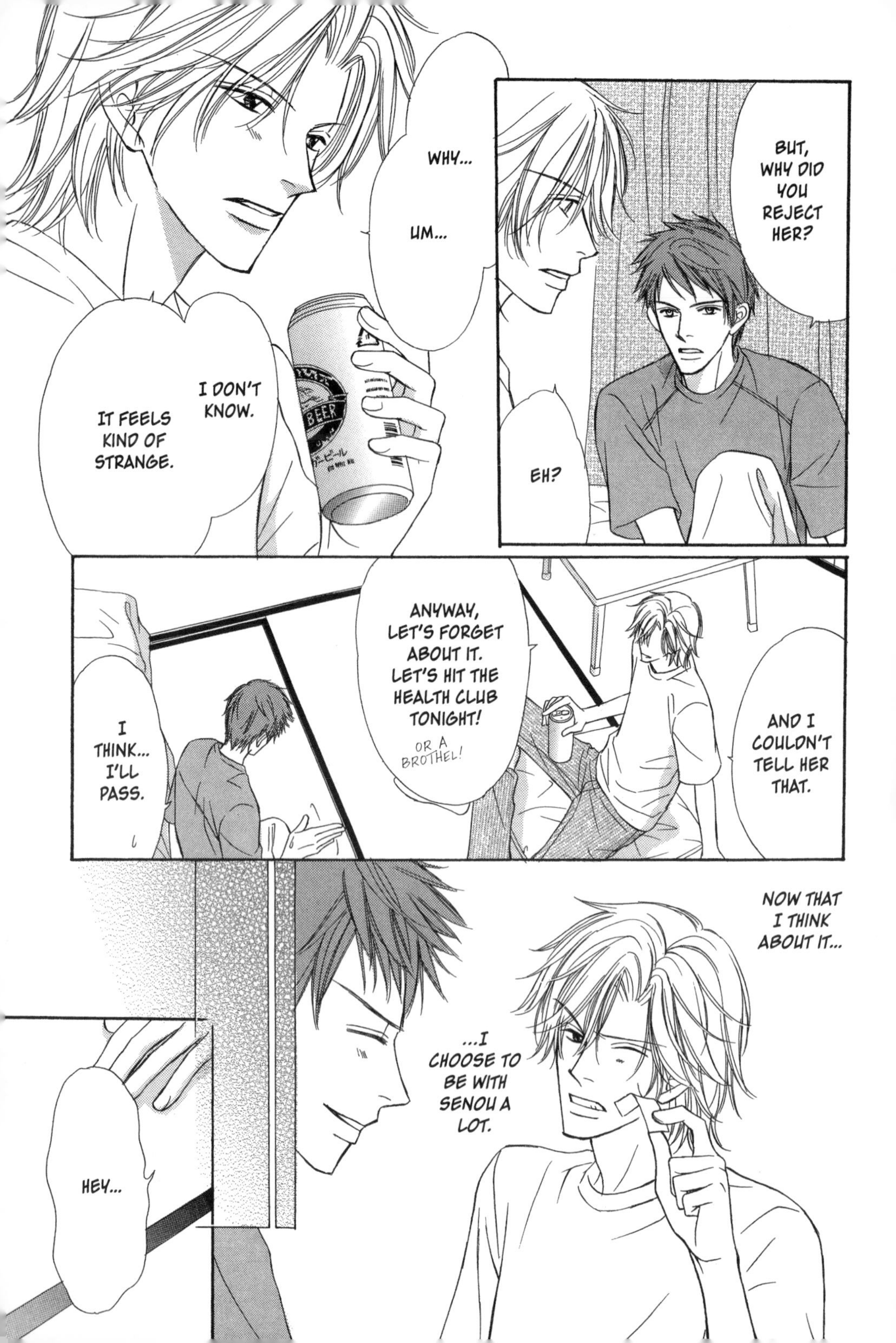
BUT, WHY DID YOU REJECT HER?
EH?
WHY...
UM...
I DON'T KNOW.
IT FEELS KIND OF STRANGE.
AND I COULDN'T TELL HER THAT.
ANYWAY, LET'S FORGET ABOUT IT. LET'S HIT THE HEALTH CLUB TONIGHT!
OR A BROTHEL!
I THINK... I'LL PASS.
NOW THAT I THINK ABOUT IT...
...I CHOOSE TO BE WITH SENOU A LOT.
HEY...

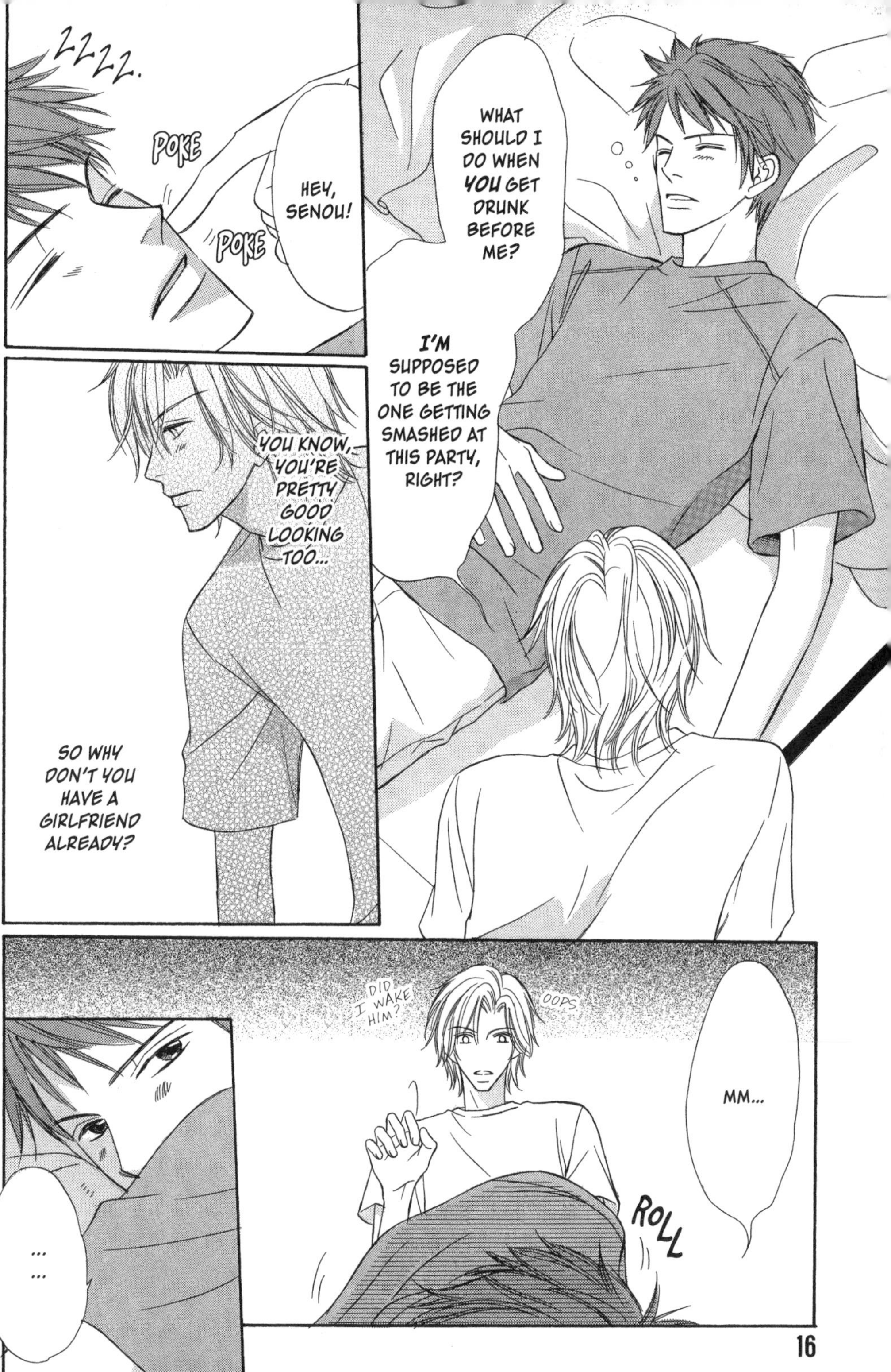
WHAT SHOULD I DO WHEN YOU GET DRUNK BEFORE ME?
I'M SUPPOSED TO BE THE ONE GETTING SMASHED AT THIS PARTY, RIGHT?
ZZZZ.
POKE
POKE
HEY, SENOU!
YOU KNOW, YOU'RE PRETTY GOOD LOOKING TOO...
SO WHY DON'T YOU HAVE A GIRLFRIEND ALREADY?
MM...
OOPS.
DID I WAKE HIM?
ROLL
... ...

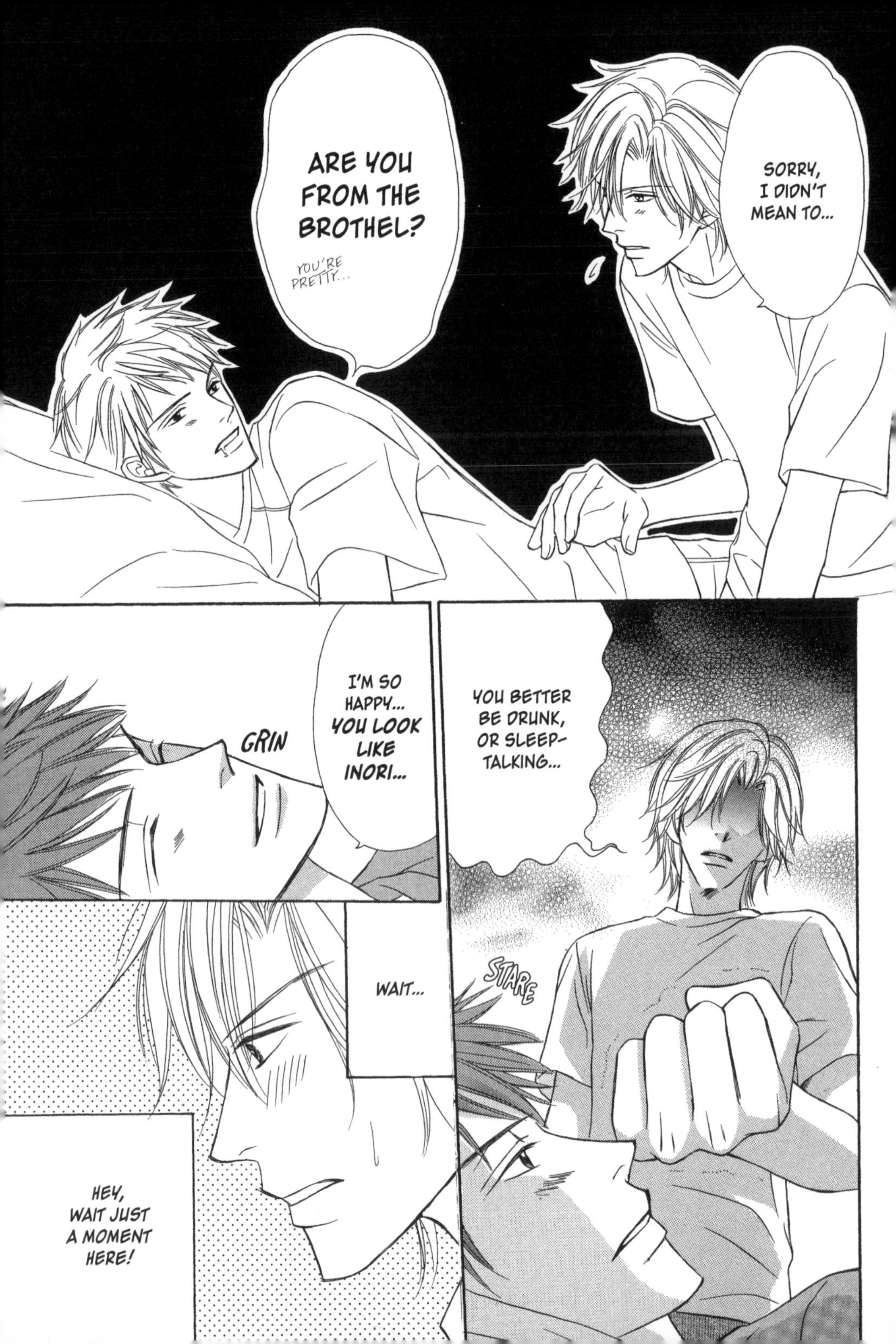
SORRY, I DIDN'T MEAN TO...
ARE YOU FROM THE BROTHEL?
YOU'RE PRETTY...
YOU BETTER BE DRUNK, OR SLEEP-TALKING...
STARE
I'M SO HAPPY... YOU LOOK LIKE INORI...
GRIN
WAIT...
HEY, WAIT JUST A MOMENT HERE!

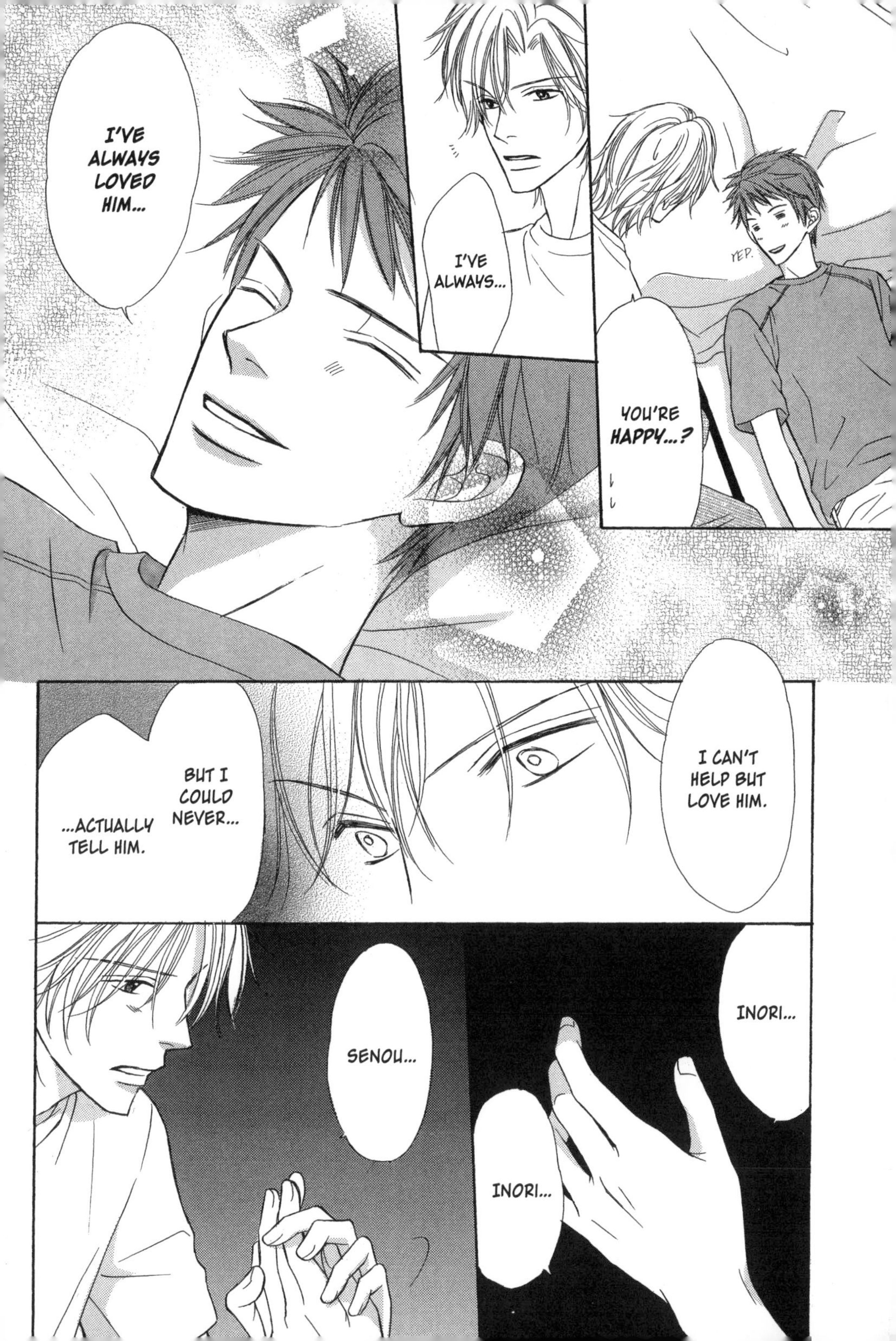
YEP.
YOU'RE HAPPY...?
I'VE ALWAYS...
I'VE ALWAYS LOVED HIM...
I CAN'T HELP BUT LOVE HIM.
BUT I COULD NEVER...
...ACTUALLY TELL HIM.
INORI...
INORI...
SENOU...

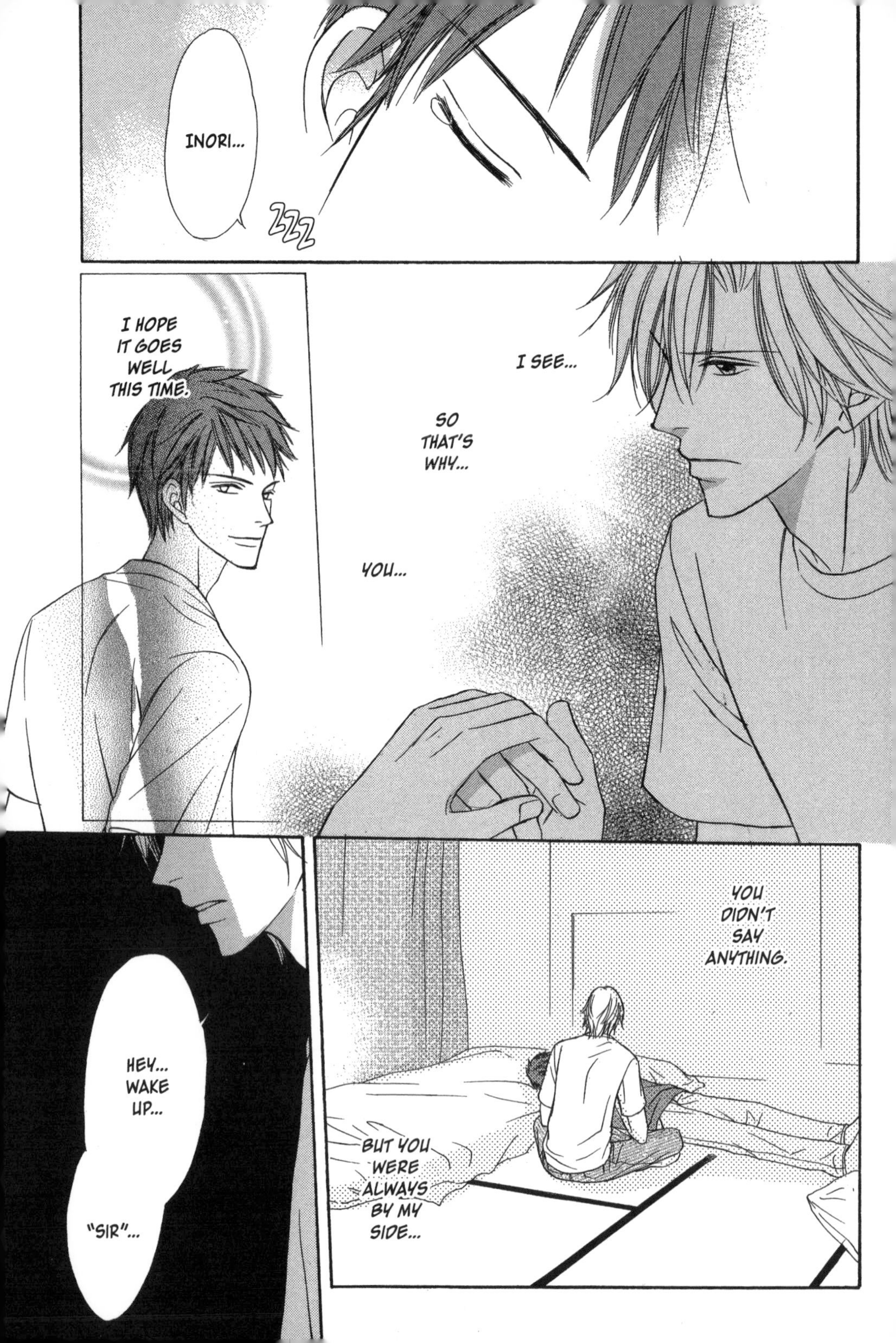
INORI...
ZZZ
I SEE...
SO THAT'S WHY...
YOU...
I HOPE IT GOES WELL THIS TIME.
YOU DIDN'T SAY ANYTHING.
BUT YOU WERE ALWAYS BY MY SIDE...
HEY... WAKE UP...
"SIR"...

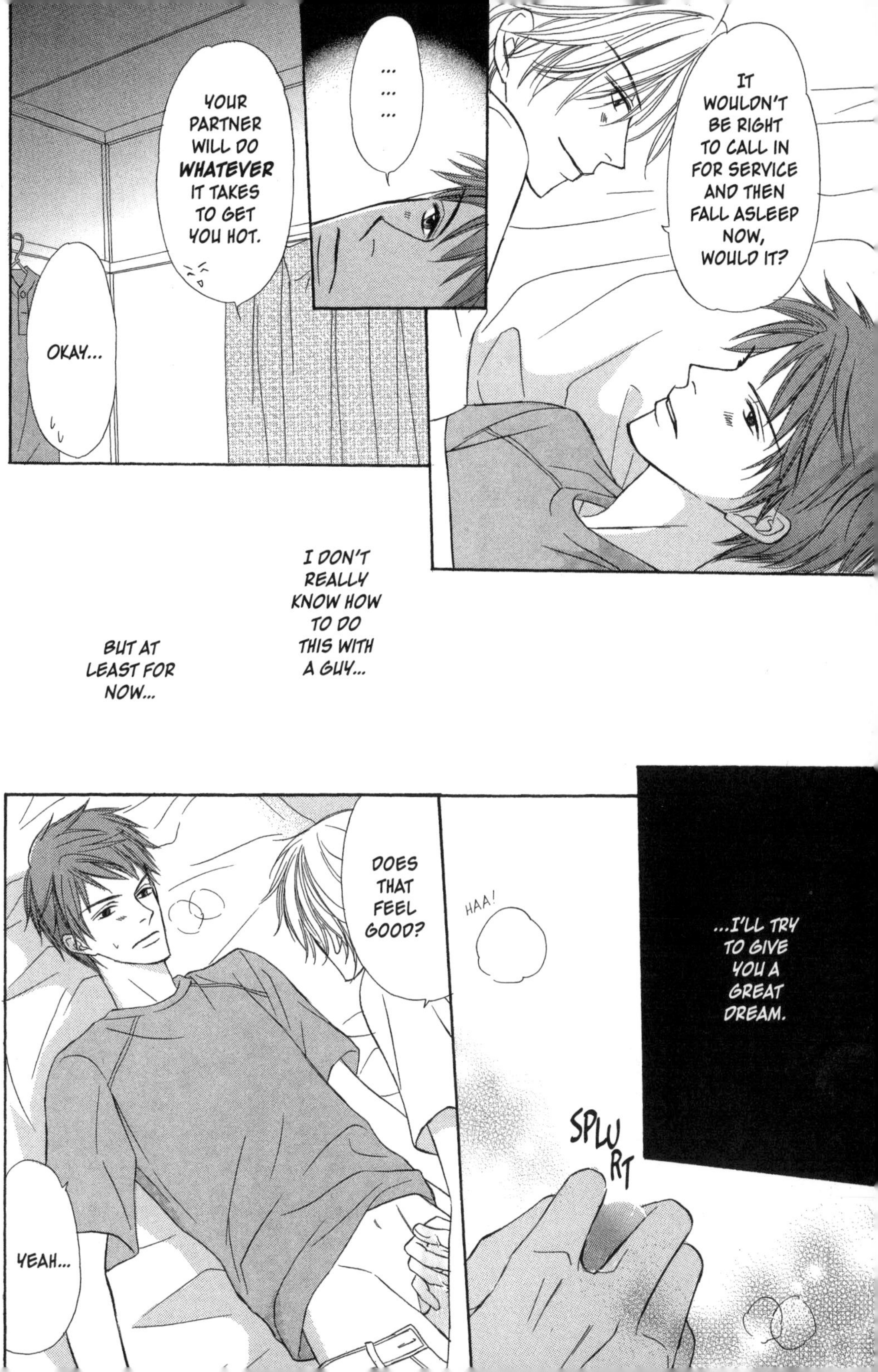
IT WOULDN'T BE RIGHT TO CALL IN FOR SERVICE AND THEN FALL ASLEEP NOW, WOULD IT?
... ...
YOUR PARTNER WILL DO **WHATEVER** IT TAKES TO GET YOU HOT.
OKAY...
I DON'T REALLY KNOW HOW TO DO THIS WITH A GUY...
BUT AT LEAST FOR NOW...
...I'LL TRY TO GIVE YOU A GREAT DREAM.
HAA!
SPLURT
DOES THAT FEEL GOOD?
YEAH...

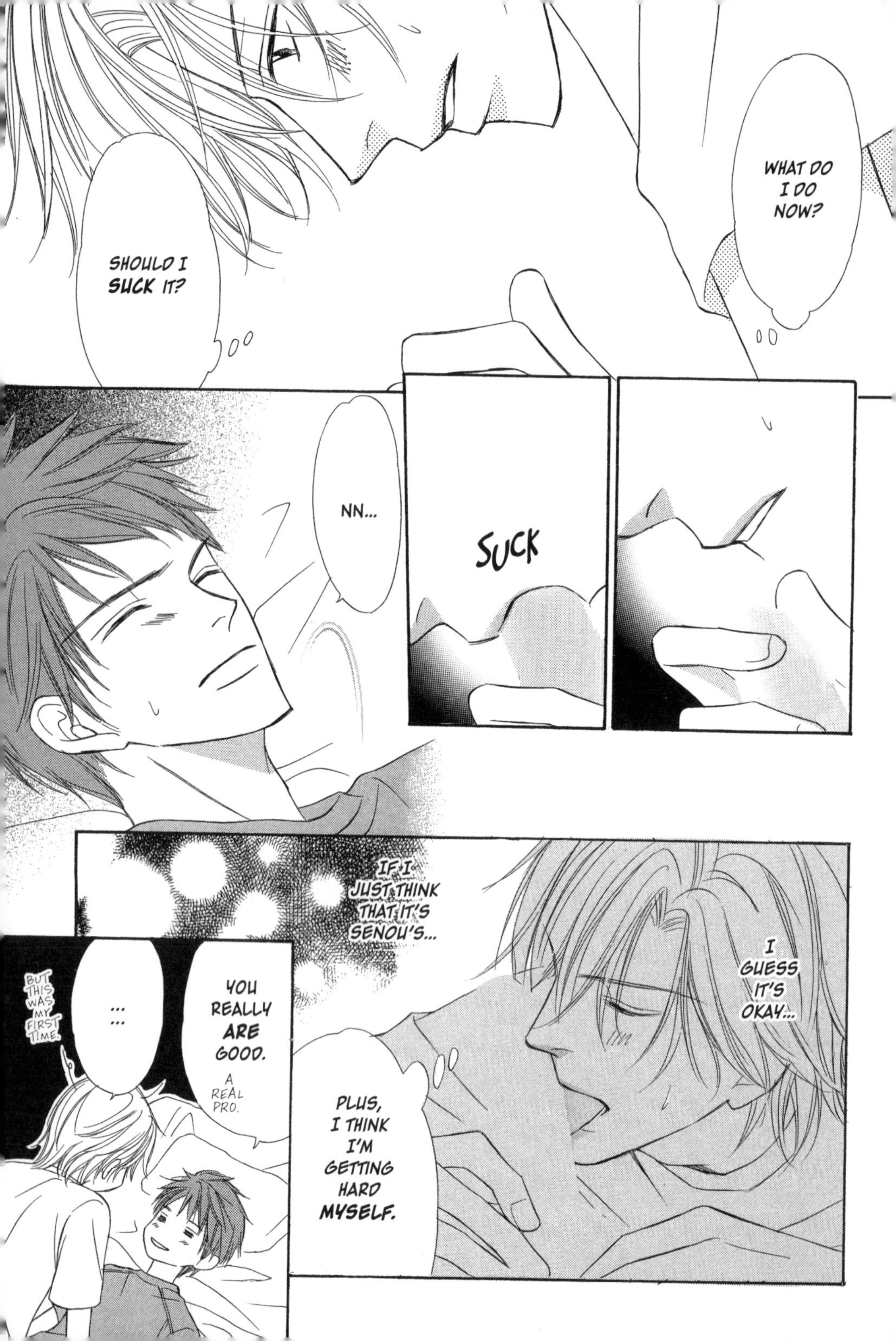
WHAT DO I DO NOW?
SHOULD I SUCK IT?
SUCK
NN...
IF I JUST THINK THAT IT'S SENOU'S...
I GUESS IT'S OKAY...
PLUS, I THINK I'M GETTING HARD MYSELF.
YOU REALLY ARE GOOD.
A REAL PRO.
... ...
BUT THIS WAS MY FIRST TIME.

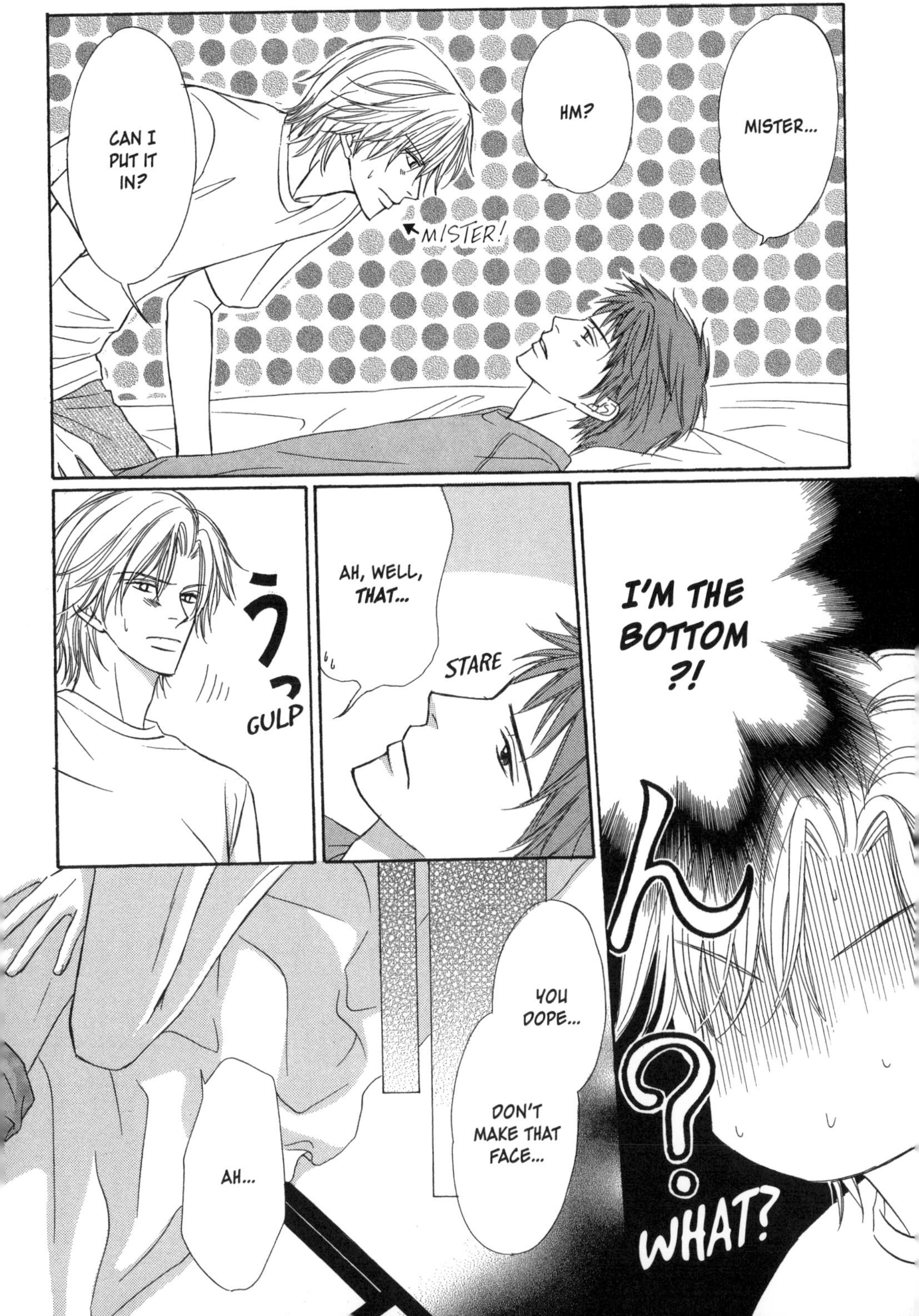
MISTER...
HM?
MISTER!
CAN I PUT IT IN?
I'M THE BOTTOM ?!
ん？
WHAT?
AH, WELL, THAT...
STARE
うっ
GULP
YOU DOPE...
DON'T MAKE THAT FACE...
AH...

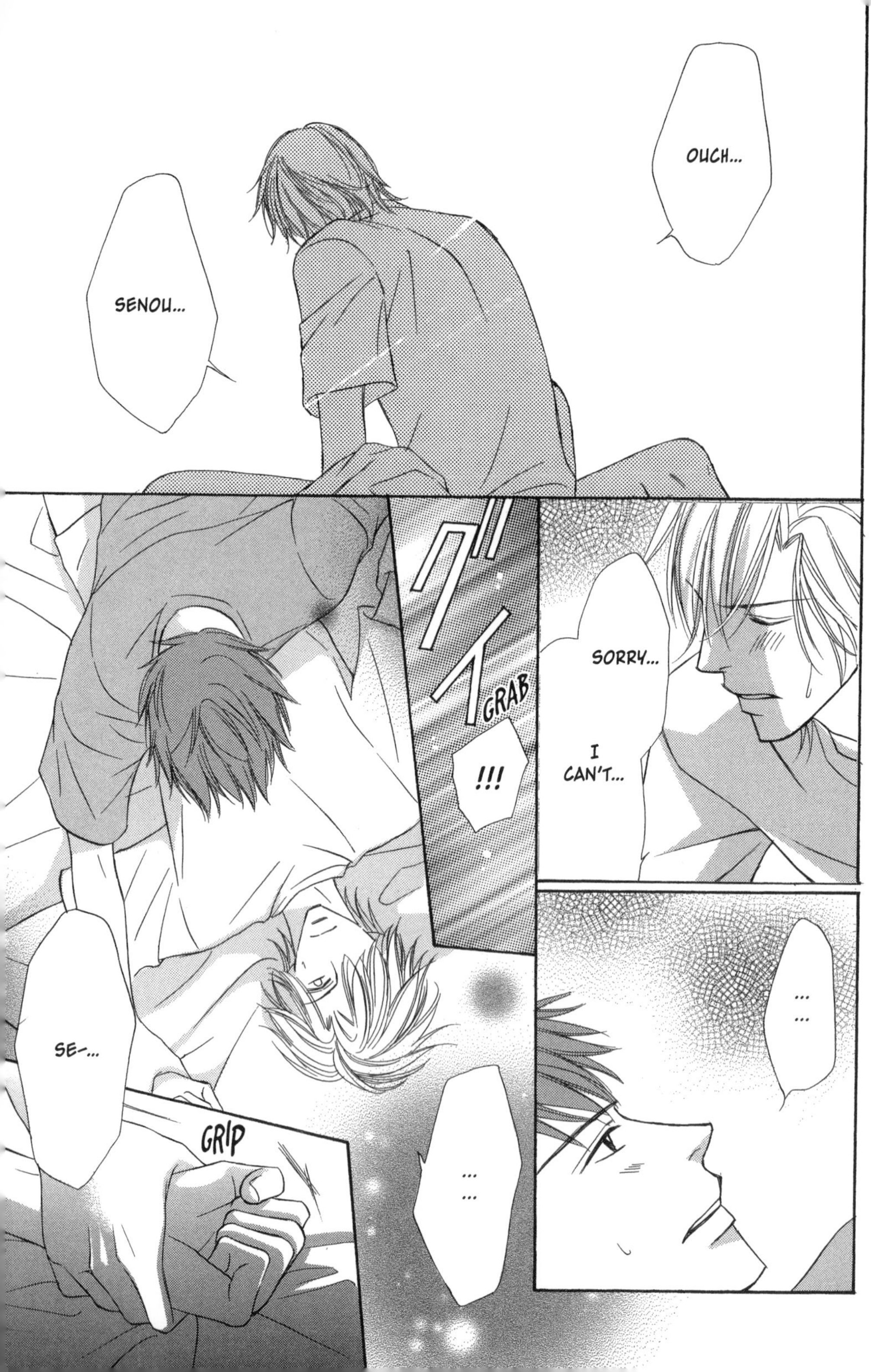
OUCH...
SENOU...
SORRY...
I CAN'T...
......
グイ
GRAB
!!!
SE-...
GRIP
......

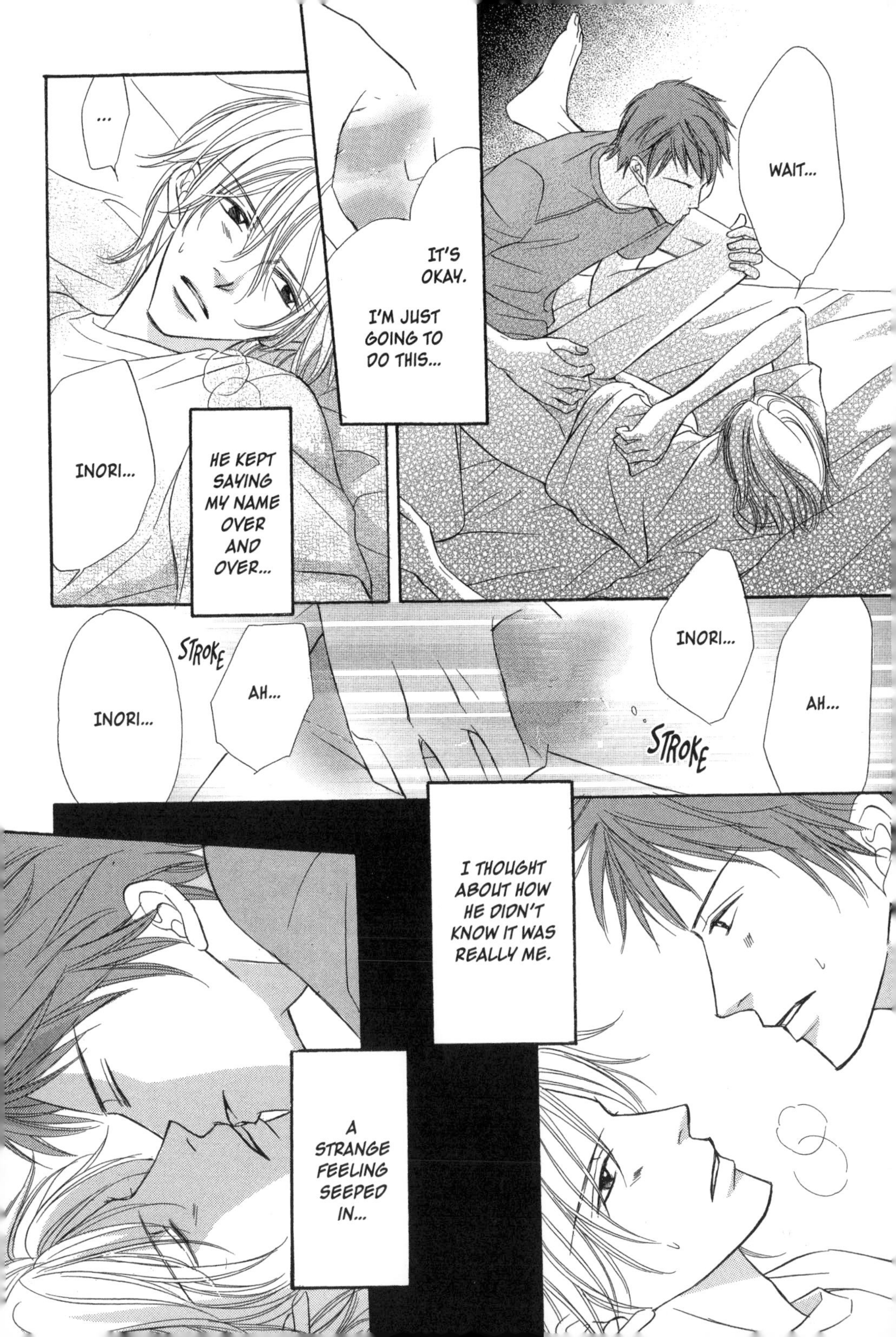
WAIT...
IT'S OKAY.
I'M JUST GOING TO DO THIS...
...
INORI...
HE KEPT SAYING MY NAME OVER AND OVER...
AH...
INORI...
STROKE
AH...
STROKE
INORI...
I THOUGHT ABOUT HOW HE DIDN'T KNOW IT WAS REALLY ME.
A STRANGE FEELING SEEPED IN...

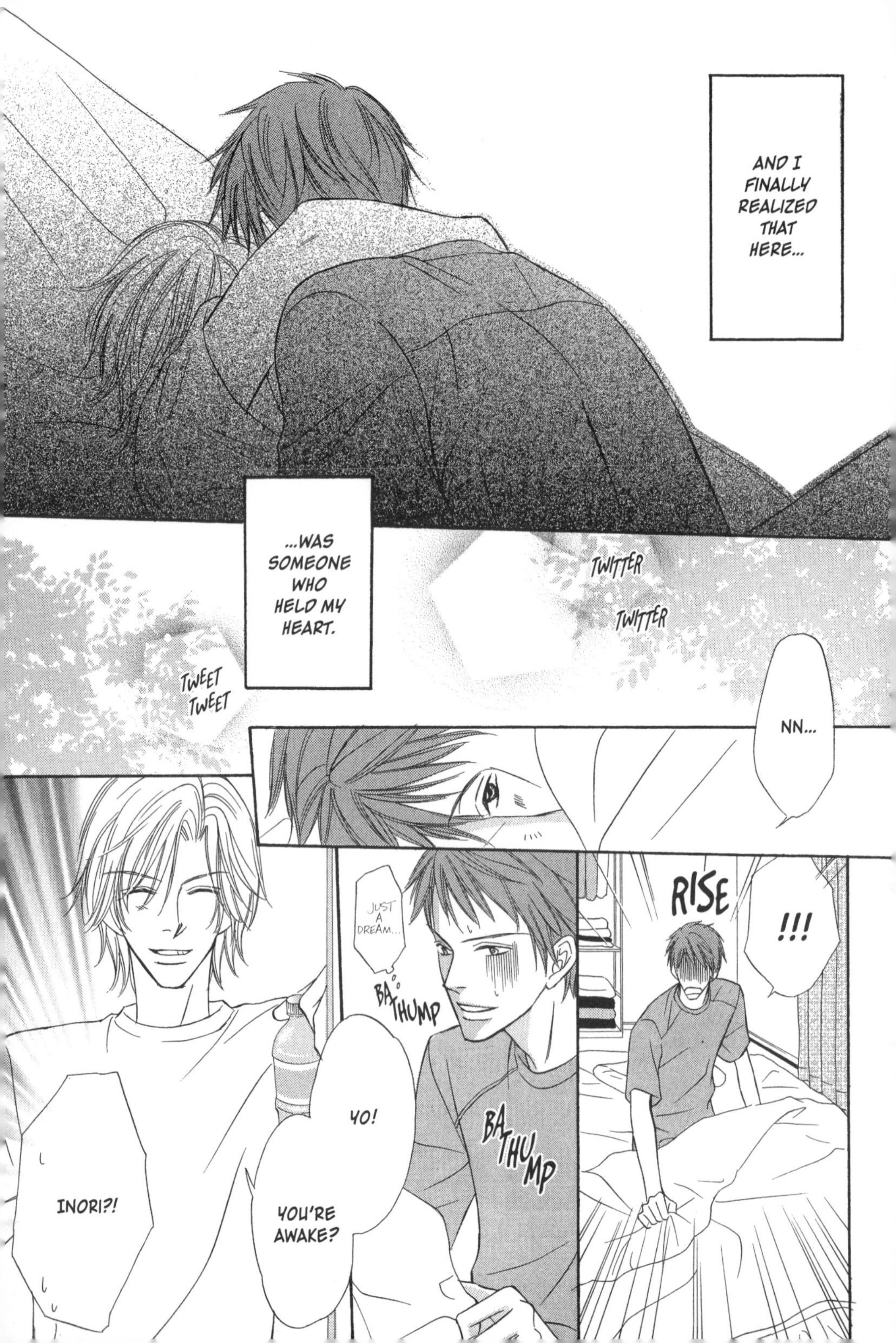
AND I FINALLY REALIZED THAT HERE...
...WAS SOMEONE WHO HELD MY HEART.
TWITTER
TWITTER
TWEET TWEET
NN...
RISE
!!!
JUST A DREAM...
BA THUMP
BA THUMP
YO!
YOU'RE AWAKE?
INORI?!

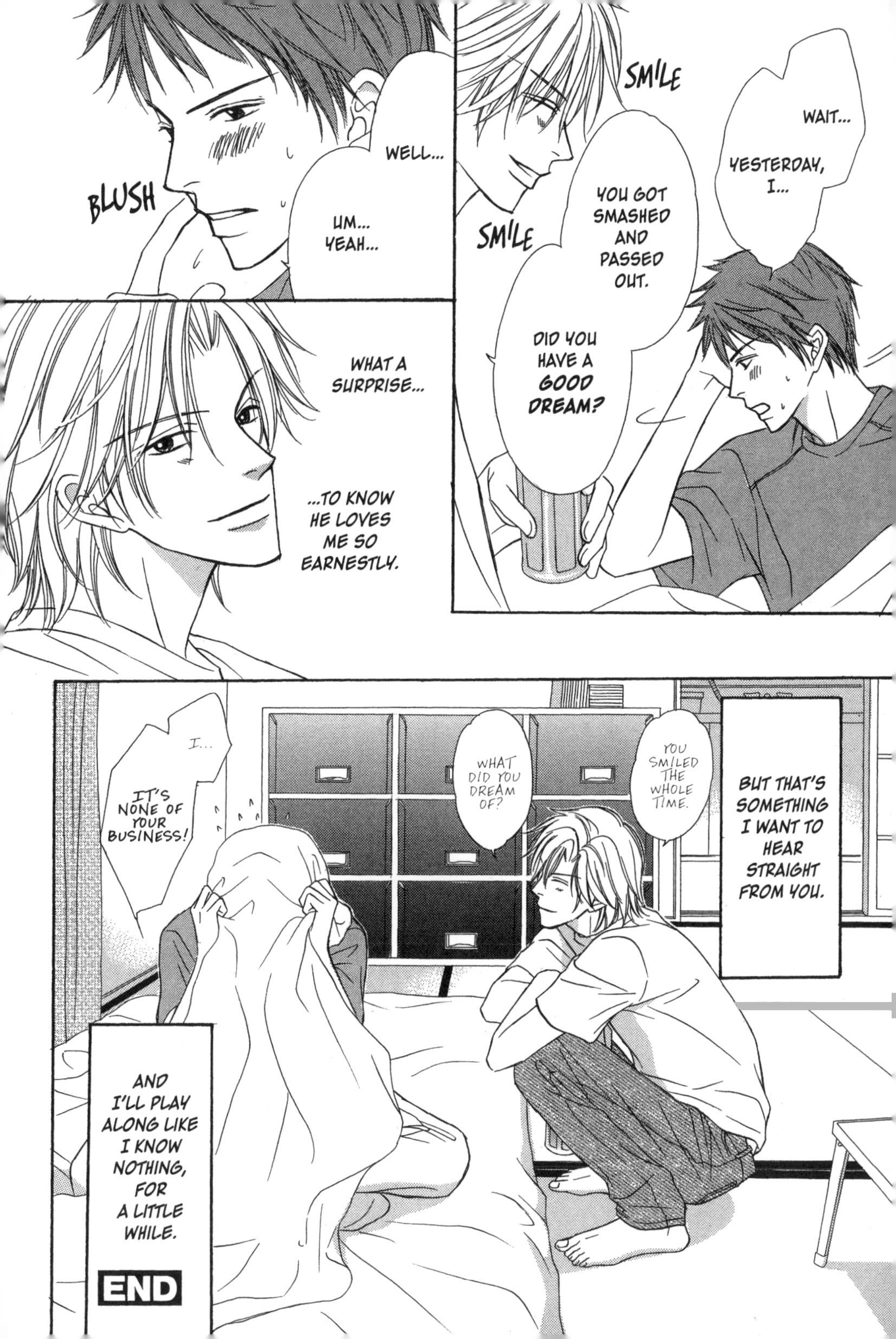
SMILE
WAIT... YESTERDAY, I...
YOU GOT SMASHED AND PASSED OUT.
SMILE
DID YOU HAVE A GOOD DREAM?
WELL...
UM... YEAH...
BLUSH
WHAT A SURPRISE...
...TO KNOW HE LOVES ME SO EARNESTLY.
BUT THAT'S SOMETHING I WANT TO HEAR STRAIGHT FROM YOU.
YOU SMILED THE WHOLE TIME.
WHAT DID YOU DREAM OF?
I...
IT'S NONE OF YOUR BUSINESS!
AND I'LL PLAY ALONG LIKE I KNOW NOTHING, FOR A LITTLE WHILE.
END

IMPOSSIBLE LOVER

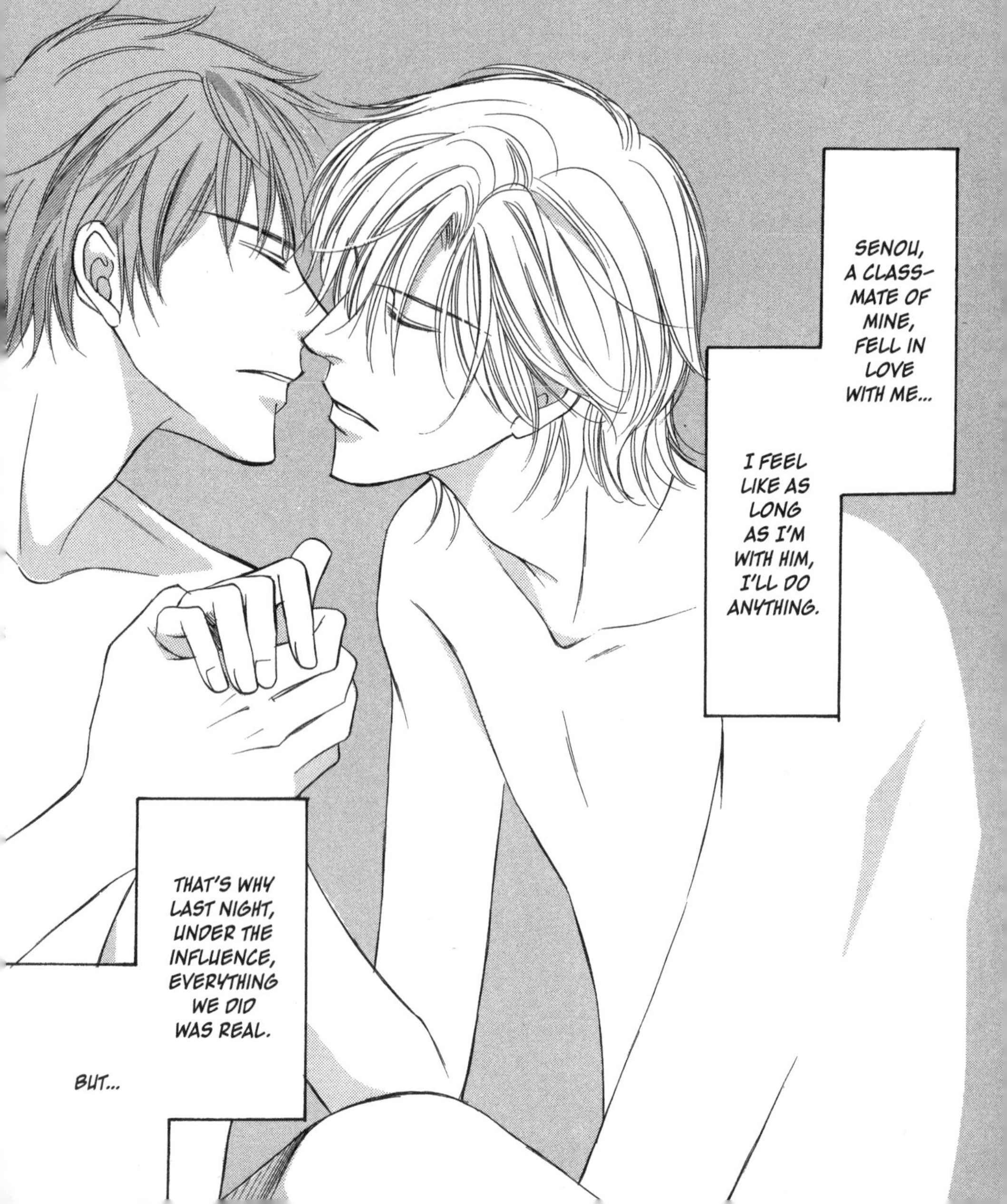
SENOU, A CLASS-MATE OF MINE, FELL IN LOVE WITH ME...
I FEEL LIKE AS LONG AS I'M WITH HIM, I'LL DO ANYTHING.
THAT'S WHY LAST NIGHT, UNDER THE INFLUENCE, EVERYTHING WE DID WAS REAL.
BUT...

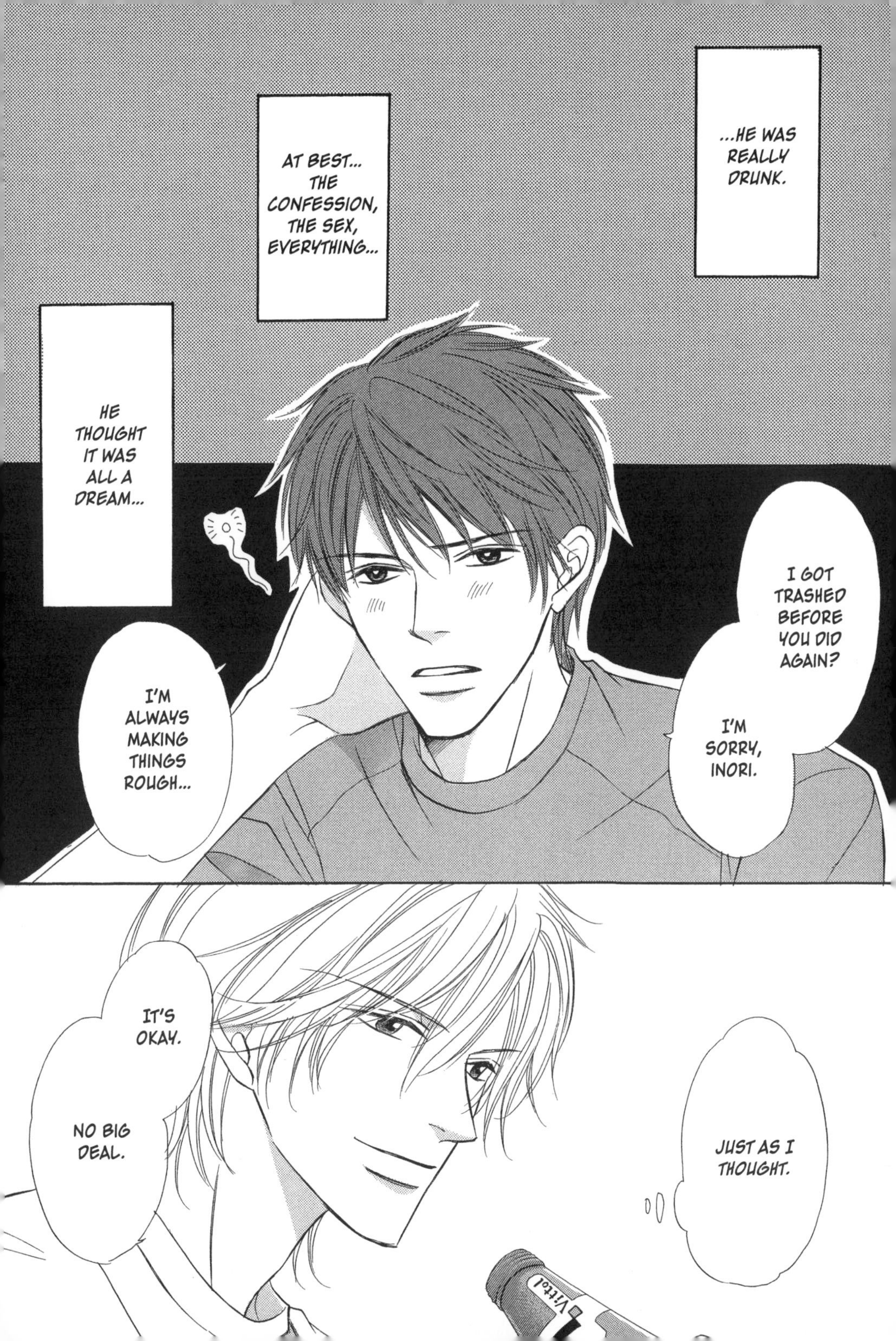
...HE WAS REALLY DRUNK.
AT BEST... THE CONFESSION, THE SEX, EVERYTHING...
HE THOUGHT IT WAS ALL A DREAM...
I GOT TRASHED BEFORE YOU DID AGAIN?
I'M SORRY, INORI.
I'M ALWAYS MAKING THINGS ROUGH...
JUST AS I THOUGHT.
IT'S OKAY.
NO BIG DEAL.
Vittel

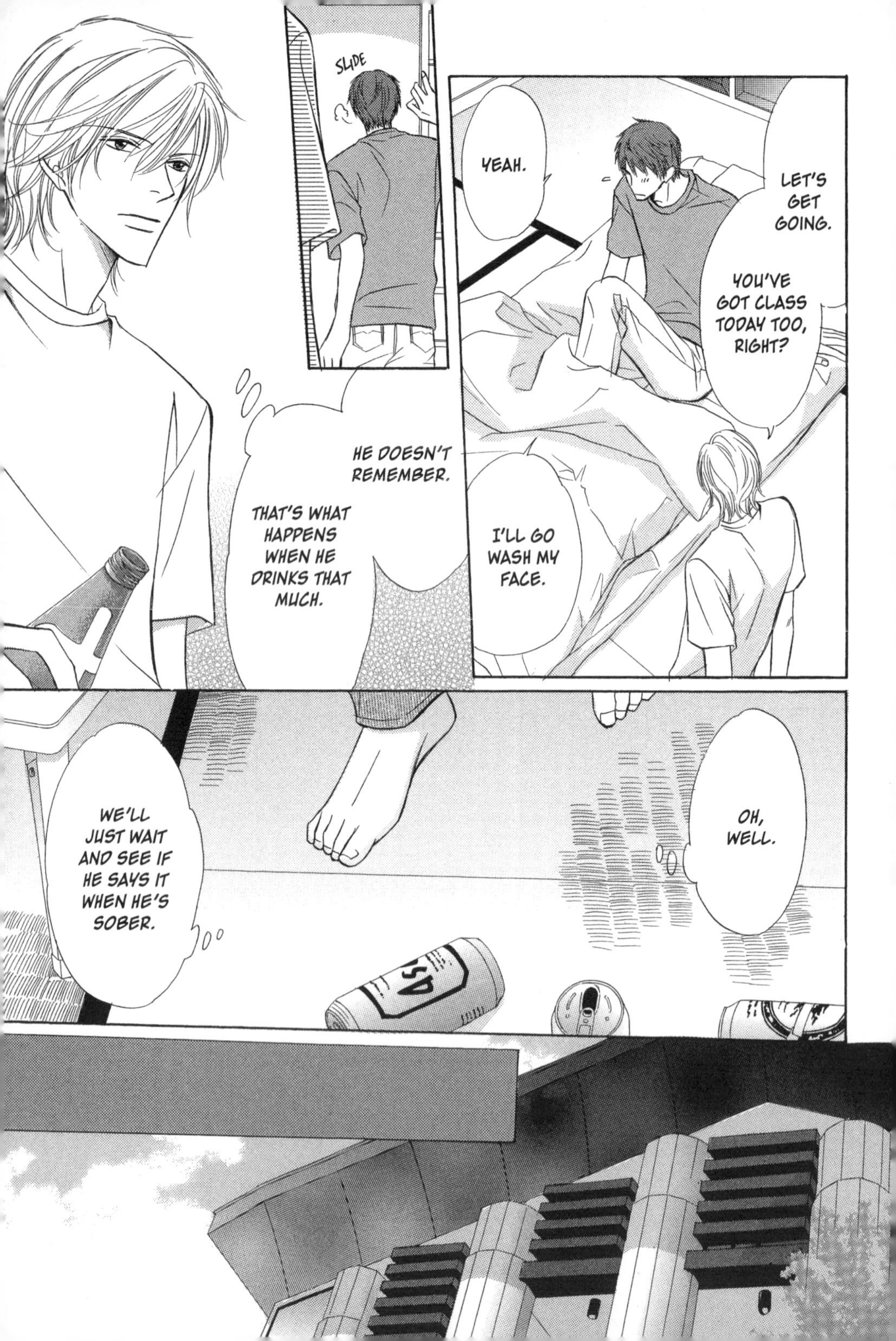
LET'S GET GOING.
YOU'VE GOT CLASS TODAY TOO, RIGHT?
YEAH.
I'LL GO WASH MY FACE.
SLIDE
HE DOESN'T REMEMBER.
THAT'S WHAT HAPPENS WHEN HE DRINKS THAT MUCH.
OH, WELL.
WE'LL JUST WAIT AND SEE IF HE SAYS IT WHEN HE'S SOBER.

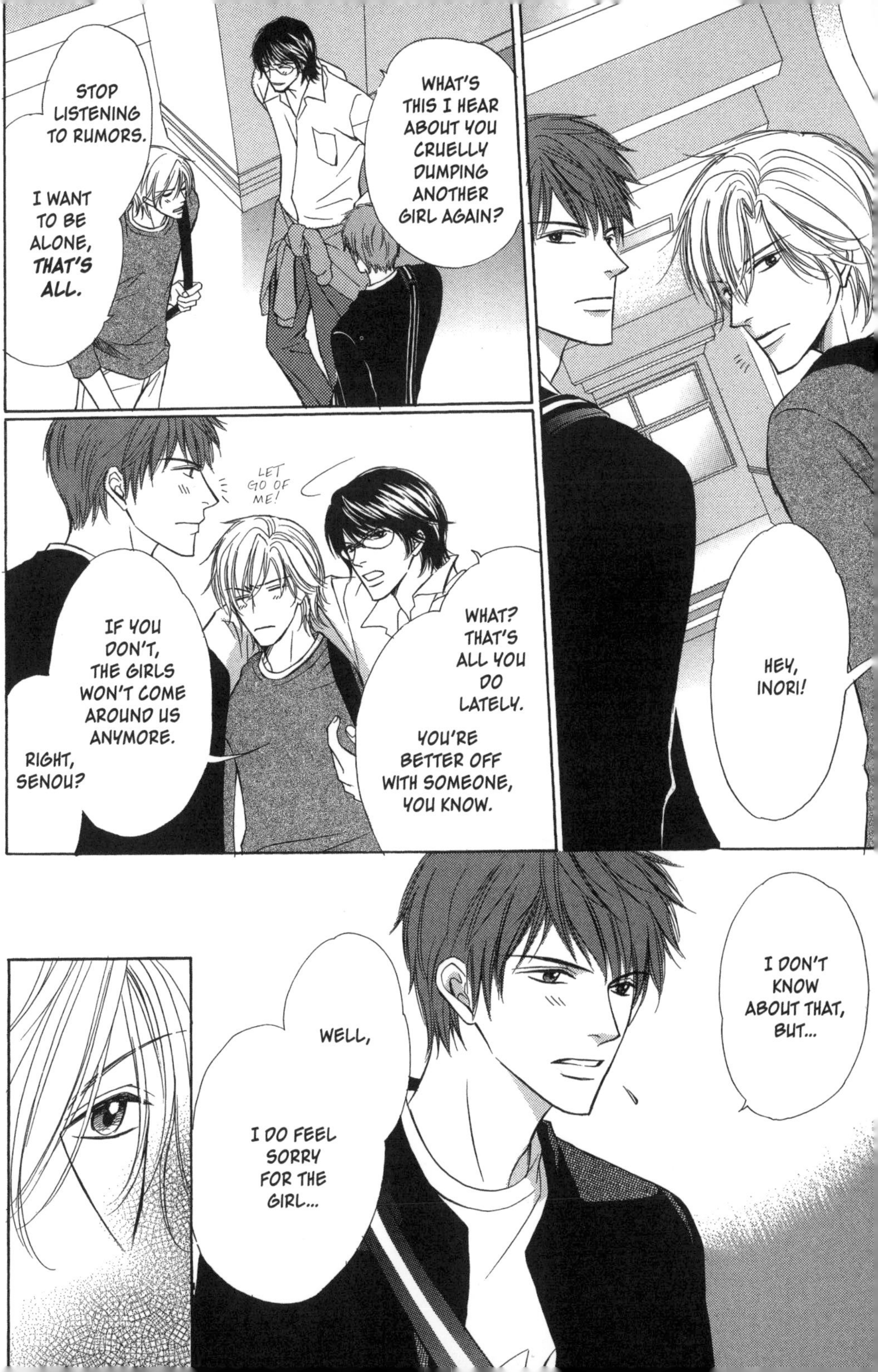
HEY, INORI!
WHAT'S THIS I HEAR ABOUT YOU CRUELLY DUMPING ANOTHER GIRL AGAIN?
STOP LISTENING TO RUMORS.
I WANT TO BE ALONE, THAT'S ALL.
LET GO OF ME!
WHAT? THAT'S ALL YOU DO LATELY.
YOU'RE BETTER OFF WITH SOMEONE, YOU KNOW.
IF YOU DON'T, THE GIRLS WON'T COME AROUND US ANYMORE.
RIGHT, SENOU?
I DON'T KNOW ABOUT THAT, BUT...
WELL,
I DO FEEL SORRY FOR THE GIRL...

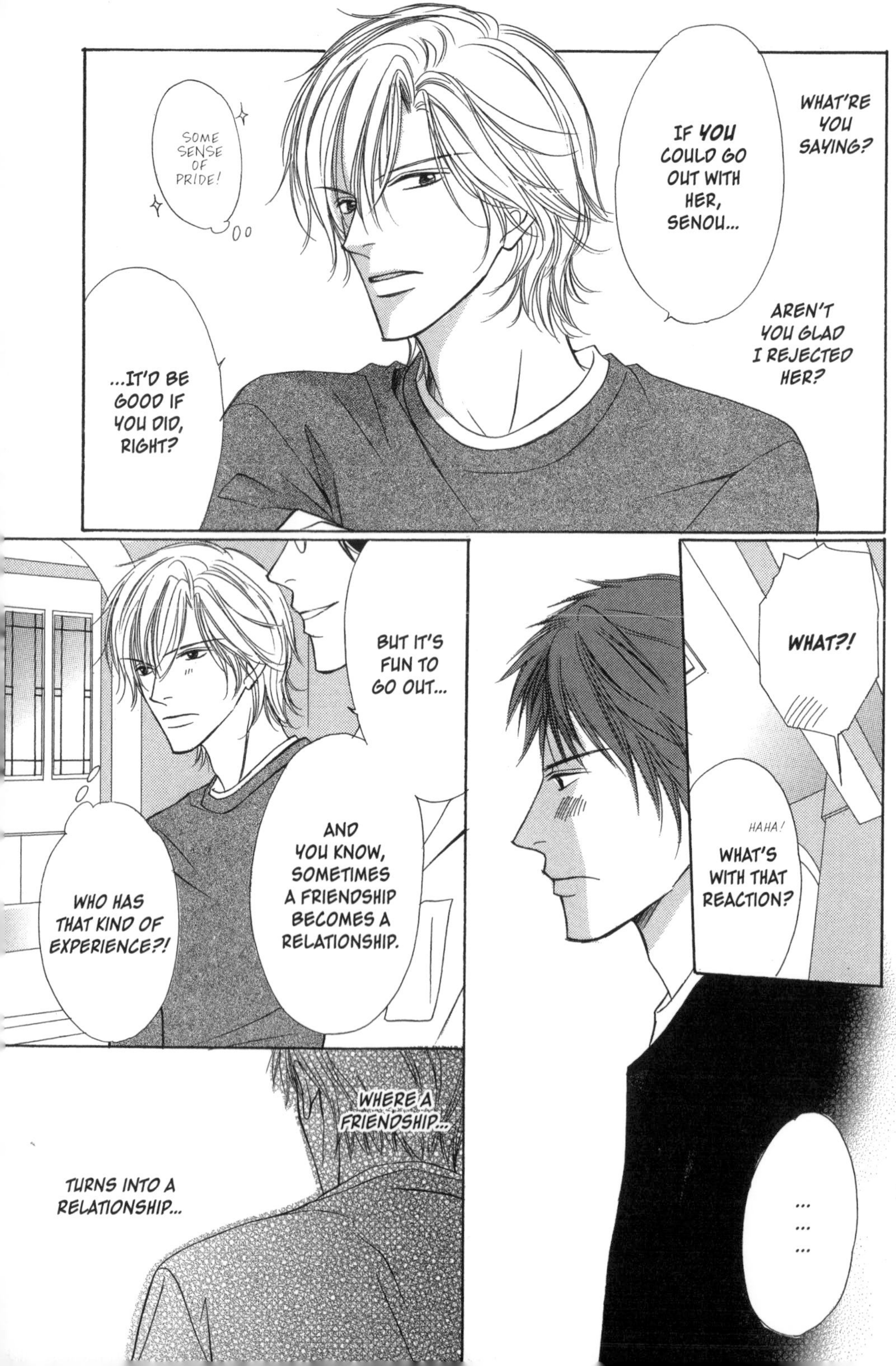
WHAT'RE YOU SAYING?
IF YOU COULD GO OUT WITH HER, SENOU...
AREN'T YOU GLAD I REJECTED HER?
SOME SENSE OF PRIDE!
...IT'D BE GOOD IF YOU DID, RIGHT?
WHAT?!
HAHA! WHAT'S WITH THAT REACTION?
... ...
BUT IT'S FUN TO GO OUT...
AND YOU KNOW, SOMETIMES A FRIENDSHIP BECOMES A RELATIONSHIP.
WHO HAS THAT KIND OF EXPERIENCE?!
WHERE A FRIENDSHIP...
TURNS INTO A RELATIONSHIP...

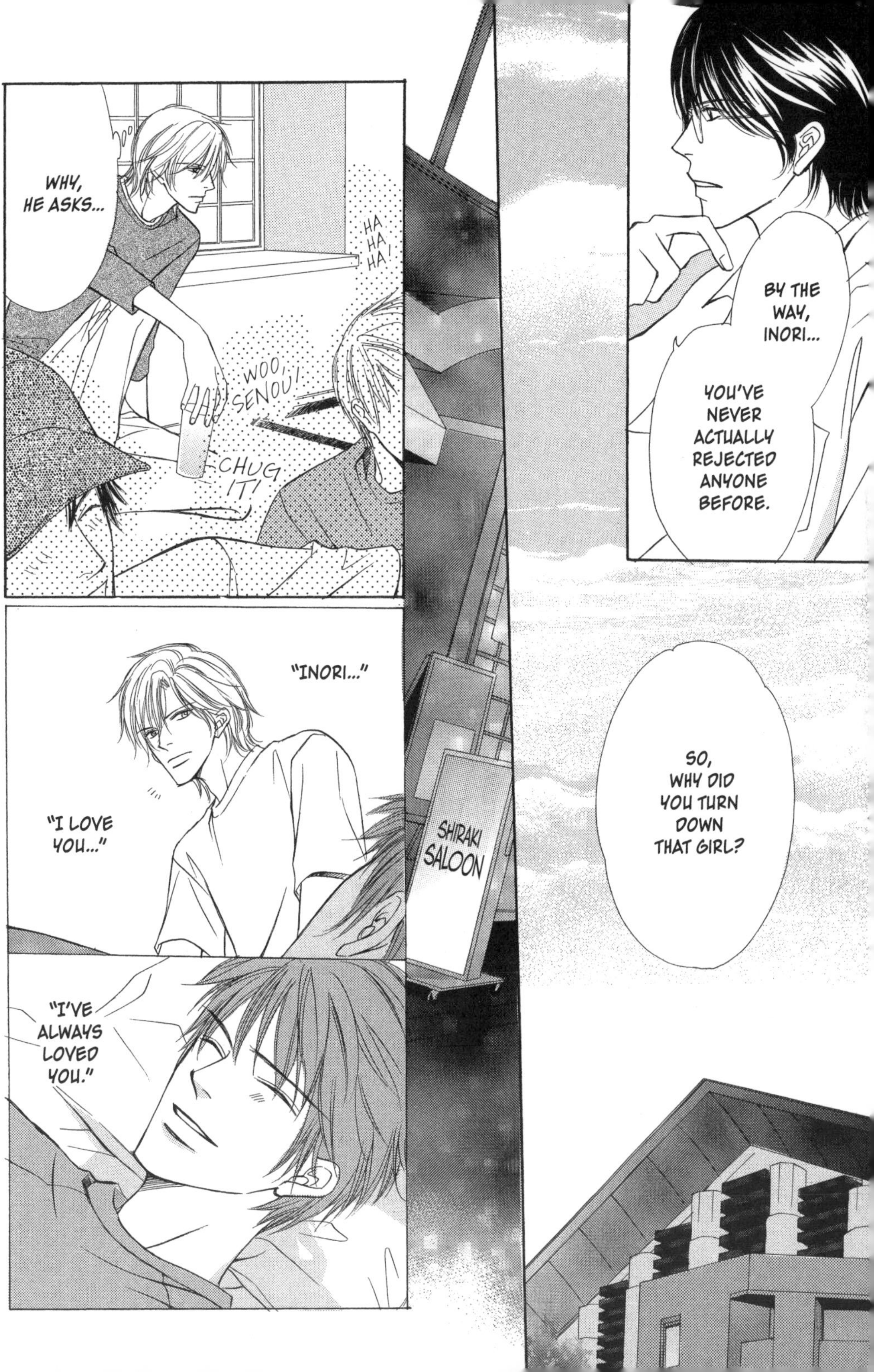
BY THE WAY, INORI...
YOU'VE NEVER ACTUALLY REJECTED ANYONE BEFORE.
SO, WHY DID YOU TURN DOWN THAT GIRL?
SHIRAKI SALOON
WHY, HE ASKS...
HA HA HA!
WOO, SENOU!
CHUG IT!
"INORI..."
"I LOVE YOU..."
"I'VE ALWAYS LOVED YOU."

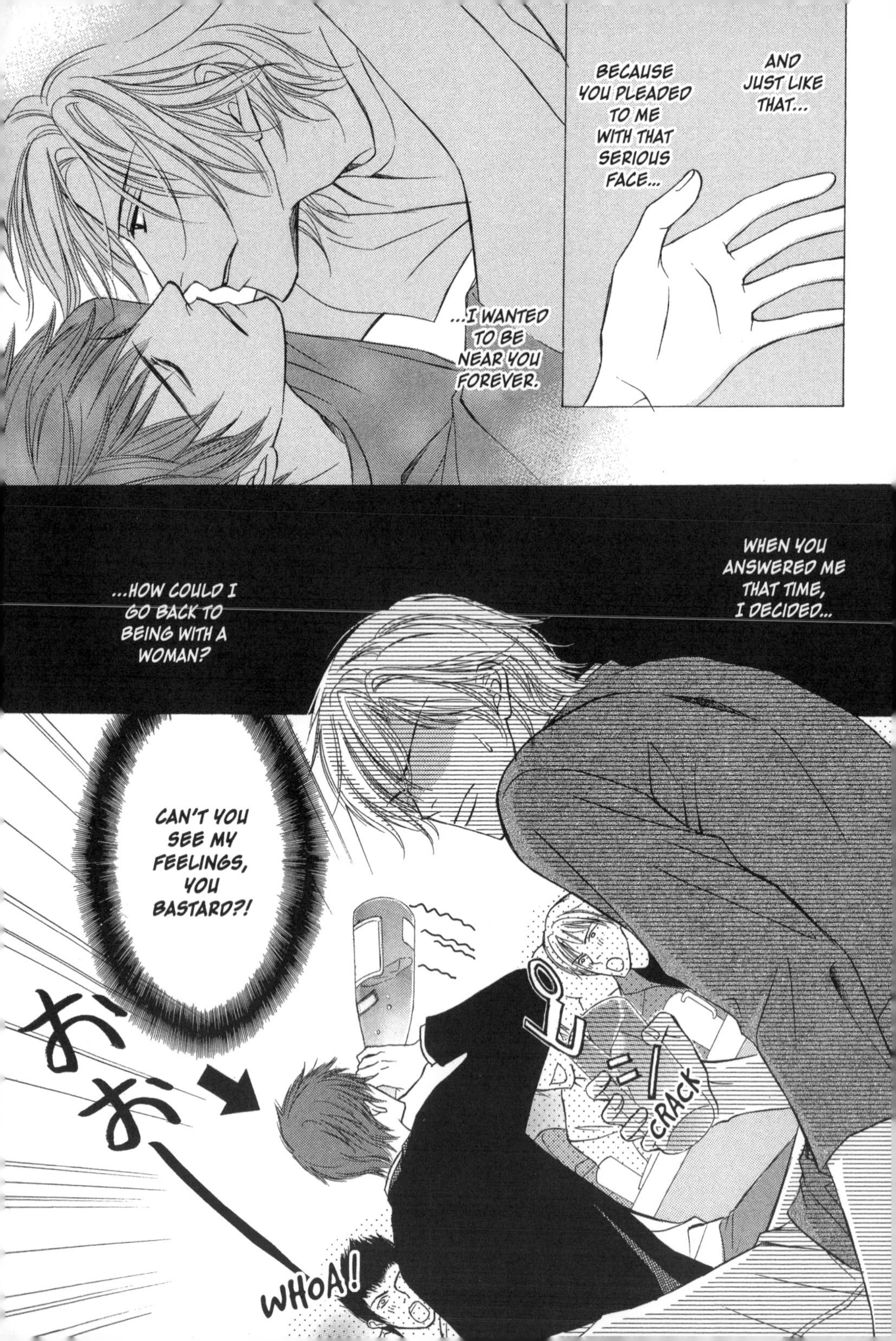
AND JUST LIKE THAT...
BECAUSE YOU PLEADED TO ME WITH THAT SERIOUS FACE...
...I WANTED TO BE NEAR YOU FOREVER.
WHEN YOU ANSWERED ME THAT TIME, I DECIDED...
...HOW COULD I GO BACK TO BEING WITH A WOMAN?
CAN'T YOU SEE MY FEELINGS, YOU BASTARD?!
CRACK
おおー
WHOA!!

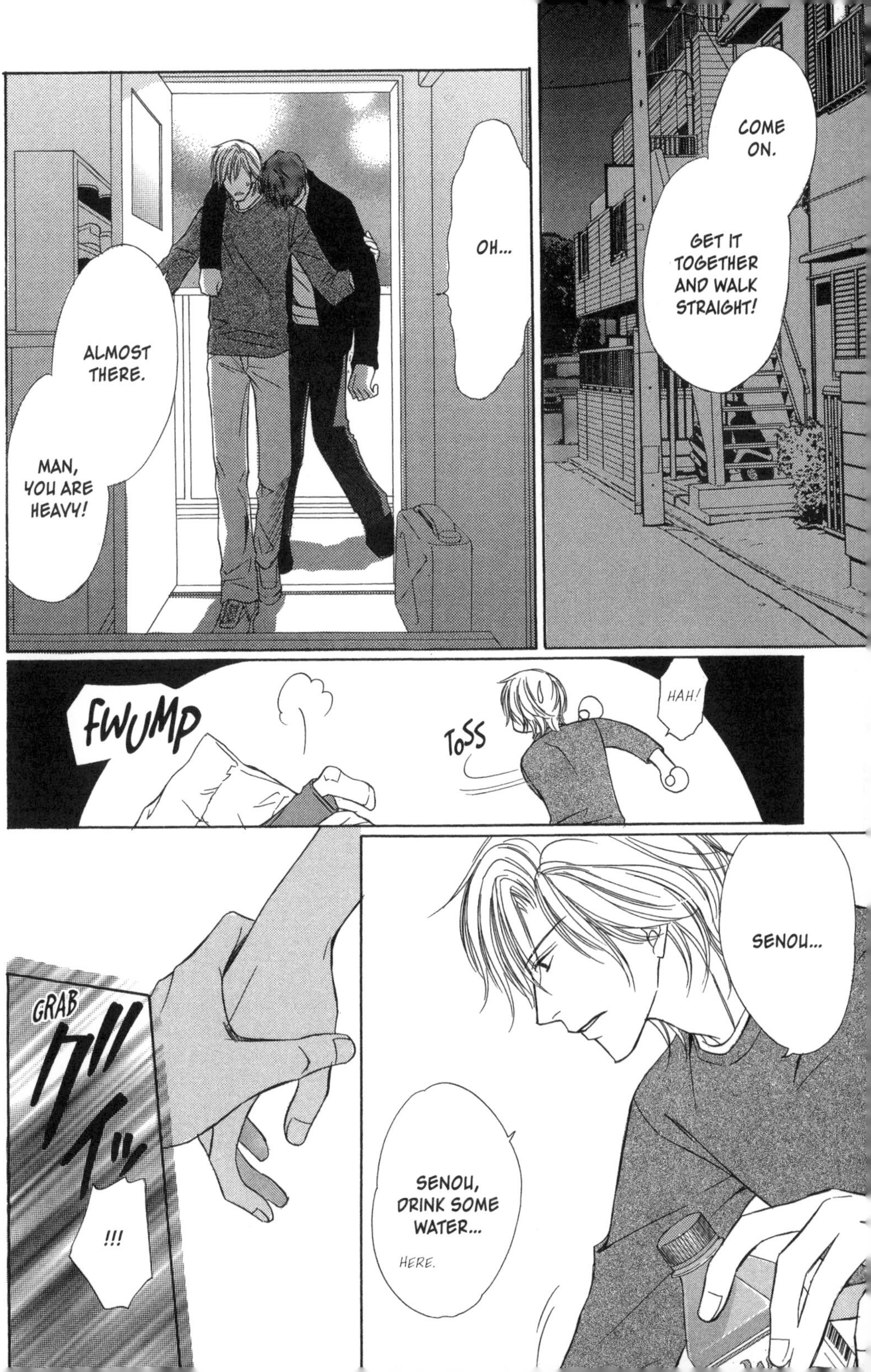
COME ON.
GET IT TOGETHER AND WALK STRAIGHT!
OH...
ALMOST THERE.
MAN, YOU ARE HEAVY!
HAH!
TOSS
FWUMP
SENOU...
SENOU, DRINK SOME WATER...
HERE.
GRAB
グイッ
!!!

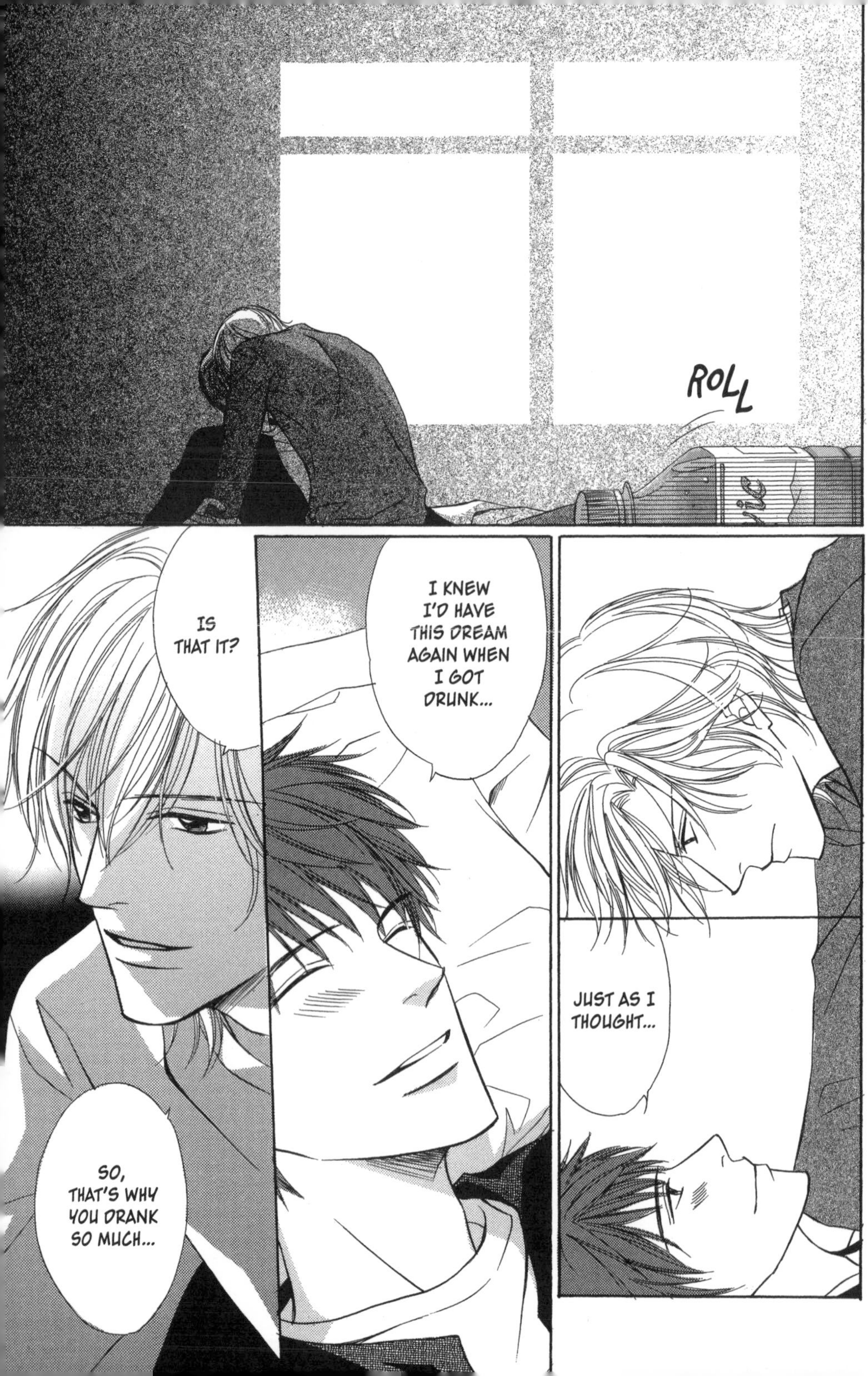
ROLL
JUST AS I THOUGHT...
I KNEW I'D HAVE THIS DREAM AGAIN WHEN I GOT DRUNK...
IS THAT IT?
SO, THAT'S WHY YOU DRANK SO MUCH...

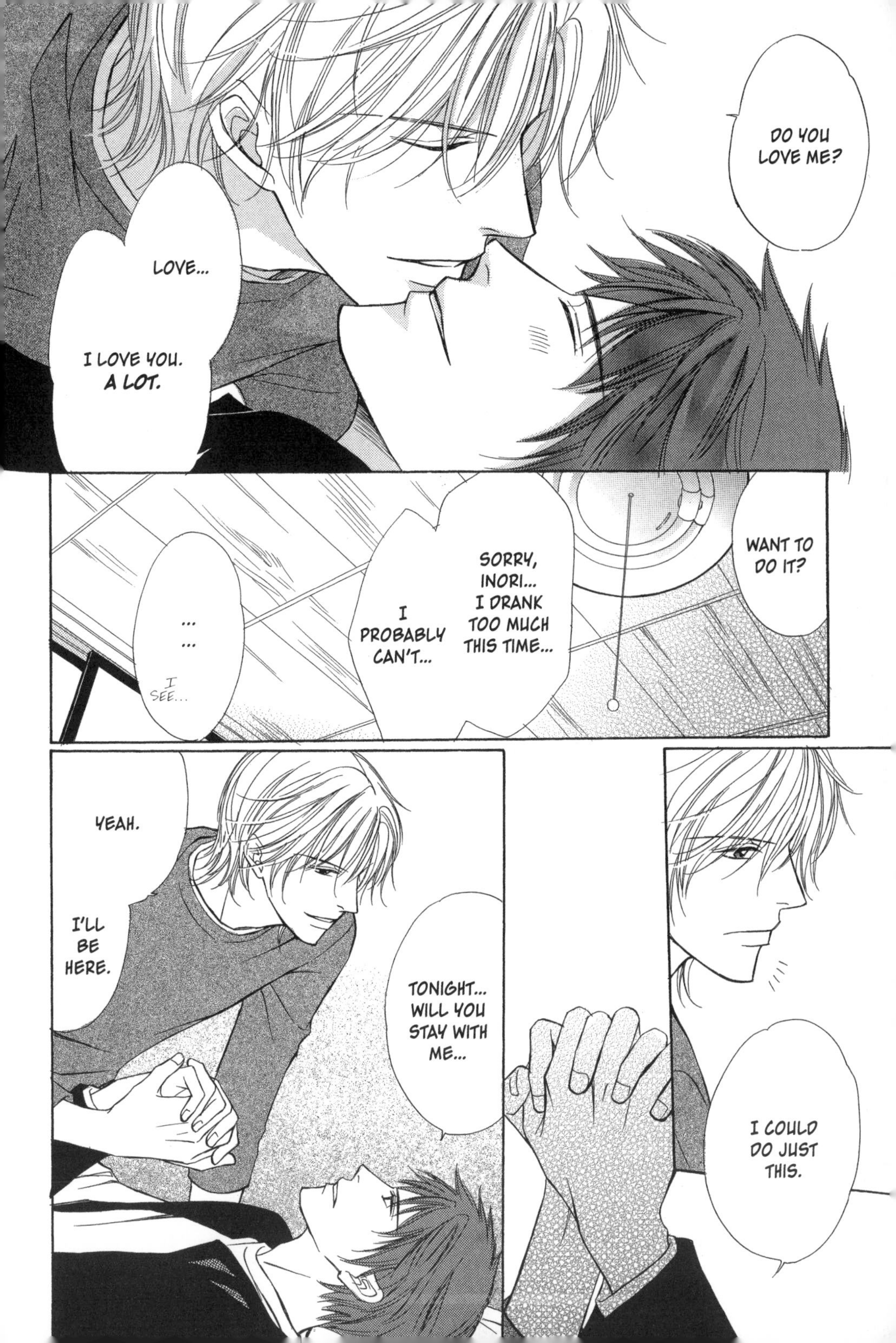
DO YOU LOVE ME?
LOVE... I LOVE YOU. A LOT.
WANT TO DO IT?
SORRY, INORI... I DRANK TOO MUCH THIS TIME... I PROBABLY CAN'T...
... ... I SEE...
I COULD DO JUST THIS.
TONIGHT... WILL YOU STAY WITH ME...
YEAH. I'LL BE HERE.

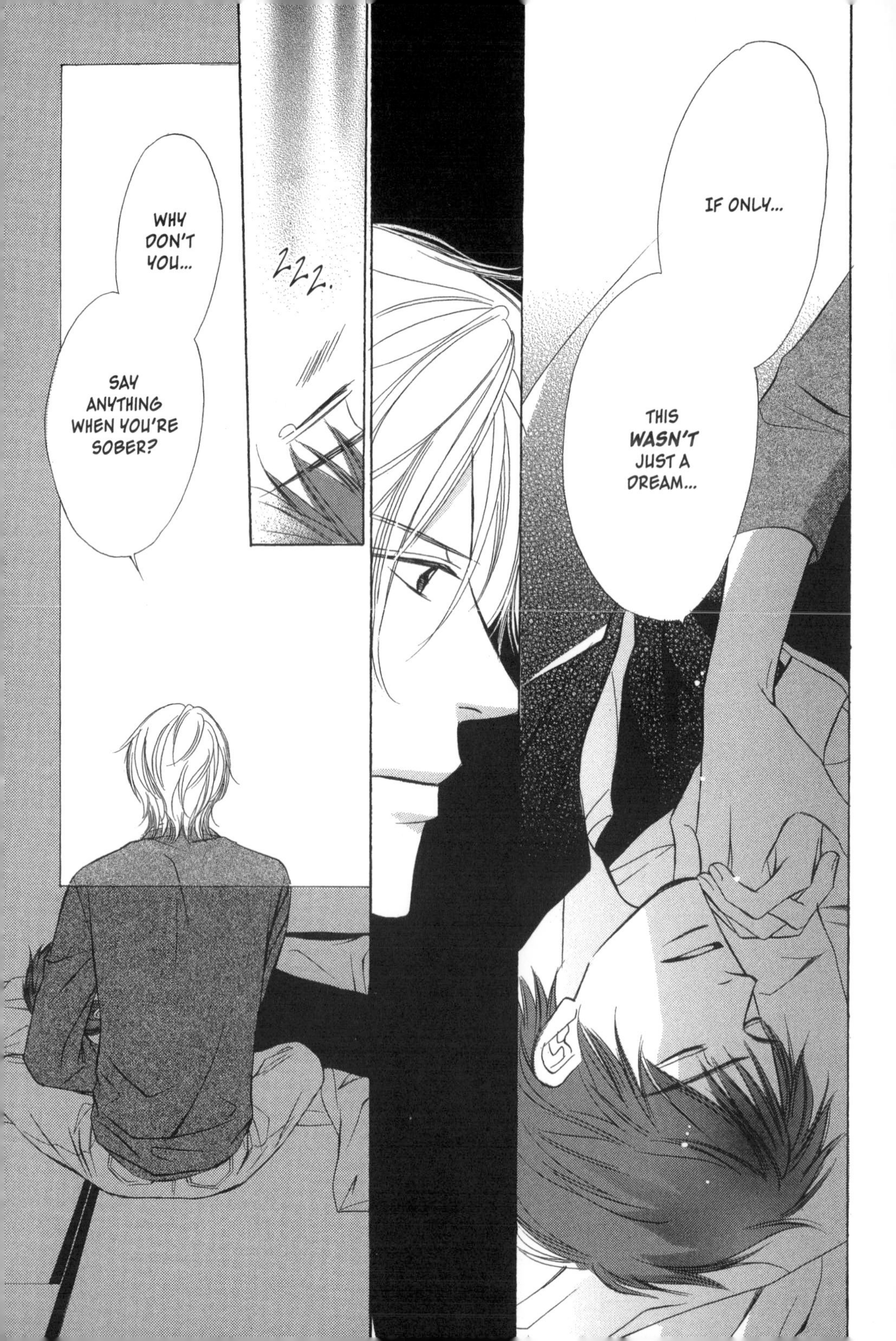
IF ONLY...
THIS WASN'T JUST A DREAM...
ZZZ.
WHY DON'T YOU...
SAY ANYTHING WHEN YOU'RE SOBER?

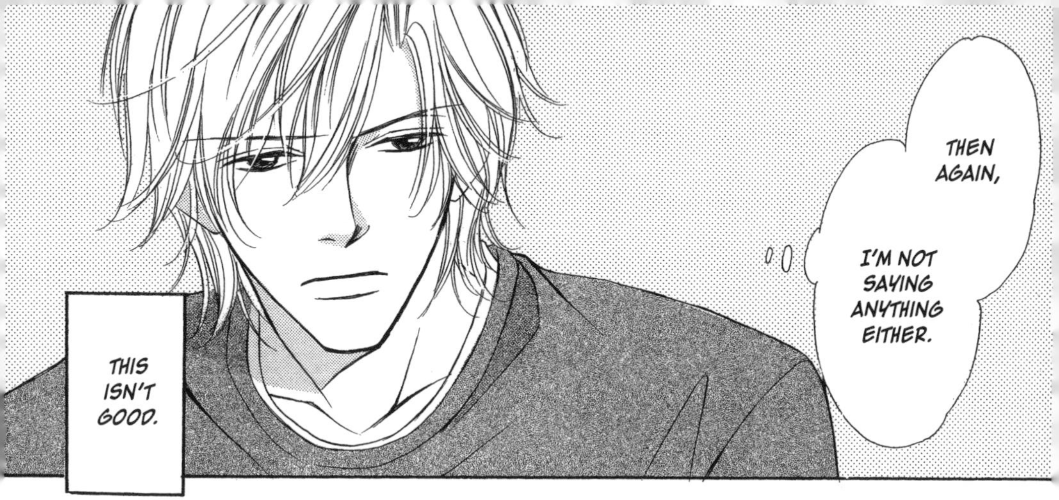
THEN AGAIN,
I'M NOT SAYING ANYTHING EITHER.
THIS ISN'T GOOD.

I'M BECOMING...

...A LITTLE BITTER.

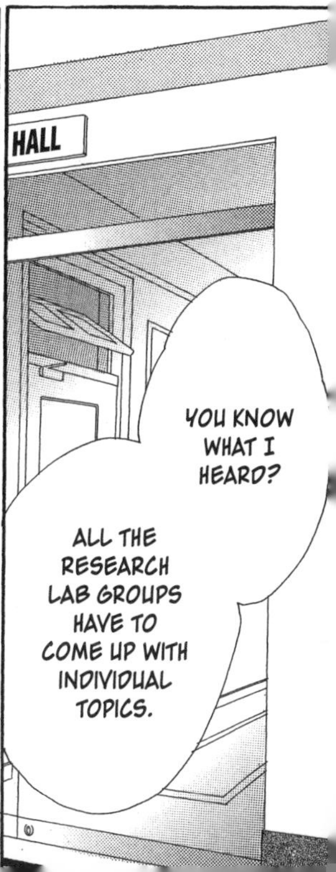
HALL
YOU KNOW WHAT I HEARD?
ALL THE RESEARCH LAB GROUPS HAVE TO COME UP WITH INDIVIDUAL TOPICS.

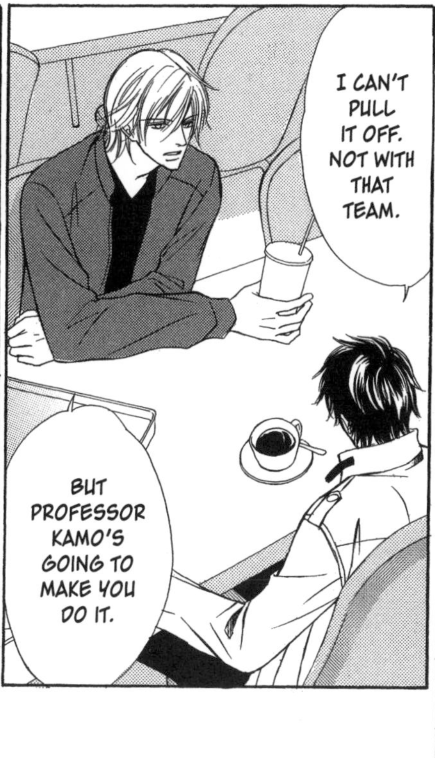
I CAN'T PULL IT OFF. NOT WITH THAT TEAM.
BUT PROFESSOR KAMO'S GOING TO MAKE YOU DO IT.

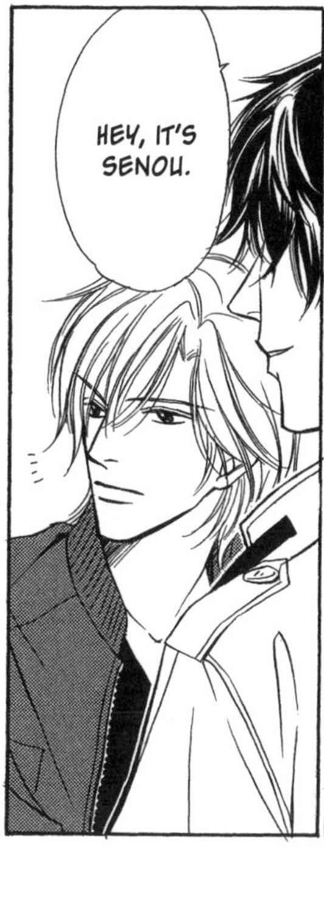
HEY, IT'S SENOU.

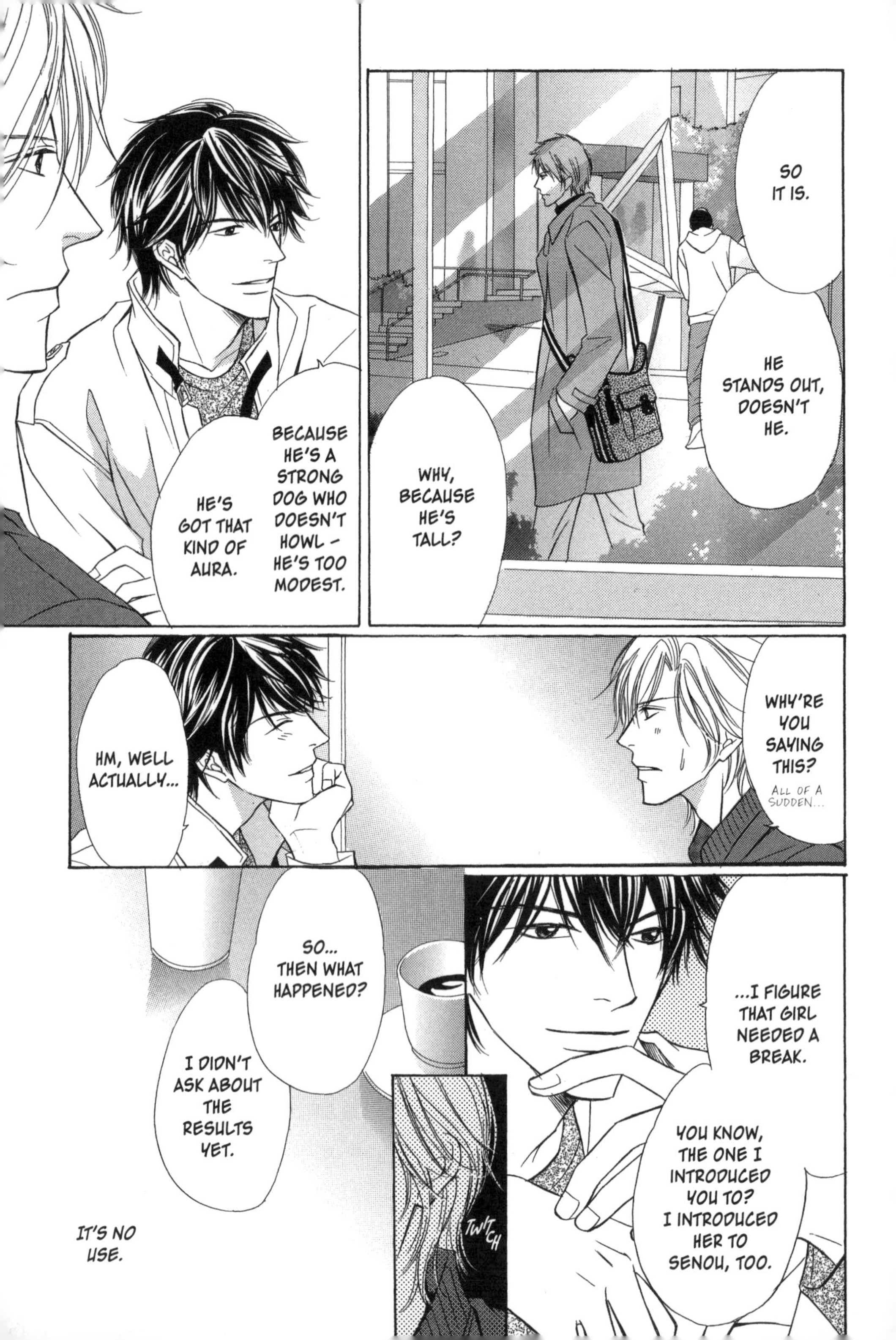
SO IT IS.
HE STANDS OUT, DOESN'T HE.
WHY, BECAUSE HE'S TALL?
BECAUSE HE'S A STRONG DOG WHO DOESN'T HOWL - HE'S TOO MODEST.
HE'S GOT THAT KIND OF AURA.
WHY'RE YOU SAYING THIS?
ALL OF A SUDDEN...
HM, WELL ACTUALLY...
...I FIGURE THAT GIRL NEEDED A BREAK.
YOU KNOW, THE ONE I INTRODUCED YOU TO? I INTRODUCED HER TO SENOU, TOO.
TWITCH
SO... THEN WHAT HAPPENED?
I DIDN'T ASK ABOUT THE RESULTS YET.
IT'S NO USE.

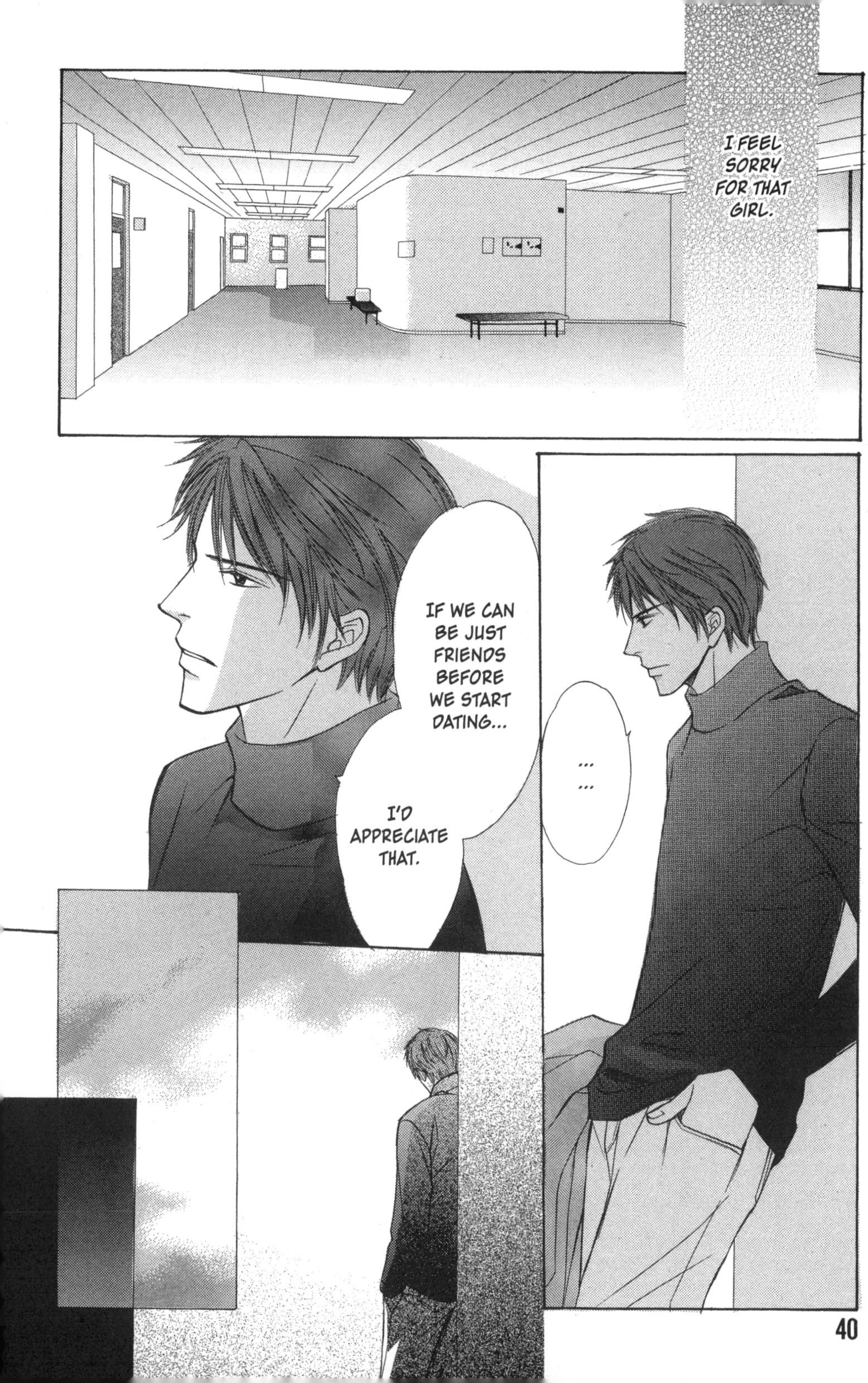
I FEEL SORRY FOR THAT GIRL.
IF WE CAN BE JUST FRIENDS BEFORE WE START DATING...
I'D APPRECIATE THAT.
... ...

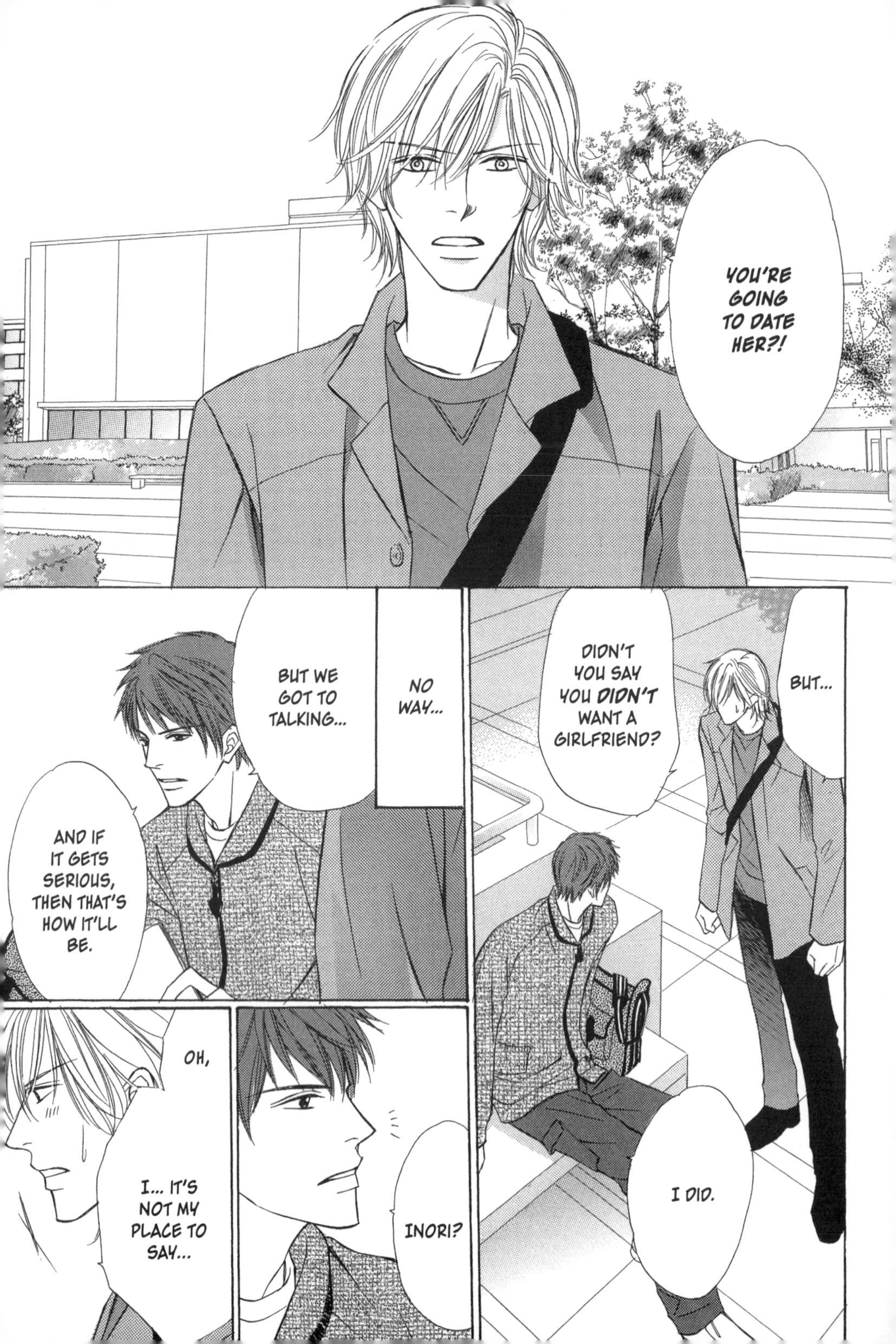

YOU'RE GOING TO DATE HER?!
BUT...
DIDN'T YOU SAY YOU DIDN'T WANT A GIRLFRIEND?
I DID.
NO WAY...
BUT WE GOT TO TALKING...
AND IF IT GETS SERIOUS, THEN THAT'S HOW IT'LL BE.
INORI?
OH,
I... IT'S NOT MY PLACE TO SAY...

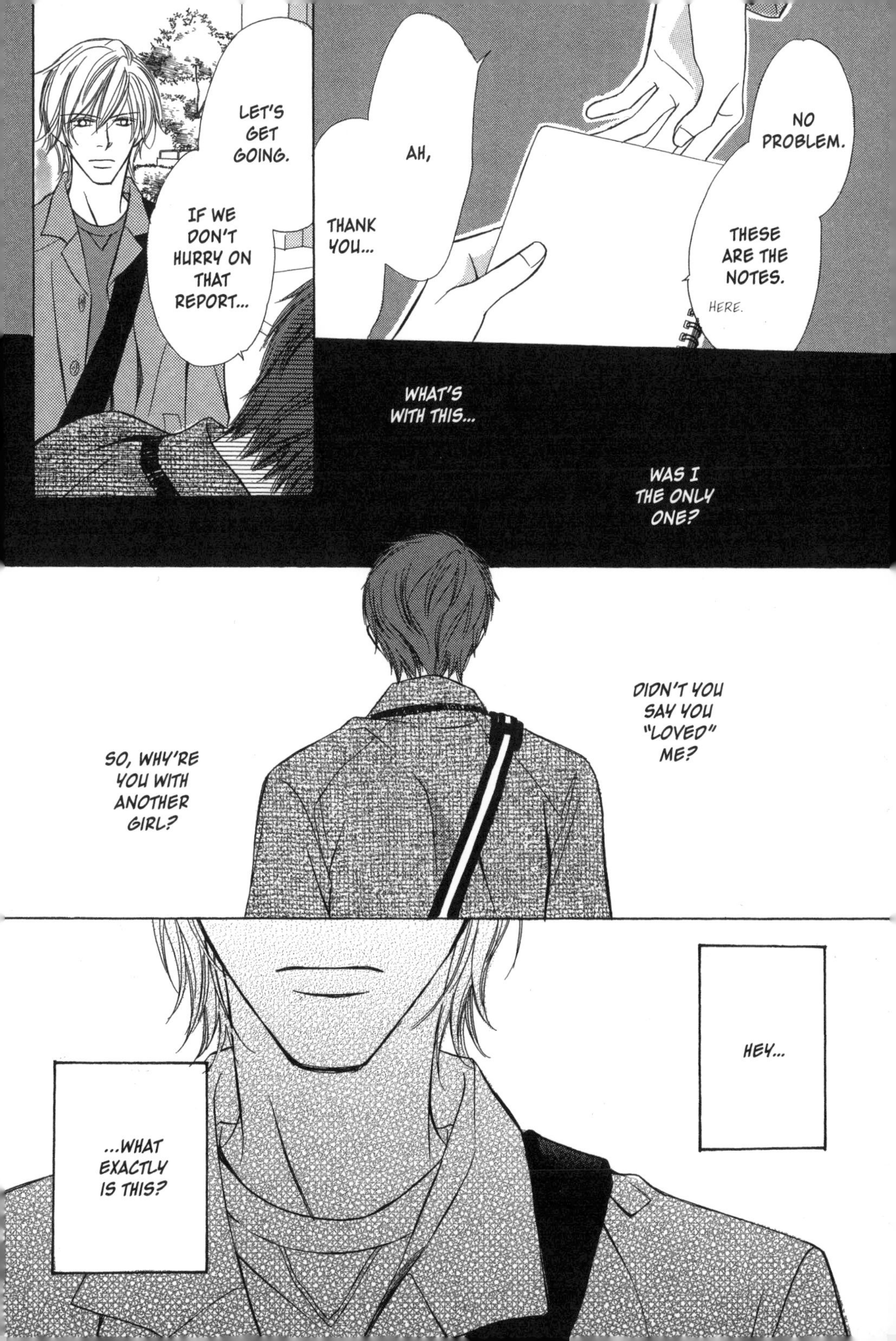

NO PROBLEM.
THESE ARE THE NOTES.
HERE.
AH,
THANK YOU...
LET'S GET GOING.
IF WE DON'T HURRY ON THAT REPORT...
WHAT'S WITH THIS...
WAS I THE ONLY ONE?
DIDN'T YOU SAY YOU "LOVED" ME?
SO, WHY'RE YOU WITH ANOTHER GIRL?
HEY...
...WHAT EXACTLY IS THIS?

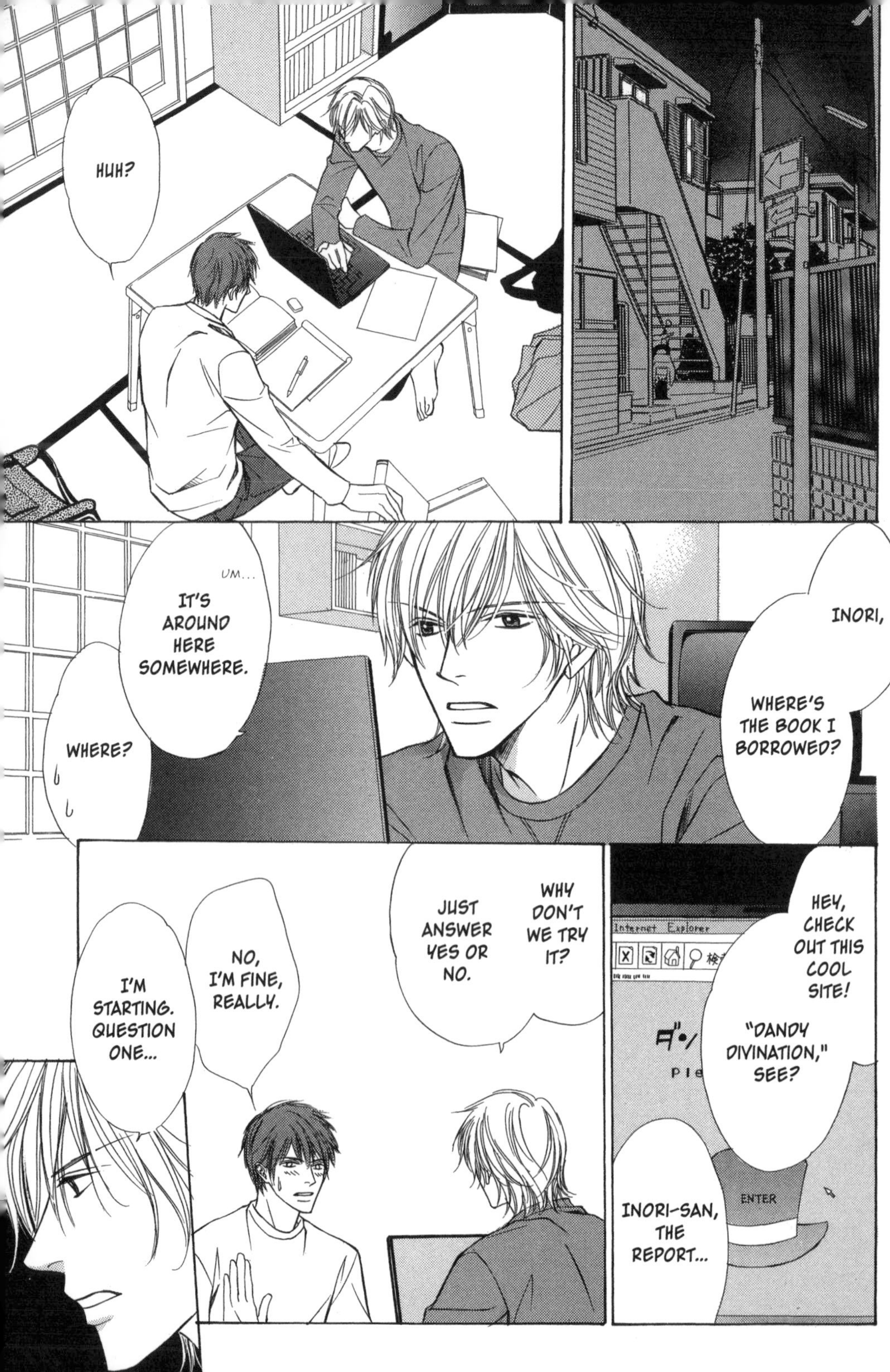
HUH?
INORI, WHERE'S THE BOOK I BORROWED?
UM...
IT'S AROUND HERE SOMEWHERE.
WHERE?
Internet Explorer
HEY, CHECK OUT THIS COOL SITE!
"DANDY DIVINATION," SEE?
ENTER
INORI-SAN, THE REPORT...
WHY DON'T WE TRY IT?
JUST ANSWER YES OR NO.
NO, I'M FINE, REALLY.
I'M STARTING. QUESTION ONE...

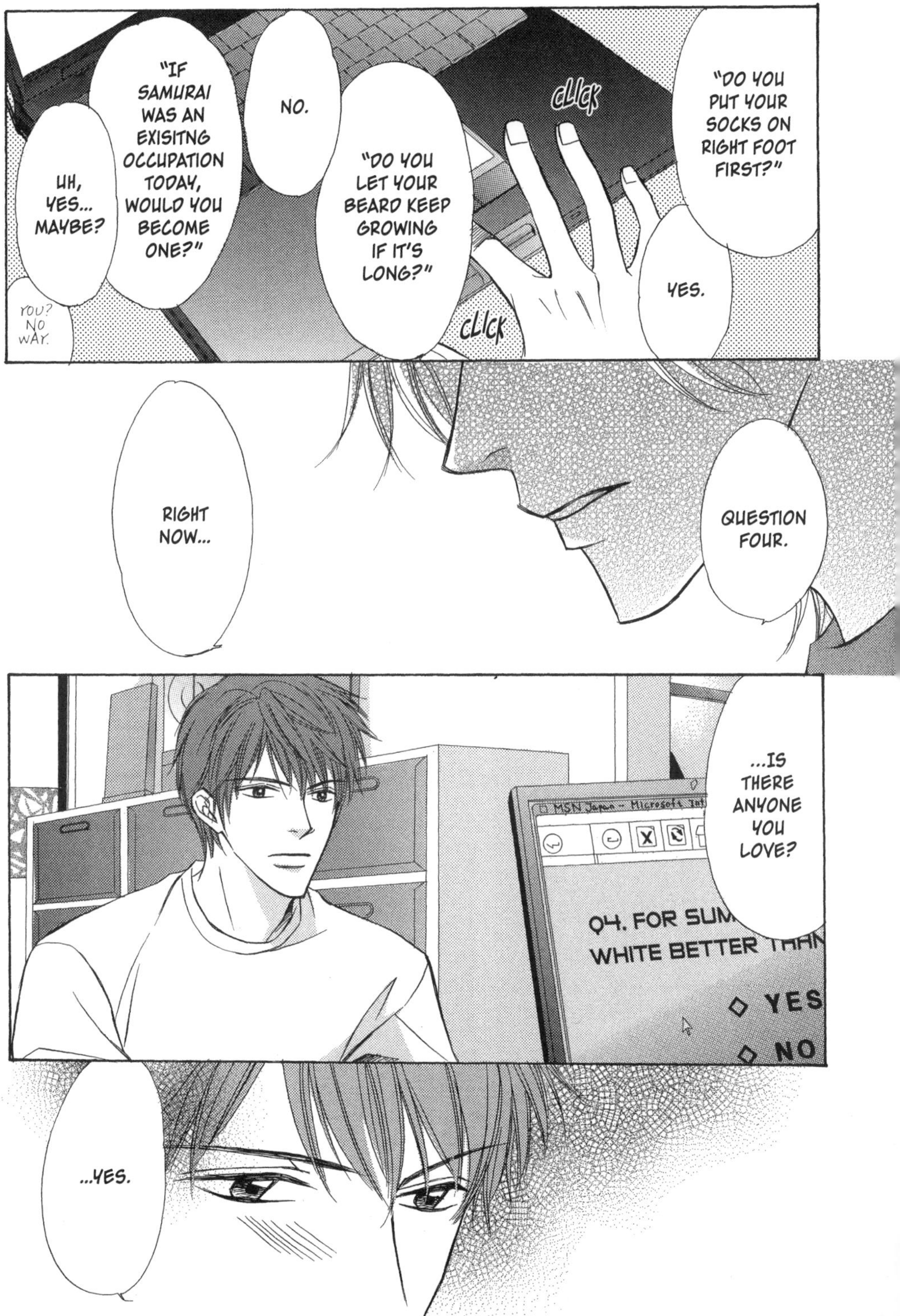
"DO YOU PUT YOUR SOCKS ON RIGHT FOOT FIRST?"
YES.
CLICK
"DO YOU LET YOUR BEARD KEEP GROWING IF IT'S LONG?"
CLICK
NO.
"IF SAMURAI WAS AN EXISITNG OCCUPATION TODAY, WOULD YOU BECOME ONE?"
UH, YES... MAYBE?
YOU? NO WAY.
QUESTION FOUR.
RIGHT NOW...
...IS THERE ANYONE YOU LOVE?
MSN Japan - Microsoft Int
Q4. FOR SUM
WHITE BETTER THAN
YES
NO
...YES.

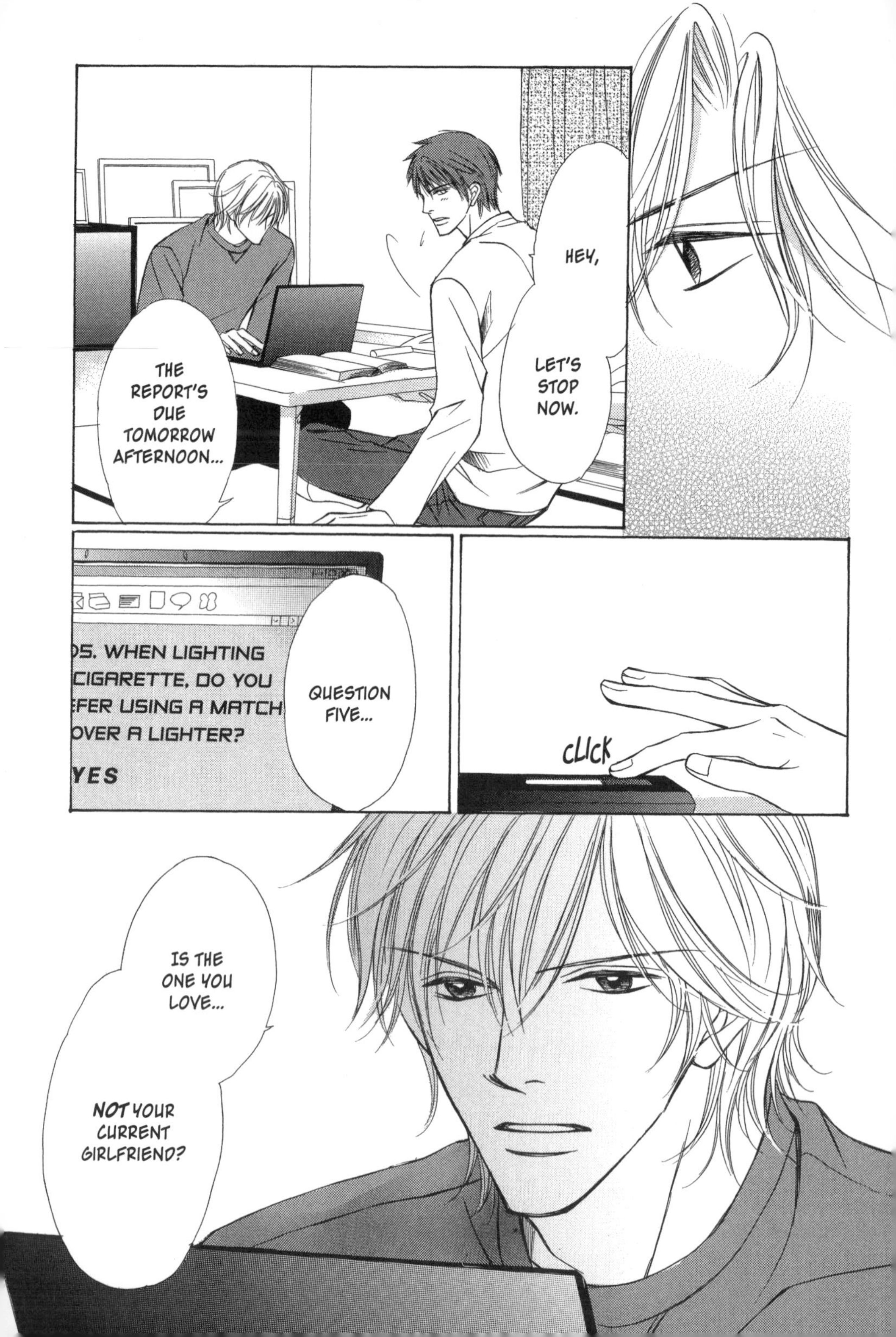
HEY,
LET'S STOP NOW.
THE REPORT'S DUE TOMORROW AFTERNOON...
CLICK
05. WHEN LIGHTING
CIGARETTE, DO YOU
EFER USING A MATCH
OVER A LIGHTER?
YES
QUESTION FIVE...
IS THE ONE YOU LOVE...
NOT YOUR CURRENT GIRLFRIEND?

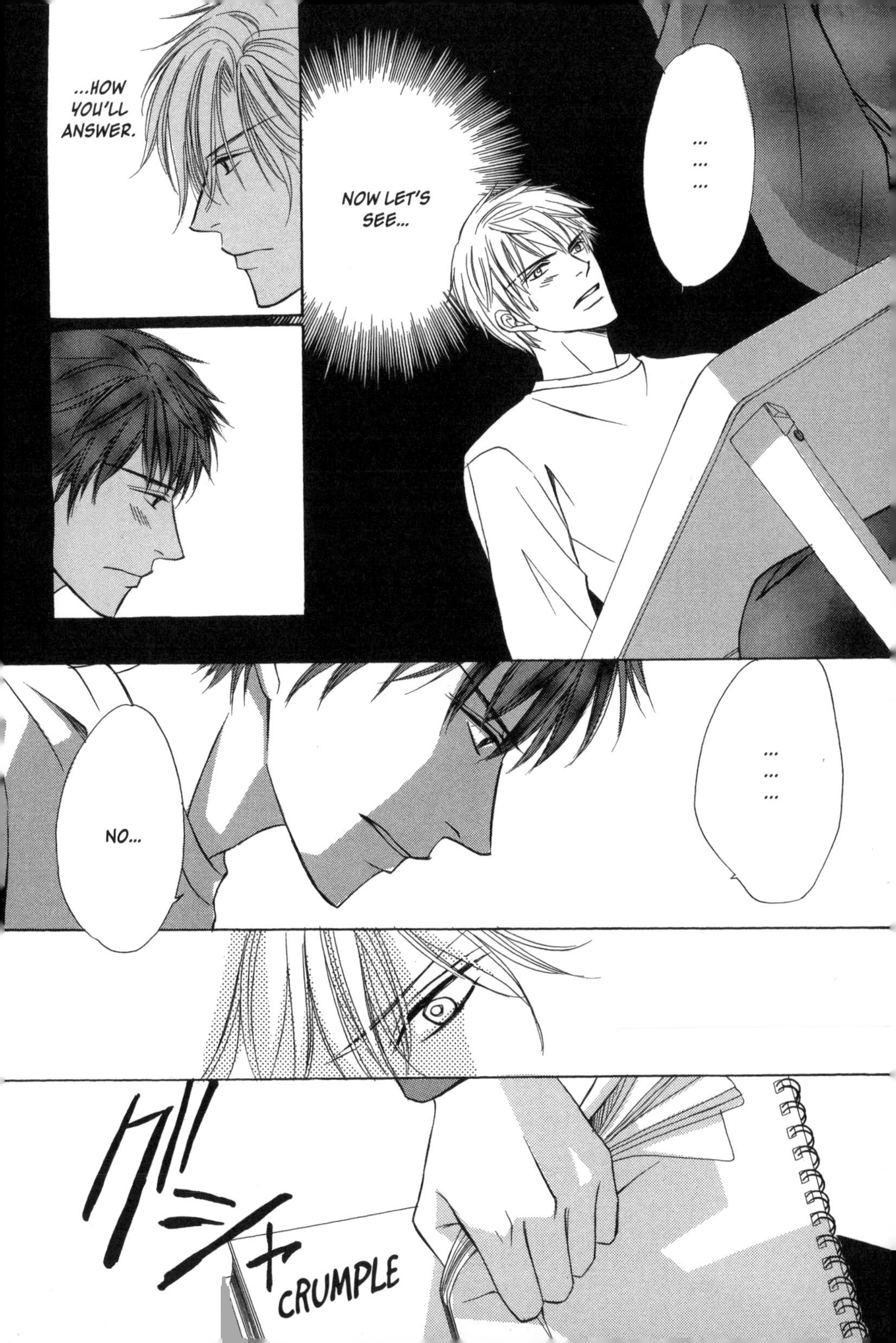

...
...
...
NOW LET'S SEE...
...HOW YOU'LL ANSWER.
...
...
...
NO...
CRUMPLE

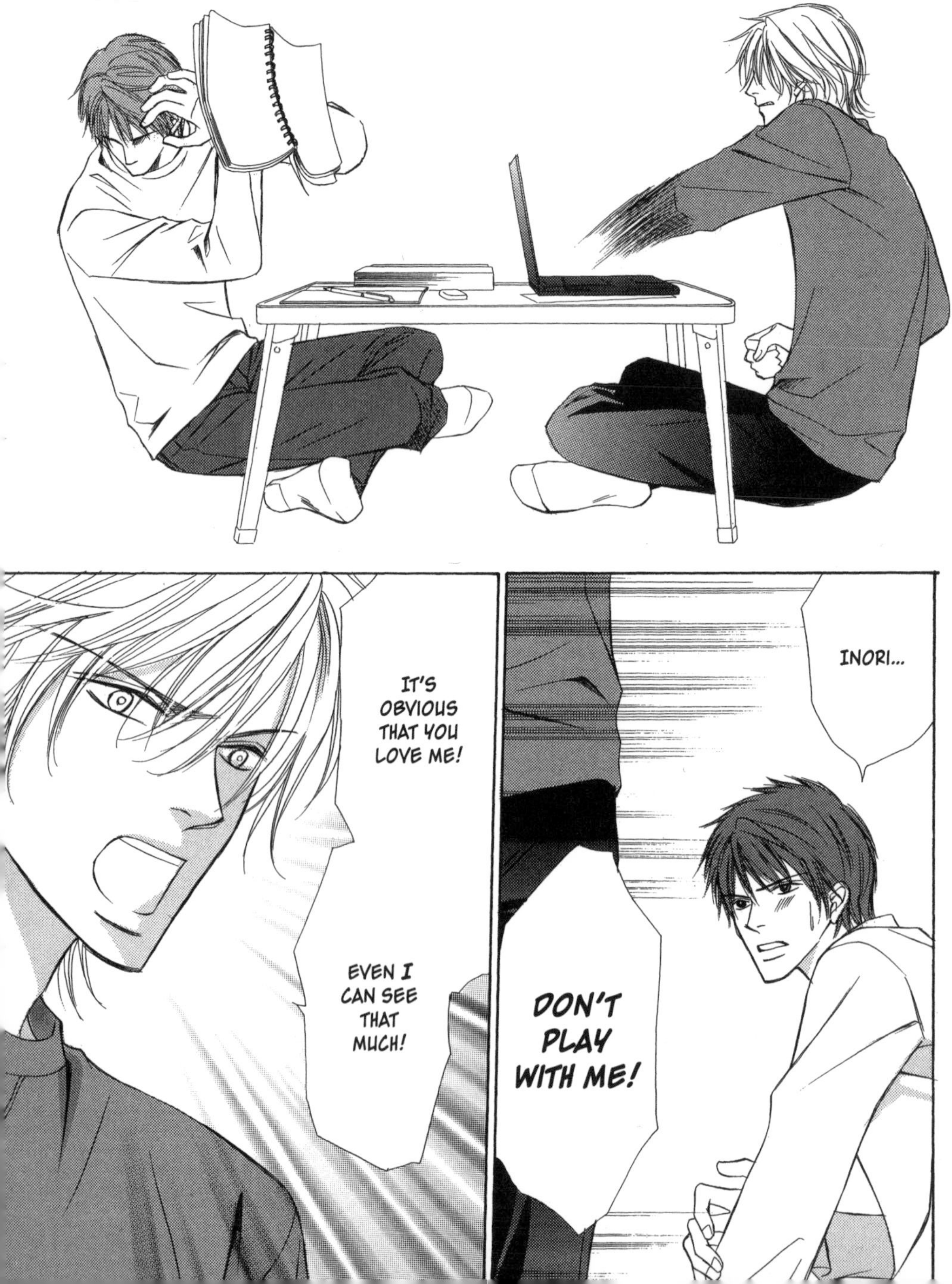
INORI...
DON'T PLAY WITH ME!
IT'S OBVIOUS THAT YOU LOVE ME!
EVEN I CAN SEE THAT MUCH!

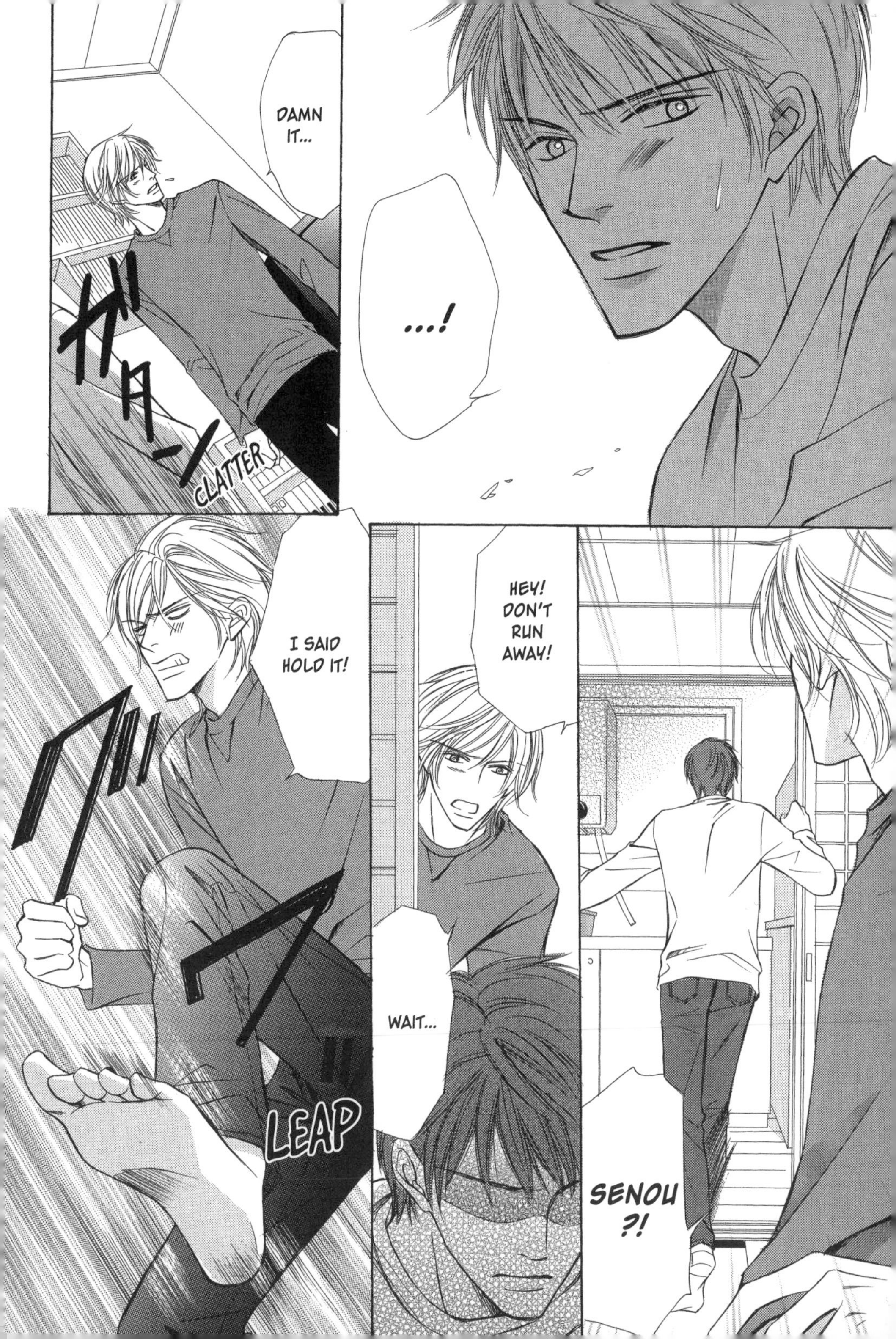
...!
DAMN IT...
CLATTER
SENOU ?!
HEY! DON'T RUN AWAY!
WAIT...
I SAID HOLD IT!
LEAP

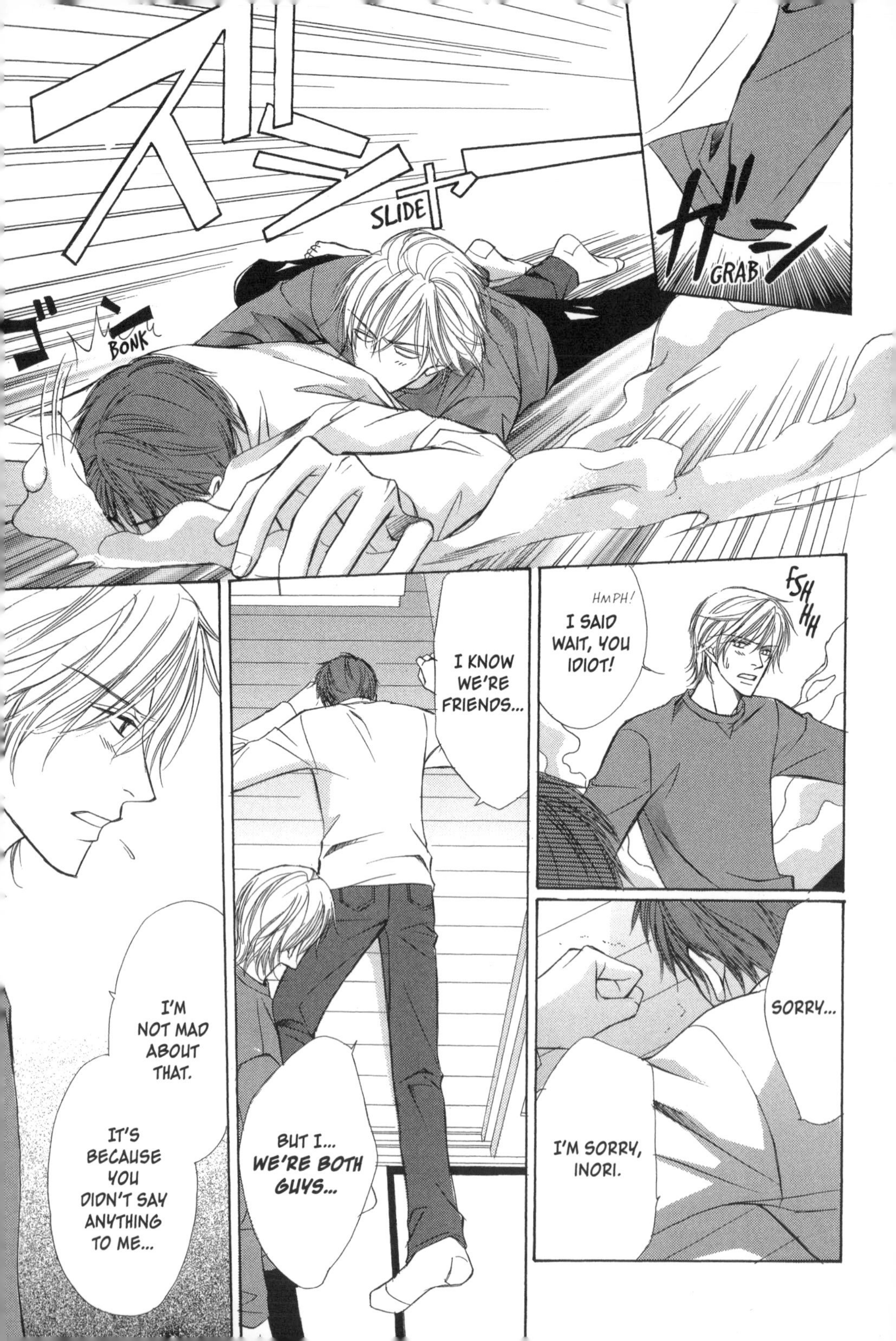
GRAB
SLIDE
BONK
HMPH!
I SAID WAIT, YOU IDIOT!
FSHHH
SORRY...
I'M SORRY, INORI.
I KNOW WE'RE FRIENDS...
BUT I... WE'RE BOTH GUYS...
I'M NOT MAD ABOUT THAT.
IT'S BECAUSE YOU DIDN'T SAY ANYTHING TO ME...

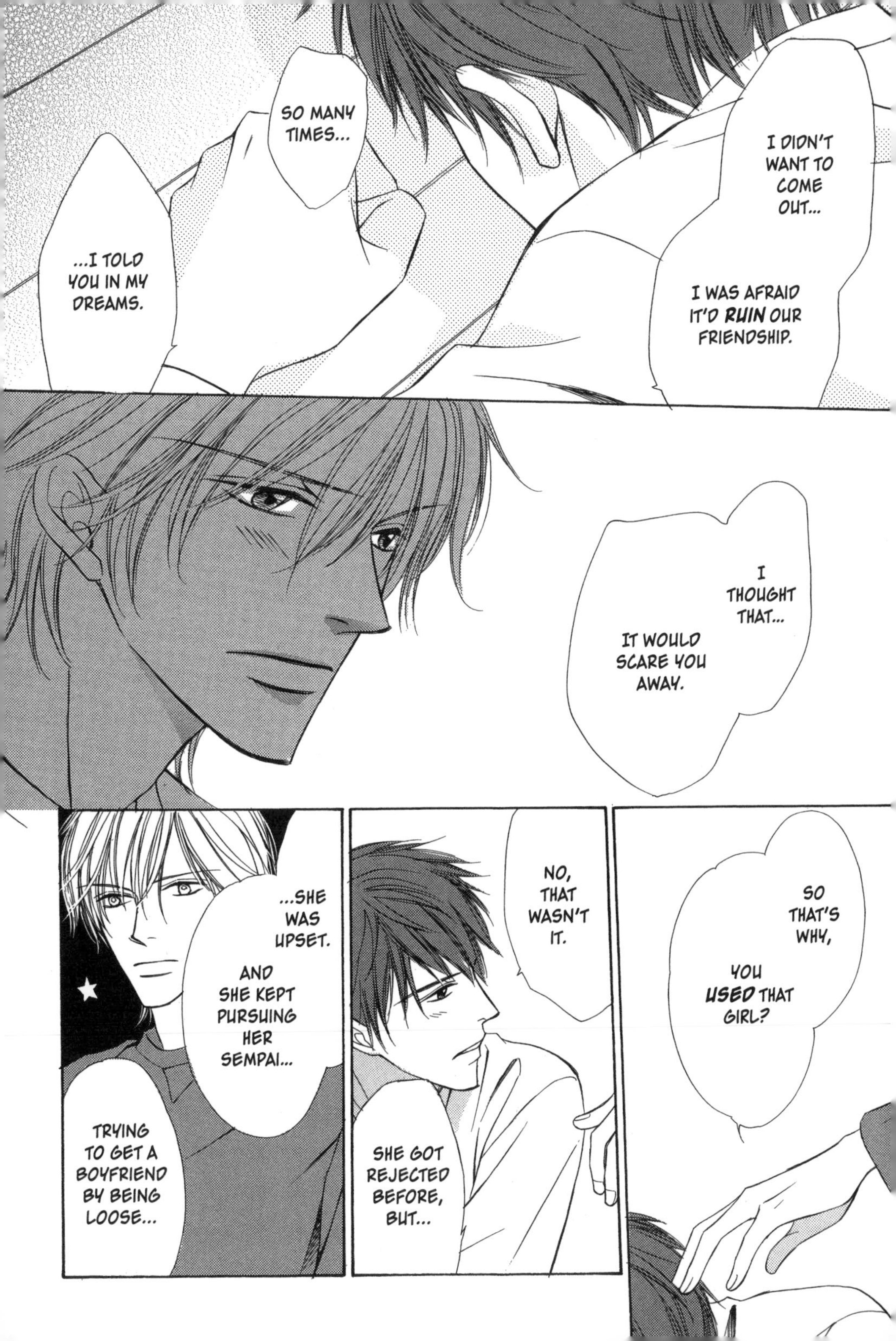
I DIDN'T WANT TO COME OUT...
I WAS AFRAID IT'D **RUIN** OUR FRIENDSHIP.
SO MANY TIMES...
...I TOLD YOU IN MY DREAMS.
I THOUGHT THAT...
IT WOULD SCARE YOU AWAY.
SO THAT'S WHY,
YOU **USED** THAT GIRL?
NO, THAT WASN'T IT.
SHE GOT REJECTED BEFORE, BUT...
...SHE WAS UPSET.
AND SHE KEPT PURSUING HER SEMPAI...
TRYING TO GET A BOYFRIEND BY BEING LOOSE...

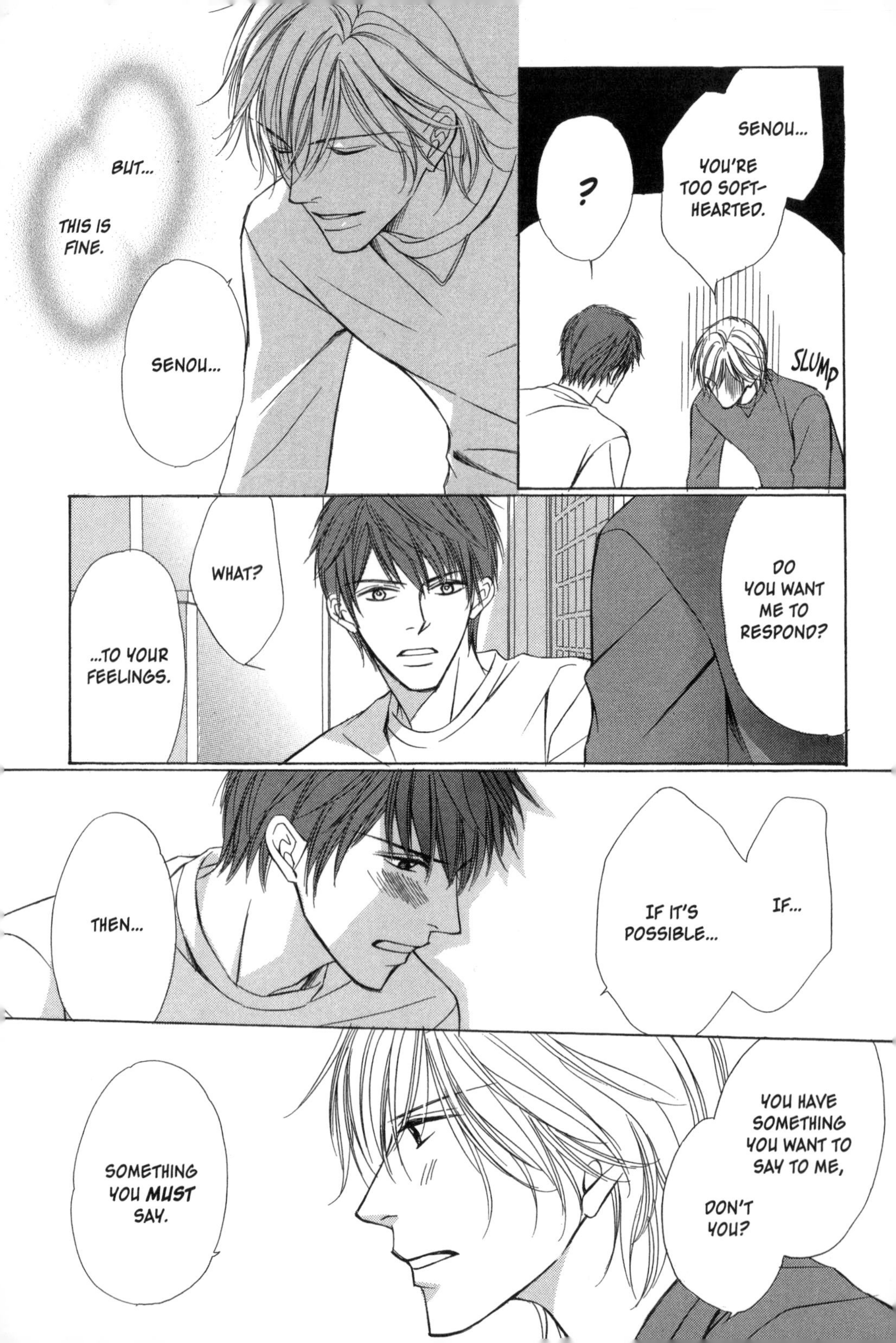
SENOU...
YOU'RE TOO SOFT-HEARTED.
?
SLUMP
BUT...
THIS IS FINE.
SENOU...
DO YOU WANT ME TO RESPOND?
WHAT?
...TO YOUR FEELINGS.
IF...
IF IT'S POSSIBLE...
THEN...
YOU HAVE SOMETHING YOU WANT TO SAY TO ME,
DON'T YOU?
SOMETHING YOU **MUST** SAY.

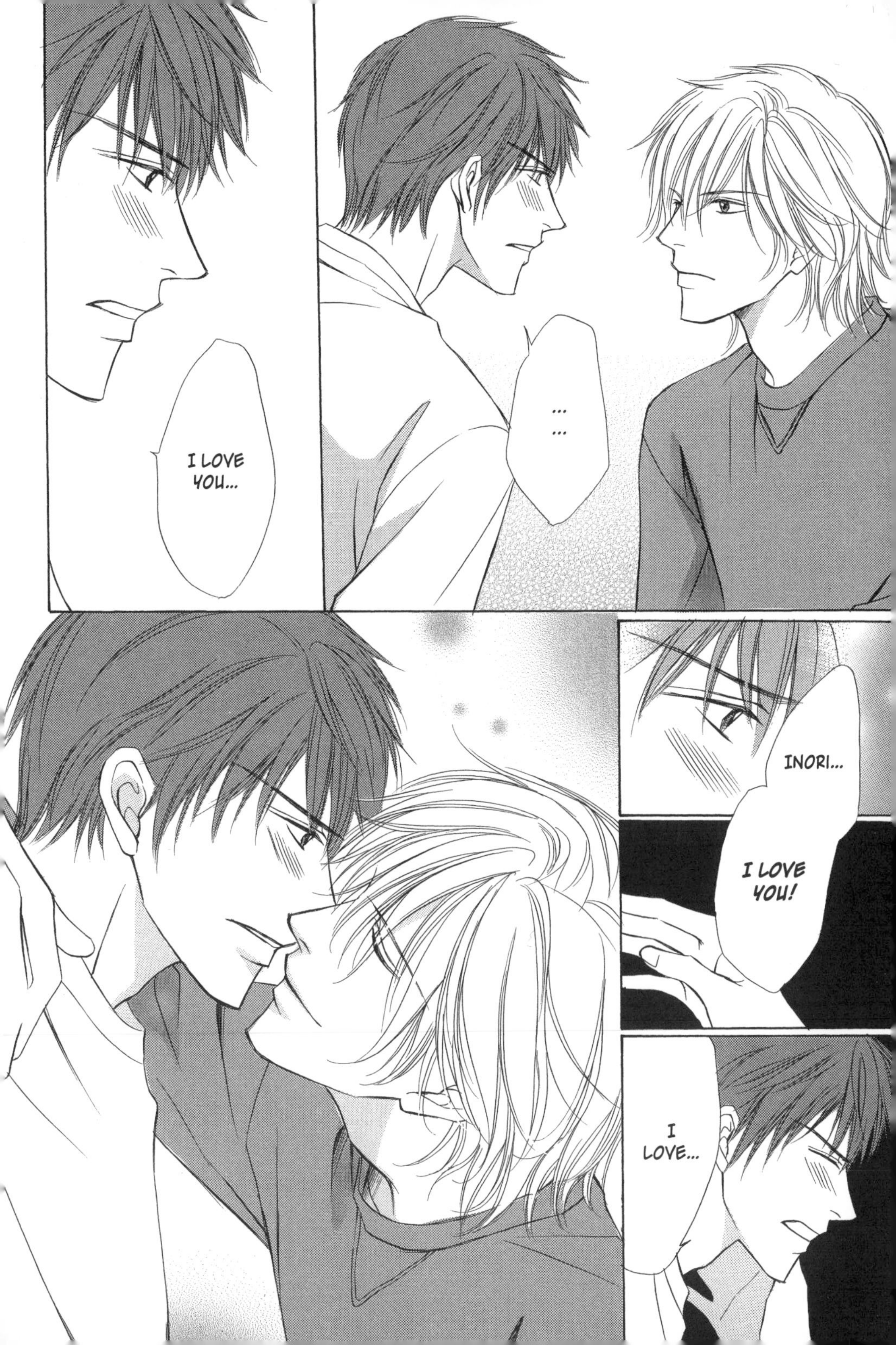
……
I LOVE YOU...
INORI...
I LOVE YOU!
I LOVE...

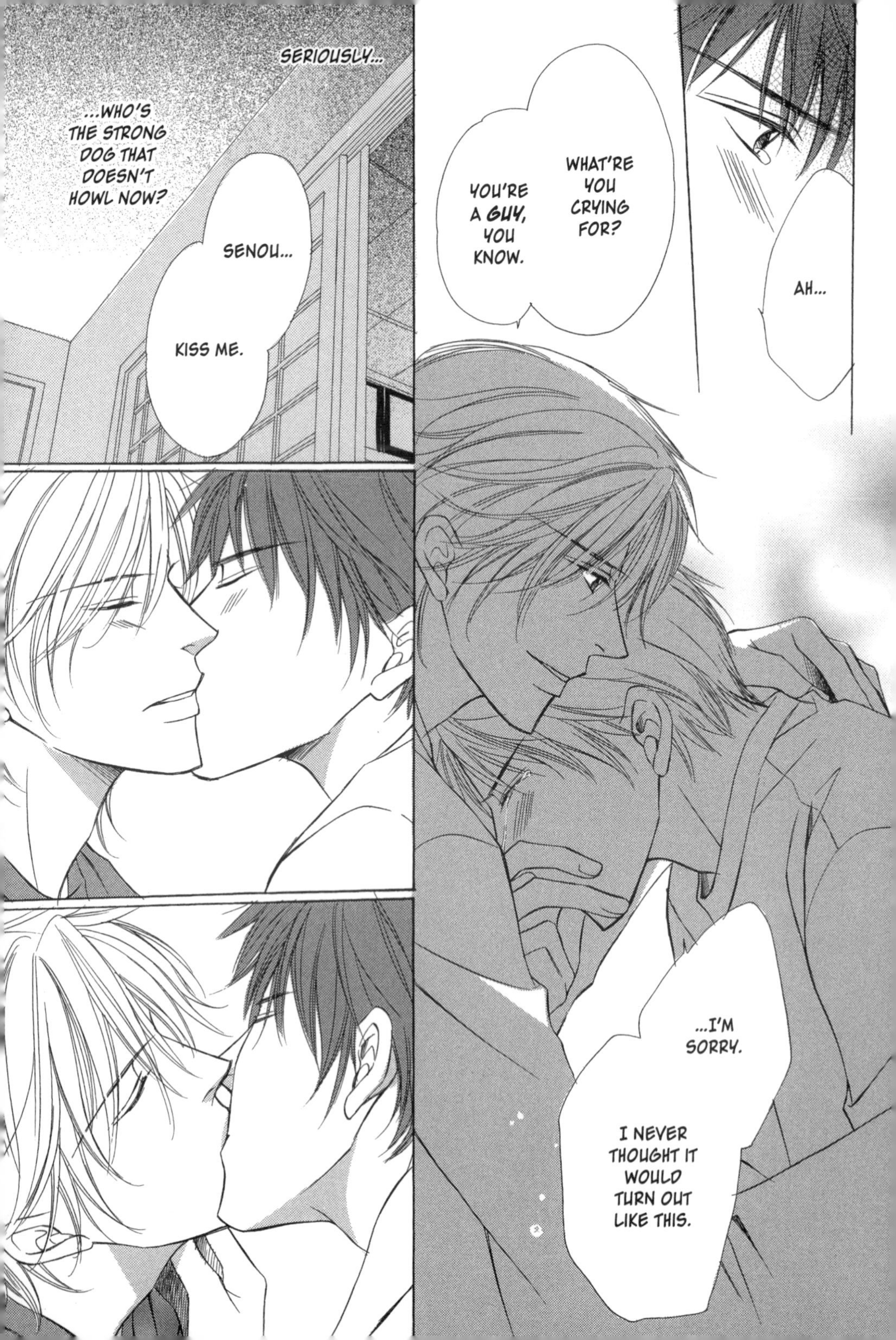
AH...
WHAT'RE YOU CRYING FOR?
YOU'RE A GUY, YOU KNOW.
...I'M SORRY.
I NEVER THOUGHT IT WOULD TURN OUT LIKE THIS.
SERIOUSLY...
...WHO'S THE STRONG DOG THAT DOESN'T HOWL NOW?
SENOU...
KISS ME.

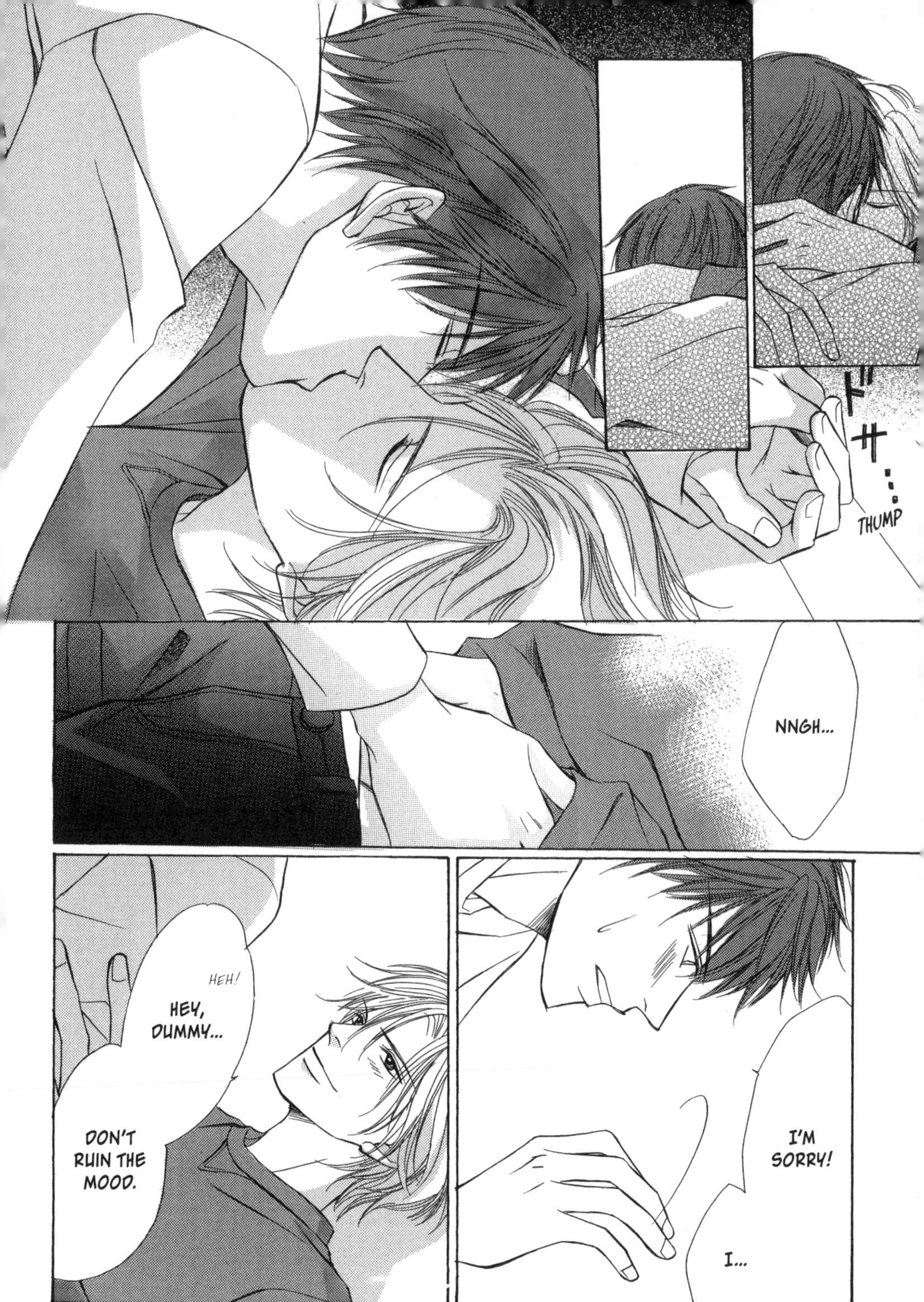
ドサ…
THUMP
NNGH...
I'M SORRY!
I...
HEH!
HEY, DUMMY...
DON'T RUIN THE MOOD.

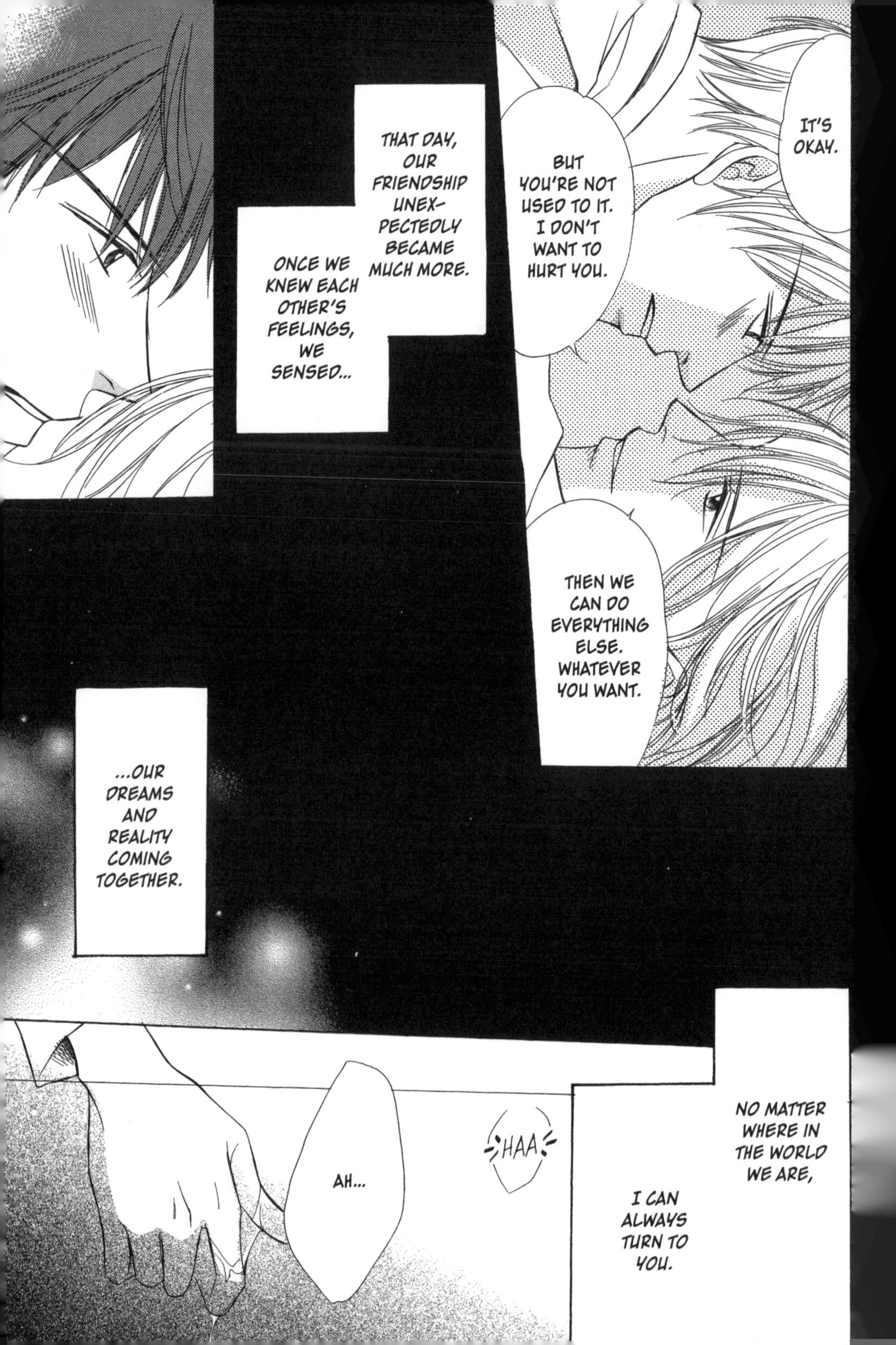

IT'S OKAY.
BUT YOU'RE NOT USED TO IT. I DON'T WANT TO HURT YOU.
THEN WE CAN DO EVERYTHING ELSE. WHATEVER YOU WANT.
THAT DAY, OUR FRIENDSHIP UNEX-PECTEDLY BECAME MUCH MORE.
ONCE WE KNEW EACH OTHER'S FEELINGS, WE SENSED...
...OUR DREAMS AND REALITY COMING TOGETHER.
NO MATTER WHERE IN THE WORLD WE ARE,
I CAN ALWAYS TURN TO YOU.
HAA
AH...

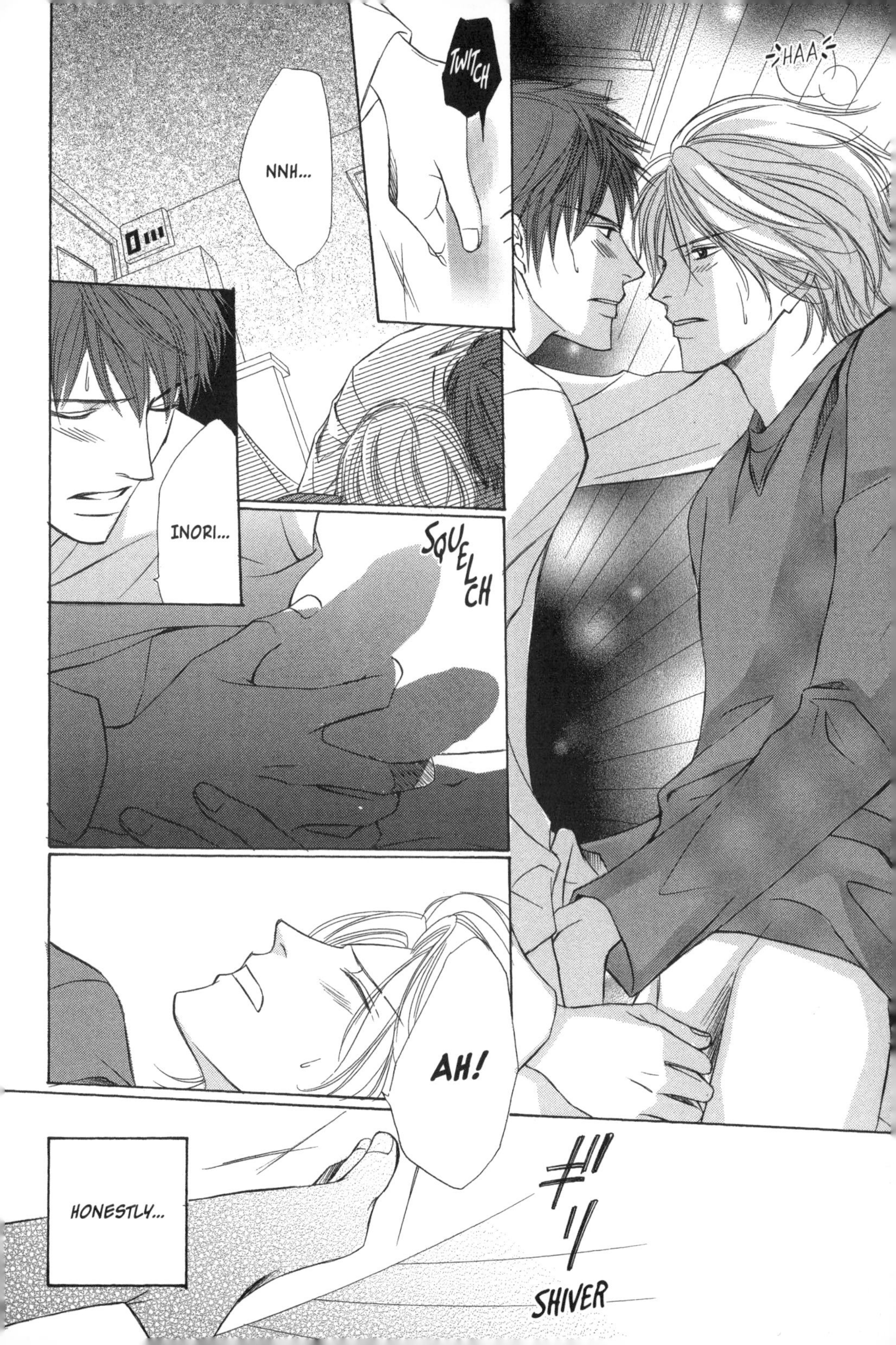
HAA
TWITCH
NNH...
INORI...
SQUELCH
AH!
ギリ
SHIVER
HONESTLY...

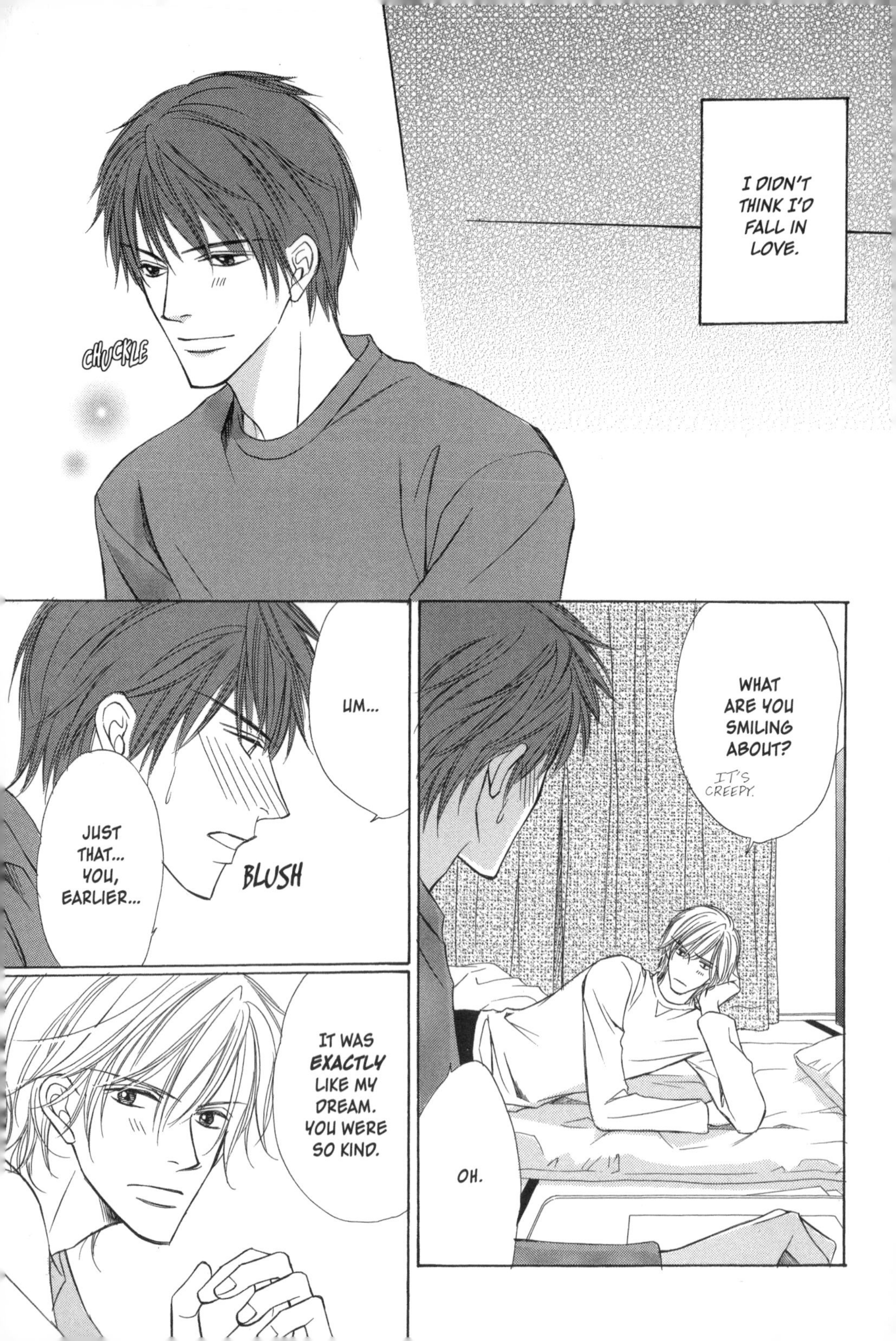
I DIDN'T THINK I'D FALL IN LOVE.
CHUCKLE
WHAT ARE YOU SMILING ABOUT?
IT'S CREEPY.
OH.
UM...
JUST THAT... YOU, EARLIER...
BLUSH
IT WAS EXACTLY LIKE MY DREAM. YOU WERE SO KIND.

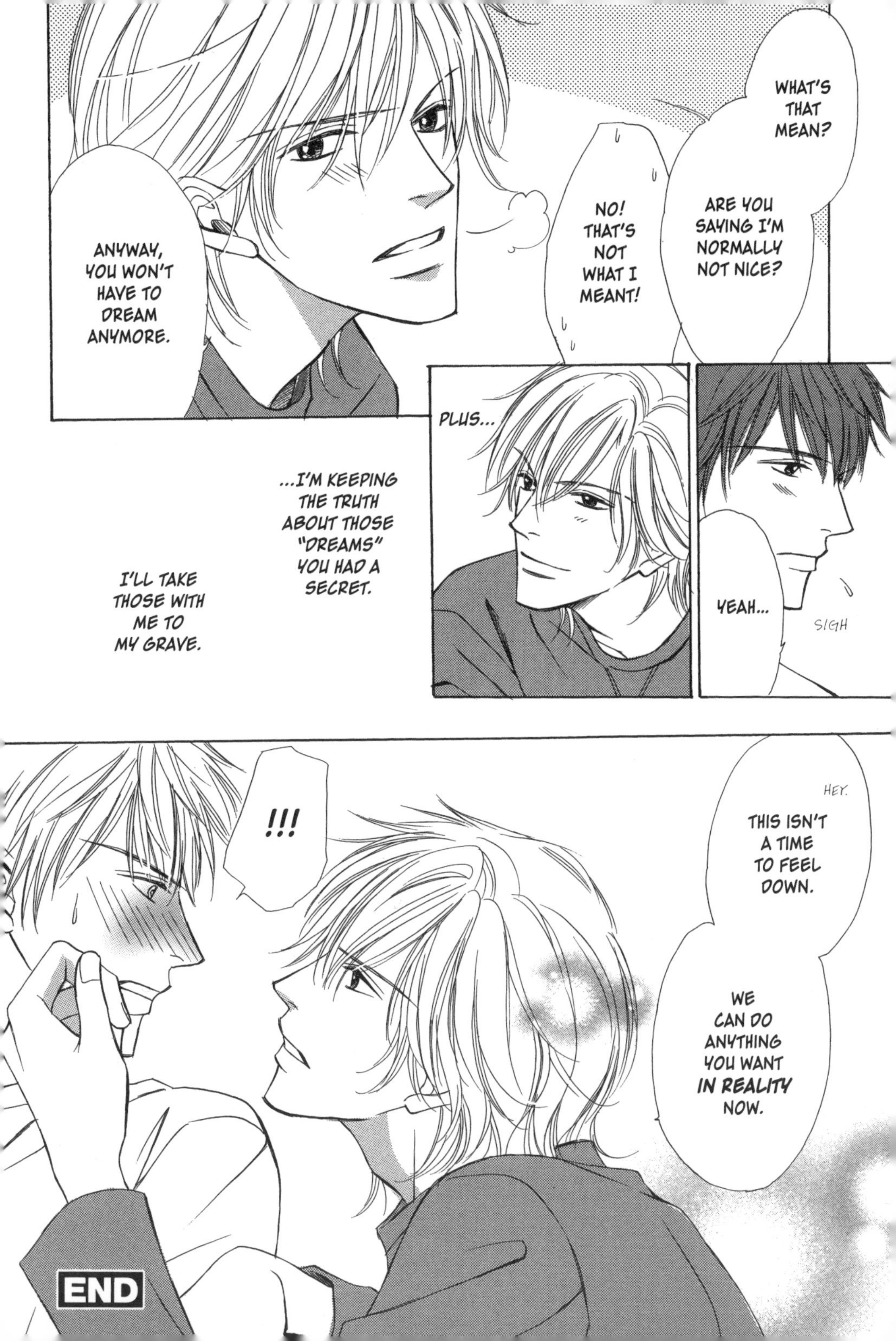
WHAT'S THAT MEAN?
ARE YOU SAYING I'M NORMALLY NOT NICE?
NO! THAT'S NOT WHAT I MEANT!
ANYWAY, YOU WON'T HAVE TO DREAM ANYMORE.
YEAH...
SIGH
PLUS...
...I'M KEEPING THE TRUTH ABOUT THOSE "DREAMS" YOU HAD A SECRET.
I'LL TAKE THOSE WITH ME TO MY GRAVE.
HEY.
THIS ISN'T A TIME TO FEEL DOWN.
WE CAN DO ANYTHING YOU WANT IN REALITY NOW.
!!!
END

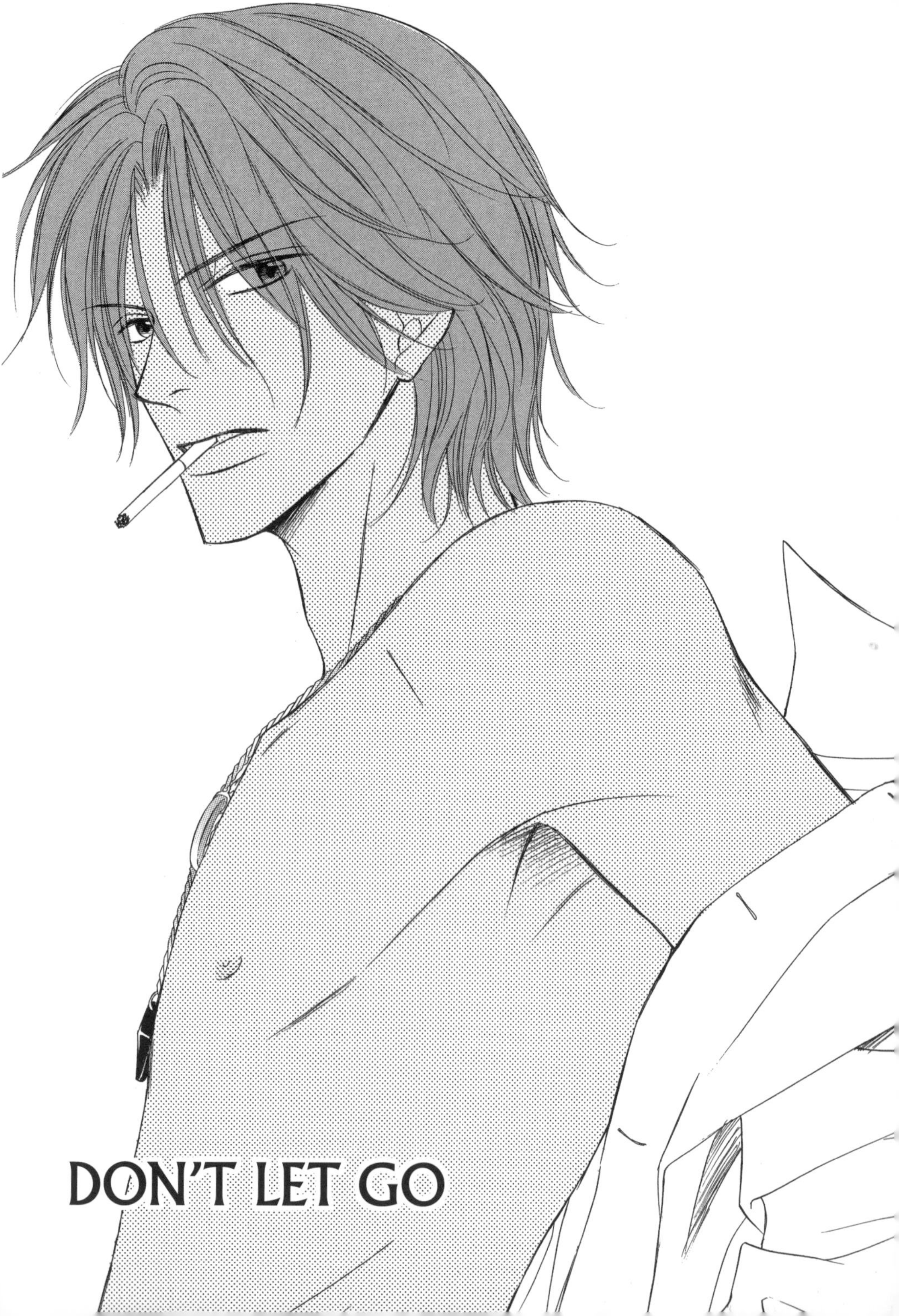

DON'T LET GO

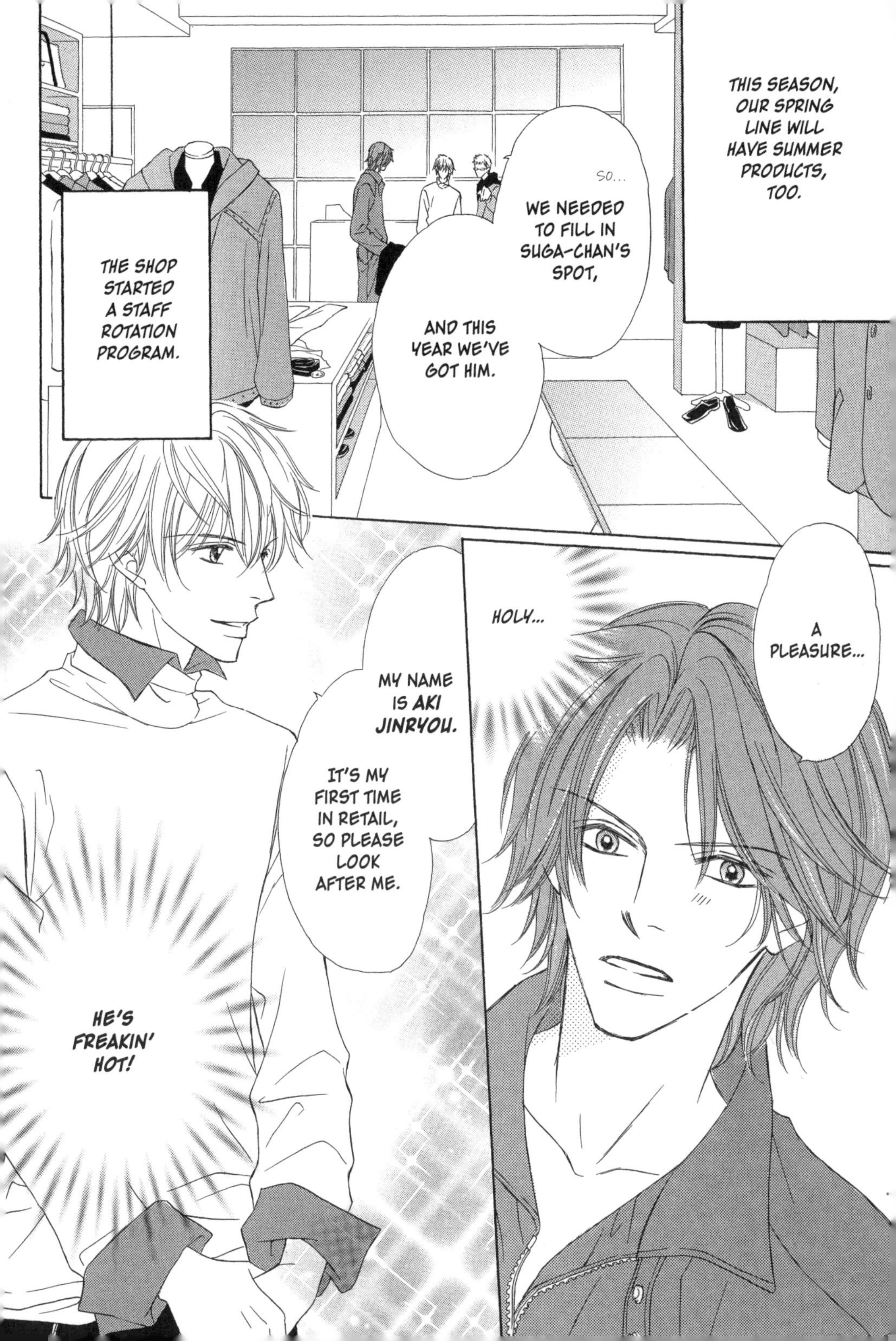
THIS SEASON, OUR SPRING LINE WILL HAVE SUMMER PRODUCTS, TOO.
SO...
WE NEEDED TO FILL IN SUGA-CHAN'S SPOT,
AND THIS YEAR WE'VE GOT HIM.
THE SHOP STARTED A STAFF ROTATION PROGRAM.
A PLEASURE...
HOLY...
MY NAME IS AKI JINRYOU.
IT'S MY FIRST TIME IN RETAIL, SO PLEASE LOOK AFTER ME.
HE'S FREAKIN' HOT!

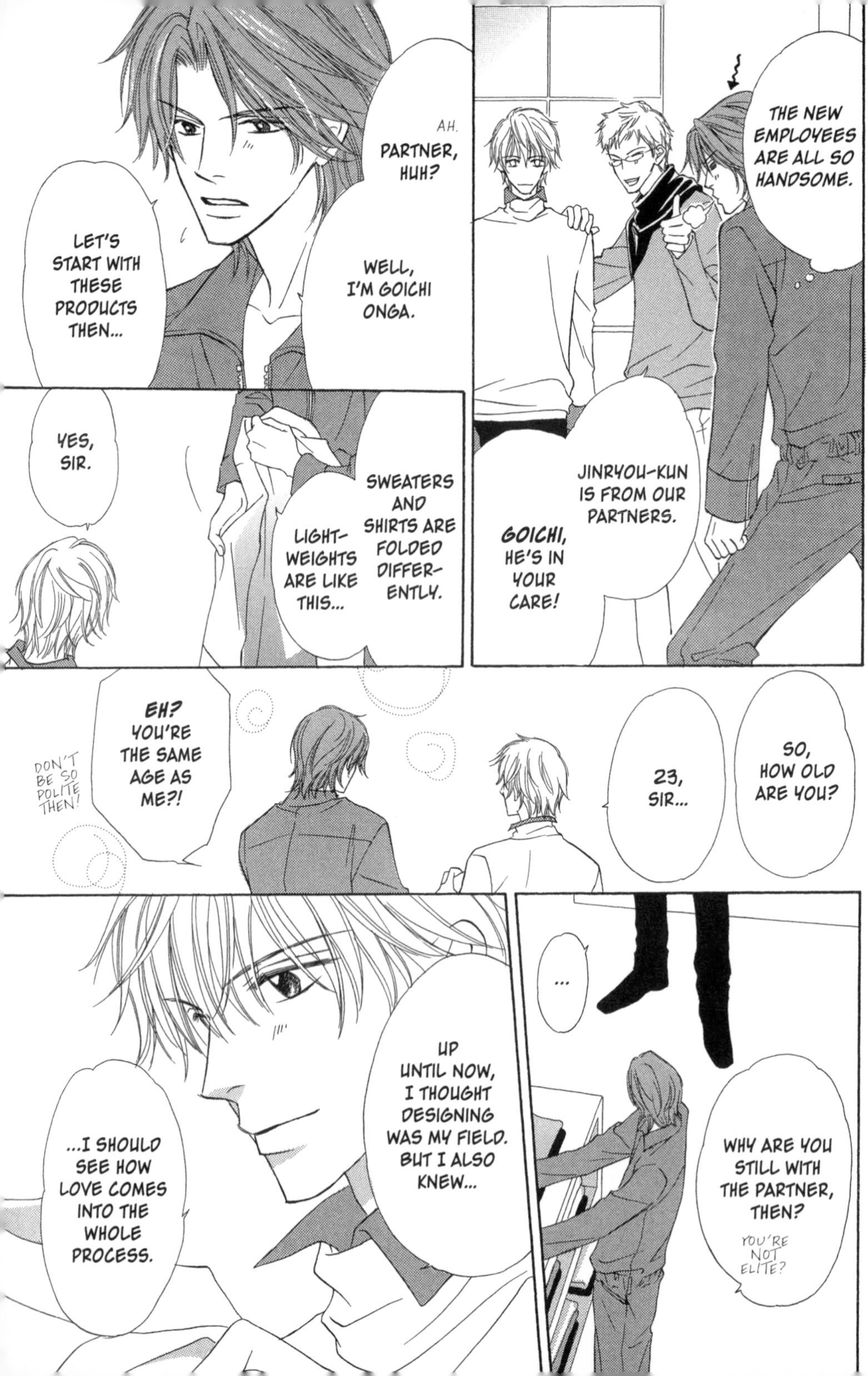
THE NEW EMPLOYEES ARE ALL SO HANDSOME.
JINRYOU-KUN IS FROM OUR PARTNERS.
GOICHI, HE'S IN YOUR CARE!
AH.
PARTNER, HUH?
WELL, I'M GOICHI ONGA.
LET'S START WITH THESE PRODUCTS THEN...
SWEATERS AND SHIRTS ARE FOLDED DIFFERENTLY.
LIGHT-WEIGHTS ARE LIKE THIS...
YES, SIR.
SO, HOW OLD ARE YOU?
23, SIR...
EH? YOU'RE THE SAME AGE AS ME?!
DON'T BE SO POLITE THEN!
...
WHY ARE YOU STILL WITH THE PARTNER, THEN?
YOU'RE NOT ELITE?
UP UNTIL NOW, I THOUGHT DESIGNING WAS MY FIELD. BUT I ALSO KNEW...
...I SHOULD SEE HOW LOVE COMES INTO THE WHOLE PROCESS.

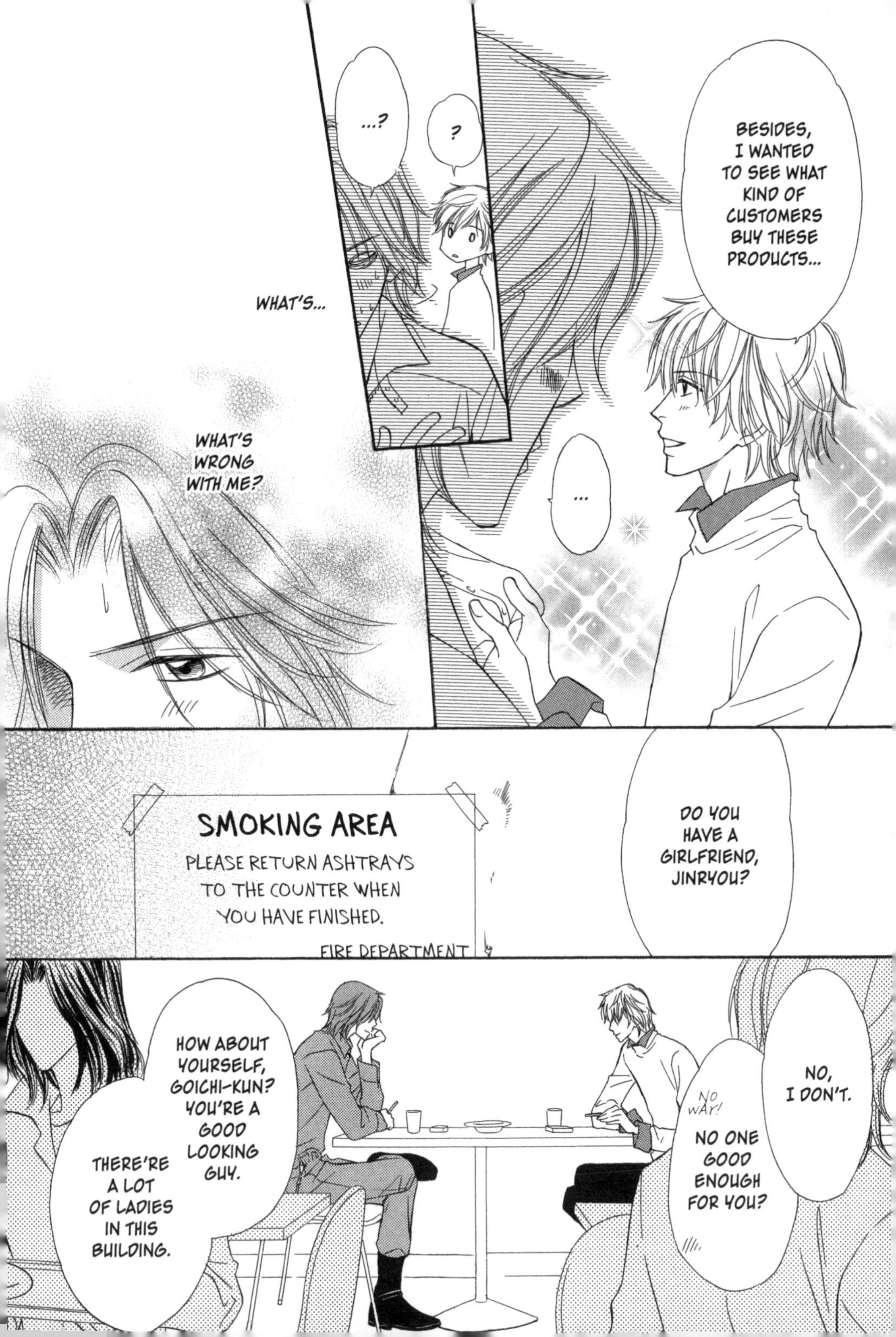

BESIDES, I WANTED TO SEE WHAT KIND OF CUSTOMERS BUY THESE PRODUCTS...
...
...?
?
WHAT'S...
WHAT'S WRONG WITH ME?
DO YOU HAVE A GIRLFRIEND, JINRYOU?
SMOKING AREA
PLEASE RETURN ASHTRAYS TO THE COUNTER WHEN YOU HAVE FINISHED.
FIRE DEPARTMENT
NO, I DON'T.
NO WAY!
NO ONE GOOD ENOUGH FOR YOU?
HOW ABOUT YOURSELF, GOICHI-KUN? YOU'RE A GOOD LOOKING GUY.
THERE'RE A LOT OF LADIES IN THIS BUILDING.

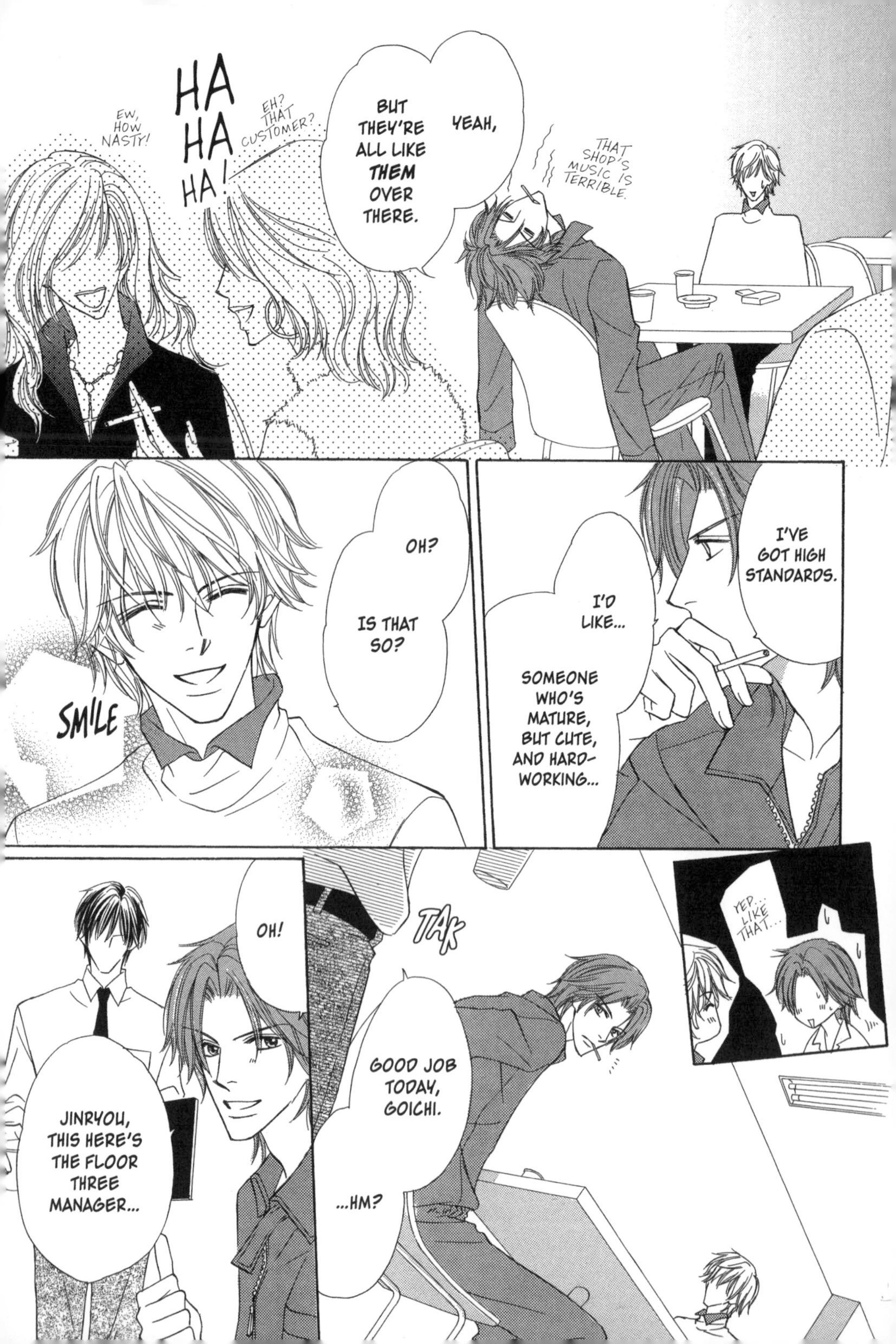
THAT SHOP'S MUSIC IS TERRIBLE.
YEAH,
BUT THEY'RE ALL LIKE THEM OVER THERE.
EH? THAT CUSTOMER?
HA HA HA!
EW, HOW NASTY!
I'VE GOT HIGH STANDARDS.
I'D LIKE...
SOMEONE WHO'S MATURE, BUT CUTE, AND HARD-WORKING...
OH?
IS THAT SO?
SMILE
YEP... LIKE THAT...
TAK
GOOD JOB TODAY, GOICHI.
...HM?
OH!
JINRYOU, THIS HERE'S THE FLOOR THREE MANAGER...

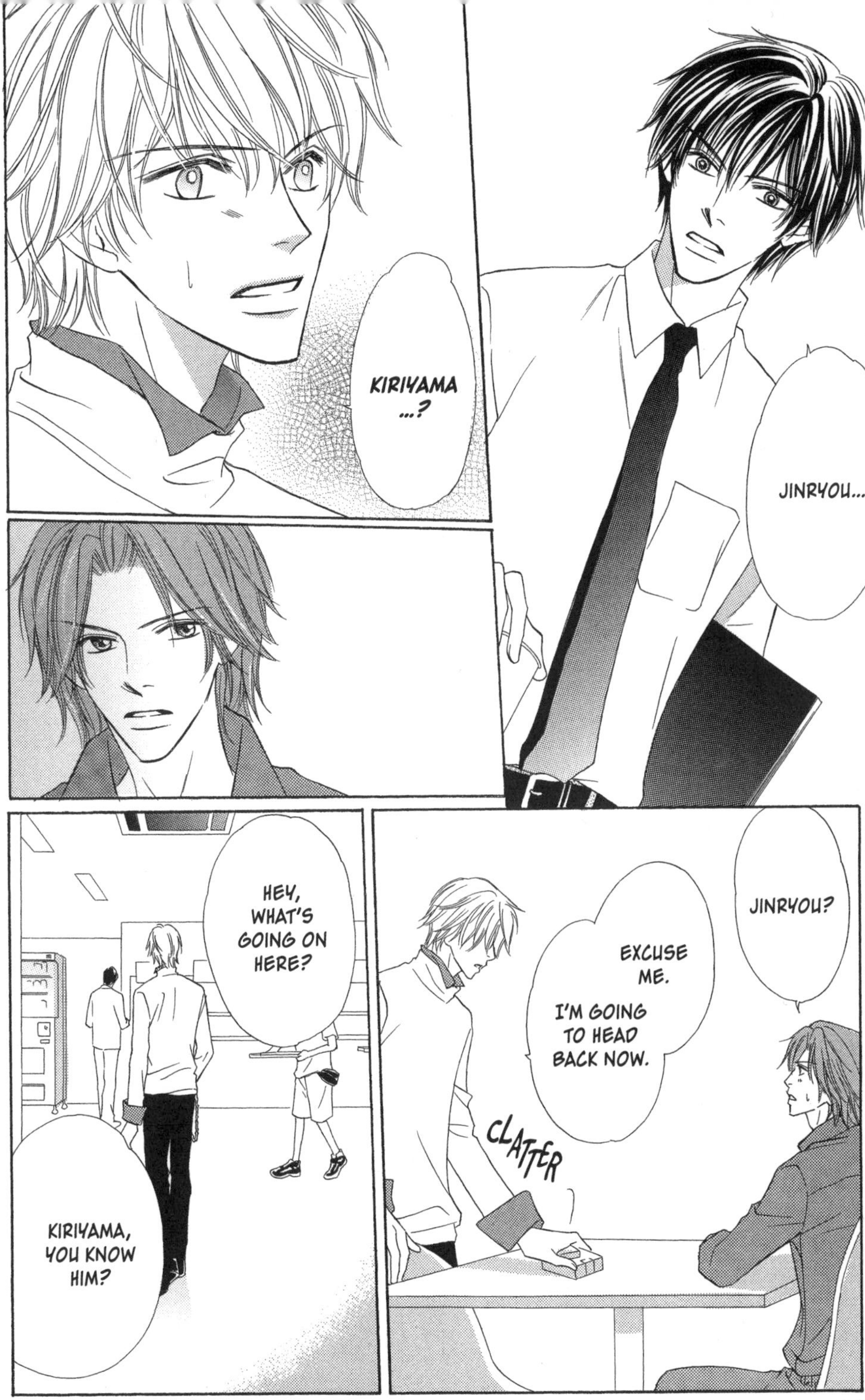
JINRYOU...
KIRIYAMA ...?
JINRYOU?
EXCUSE ME. I'M GOING TO HEAD BACK NOW.
CLATTER
HEY, WHAT'S GOING ON HERE?
KIRIYAMA, YOU KNOW HIM?

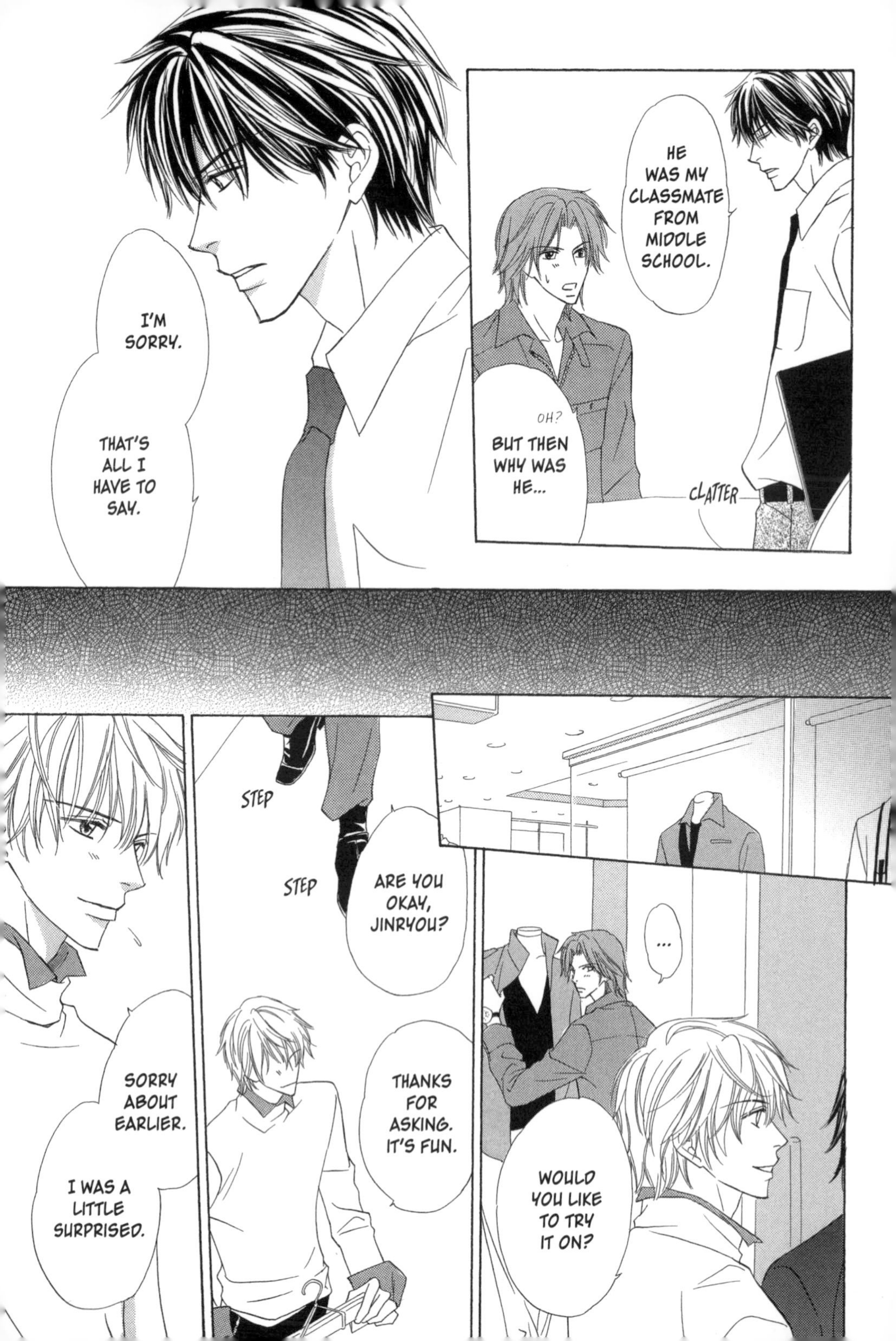
HE WAS MY CLASSMATE FROM MIDDLE SCHOOL.
OH?
BUT THEN WHY WAS HE...
CLATTER
I'M SORRY.
THAT'S ALL I HAVE TO SAY.
...
WOULD YOU LIKE TO TRY IT ON?
STEP
STEP
ARE YOU OKAY, JINRYOU?
THANKS FOR ASKING. IT'S FUN.
SORRY ABOUT EARLIER.
I WAS A LITTLE SURPRISED.

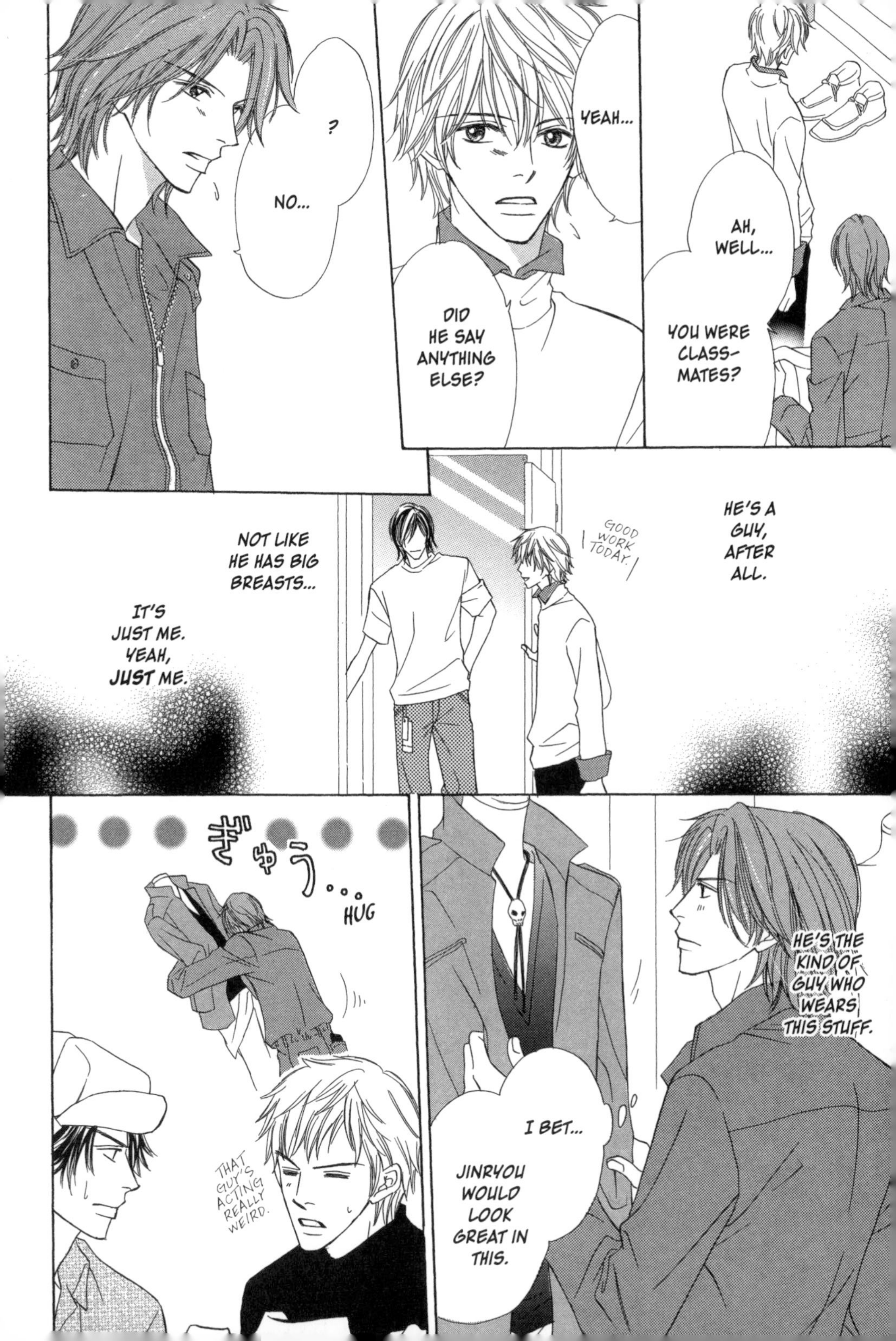
AH, WELL...
YOU WERE CLASS-MATES?
YEAH...
DID HE SAY ANYTHING ELSE?
?
NO...
HE'S A GUY, AFTER ALL.
GOOD WORK TODAY.
NOT LIKE HE HAS BIG BREASTS...
IT'S JUST ME. YEAH, JUST ME.
HE'S THE KIND OF GUY WHO WEARS THIS STUFF.
I BET...
JINRYOU WOULD LOOK GREAT IN THIS.
ぎゅう...
HUG
THAT GUY'S ACTING REALLY WEIRD.

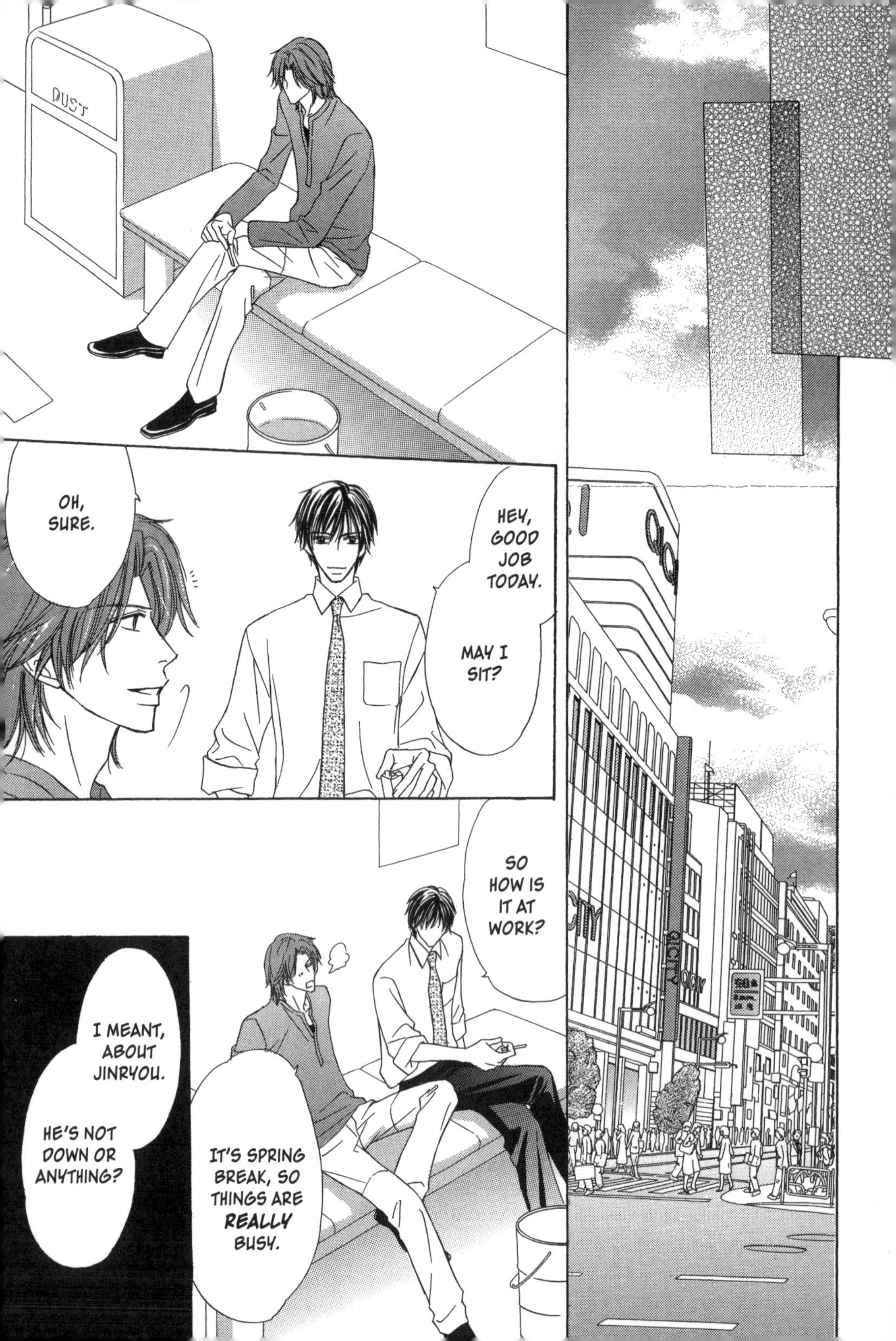
DUST
HEY, GOOD JOB TODAY.
MAY I SIT?
OH, SURE.
SO HOW IS IT AT WORK?
IT'S SPRING BREAK, SO THINGS ARE **REALLY** BUSY.
I MEANT, ABOUT JINRYOU.
HE'S NOT DOWN OR ANYTHING?

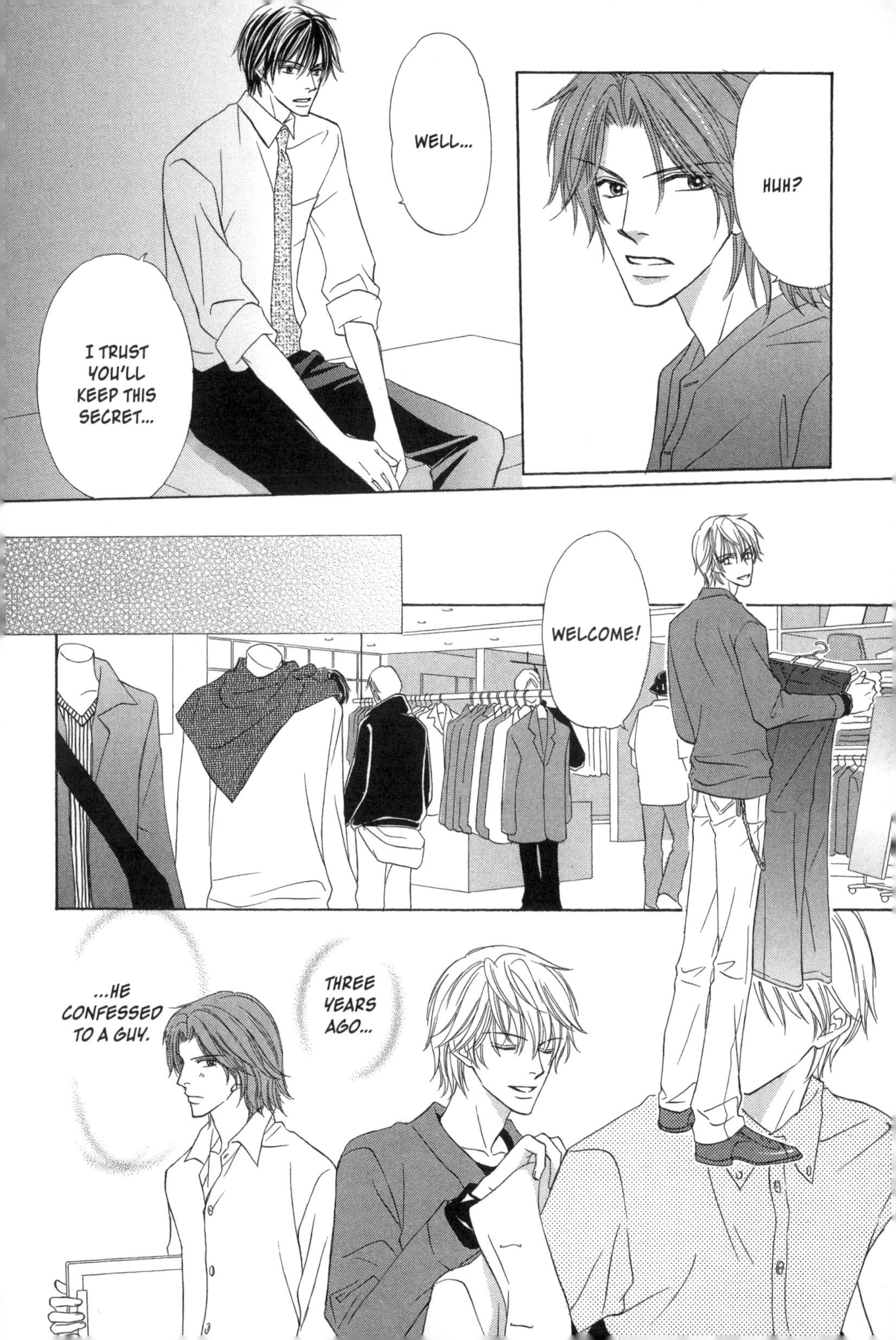
HUH?
WELL...
I TRUST YOU'LL KEEP THIS SECRET...
WELCOME!
THREE YEARS AGO...
...HE CONFESSED TO A GUY.

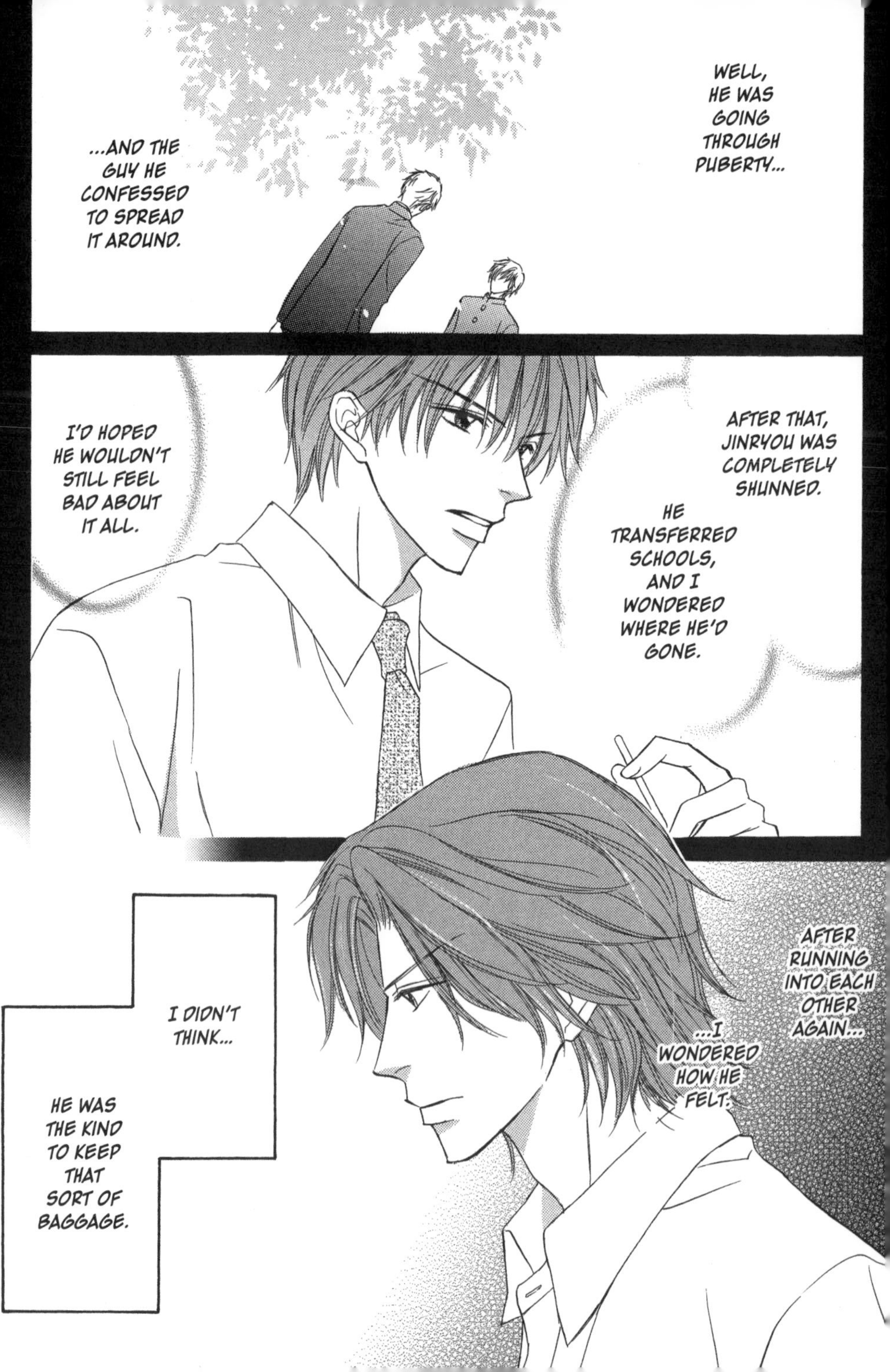
WELL, HE WAS GOING THROUGH PUBERTY...
...AND THE GUY HE CONFESSED TO SPREAD IT AROUND.
AFTER THAT, JINRYOU WAS COMPLETELY SHUNNED.
HE TRANSFERRED SCHOOLS, AND I WONDERED WHERE HE'D GONE.
I'D HOPED HE WOULDN'T STILL FEEL BAD ABOUT IT ALL.
AFTER RUNNING INTO EACH OTHER AGAIN...
...I WONDERED HOW HE FELT.
I DIDN'T THINK...
HE WAS THE KIND TO KEEP THAT SORT OF BAGGAGE.

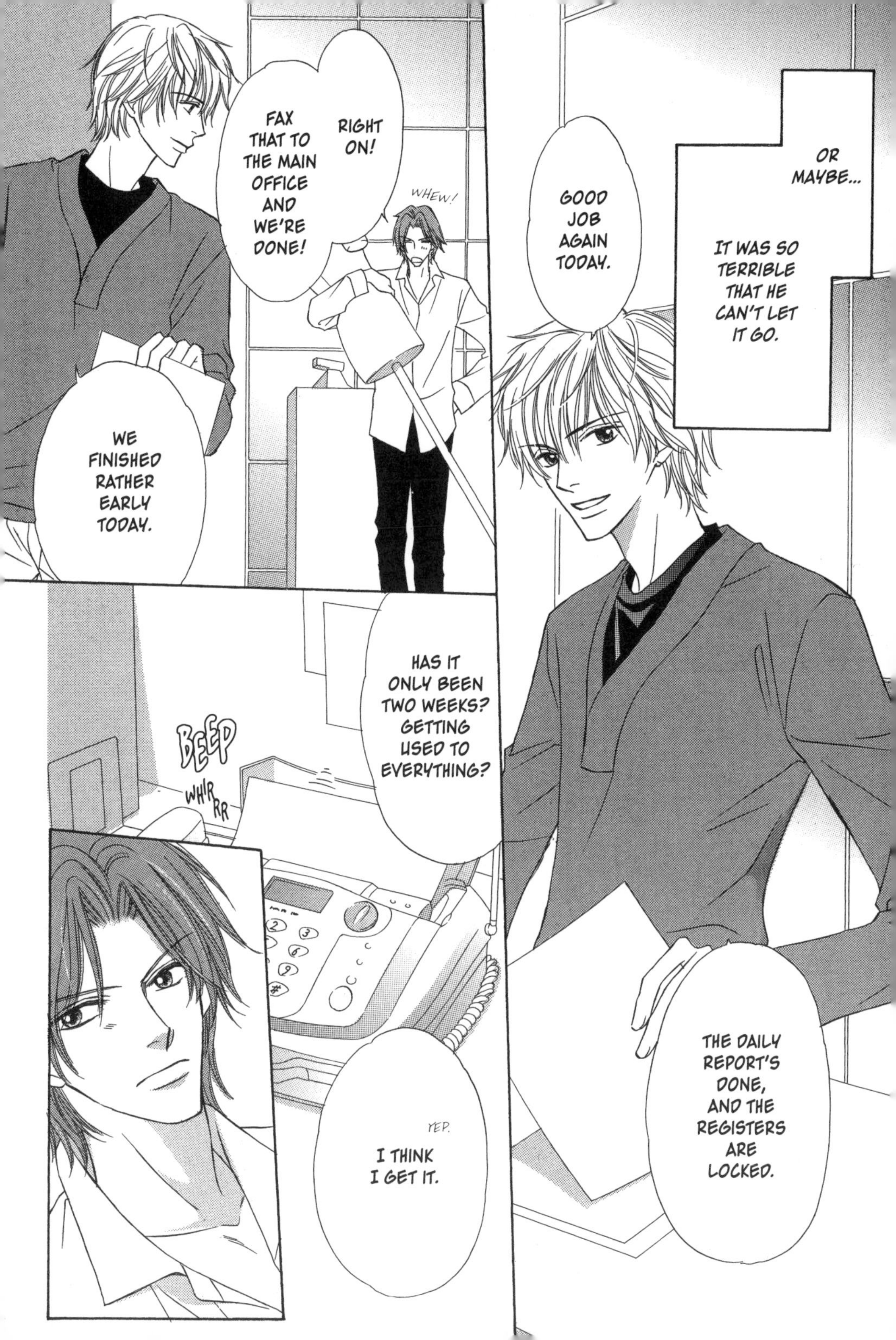
OR MAYBE...
IT WAS SO TERRIBLE THAT HE CAN'T LET IT GO.
GOOD JOB AGAIN TODAY.
THE DAILY REPORT'S DONE, AND THE REGISTERS ARE LOCKED.
RIGHT ON!
FAX THAT TO THE MAIN OFFICE AND WE'RE DONE!
WHEW!
WE FINISHED RATHER EARLY TODAY.
HAS IT ONLY BEEN TWO WEEKS? GETTING USED TO EVERYTHING?
BEEP
WHIRRR
YEP.
I THINK I GET IT.

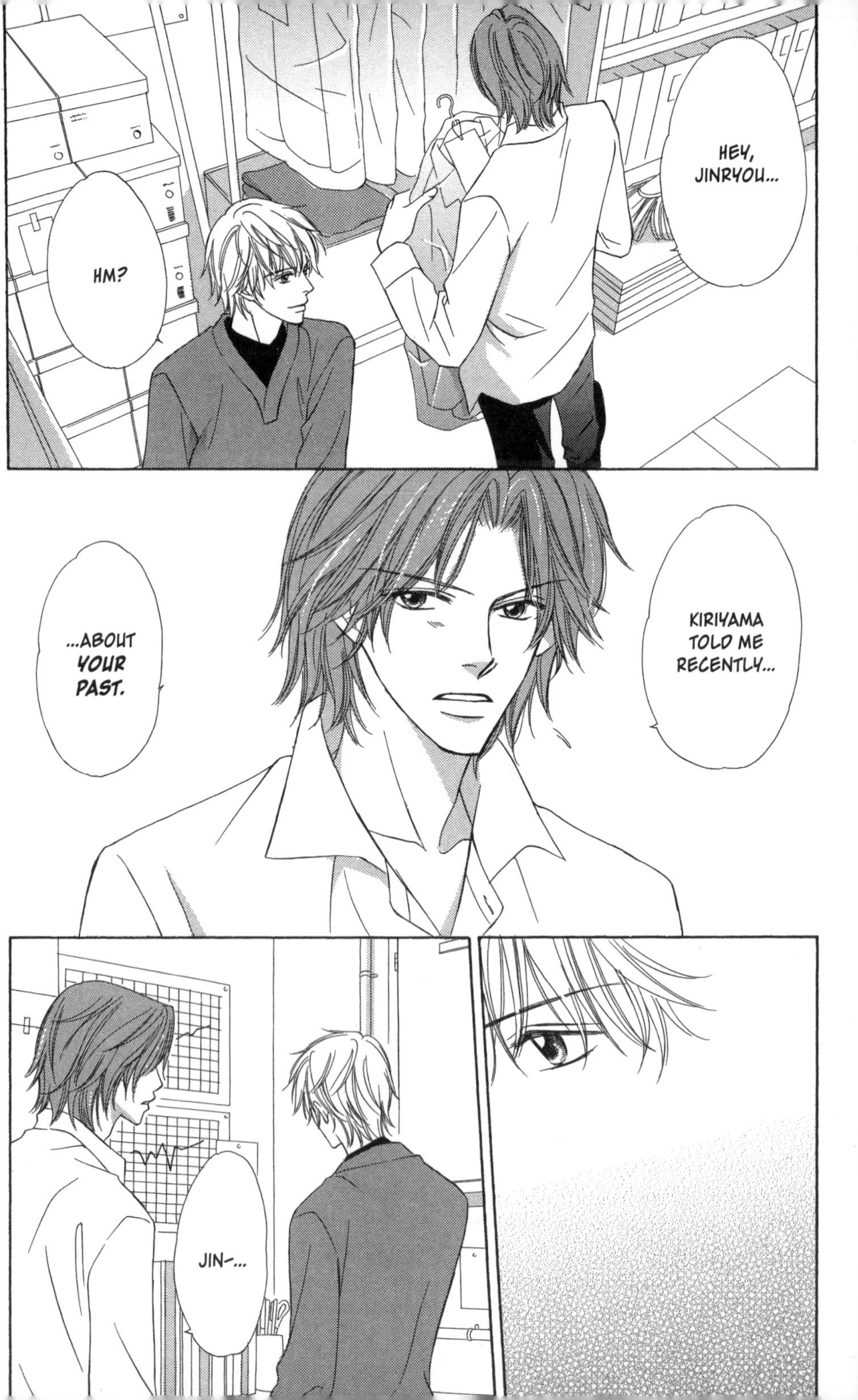
HEY, JINRYOU...
HM?
KIRIYAMA TOLD ME RECENTLY...
...ABOUT YOUR PAST.
JIN-...

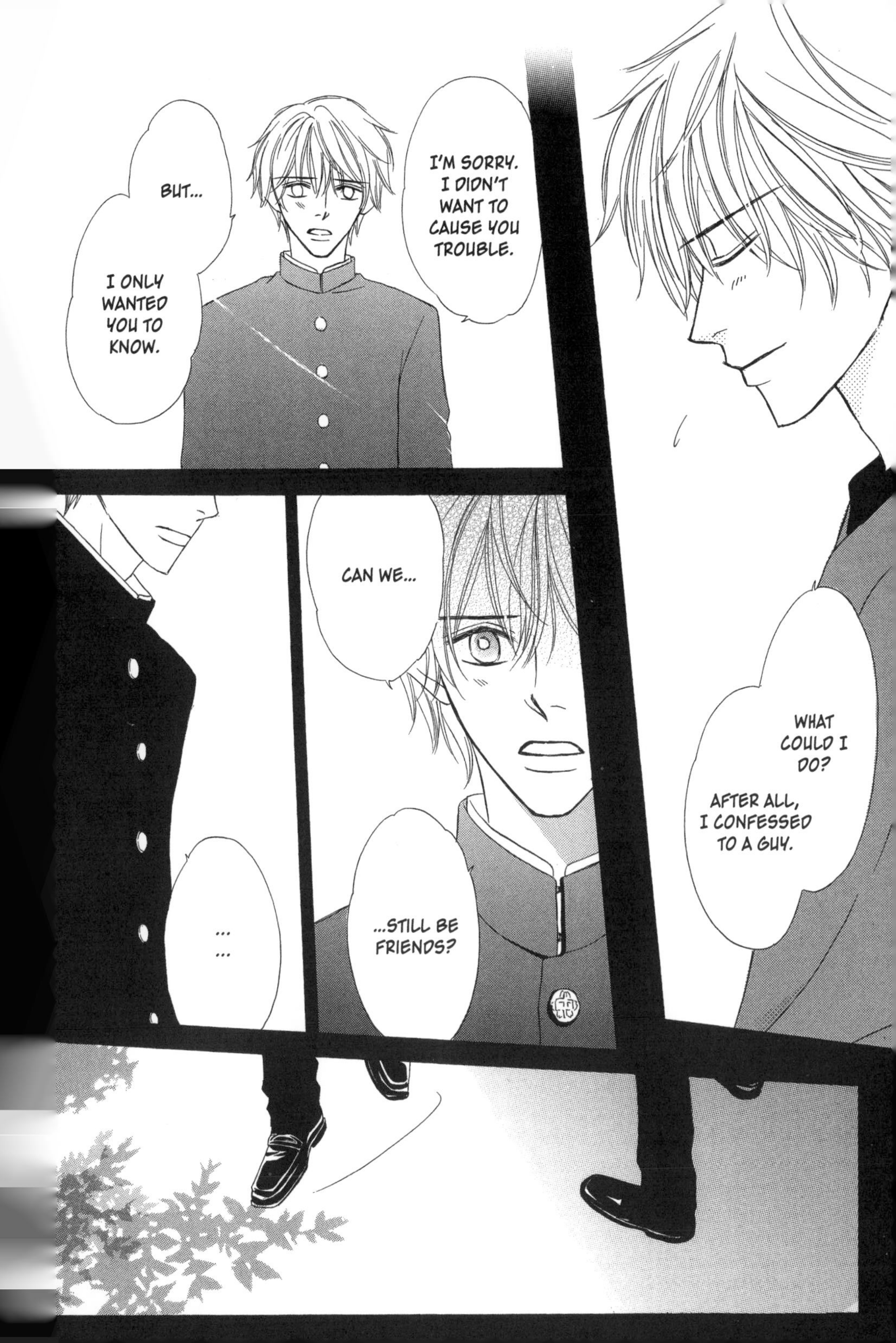
WHAT COULD I DO?
AFTER ALL, I CONFESSED TO A GUY.
I'M SORRY. I DIDN'T WANT TO CAUSE YOU TROUBLE.
BUT...
I ONLY WANTED YOU TO KNOW.
CAN WE...
...STILL BE FRIENDS?
... ...

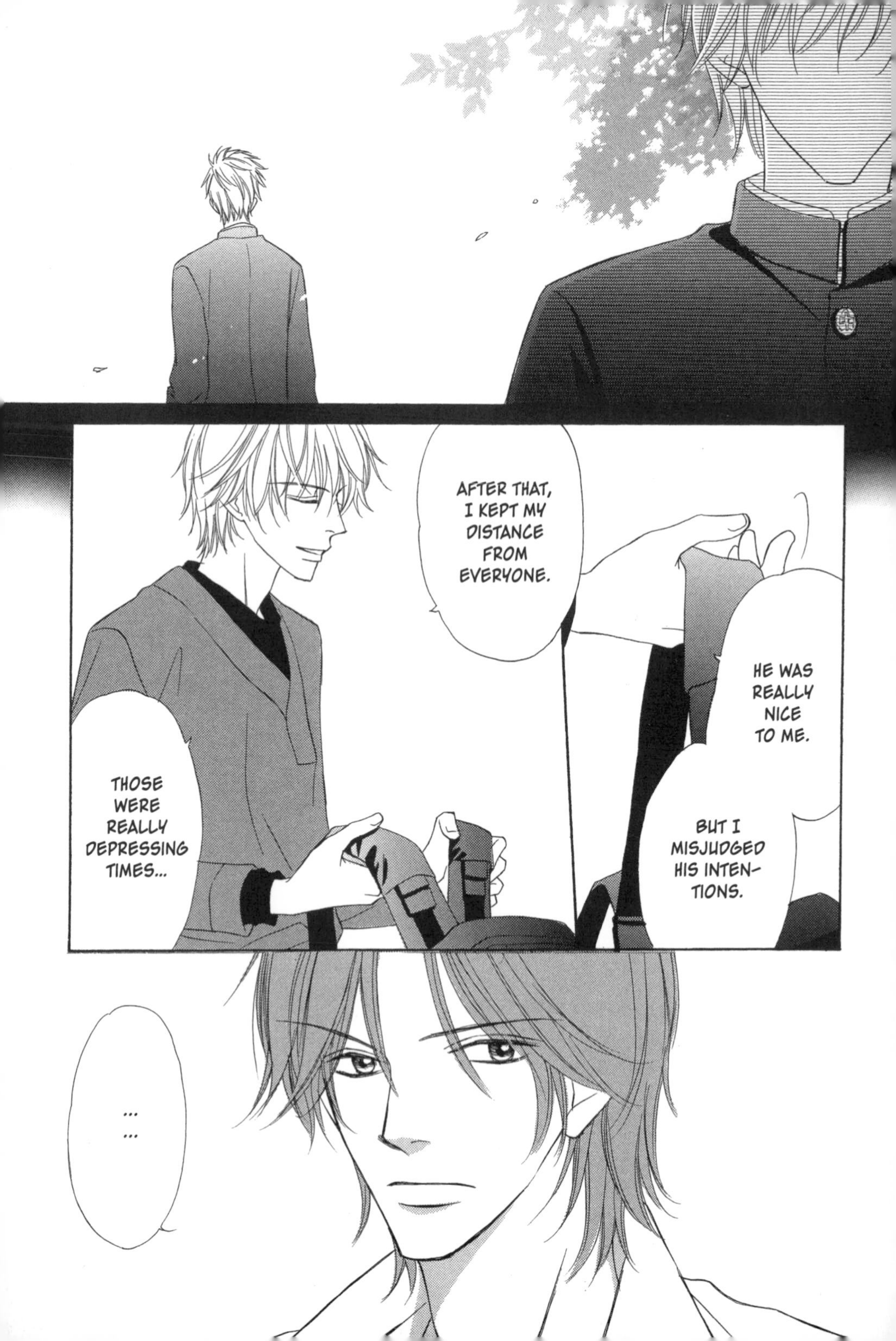
HE WAS REALLY NICE TO ME.
BUT I MISJUDGED HIS INTEN-TIONS.
AFTER THAT, I KEPT MY DISTANCE FROM EVERYONE.
THOSE WERE REALLY DEPRESSING TIMES...
...
...

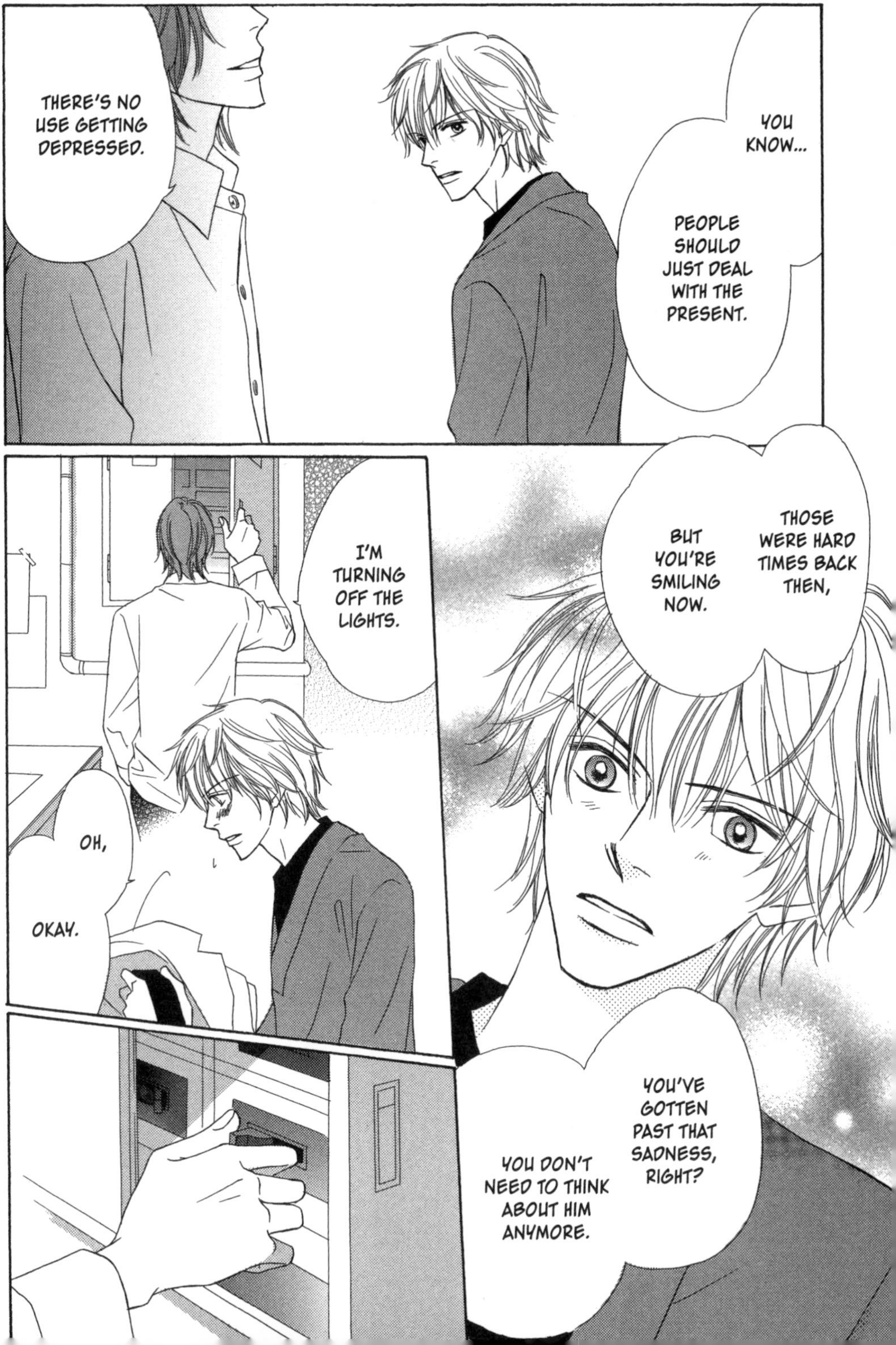
YOU KNOW...
PEOPLE SHOULD JUST DEAL WITH THE PRESENT.
THERE'S NO USE GETTING DEPRESSED.
THOSE WERE HARD TIMES BACK THEN,
BUT YOU'RE SMILING NOW.
YOU'VE GOTTEN PAST THAT SADNESS, RIGHT?
YOU DON'T NEED TO THINK ABOUT HIM ANYMORE.
I'M TURNING OFF THE LIGHTS.
OH,
OKAY.

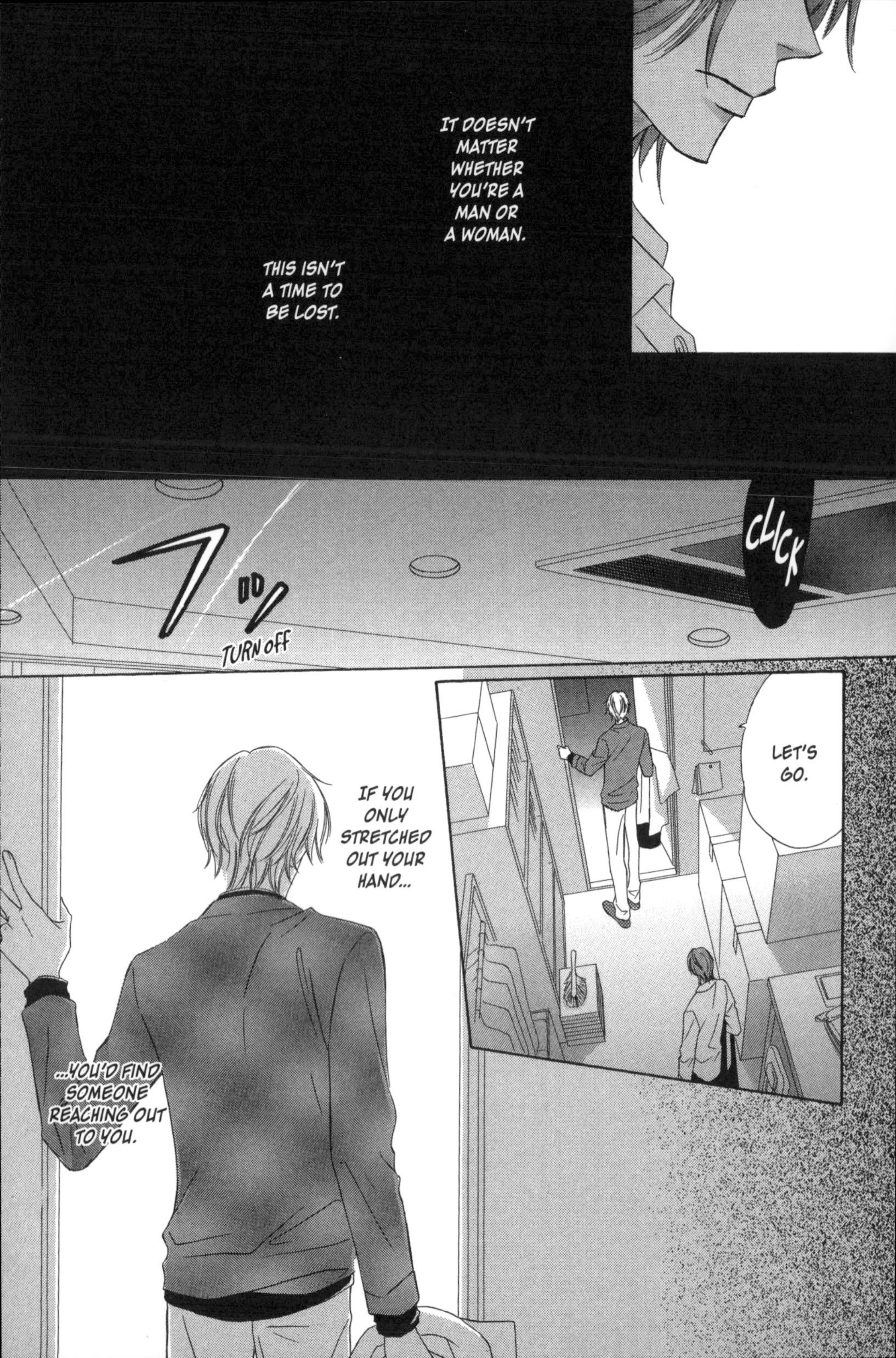
IT DOESN'T MATTER WHETHER YOU'RE A MAN OR A WOMAN.
THIS ISN'T A TIME TO BE LOST.
CLICK
TURN OFF
LET'S GO.
IF YOU ONLY STRETCHED OUT YOUR HAND...
...YOU'D FIND SOMEONE REACHING OUT TO YOU.

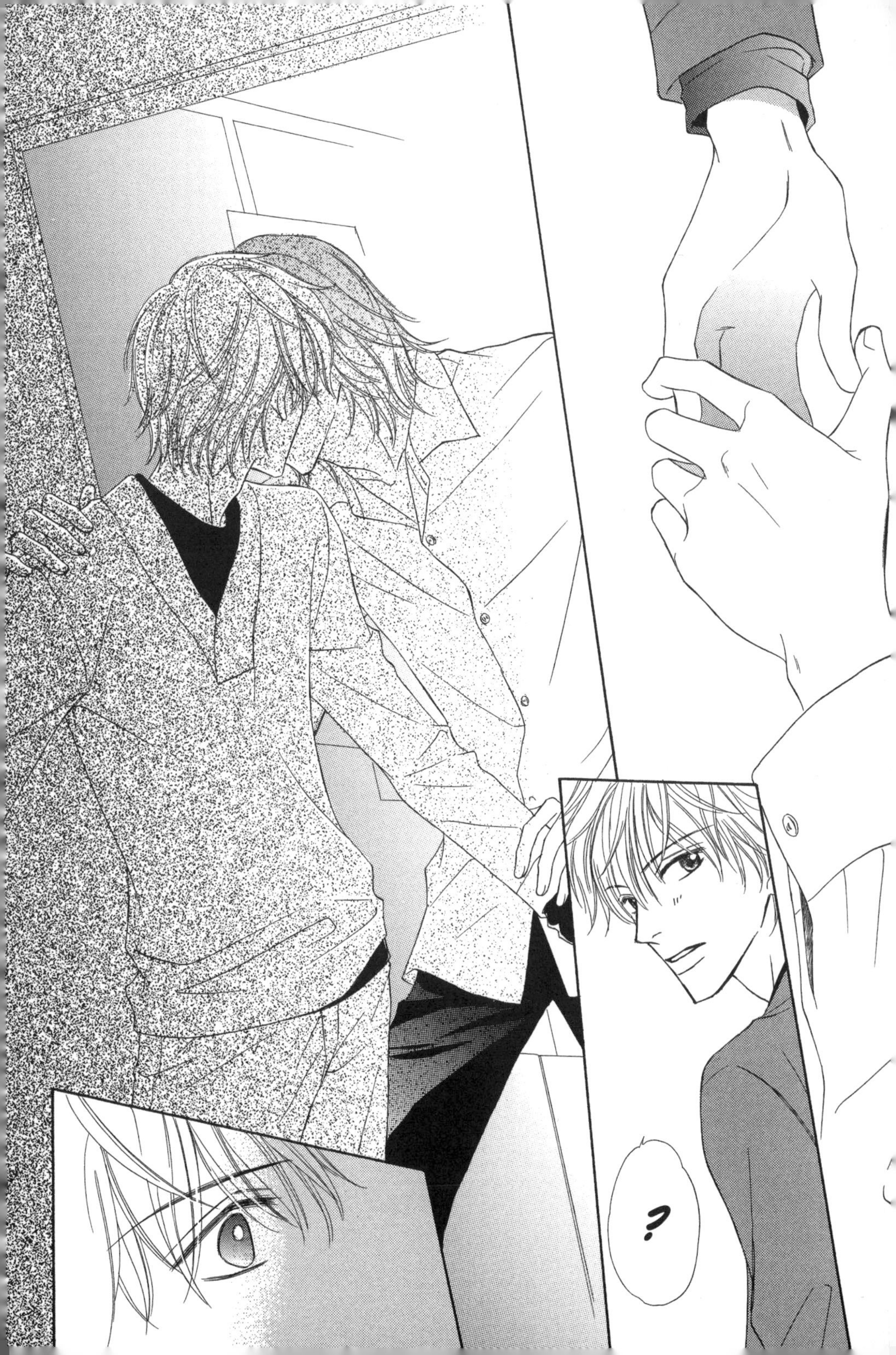
?

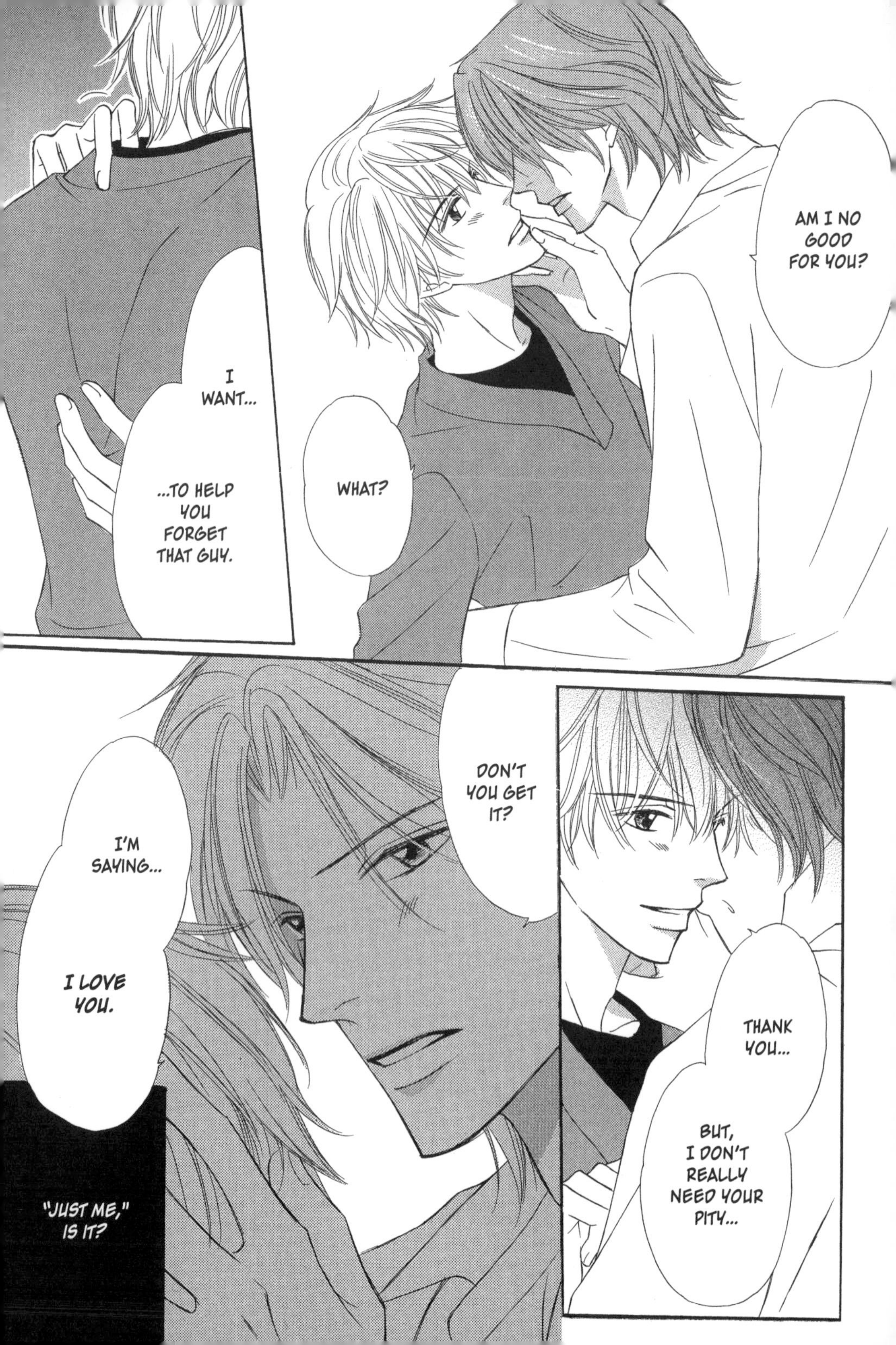
AM I NO GOOD FOR YOU?
WHAT?
I WANT...
...TO HELP YOU FORGET THAT GUY.
THANK YOU...
BUT, I DON'T REALLY NEED YOUR PITY...
DON'T YOU GET IT?
I'M SAYING...
I LOVE YOU.
"JUST ME," IS IT?

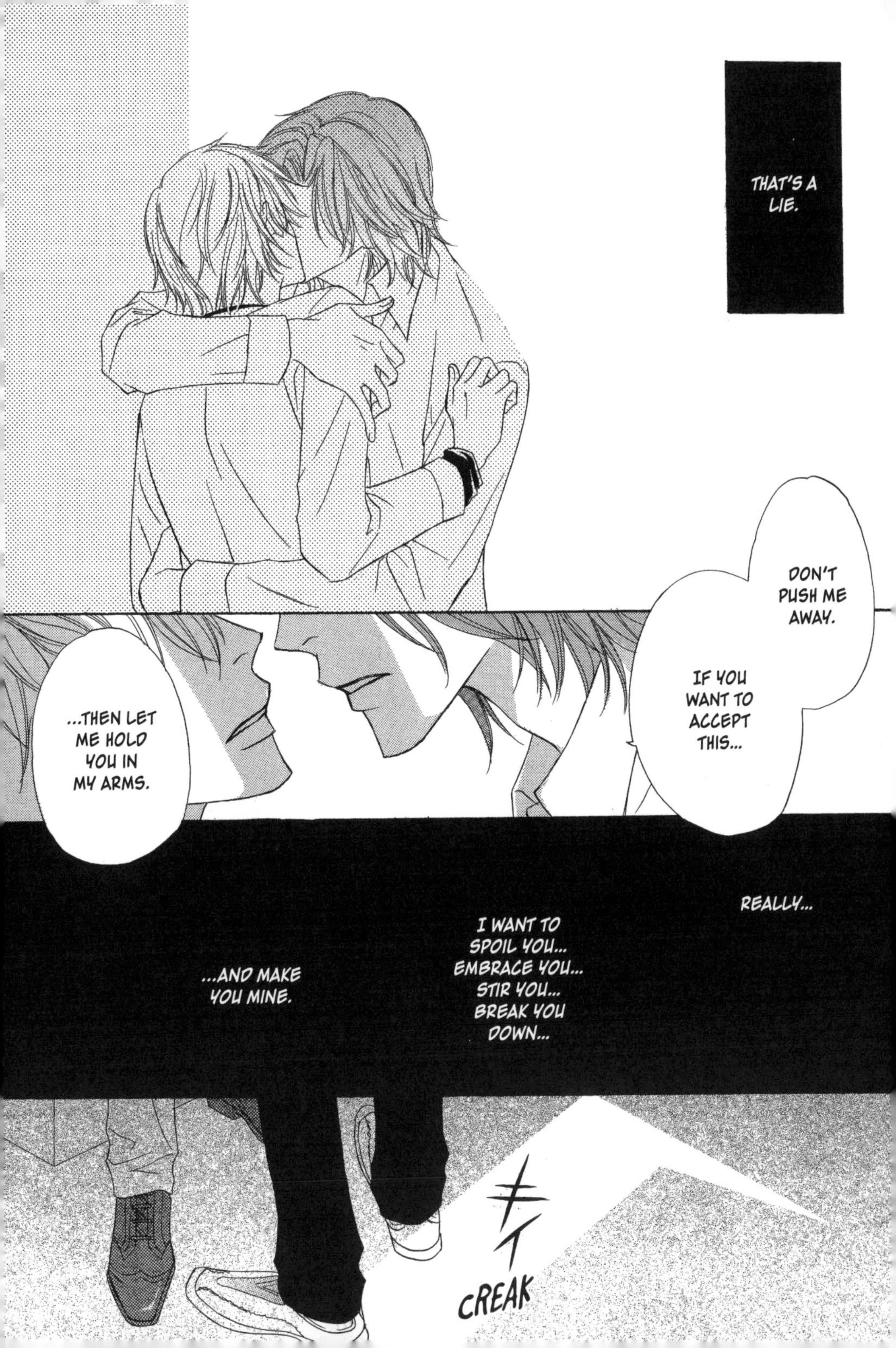
THAT'S A LIE.
DON'T PUSH ME AWAY.
IF YOU WANT TO ACCEPT THIS...
...THEN LET ME HOLD YOU IN MY ARMS.
REALLY...
I WANT TO SPOIL YOU... EMBRACE YOU... STIR YOU... BREAK YOU DOWN...
...AND MAKE YOU MINE.
キイ
CREAK

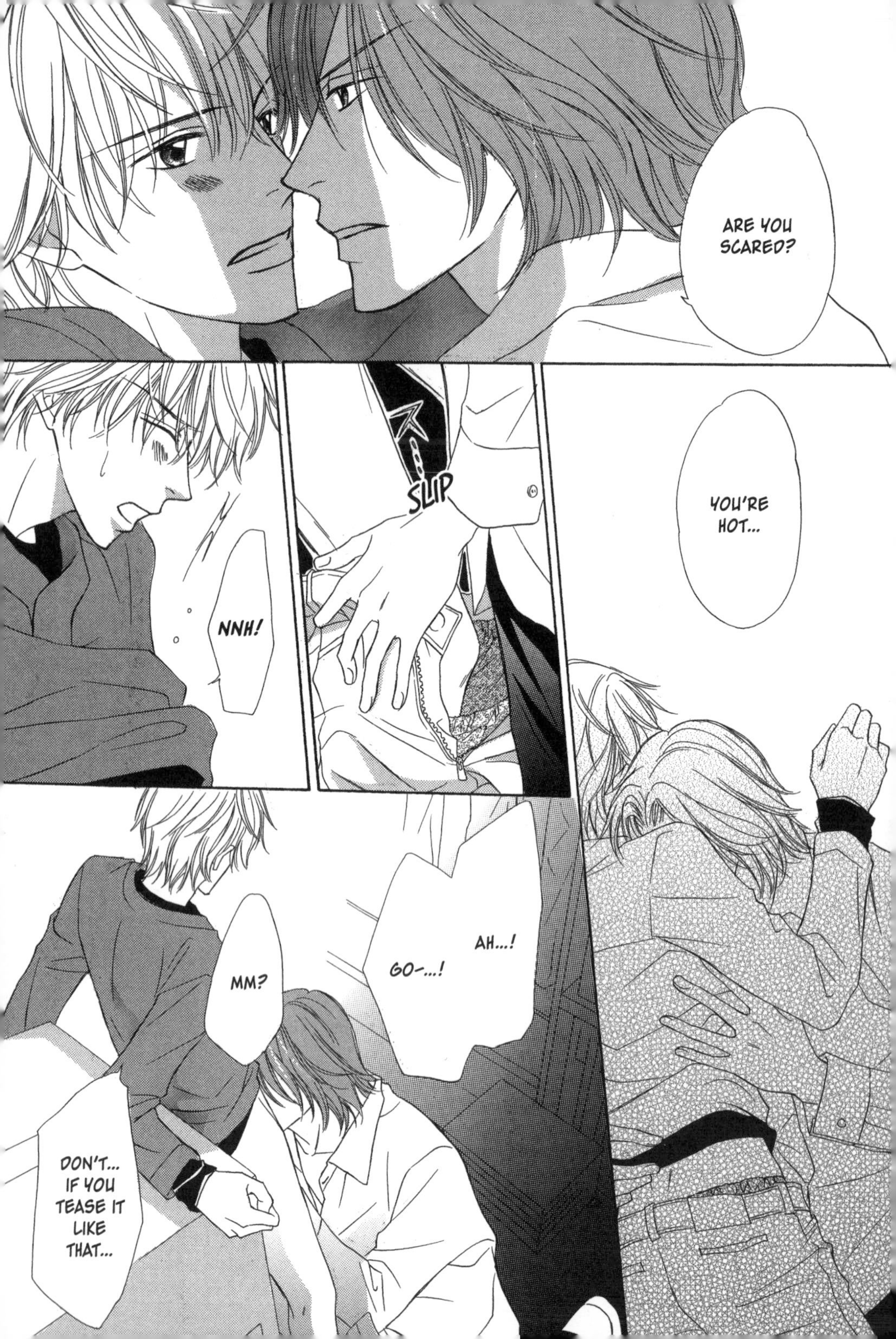
ARE YOU SCARED?
YOU'RE HOT...
SLIP
NNH!
AH...!
GO-...!
MM?
DON'T... IF YOU TEASE IT LIKE THAT...

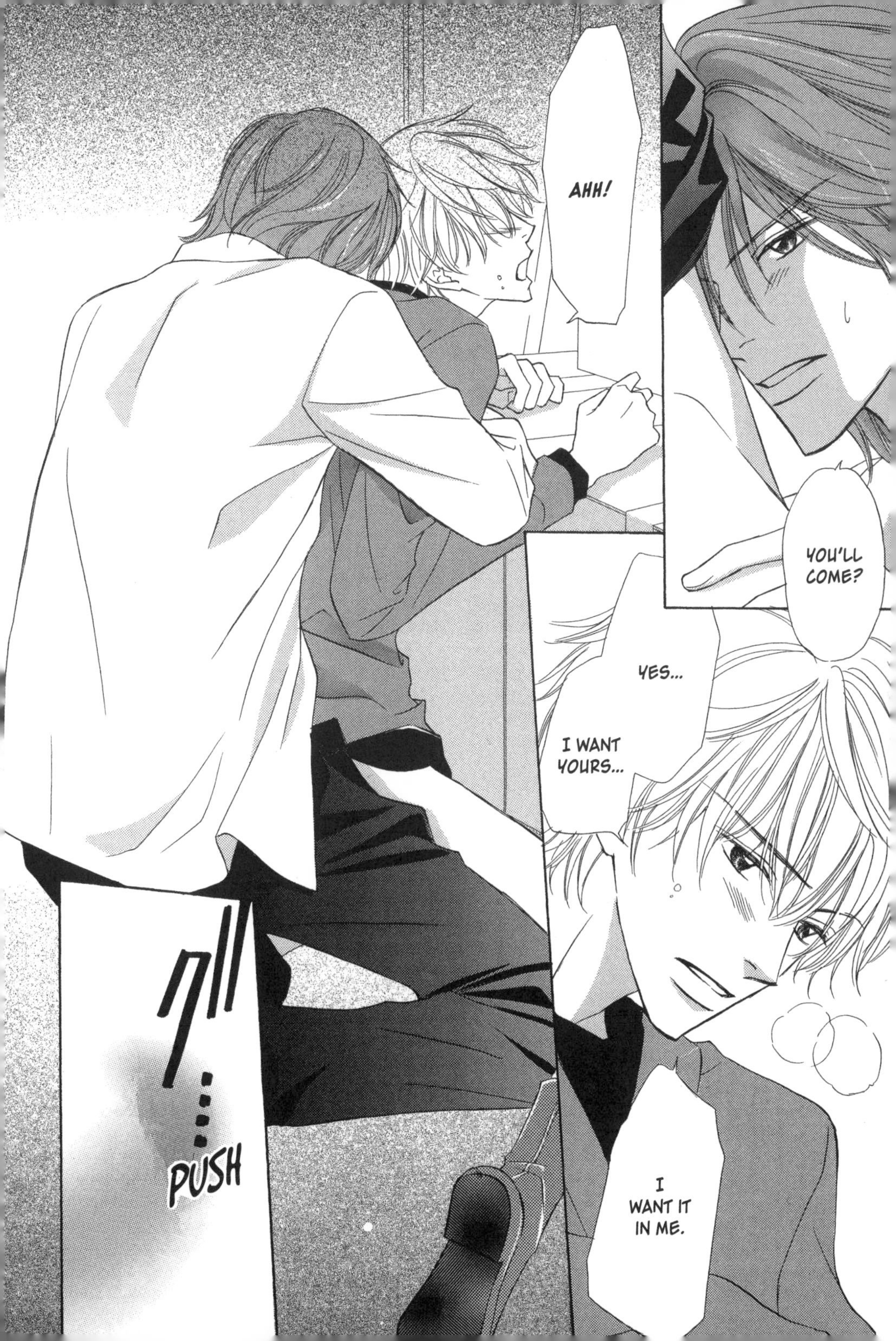
YOU'LL COME?
YES...
I WANT YOURS...
I WANT IT IN ME.
AHH!
PUSH

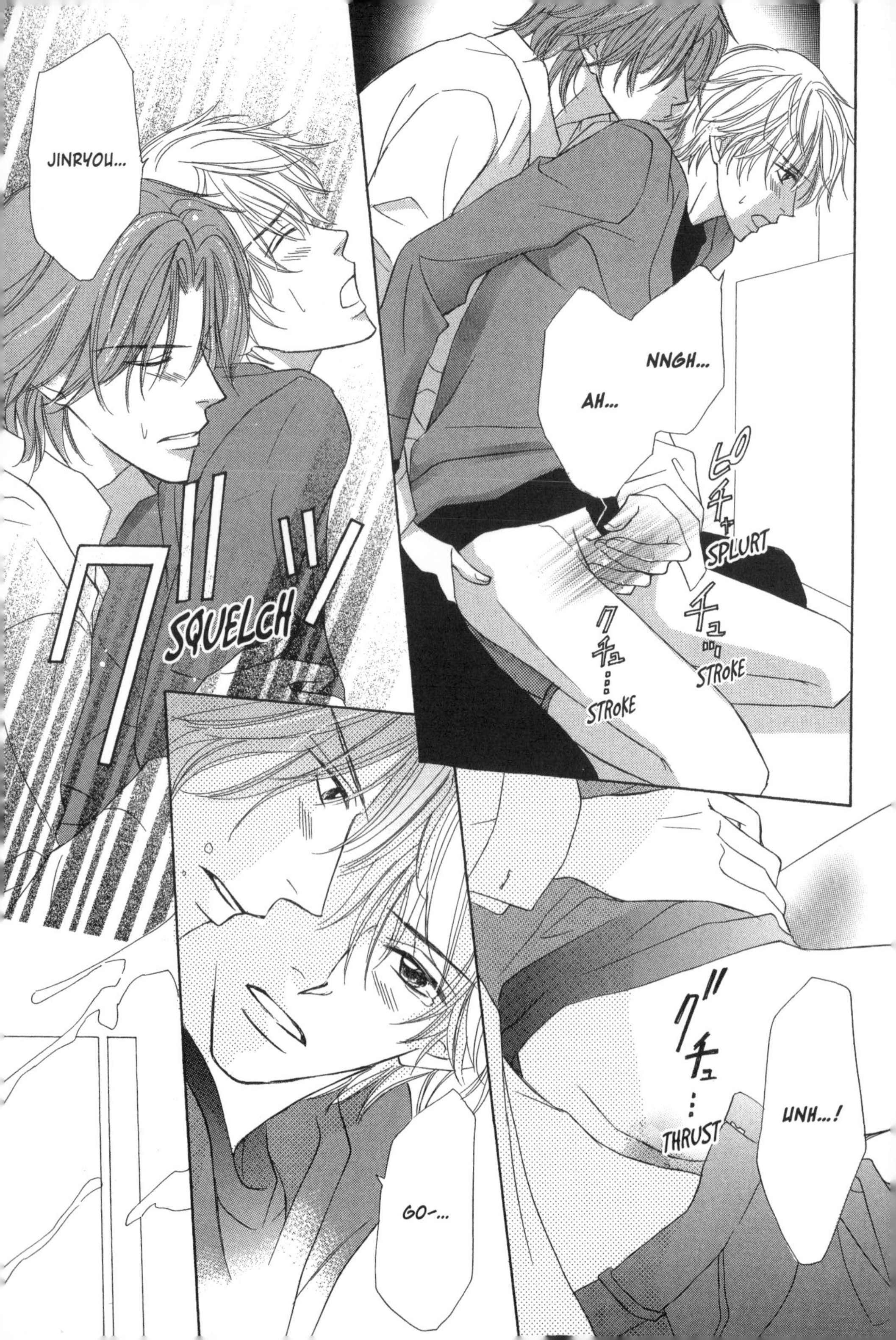

NNGH...
AH...
ピチャ
SPLURT
チュ...
STROKE
クチュ...
STROKE
JINRYOU...
グリッ
SQUELCH
グチュ...
THRUST
UNH...!
GO-...

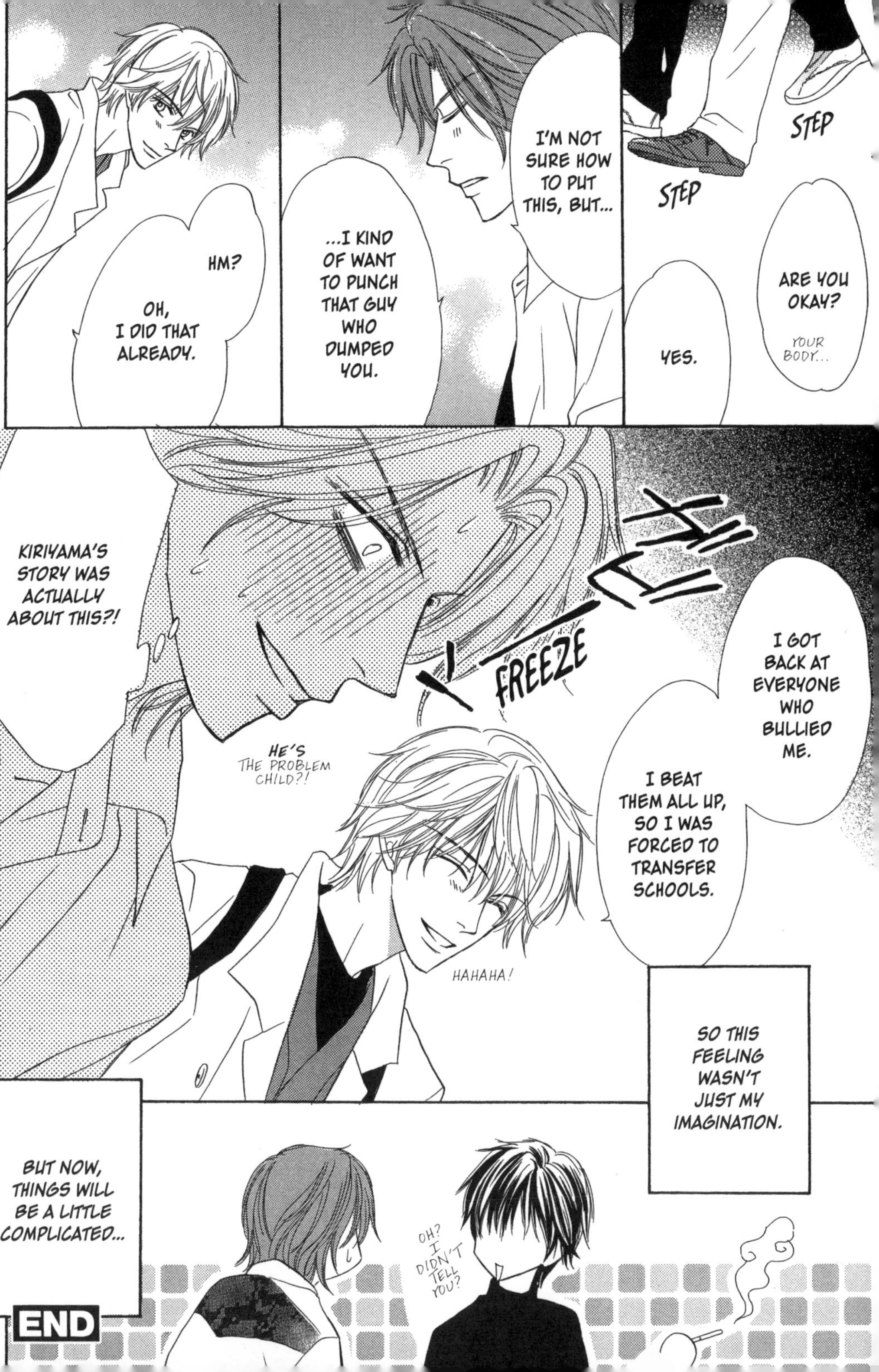
STEP
STEP
ARE YOU OKAY? YOUR BODY...
YES.
I'M NOT SURE HOW TO PUT THIS, BUT...
...I KIND OF WANT TO PUNCH THAT GUY WHO DUMPED YOU.
HM?
OH, I DID THAT ALREADY.
I GOT BACK AT EVERYONE WHO BULLIED ME.
I BEAT THEM ALL UP, SO I WAS FORCED TO TRANSFER SCHOOLS.
FREEZE
HAHAHA!
KIRIYAMA'S STORY WAS ACTUALLY ABOUT THIS?!
HE'S THE PROBLEM CHILD?!
SO THIS FEELING WASN'T JUST MY IMAGINATION.
OH? I DIDN'T TELL YOU?
BUT NOW, THINGS WILL BE A LITTLE COMPLICATED...
END

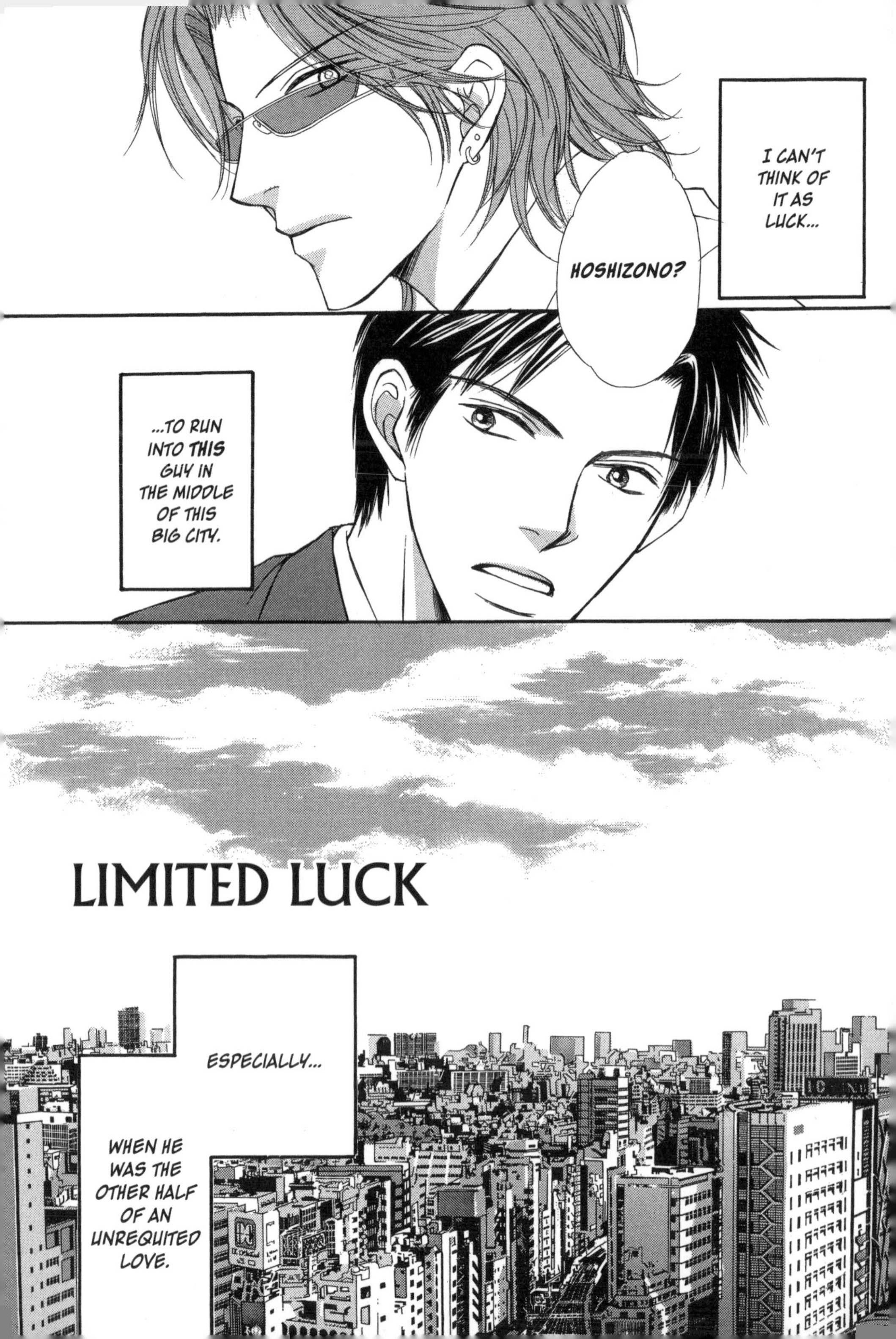
I CAN'T THINK OF IT AS LUCK...
HOSHIZONO?
...TO RUN INTO THIS GUY IN THE MIDDLE OF THIS BIG CITY.
LIMITED LUCK
ESPECIALLY...
WHEN HE WAS THE OTHER HALF OF AN UNREQUITED LOVE.

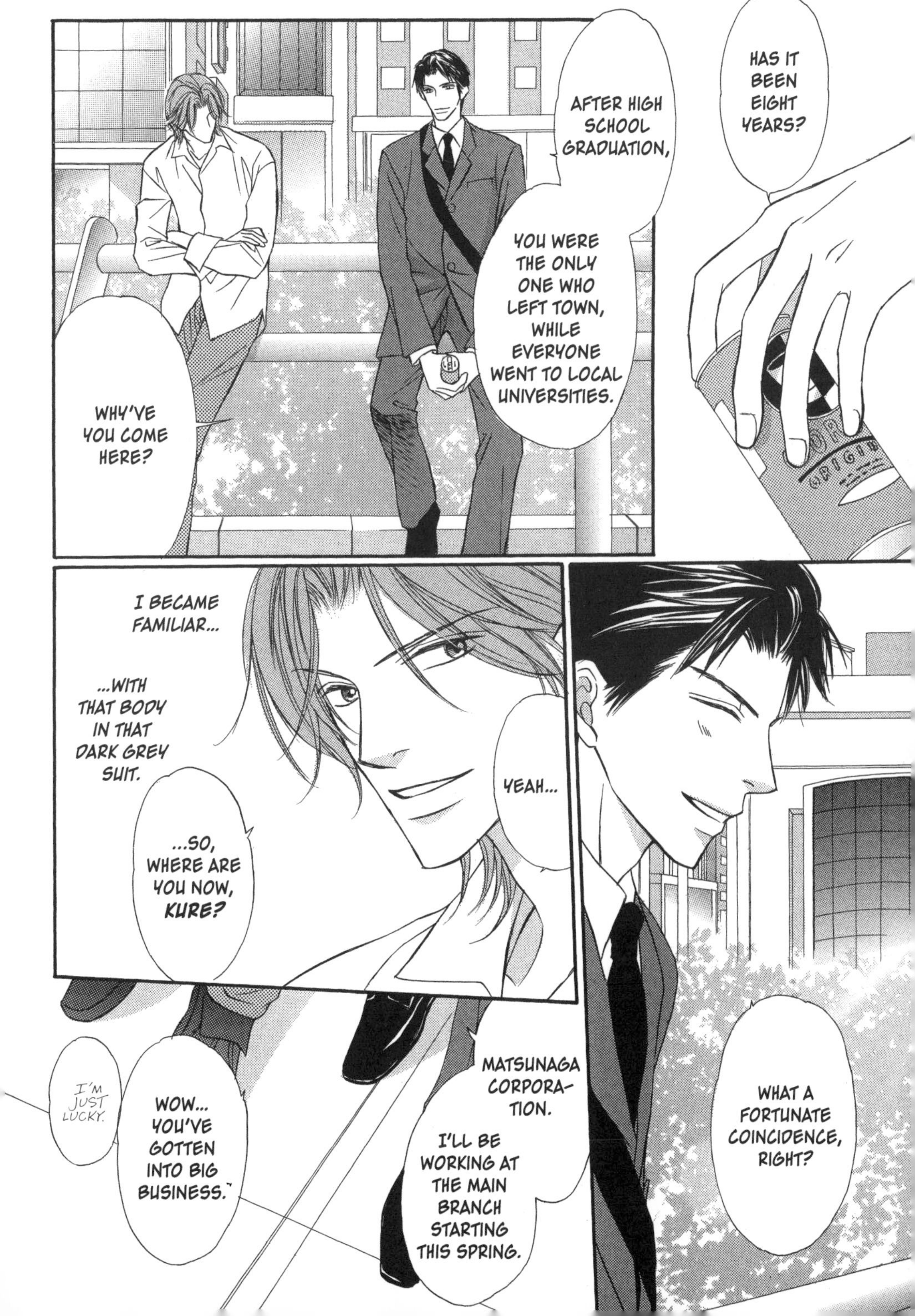
HAS IT BEEN EIGHT YEARS?
AFTER HIGH SCHOOL GRADUATION,
YOU WERE THE ONLY ONE WHO LEFT TOWN, WHILE EVERYONE WENT TO LOCAL UNIVERSITIES.
WHY'VE YOU COME HERE?
I BECAME FAMILIAR...
...WITH THAT BODY IN THAT DARK GREY SUIT.
...SO, WHERE ARE YOU NOW, KURE?
YEAH...
MATSUNAGA CORPORATION.
I'LL BE WORKING AT THE MAIN BRANCH STARTING THIS SPRING.
WOW... YOU'VE GOTTEN INTO BIG BUSINESS.
I'M JUST LUCKY.
WHAT A FORTUNATE COINCIDENCE, RIGHT?

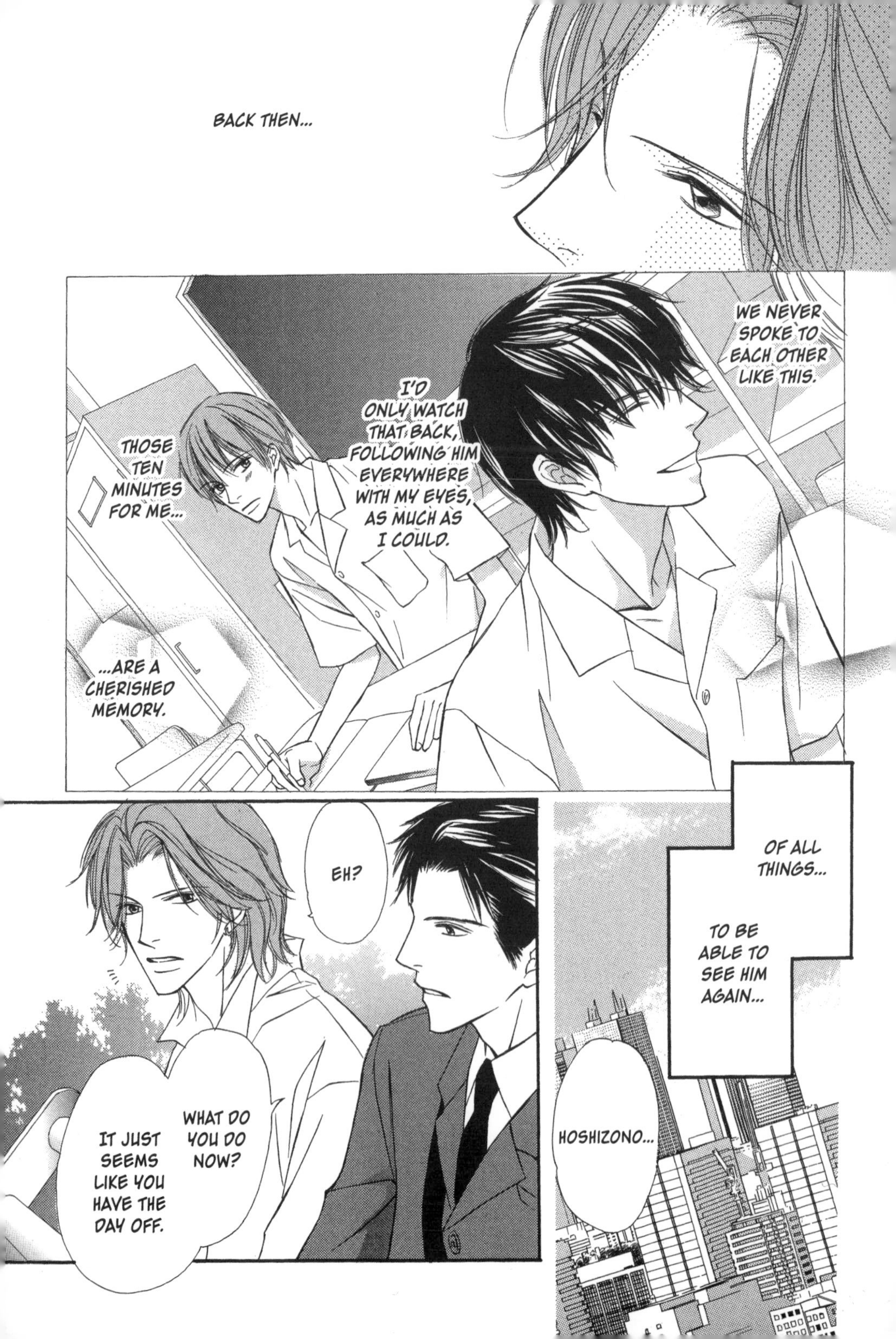
BACK THEN...
WE NEVER SPOKE TO EACH OTHER LIKE THIS.
I'D ONLY WATCH THAT BACK, FOLLOWING HIM EVERYWHERE WITH MY EYES, AS MUCH AS I COULD.
THOSE TEN MINUTES FOR ME...
...ARE A CHERISHED MEMORY.
OF ALL THINGS...
TO BE ABLE TO SEE HIM AGAIN...
HOSHIZONO...
EH?
WHAT DO YOU DO NOW?
IT JUST SEEMS LIKE YOU HAVE THE DAY OFF.

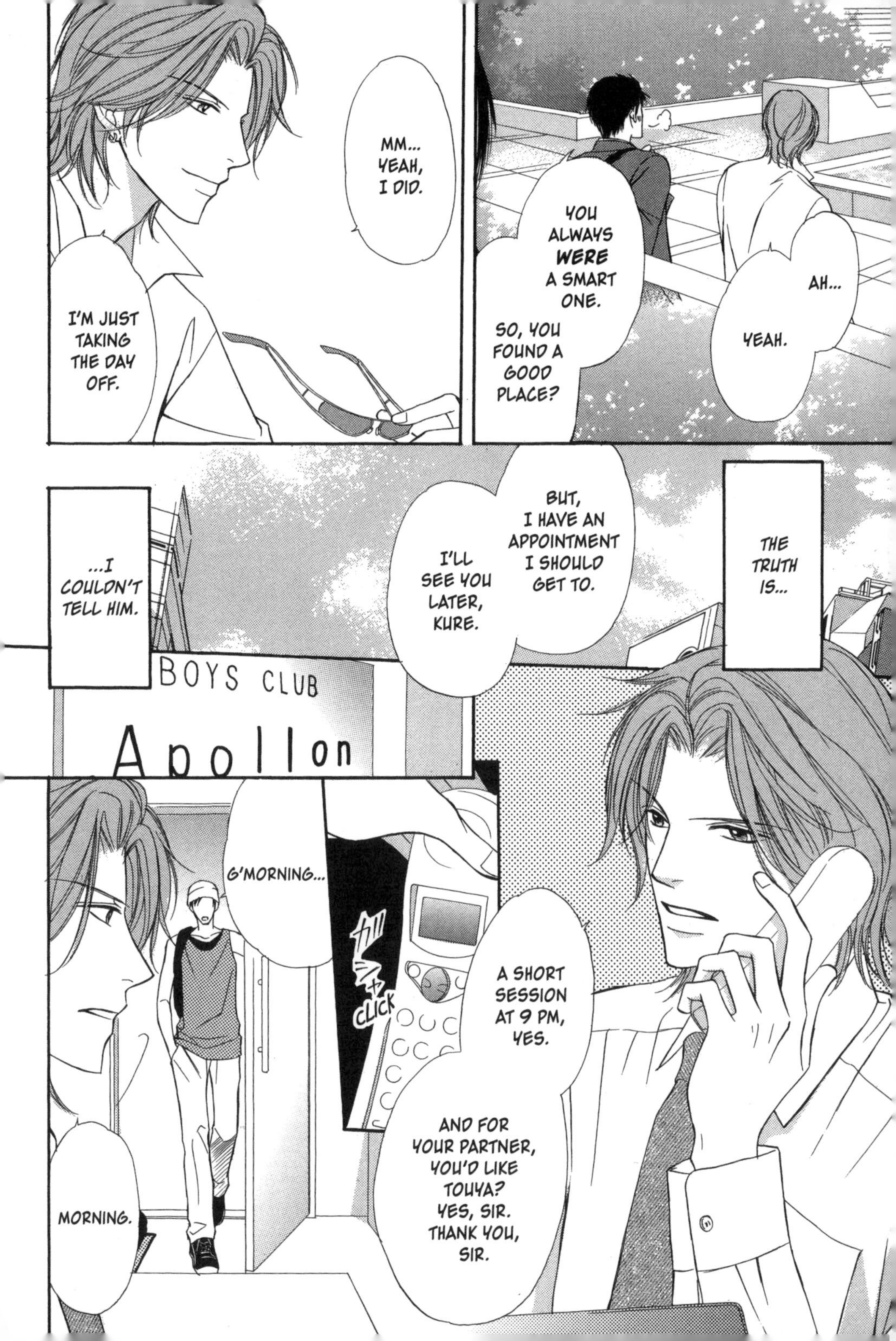

YOU ALWAYS WERE A SMART ONE.
SO, YOU FOUND A GOOD PLACE?
AH... YEAH.
MM... YEAH, I DID.
I'M JUST TAKING THE DAY OFF.
THE TRUTH IS...
BUT, I HAVE AN APPOINTMENT I SHOULD GET TO.
I'LL SEE YOU LATER, KURE.
...I COULDN'T TELL HIM.
BOYS CLUB
Apollon
A SHORT SESSION AT 9 PM, YES.
AND FOR YOUR PARTNER, YOU'D LIKE TOUYA? YES, SIR. THANK YOU, SIR.
CLICK
G'MORNING...
MORNING.

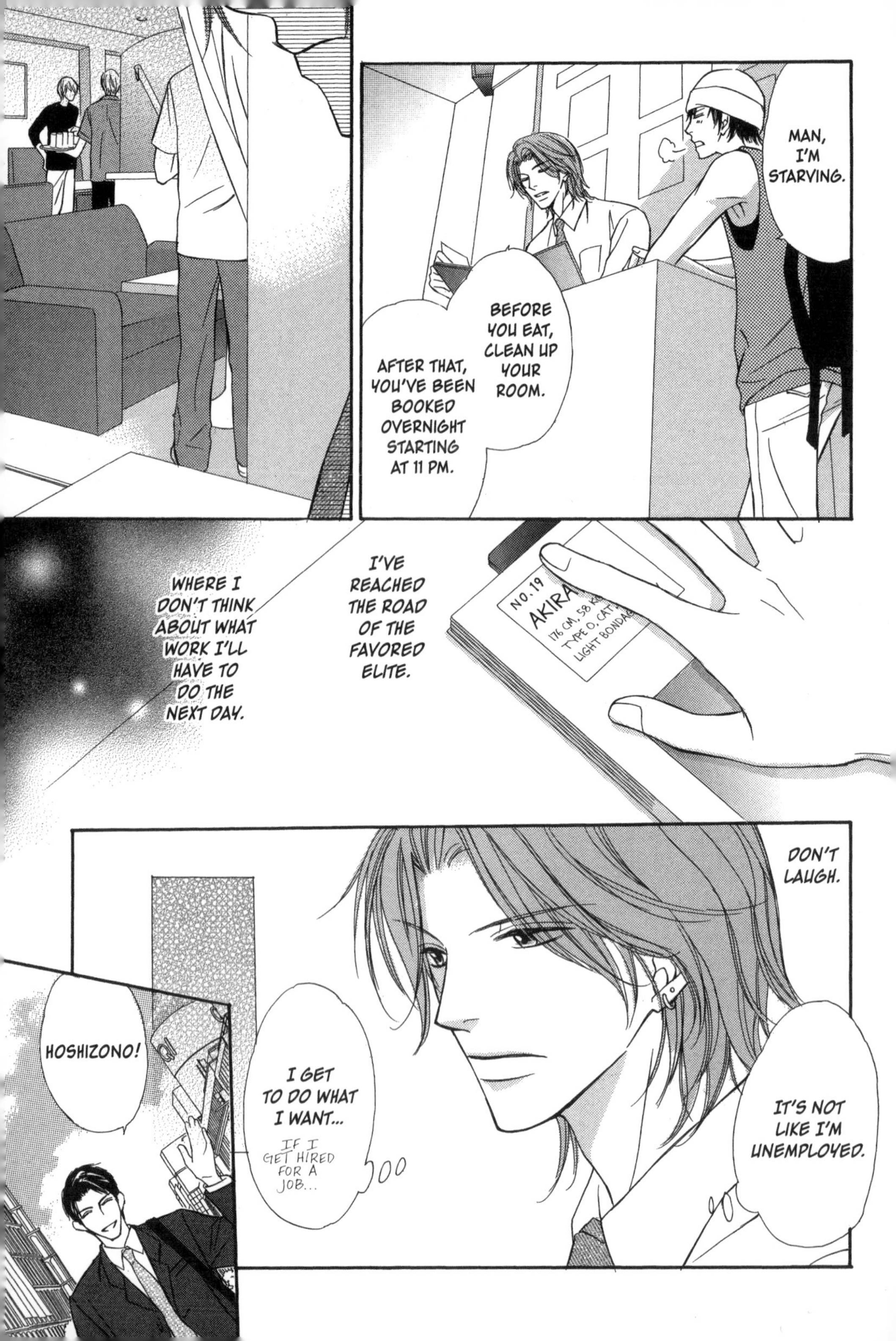
MAN, I'M STARVING.
BEFORE YOU EAT, CLEAN UP YOUR ROOM.
AFTER THAT, YOU'VE BEEN BOOKED OVERNIGHT STARTING AT 11 PM.
NO.19
AKIRA
I'VE REACHED THE ROAD OF THE FAVORED ELITE.
WHERE I DON'T THINK ABOUT WHAT WORK I'LL HAVE TO DO THE NEXT DAY.
DON'T LAUGH.
IT'S NOT LIKE I'M UNEMPLOYED.
I GET TO DO WHAT I WANT...
IF I GET HIRED FOR A JOB...
HOSHIZONO!

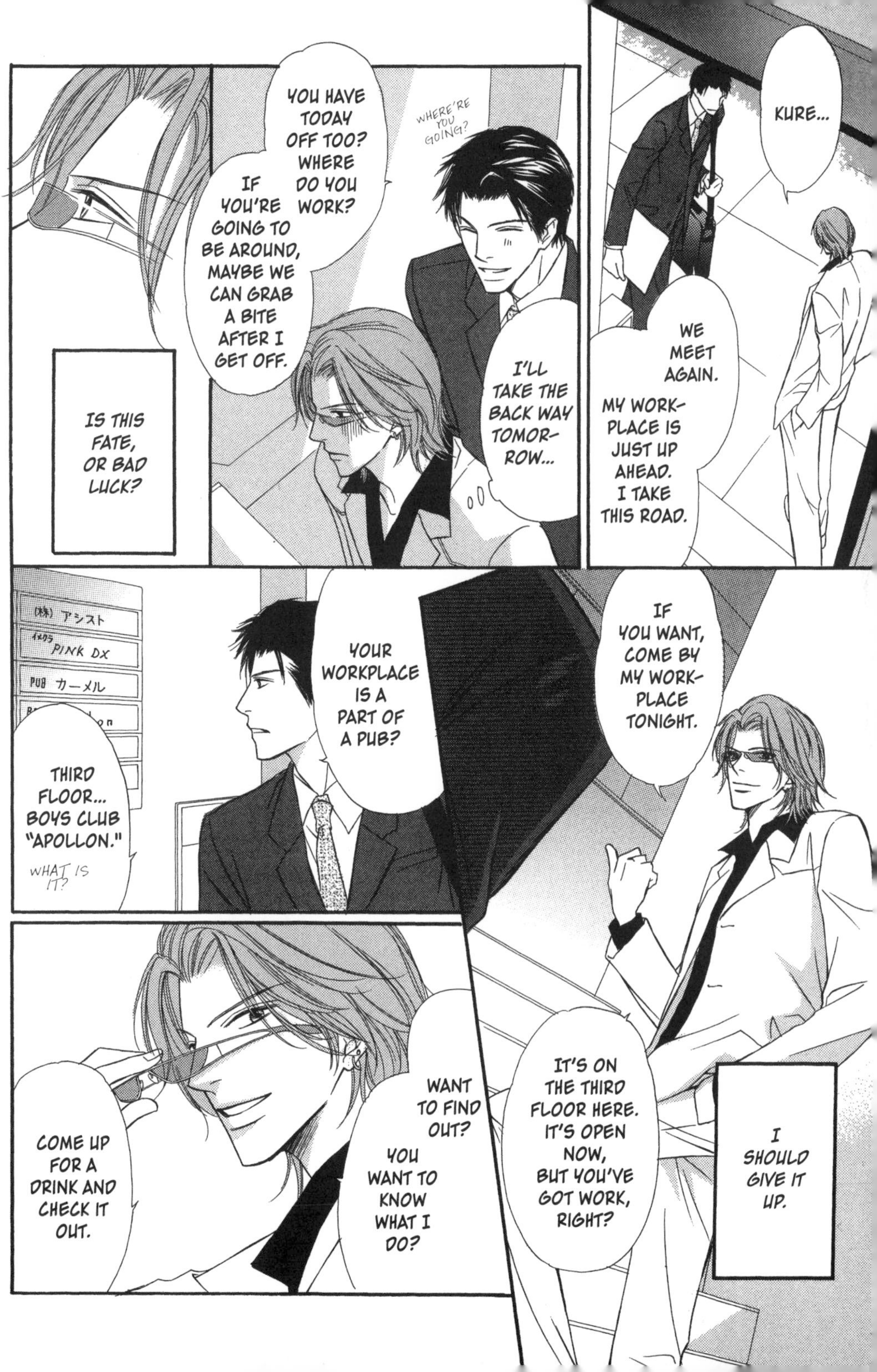
KURE...
WE MEET AGAIN.
MY WORK-PLACE IS JUST UP AHEAD. I TAKE THIS ROAD.
WHERE'RE YOU GOING?
YOU HAVE TODAY OFF TOO? WHERE DO YOU WORK?
IF YOU'RE GOING TO BE AROUND, MAYBE WE CAN GRAB A BITE AFTER I GET OFF.
I'LL TAKE THE BACK WAY TOMOR-ROW...
IS THIS FATE, OR BAD LUCK?
IF YOU WANT, COME BY MY WORK-PLACE TONIGHT.
(株)アシスト
PINK DX
PUB カーメル
YOUR WORKPLACE IS A PART OF A PUB?
THIRD FLOOR... BOYS CLUB "APOLLON."
WHAT IS IT?
IT'S ON THE THIRD FLOOR HERE. IT'S OPEN NOW, BUT YOU'VE GOT WORK, RIGHT?
I SHOULD GIVE IT UP.
WANT TO FIND OUT?
YOU WANT TO KNOW WHAT I DO?
COME UP FOR A DRINK AND CHECK IT OUT.

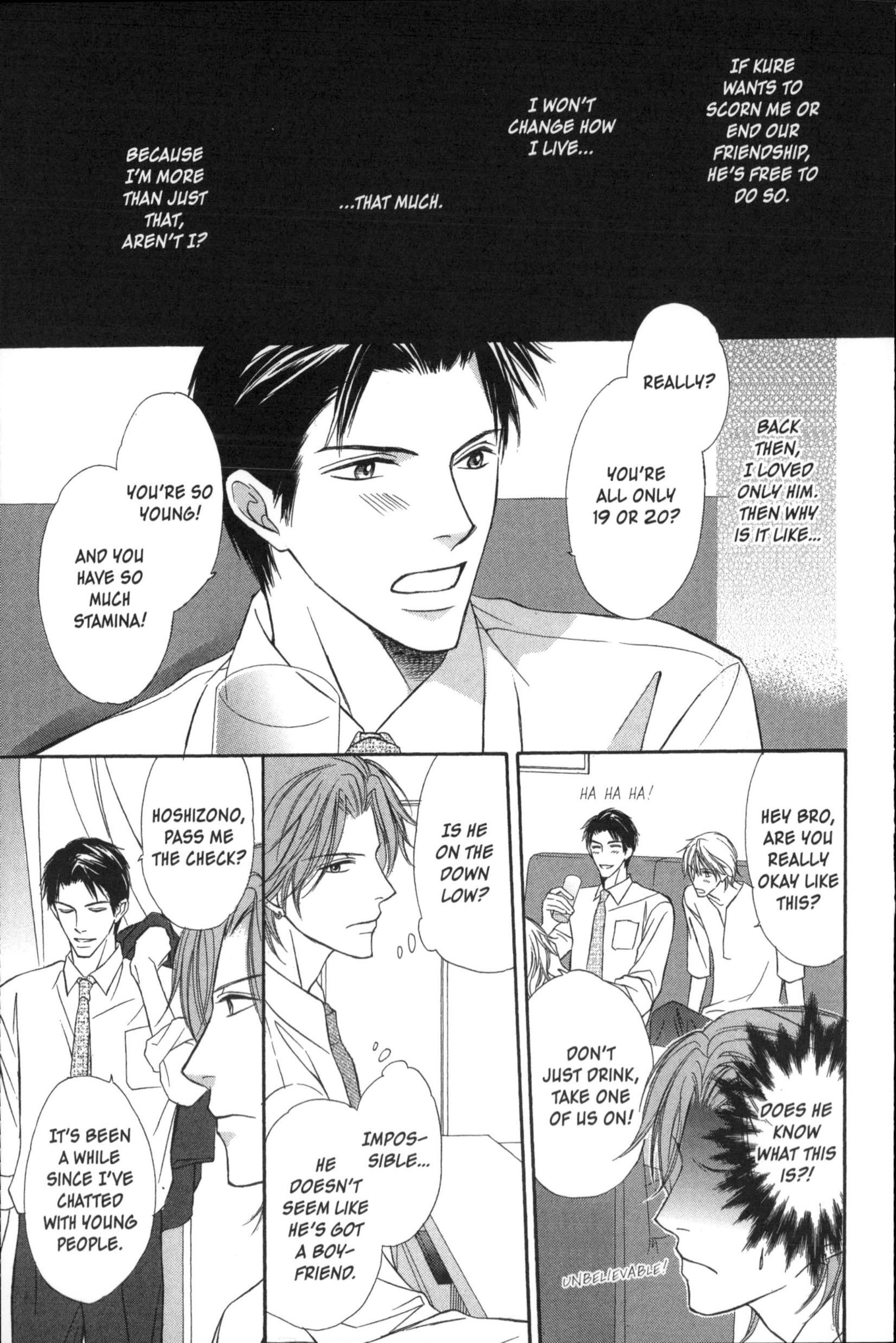
IF KURE WANTS TO SCORN ME OR END OUR FRIENDSHIP, HE'S FREE TO DO SO.
I WON'T CHANGE HOW I LIVE...
...THAT MUCH.
BECAUSE I'M MORE THAN JUST THAT, AREN'T I?
BACK THEN, I LOVED ONLY HIM. THEN WHY IS IT LIKE...
REALLY?
YOU'RE ALL ONLY 19 OR 20?
YOU'RE SO YOUNG!
AND YOU HAVE SO MUCH STAMINA!
HA HA HA!
HEY BRO, ARE YOU REALLY OKAY LIKE THIS?
DOES HE KNOW WHAT THIS IS?!
DON'T JUST DRINK, TAKE ONE OF US ON!
UNBELIEVABLE!
IS HE ON THE DOWN LOW?
IMPOS-SIBLE...
HE DOESN'T SEEM LIKE HE'S GOT A BOY-FRIEND.
HOSHIZONO, PASS ME THE CHECK?
IT'S BEEN A WHILE SINCE I'VE CHATTED WITH YOUNG PEOPLE.

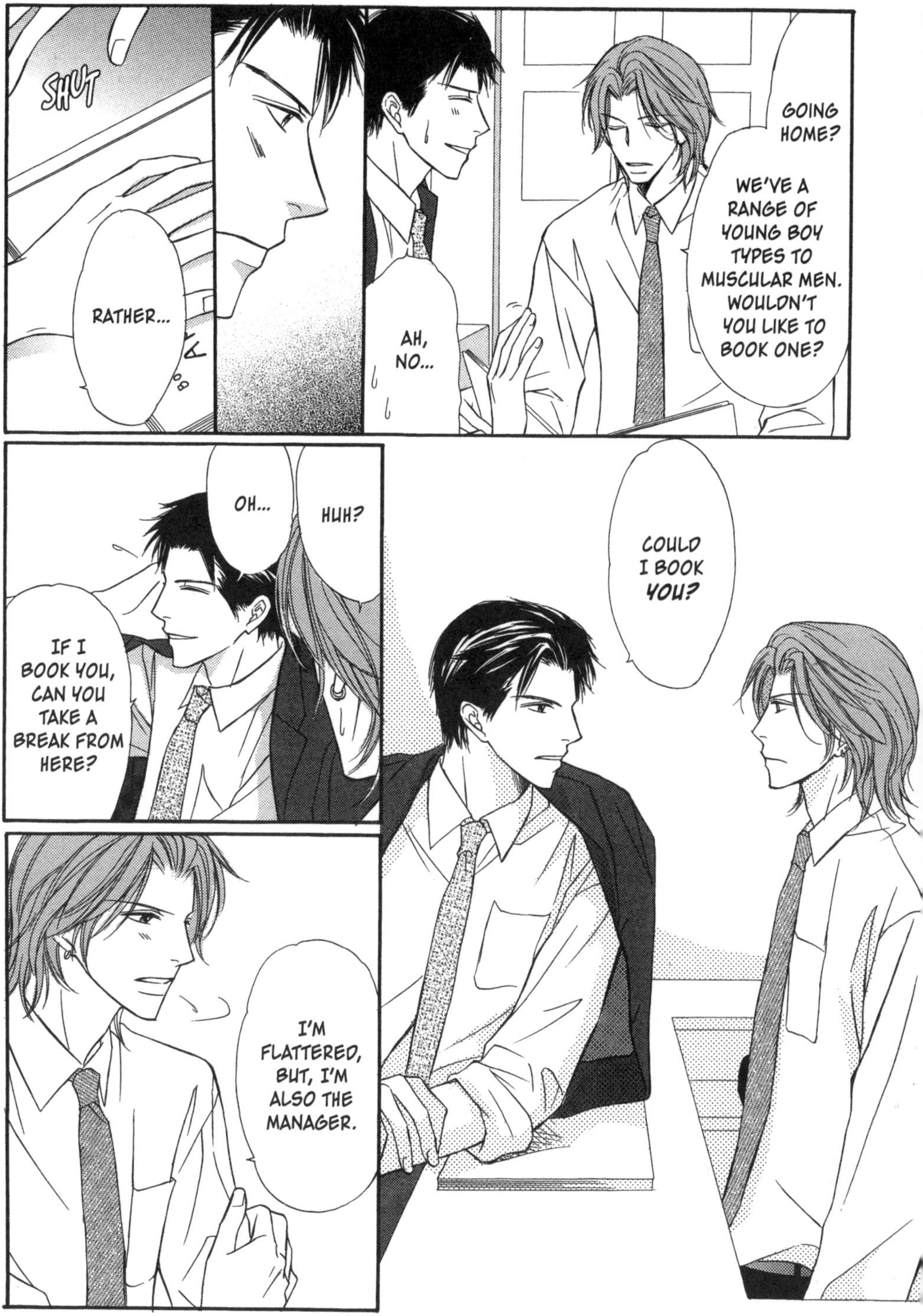
GOING HOME?
WE'VE A RANGE OF YOUNG BOY TYPES TO MUSCULAR MEN. WOULDN'T YOU LIKE TO BOOK ONE?
AH, NO...
SHUT
RATHER...
COULD I BOOK *YOU?*
HUH?
OH...
IF I BOOK YOU, CAN YOU TAKE A BREAK FROM HERE?
I'M FLATTERED, BUT, I'M ALSO THE MANAGER.

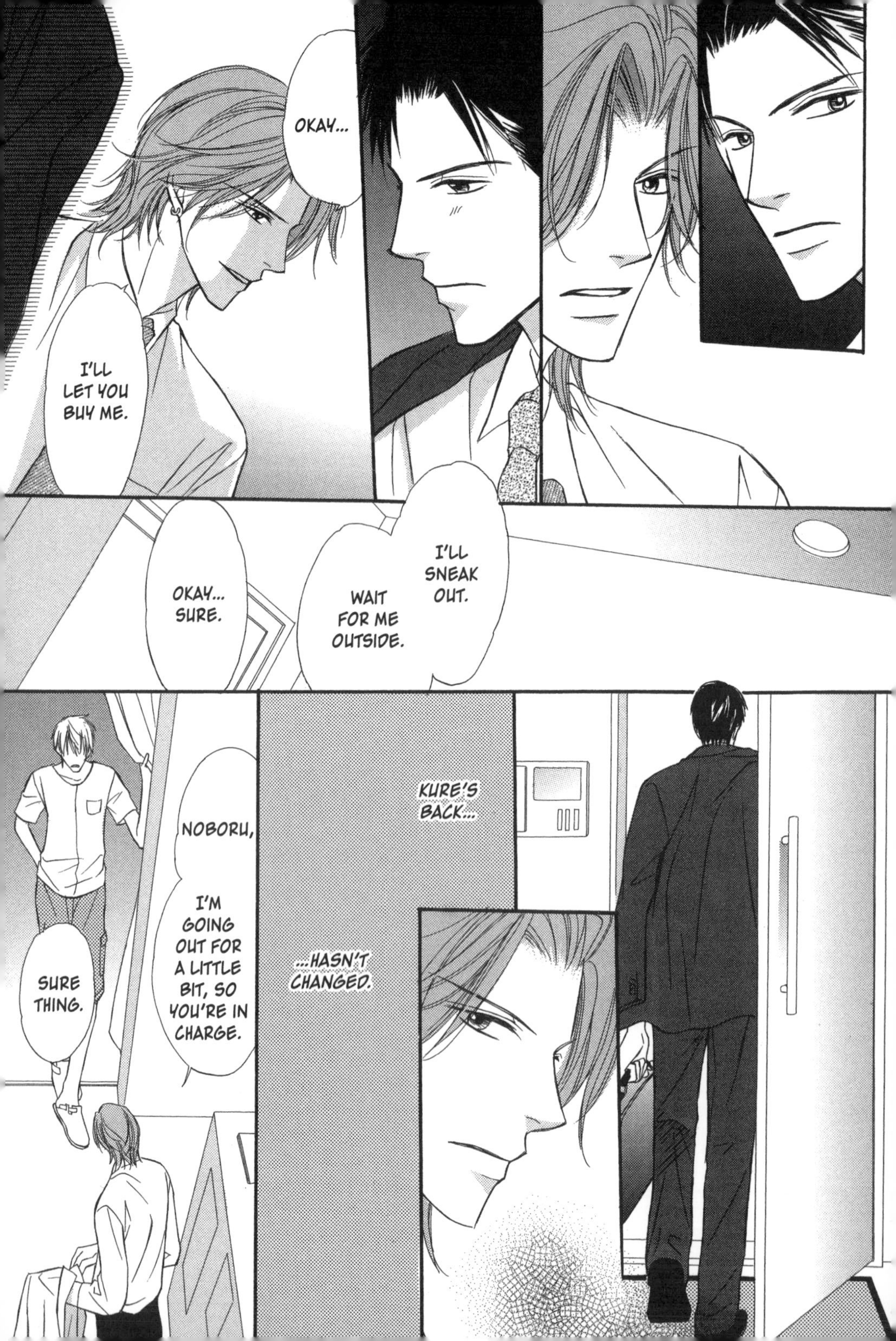
OKAY...
I'LL LET YOU BUY ME.
I'LL SNEAK OUT.
WAIT FOR ME OUTSIDE.
OKAY... SURE.
KURE'S BACK...
...HASN'T CHANGED.
NOBORU,
I'M GOING OUT FOR A LITTLE BIT, SO YOU'RE IN CHARGE.
SURE THING.

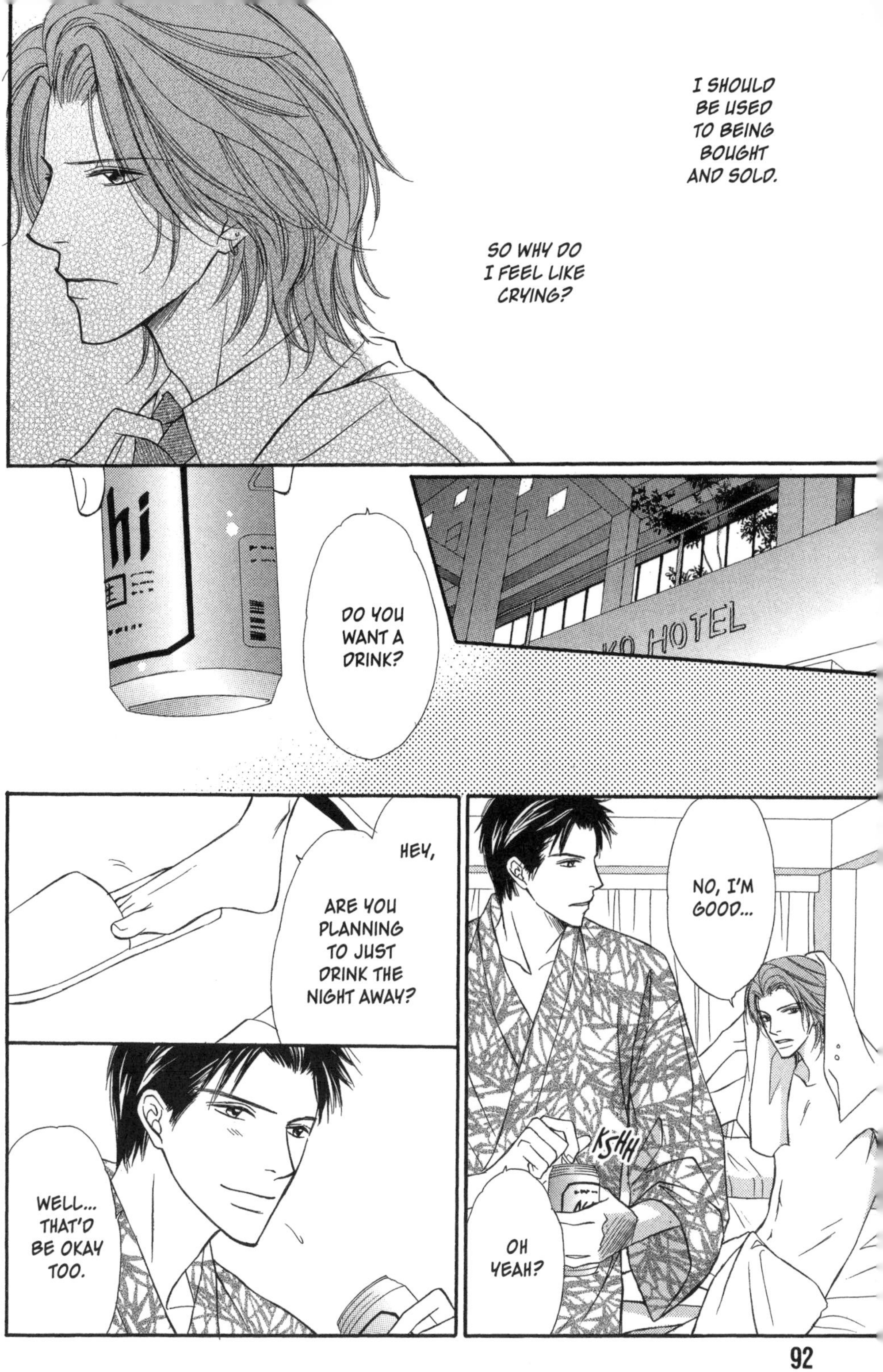
I SHOULD BE USED TO BEING BOUGHT AND SOLD.
SO WHY DO I FEEL LIKE CRYING?
KO HOTEL
hi
DO YOU WANT A DRINK?
NO, I'M GOOD...
KSHH
OH YEAH?
HEY,
ARE YOU PLANNING TO JUST DRINK THE NIGHT AWAY?
WELL... THAT'D BE OKAY TOO.

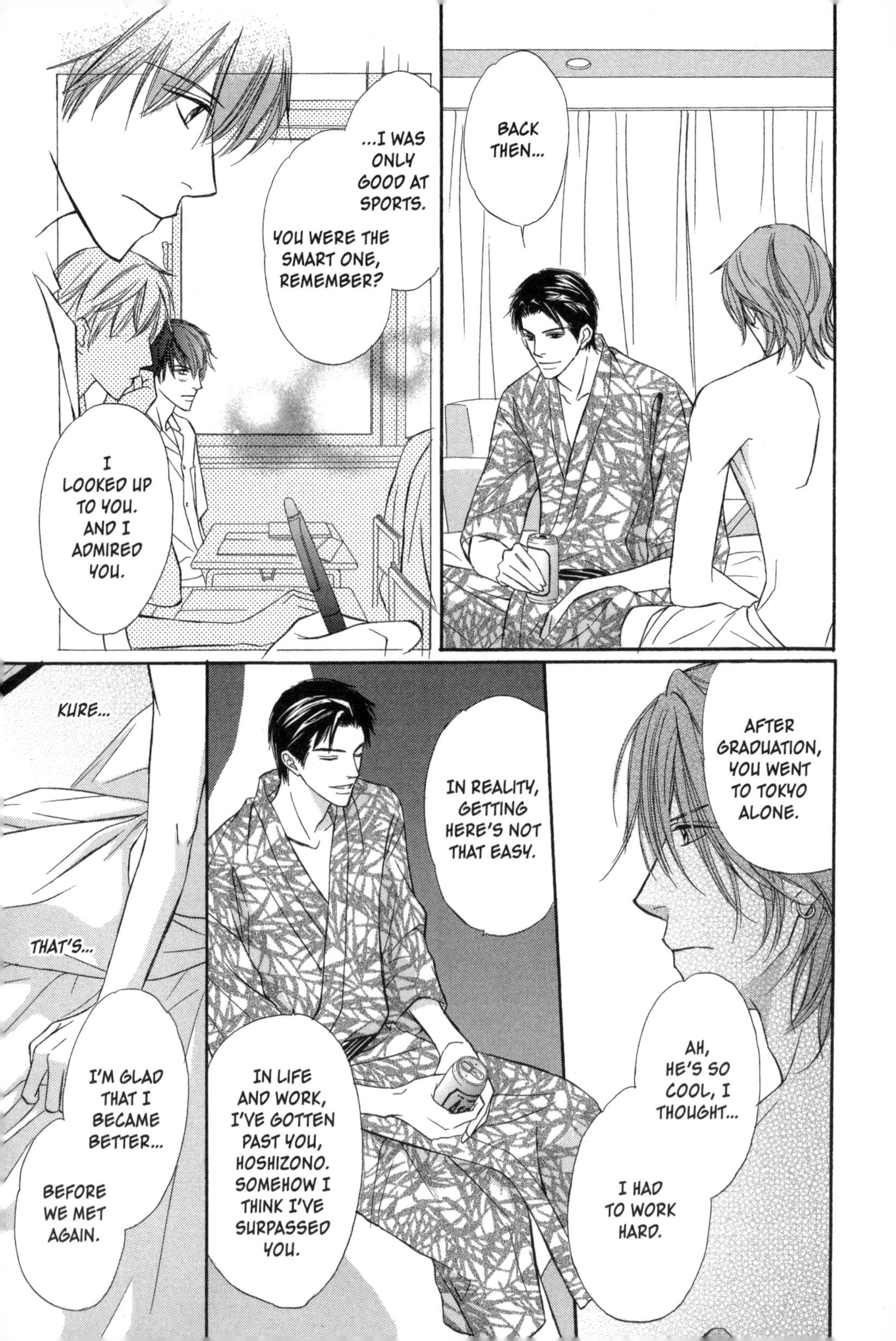
BACK THEN...
...I WAS ONLY GOOD AT SPORTS.
YOU WERE THE SMART ONE, REMEMBER?
I LOOKED UP TO YOU. AND I ADMIRED YOU.
AFTER GRADUATION, YOU WENT TO TOKYO ALONE.
AH, HE'S SO COOL, I THOUGHT...
I HAD TO WORK HARD.
IN REALITY, GETTING HERE'S NOT THAT EASY.
IN LIFE AND WORK, I'VE GOTTEN PAST YOU, HOSHIZONO. SOMEHOW I THINK I'VE SURPASSED YOU.
KURE...
THAT'S...
I'M GLAD THAT I BECAME BETTER...
BEFORE WE MET AGAIN.

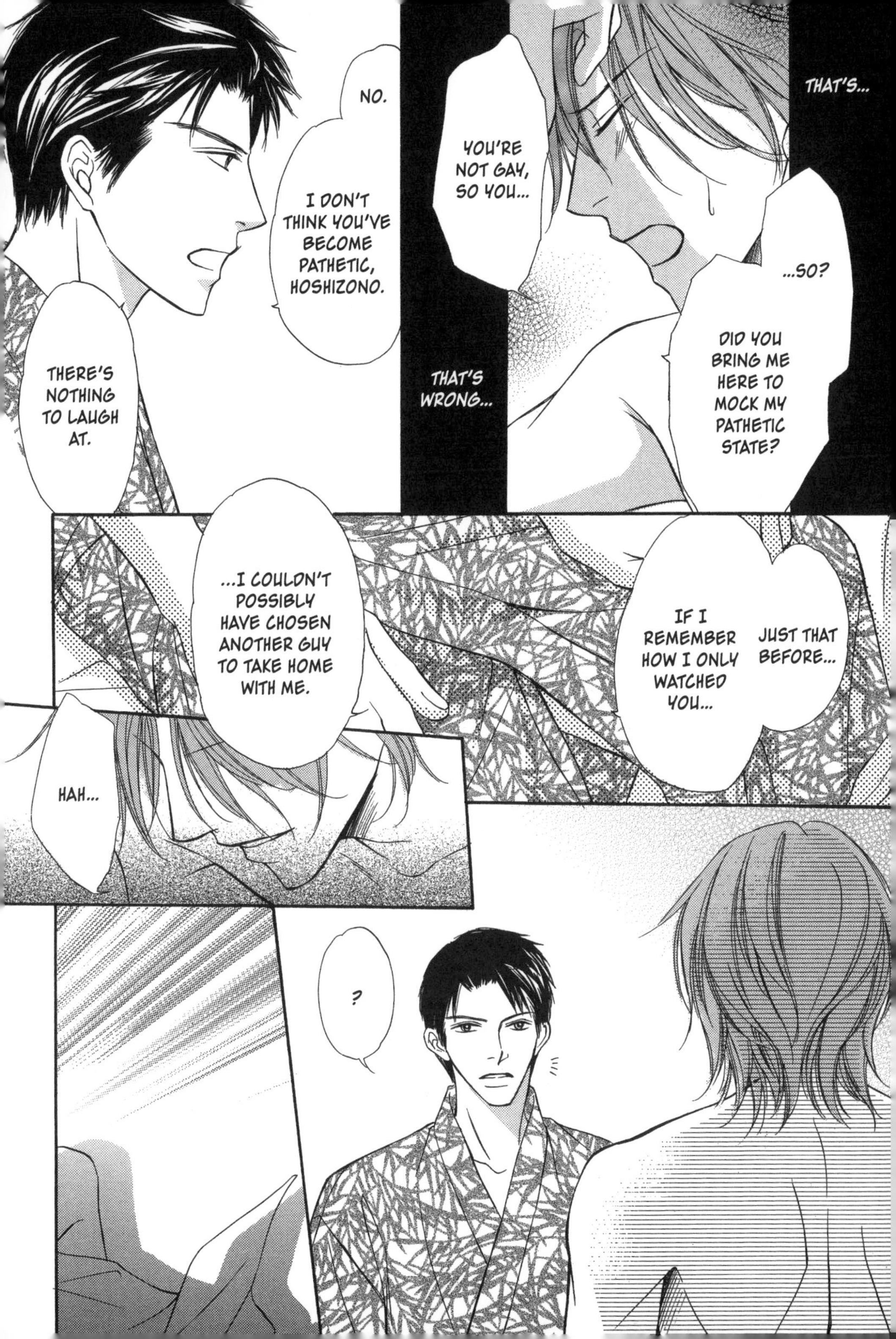
THAT'S...
YOU'RE NOT GAY, SO YOU...
...SO?
DID YOU BRING ME HERE TO MOCK MY PATHETIC STATE?
THAT'S WRONG...
NO.
I DON'T THINK YOU'VE BECOME PATHETIC, HOSHIZONO.
THERE'S NOTHING TO LAUGH AT.
JUST THAT BEFORE...
IF I REMEMBER HOW I ONLY WATCHED YOU...
...I COULDN'T POSSIBLY HAVE CHOSEN ANOTHER GUY TO TAKE HOME WITH ME.
HAH...
?

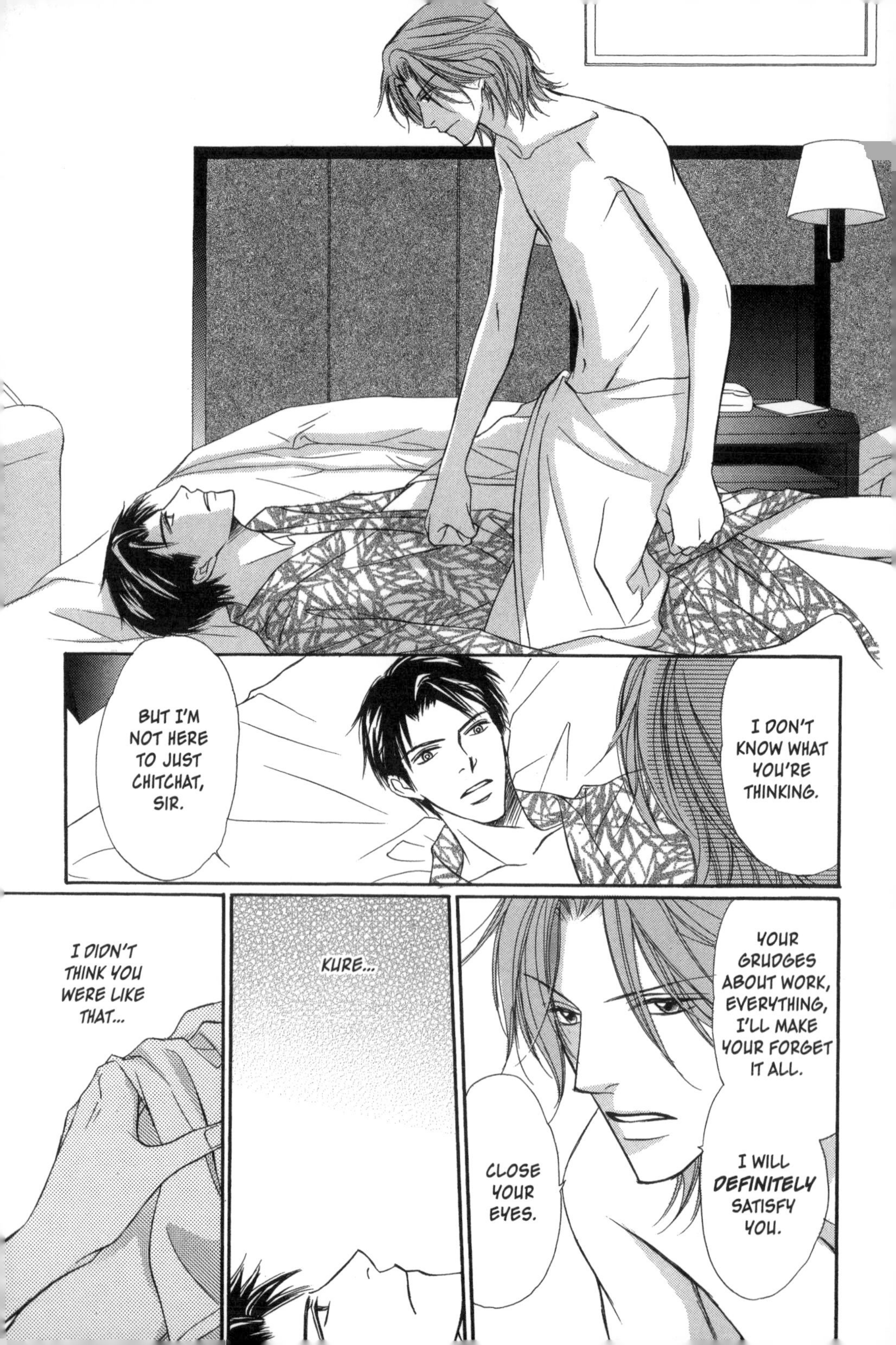
I DON'T KNOW WHAT YOU'RE THINKING.
BUT I'M NOT HERE TO JUST CHITCHAT, SIR.
YOUR GRUDGES ABOUT WORK, EVERYTHING, I'LL MAKE YOUR FORGET IT ALL.
I WILL **DEFINITELY** SATISFY YOU.
CLOSE YOUR EYES.
KURE...
I DIDN'T THINK YOU WERE LIKE THAT...

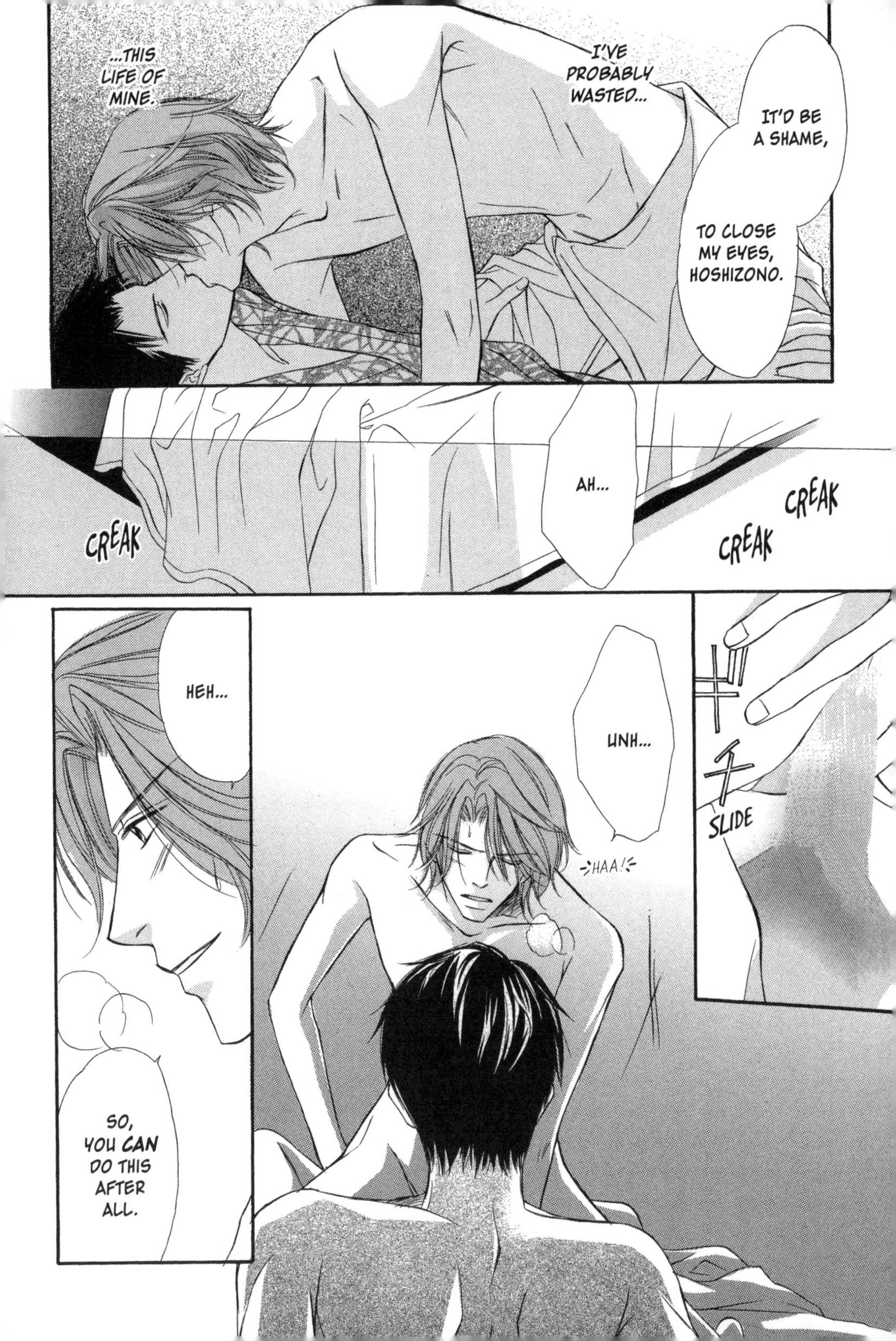
IT'D BE A SHAME,
TO CLOSE MY EYES, HOSHIZONO.
I'VE PROBABLY WASTED...
...THIS LIFE OF MINE.
CREAK
CREAK
AH...
CREAK
SLIDE
UNH...
HAA!
HEH...
SO, YOU **CAN** DO THIS AFTER ALL.

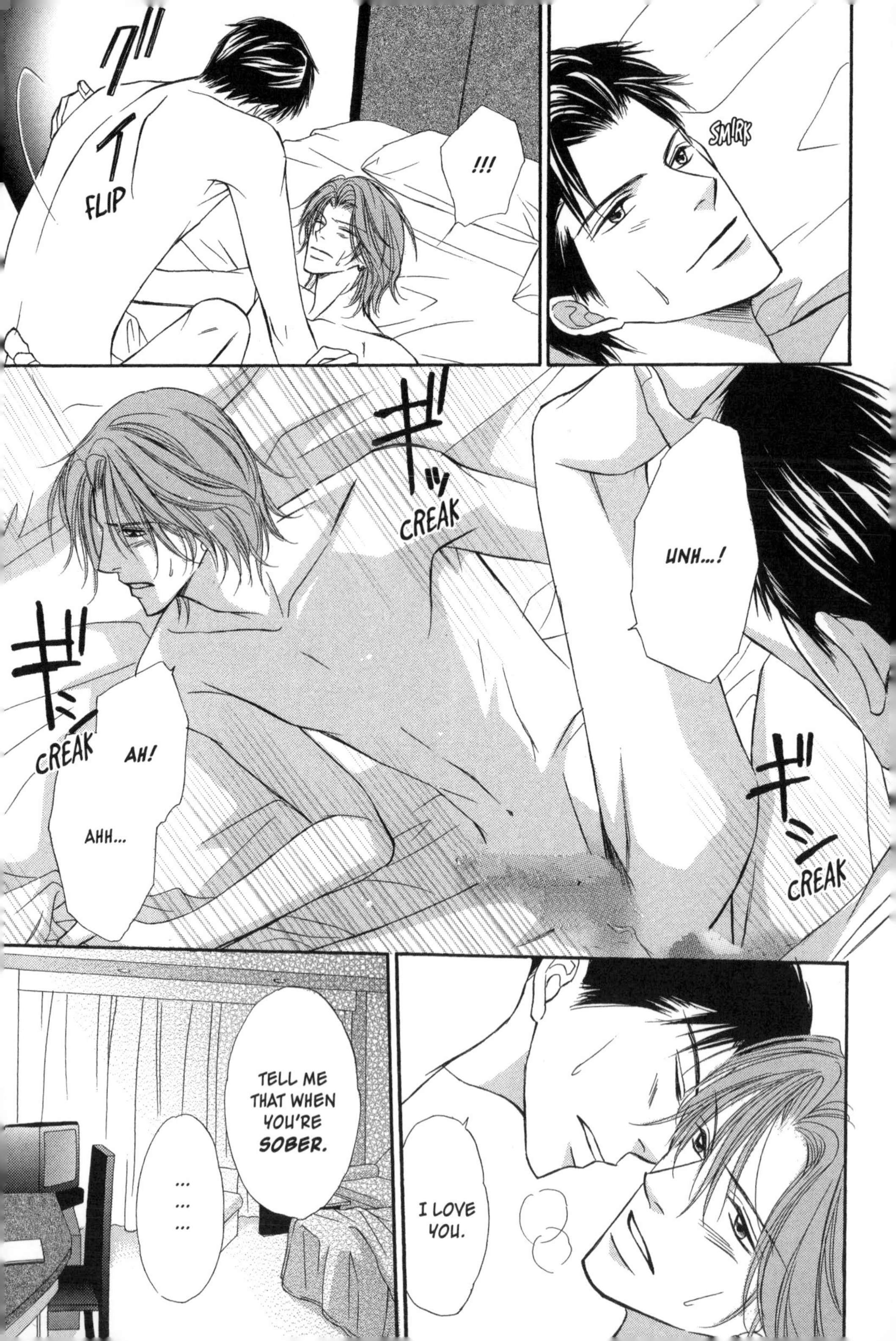
SMIRK
FLIP
!!!
UNH...!
CREAK
CREAK
CREAK
AH!
AHH...
I LOVE YOU.
TELL ME THAT WHEN YOU'RE SOBER.
...
...
...

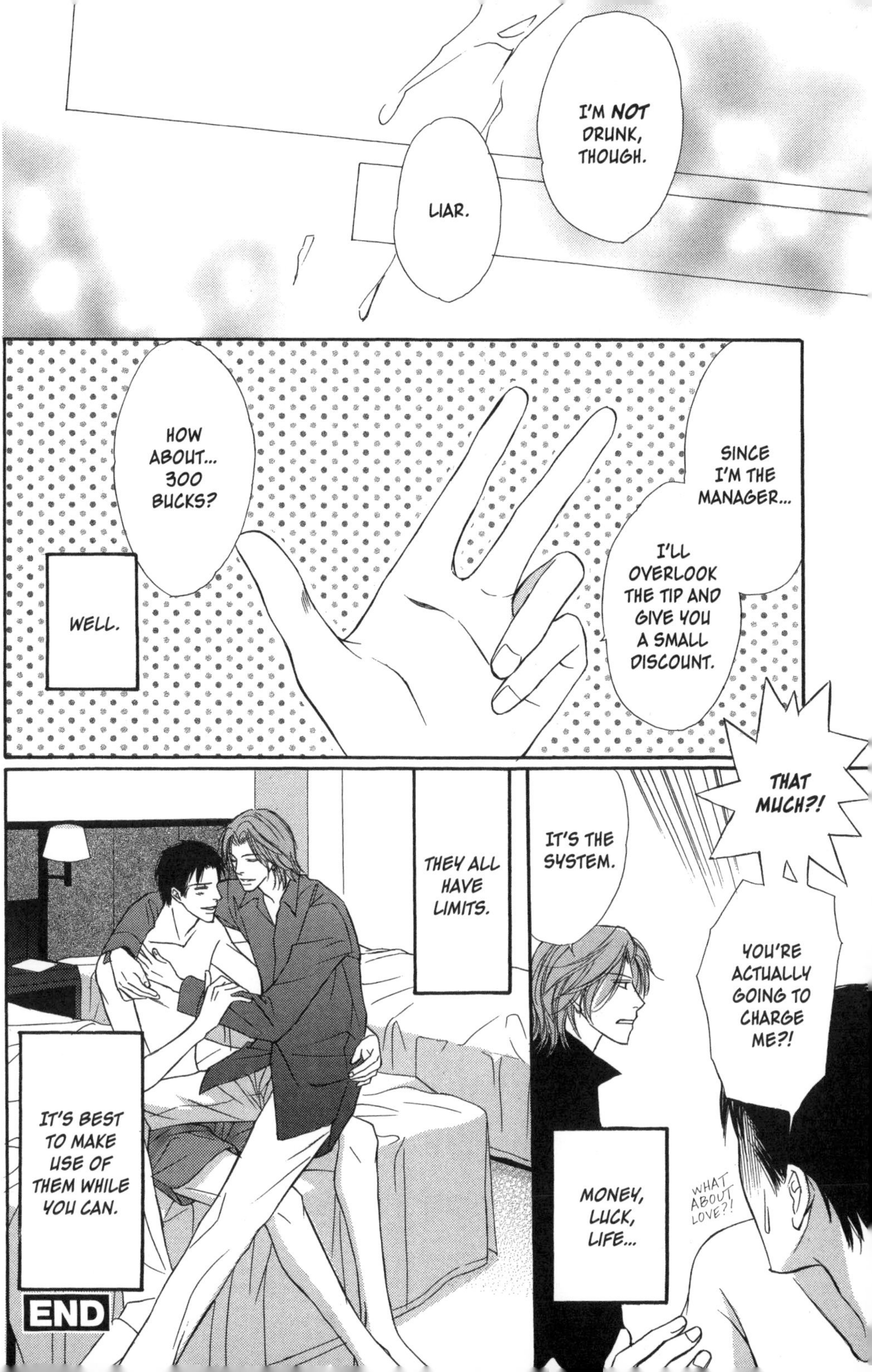
I'M NOT DRUNK, THOUGH.
LIAR.
SINCE I'M THE MANAGER...
I'LL OVERLOOK THE TIP AND GIVE YOU A SMALL DISCOUNT.
HOW ABOUT... 300 BUCKS?
WELL.
THAT MUCH?!
YOU'RE ACTUALLY GOING TO CHARGE ME?!
IT'S THE SYSTEM.
WHAT ABOUT LOVE?!
MONEY, LUCK, LIFE...
THEY ALL HAVE LIMITS.
IT'S BEST TO MAKE USE OF THEM WHILE YOU CAN.
END

THERE'S NO BREAK FROM LOVE

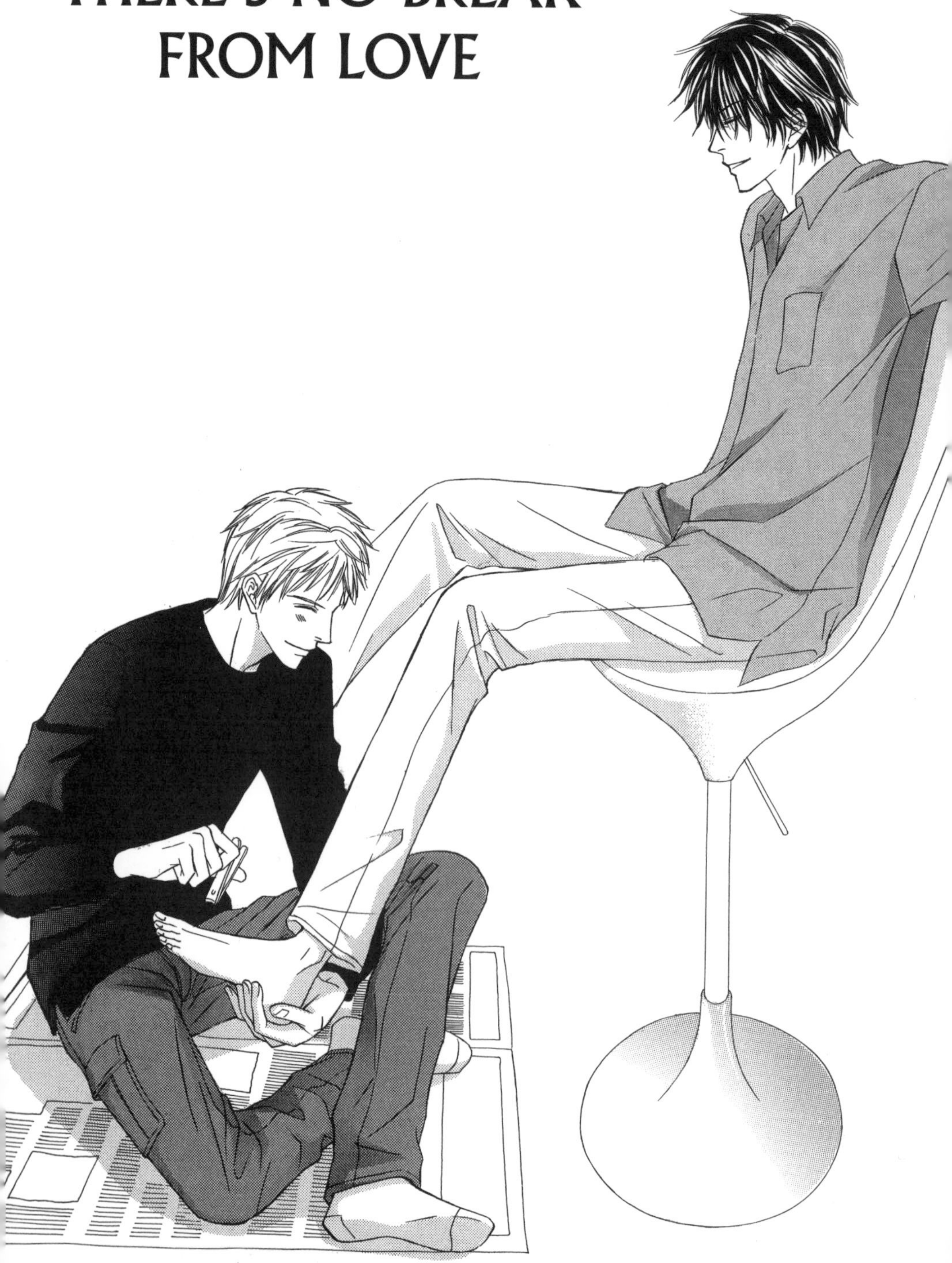

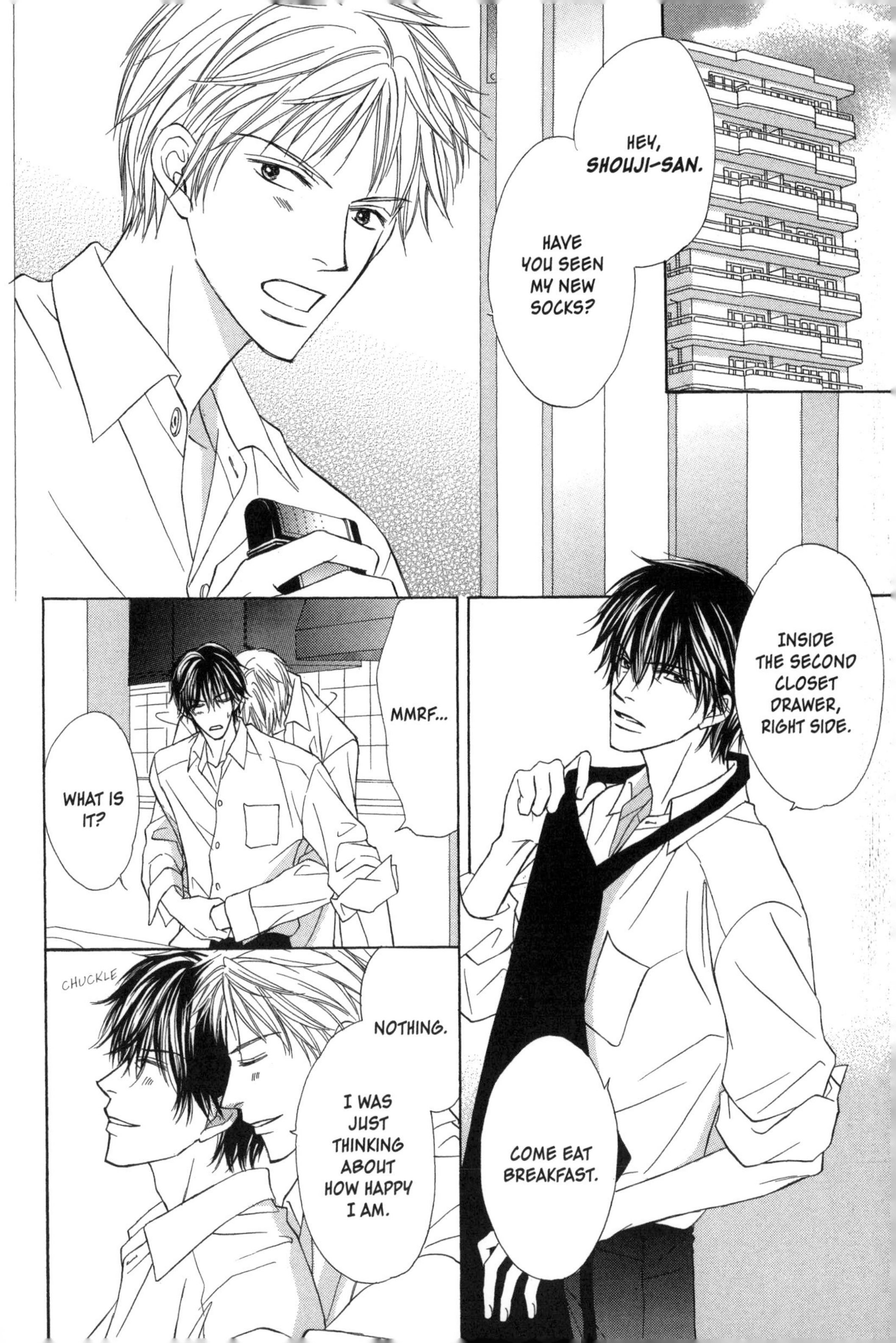
HEY, SHOUJI-SAN.
HAVE YOU SEEN MY NEW SOCKS?
INSIDE THE SECOND CLOSET DRAWER, RIGHT SIDE.
COME EAT BREAKFAST.
MMRF...
WHAT IS IT?
CHUCKLE
NOTHING.
I WAS JUST THINKING ABOUT HOW HAPPY I AM.

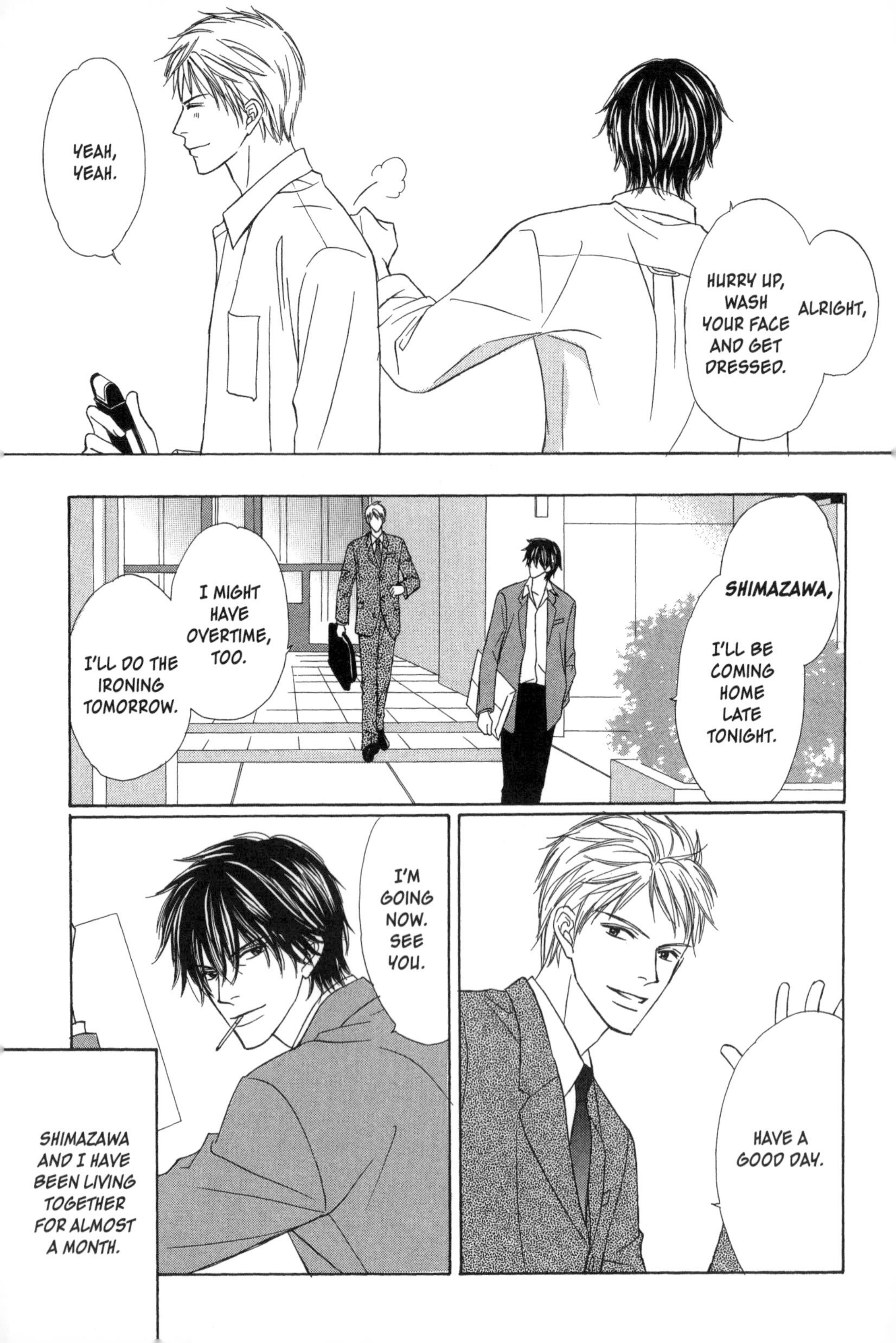
ALRIGHT,
HURRY UP, WASH YOUR FACE AND GET DRESSED.
YEAH, YEAH.
SHIMAZAWA,
I'LL BE COMING HOME LATE TONIGHT.
I MIGHT HAVE OVERTIME, TOO.
I'LL DO THE IRONING TOMORROW.
HAVE A GOOD DAY.
I'M GOING NOW. SEE YOU.
SHIMAZAWA AND I HAVE BEEN LIVING TOGETHER FOR ALMOST A MONTH.

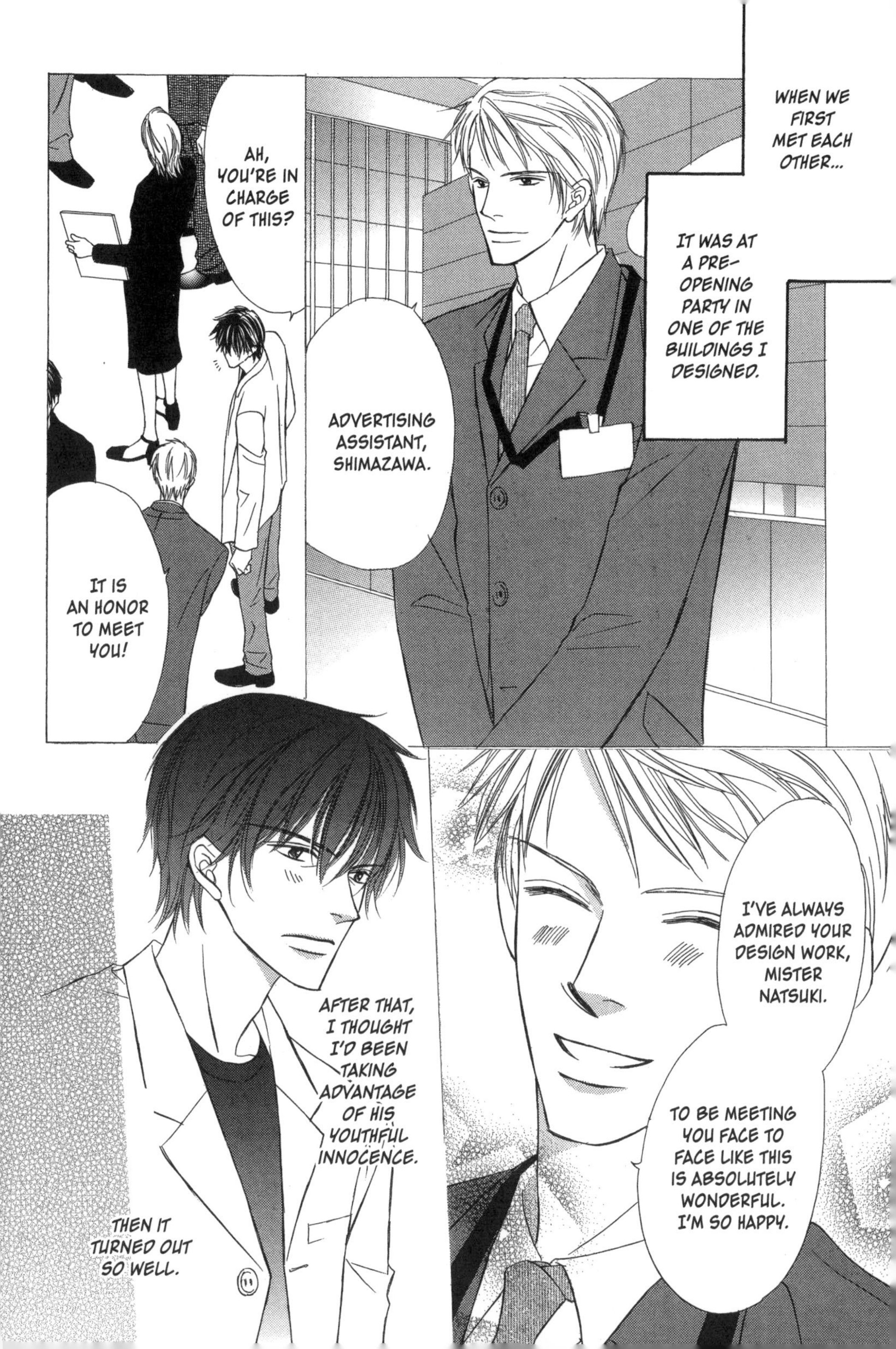
WHEN WE FIRST MET EACH OTHER...
IT WAS AT A PRE-OPENING PARTY IN ONE OF THE BUILDINGS I DESIGNED.
ADVERTISING ASSISTANT, SHIMAZAWA.
AH, YOU'RE IN CHARGE OF THIS?
IT IS AN HONOR TO MEET YOU!
I'VE ALWAYS ADMIRED YOUR DESIGN WORK, MISTER NATSUKI.
TO BE MEETING YOU FACE TO FACE LIKE THIS IS ABSOLUTELY WONDERFUL. I'M SO HAPPY.
AFTER THAT, I THOUGHT I'D BEEN TAKING ADVANTAGE OF HIS YOUTHFUL INNOCENCE.
THEN IT TURNED OUT SO WELL.

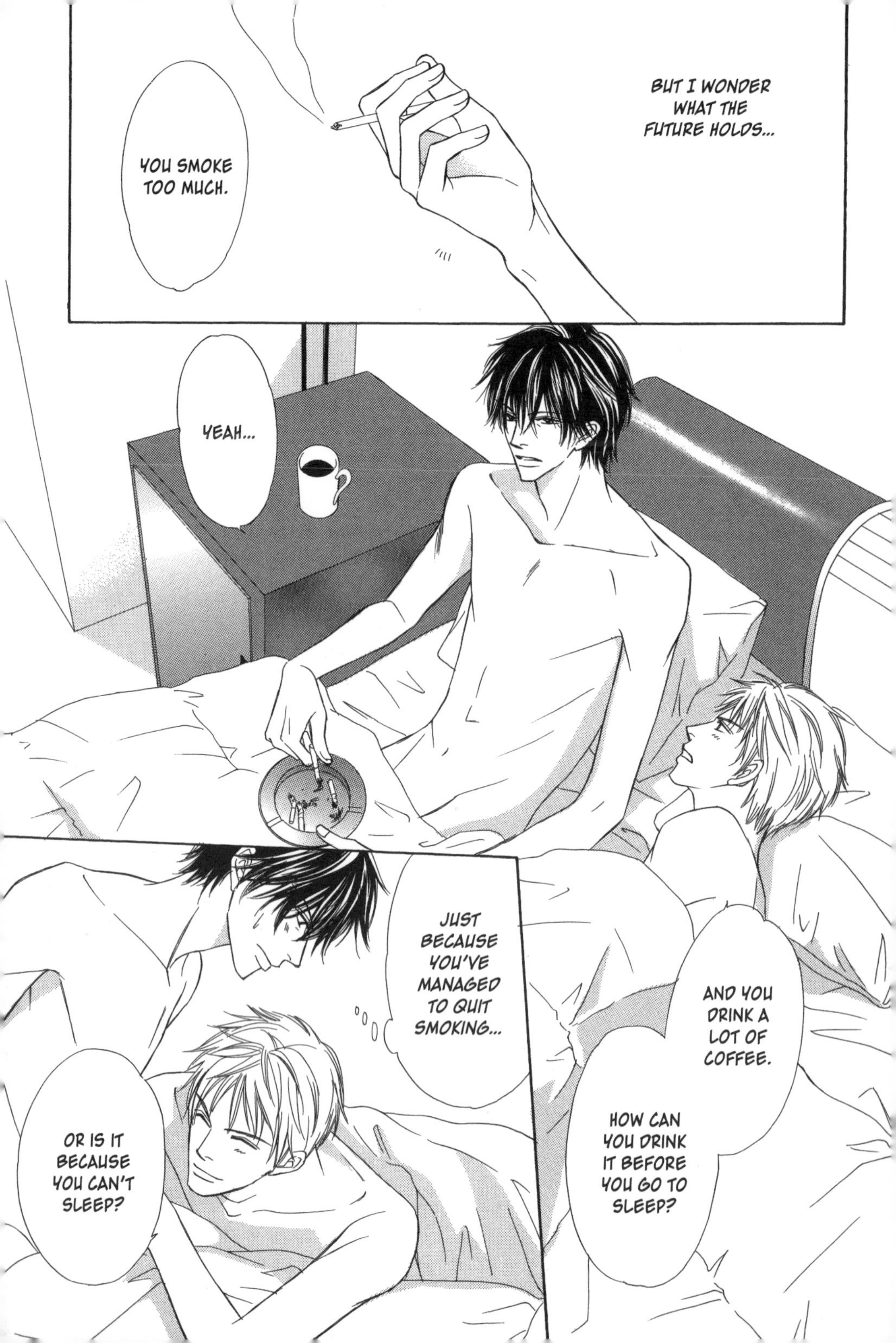
BUT I WONDER WHAT THE FUTURE HOLDS...
YOU SMOKE TOO MUCH.
YEAH...
AND YOU DRINK A LOT OF COFFEE.
HOW CAN YOU DRINK IT BEFORE YOU GO TO SLEEP?
JUST BECAUSE YOU'VE MANAGED TO QUIT SMOKING...
OR IS IT BECAUSE YOU CAN'T SLEEP?

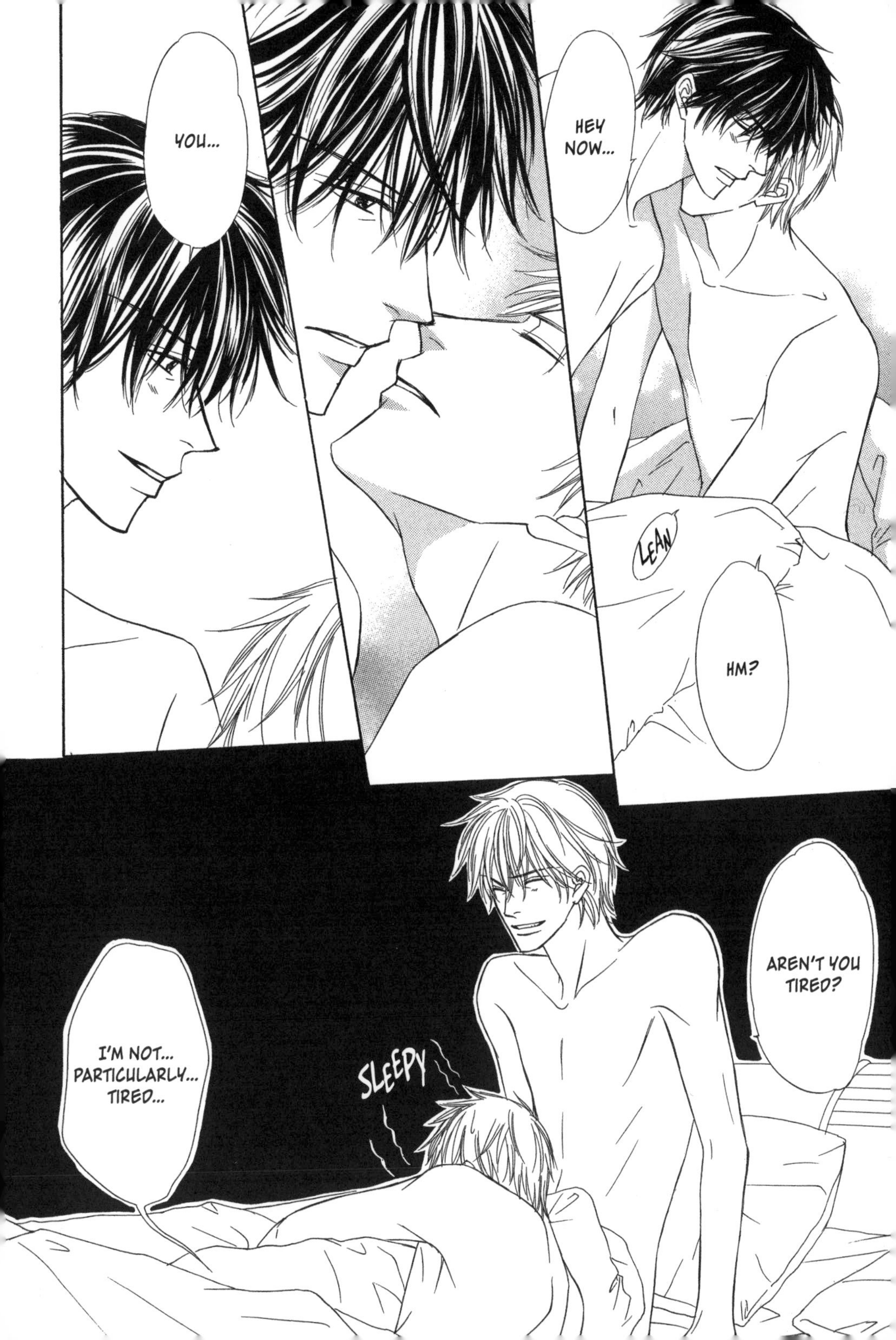
HEY NOW...
LEAN
HM?
YOU...
AREN'T YOU TIRED?
SLEEPY
I'M NOT... PARTICULARLY... TIRED...

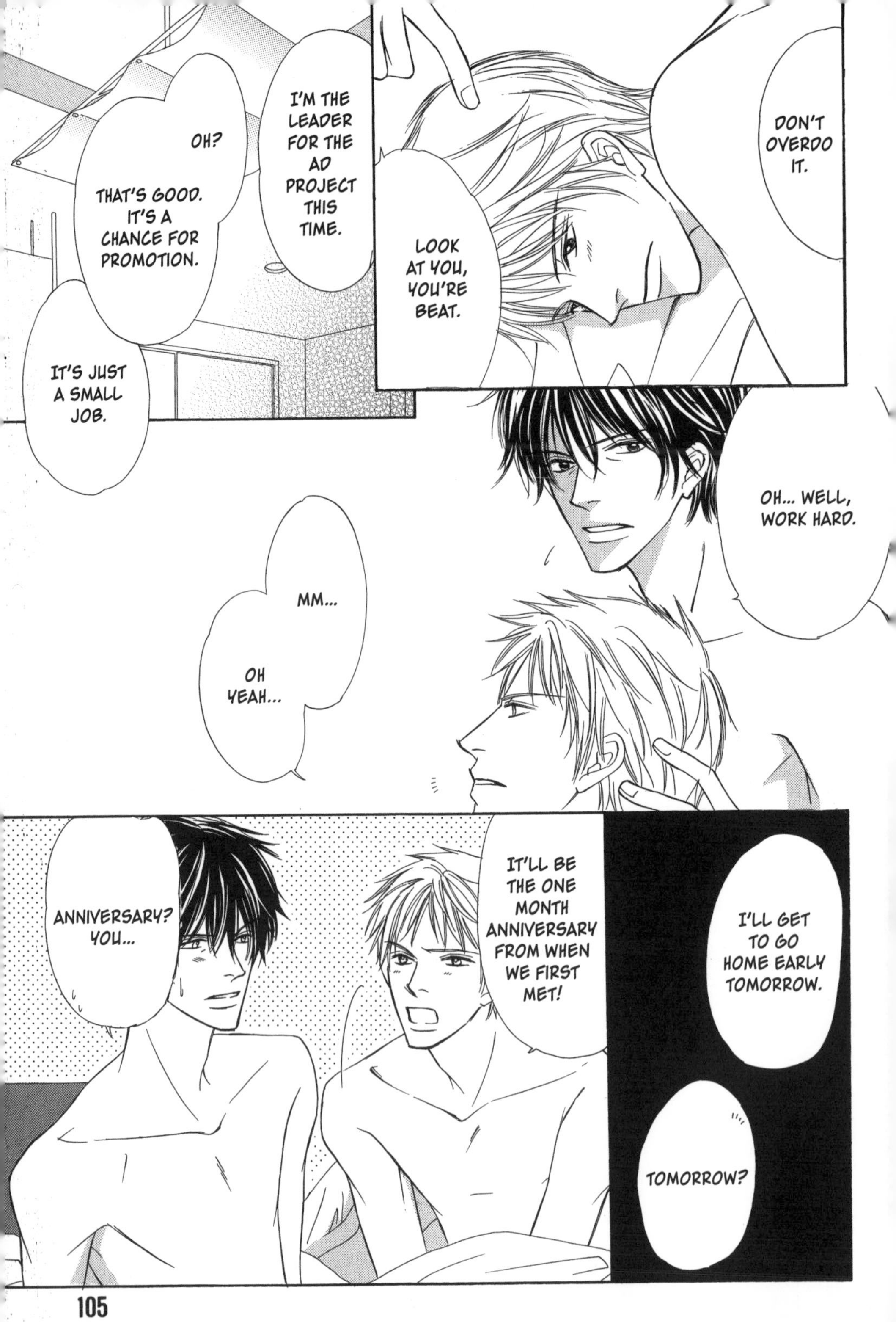
DON'T OVERDO IT.
LOOK AT YOU, YOU'RE BEAT.
I'M THE LEADER FOR THE AD PROJECT THIS TIME.
OH?
THAT'S GOOD. IT'S A CHANCE FOR PROMOTION.
IT'S JUST A SMALL JOB.
OH... WELL, WORK HARD.
MM...
OH YEAH...
I'LL GET TO GO HOME EARLY TOMORROW.
TOMORROW?
IT'LL BE THE ONE MONTH ANNIVERSARY FROM WHEN WE FIRST MET!
ANNIVERSARY? YOU...

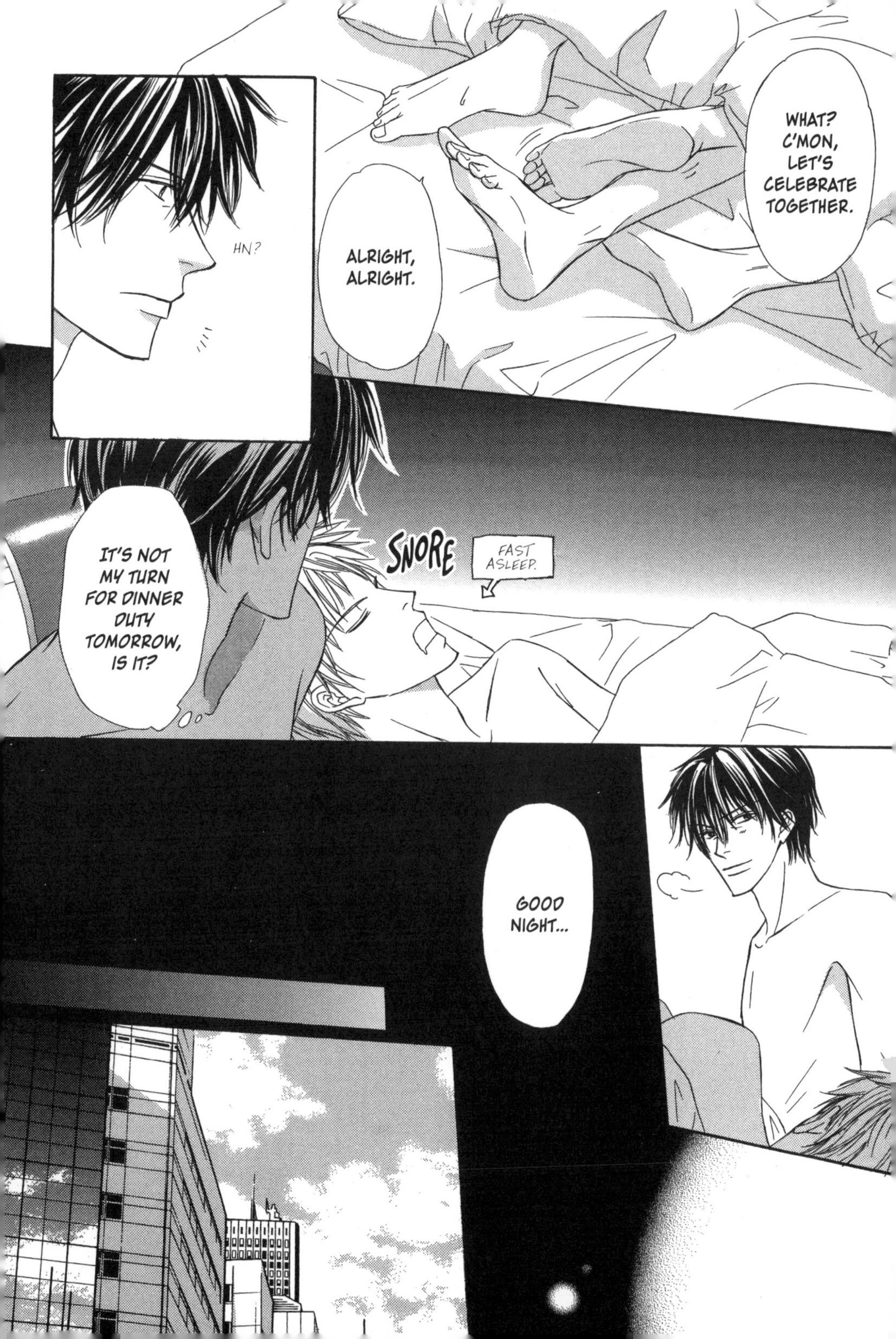
WHAT? C'MON, LET'S CELEBRATE TOGETHER.
ALRIGHT, ALRIGHT.
HN?
IT'S NOT MY TURN FOR DINNER DUTY TOMORROW, IS IT?
SNORE
FAST ASLEEP.
GOOD NIGHT...

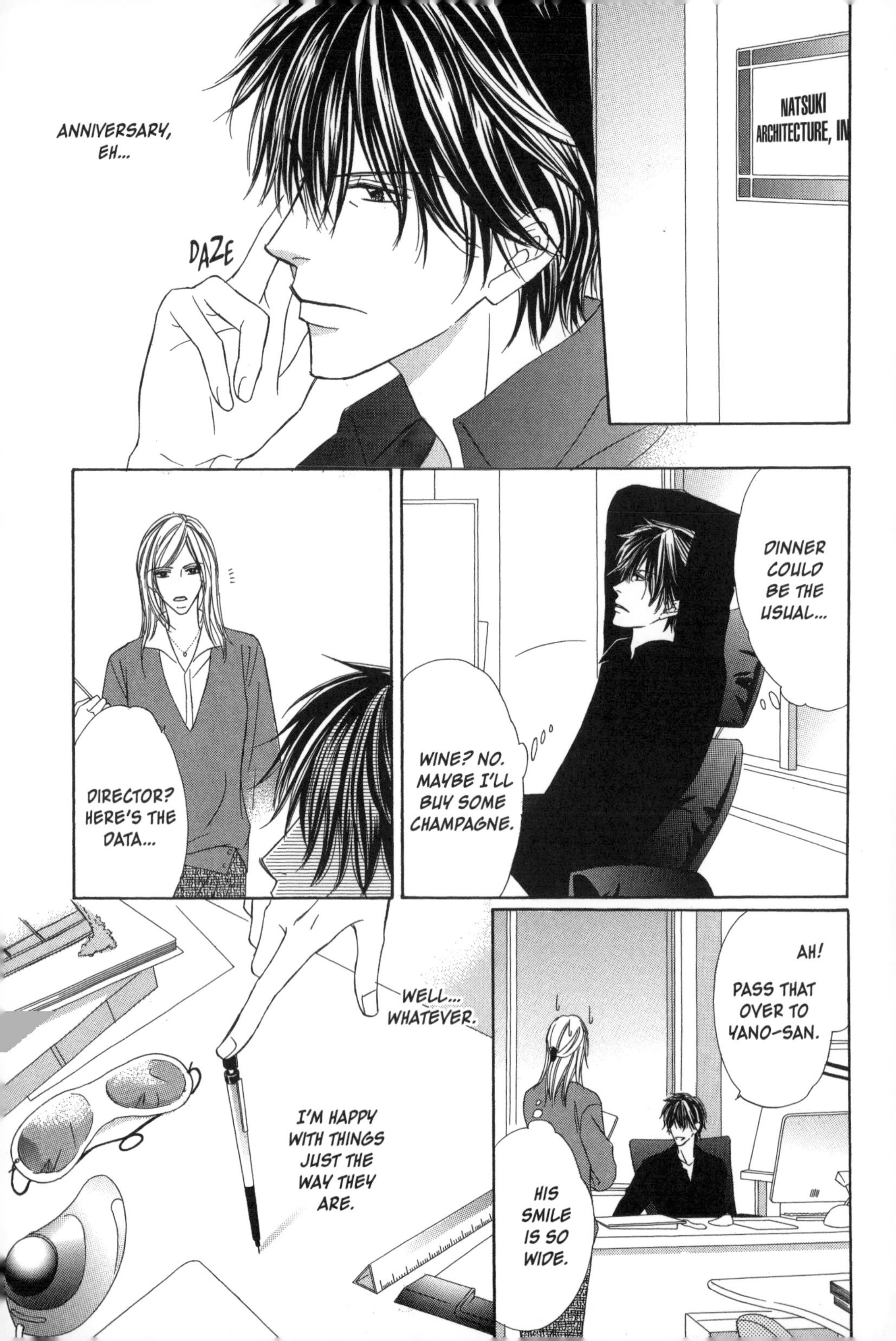
NATSUKI ARCHITECTURE, IN
ANNIVERSARY, EH...
DAZE
DINNER COULD BE THE USUAL...
WINE? NO. MAYBE I'LL BUY SOME CHAMPAGNE.
DIRECTOR? HERE'S THE DATA...
AH!
PASS THAT OVER TO YANO-SAN.
HIS SMILE IS SO WIDE.
WELL... WHATEVER.
I'M HAPPY WITH THINGS JUST THE WAY THEY ARE.

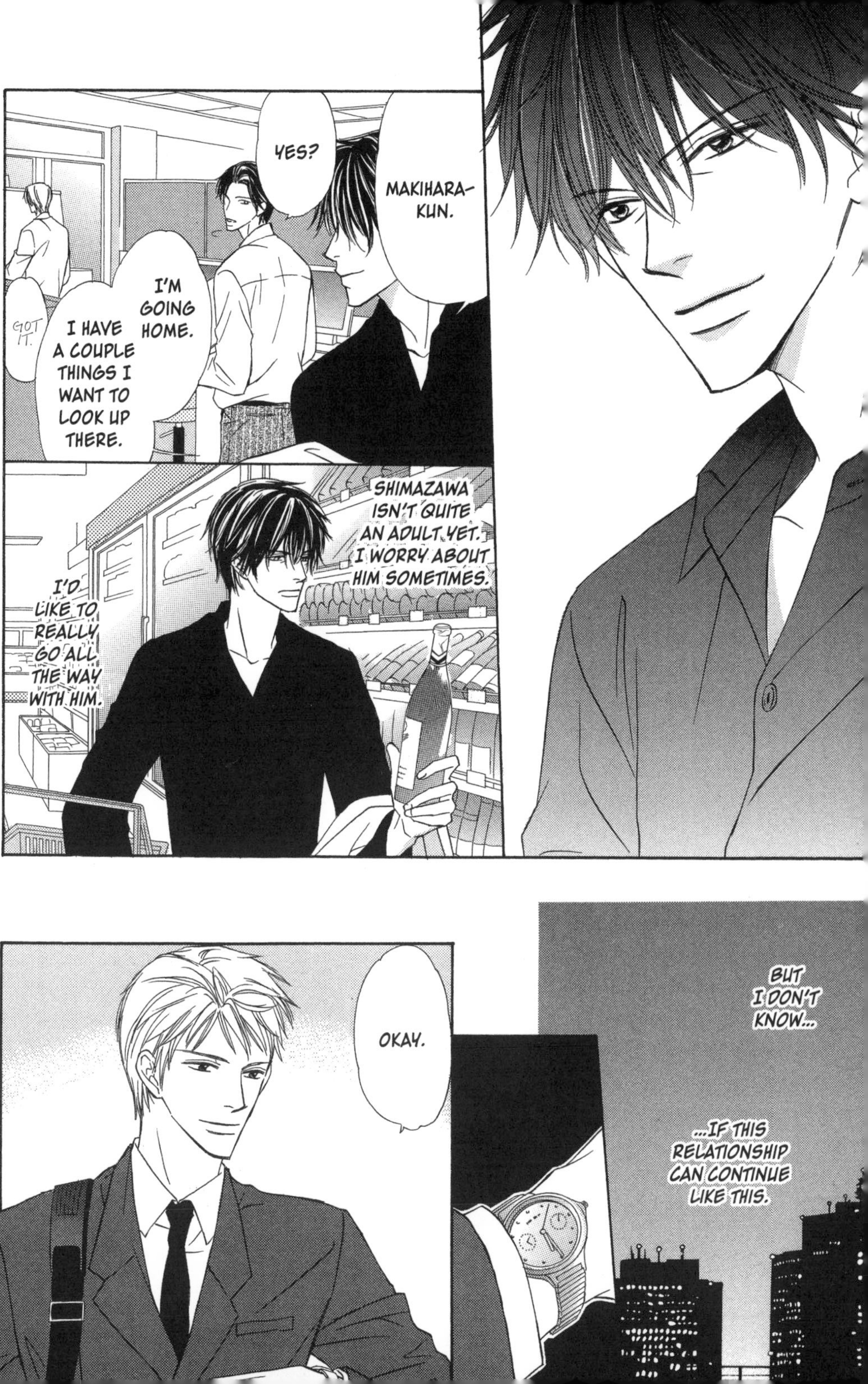
MAKIHARA-KUN.
YES?
I'M GOING HOME.
I HAVE A COUPLE THINGS I WANT TO LOOK UP THERE.
GOT IT.
SHIMAZAWA ISN'T QUITE AN ADULT YET. I WORRY ABOUT HIM SOMETIMES.
I'D LIKE TO REALLY GO ALL THE WAY WITH HIM.
BUT I DON'T KNOW...
...IF THIS RELATIONSHIP CAN CONTINUE LIKE THIS.
OKAY.

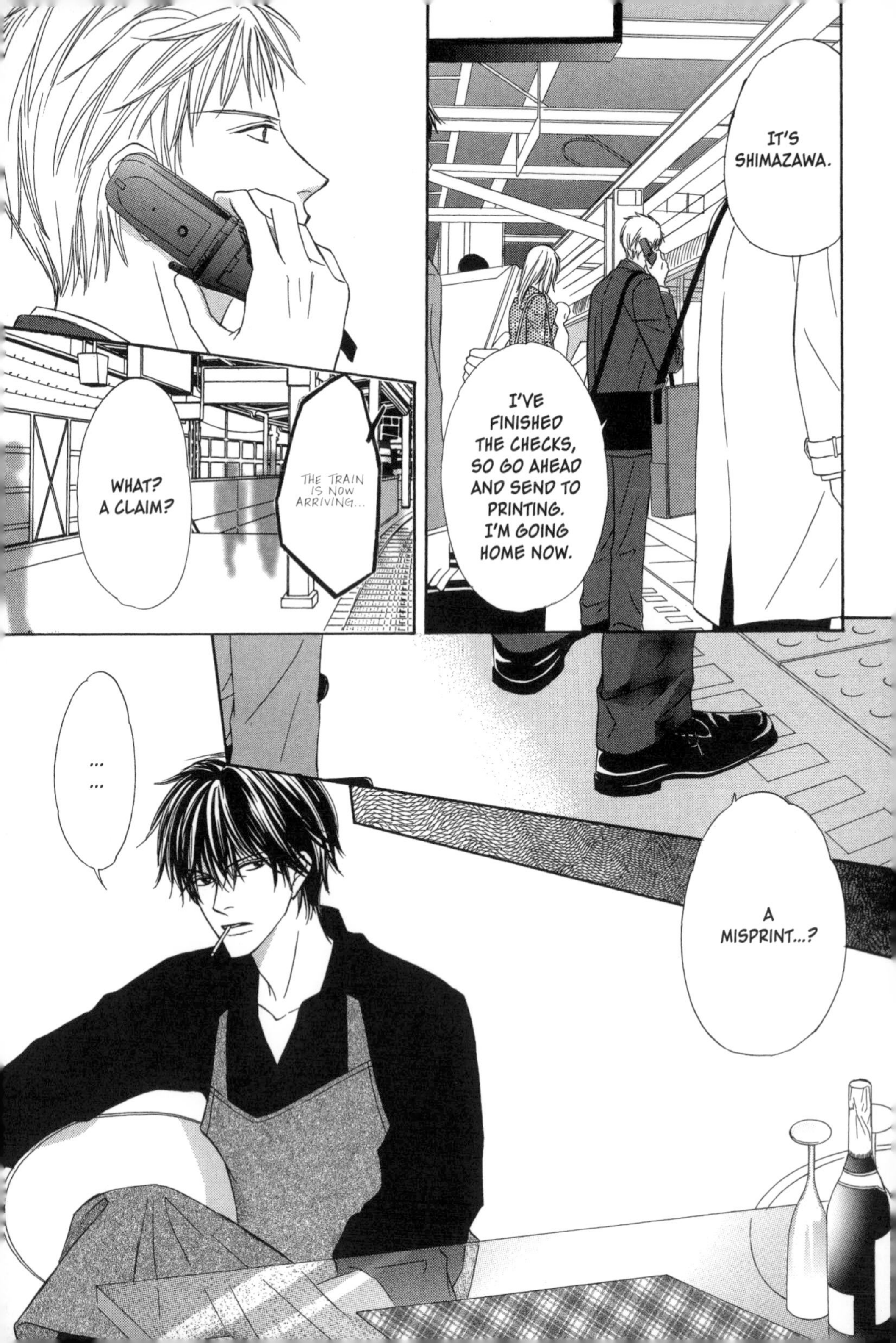
IT'S SHIMAZAWA.
I'VE FINISHED THE CHECKS, SO GO AHEAD AND SEND TO PRINTING. I'M GOING HOME NOW.
THE TRAIN IS NOW ARRIVING...
WHAT? A CLAIM?
A MISPRINT...?
... ...

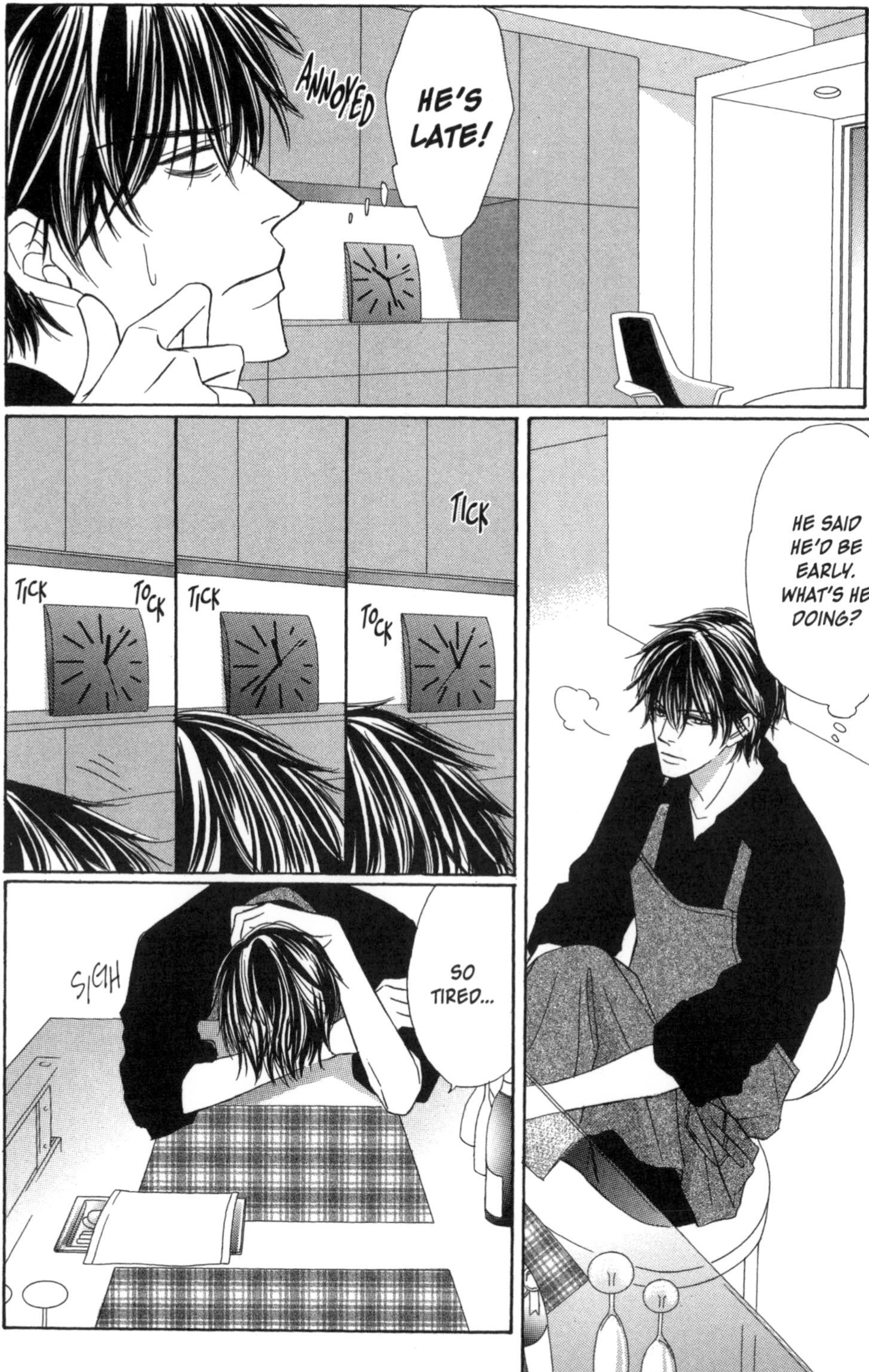
HE'S LATE!
ANNOYED
HE SAID HE'D BE EARLY. WHAT'S HE DOING?
TICK
TOCK
TICK
TOCK
TICK
SO TIRED...
SIGH

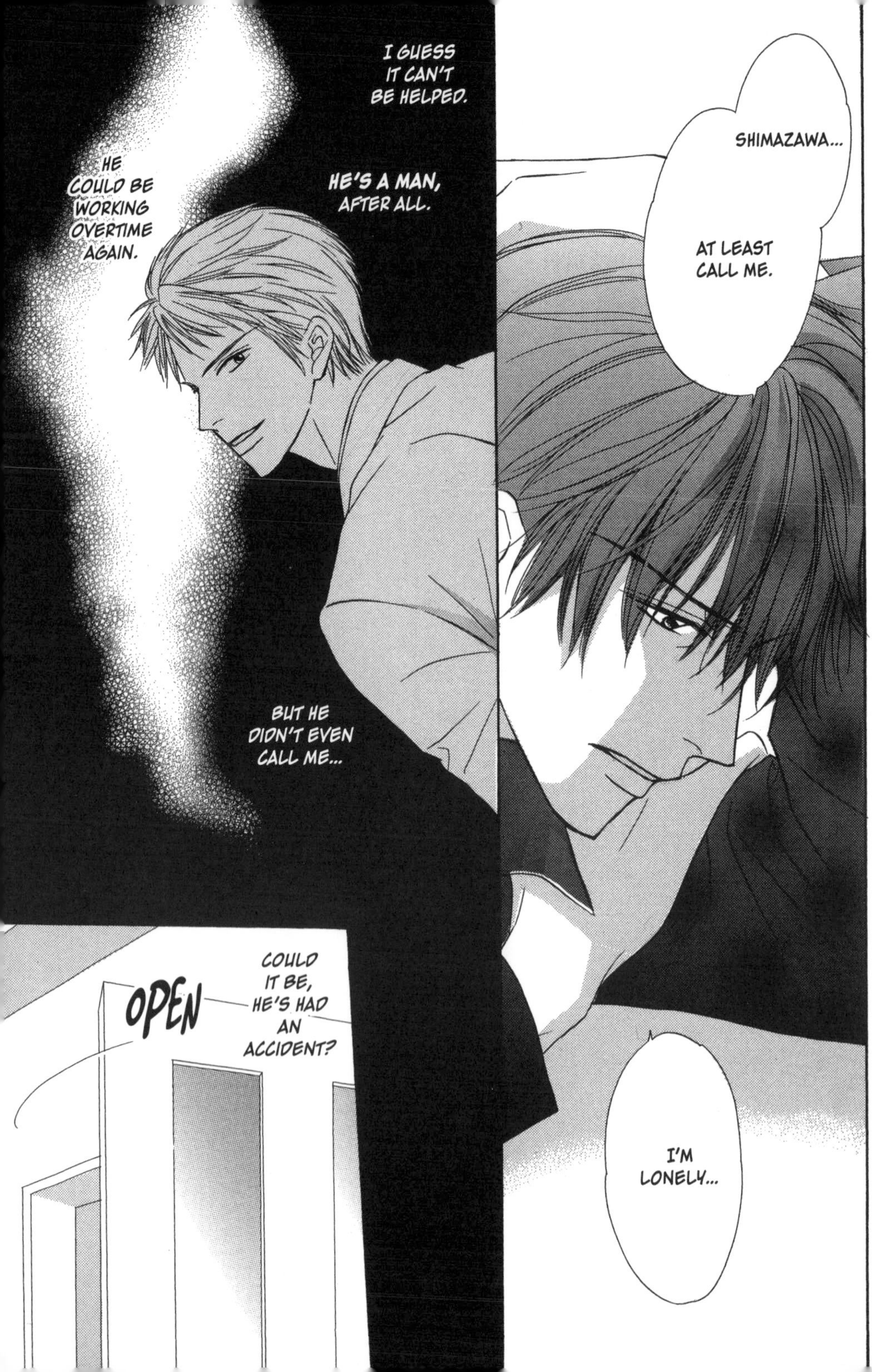
SHIMAZAWA...
AT LEAST CALL ME.
I'M LONELY...
I GUESS IT CAN'T BE HELPED.
HE'S A MAN, AFTER ALL.
HE COULD BE WORKING OVERTIME AGAIN.
BUT HE DIDN'T EVEN CALL ME...
COULD IT BE, HE'S HAD AN ACCIDENT?
OPEN

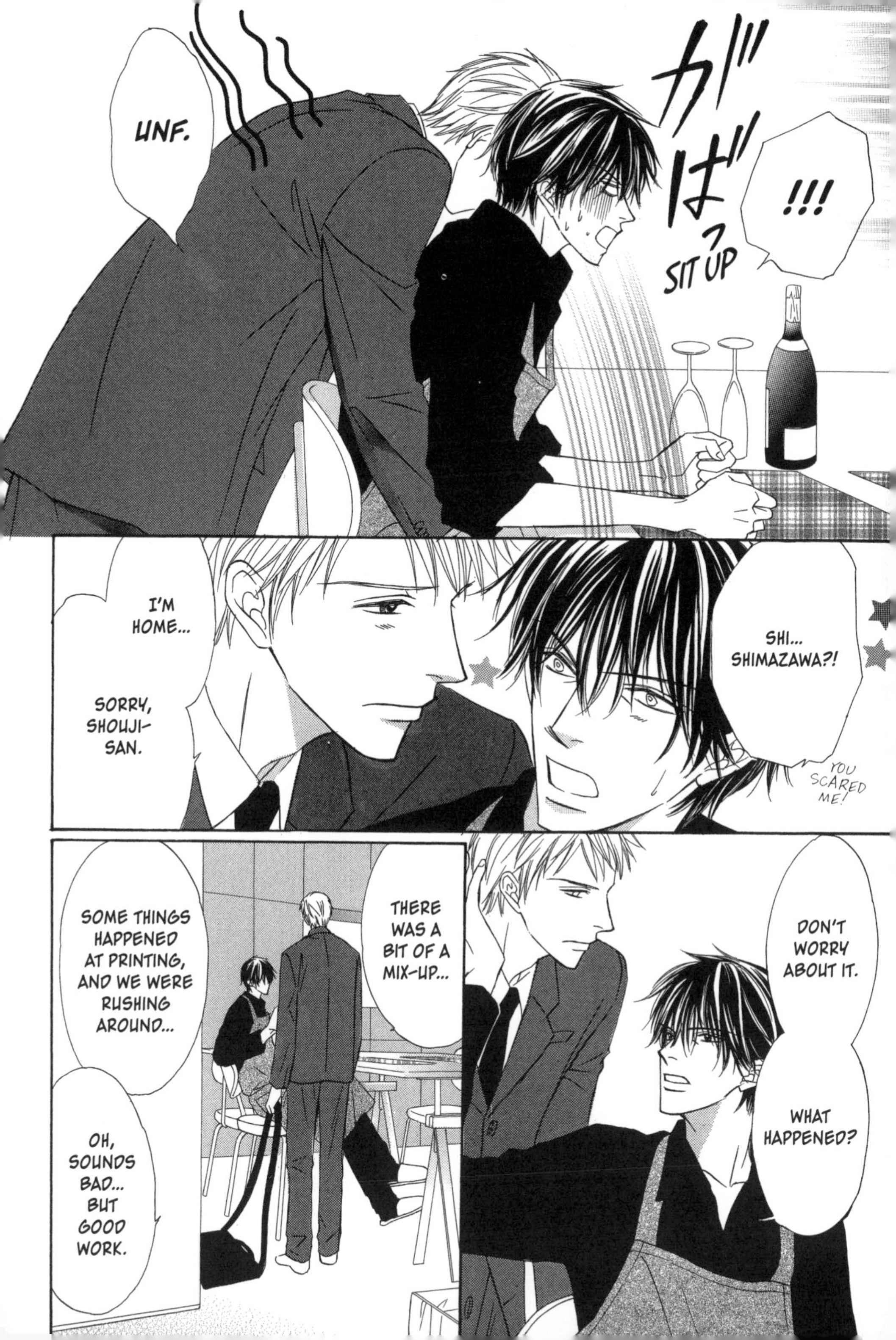
ガばっ
SIT UP
!!!
UNF.
SHI... SHIMAZAWA?!
YOU SCARED ME!
I'M HOME...
SORRY, SHOUJI-SAN.
DON'T WORRY ABOUT IT.
WHAT HAPPENED?
THERE WAS A BIT OF A MIX-UP...
SOME THINGS HAPPENED AT PRINTING, AND WE WERE RUSHING AROUND...
OH, SOUNDS BAD... BUT GOOD WORK.

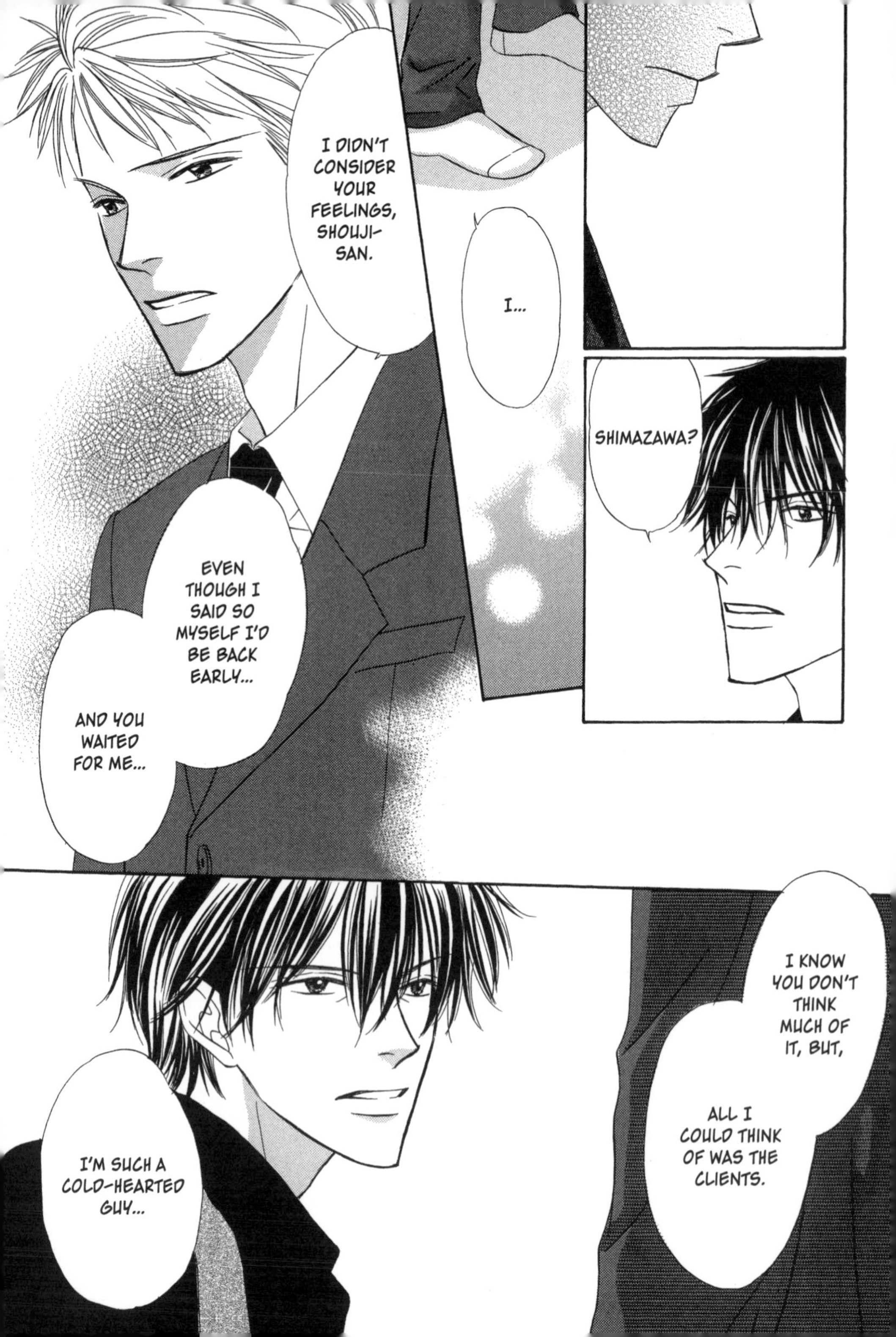
SHIMAZAWA?
I...
I DIDN'T CONSIDER YOUR FEELINGS, SHOUJI-SAN.
EVEN THOUGH I SAID SO MYSELF I'D BE BACK EARLY...
AND YOU WAITED FOR ME...
I KNOW YOU DON'T THINK MUCH OF IT, BUT,
ALL I COULD THINK OF WAS THE CLIENTS.
I'M SUCH A COLD-HEARTED GUY...

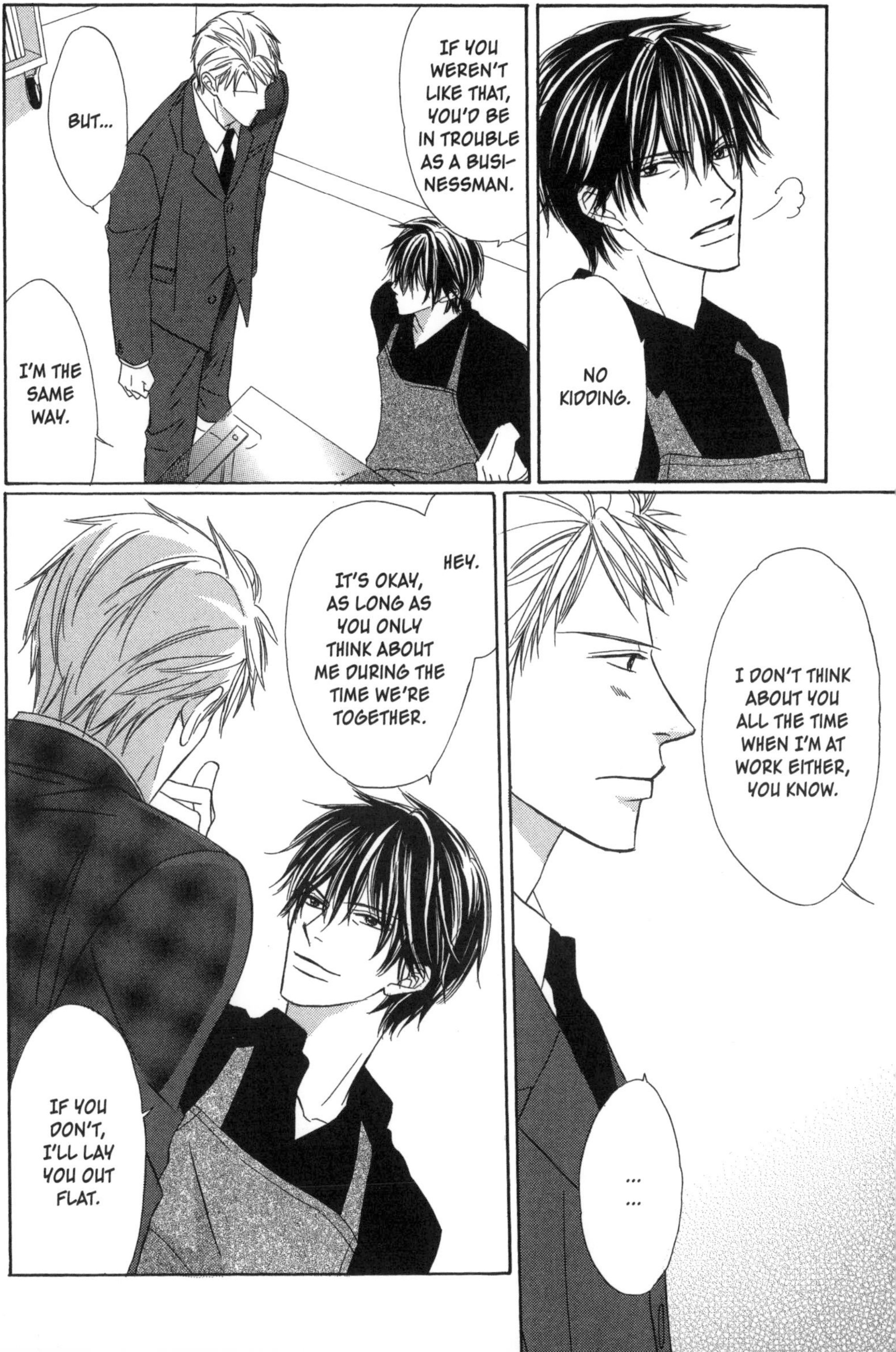
NO KIDDING.
IF YOU WEREN'T LIKE THAT, YOU'D BE IN TROUBLE AS A BUSINESSMAN.
BUT...
I'M THE SAME WAY.
I DON'T THINK ABOUT YOU ALL THE TIME WHEN I'M AT WORK EITHER, YOU KNOW.
......
HEY.
IT'S OKAY, AS LONG AS YOU ONLY THINK ABOUT ME DURING THE TIME WE'RE TOGETHER.
IF YOU DON'T, I'LL LAY YOU OUT FLAT.

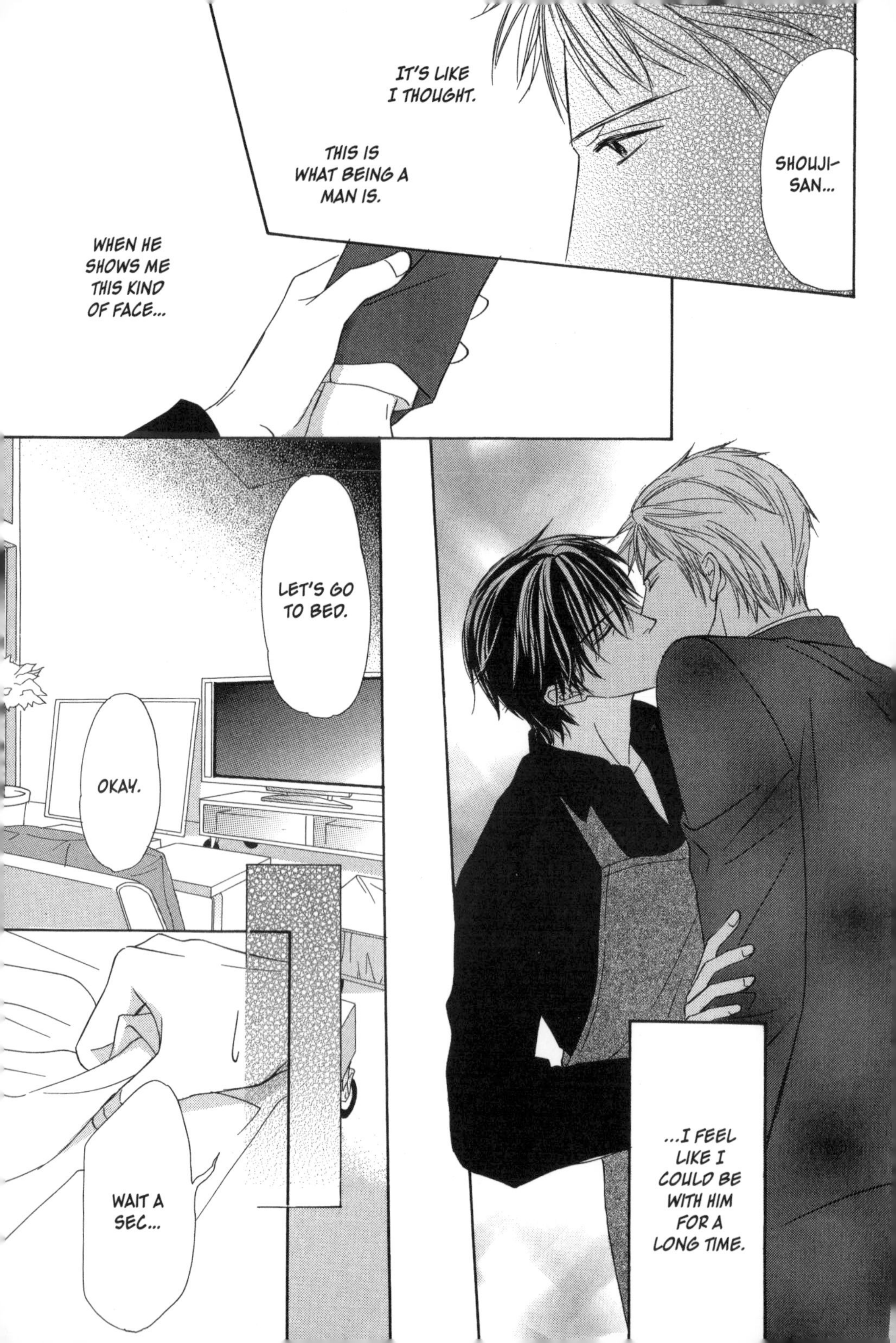
SHOUJI-SAN...
IT'S LIKE I THOUGHT.
THIS IS WHAT BEING A MAN IS.
WHEN HE SHOWS ME THIS KIND OF FACE...
...I FEEL LIKE I COULD BE WITH HIM FOR A LONG TIME.
LET'S GO TO BED.
OKAY.
WAIT A SEC...

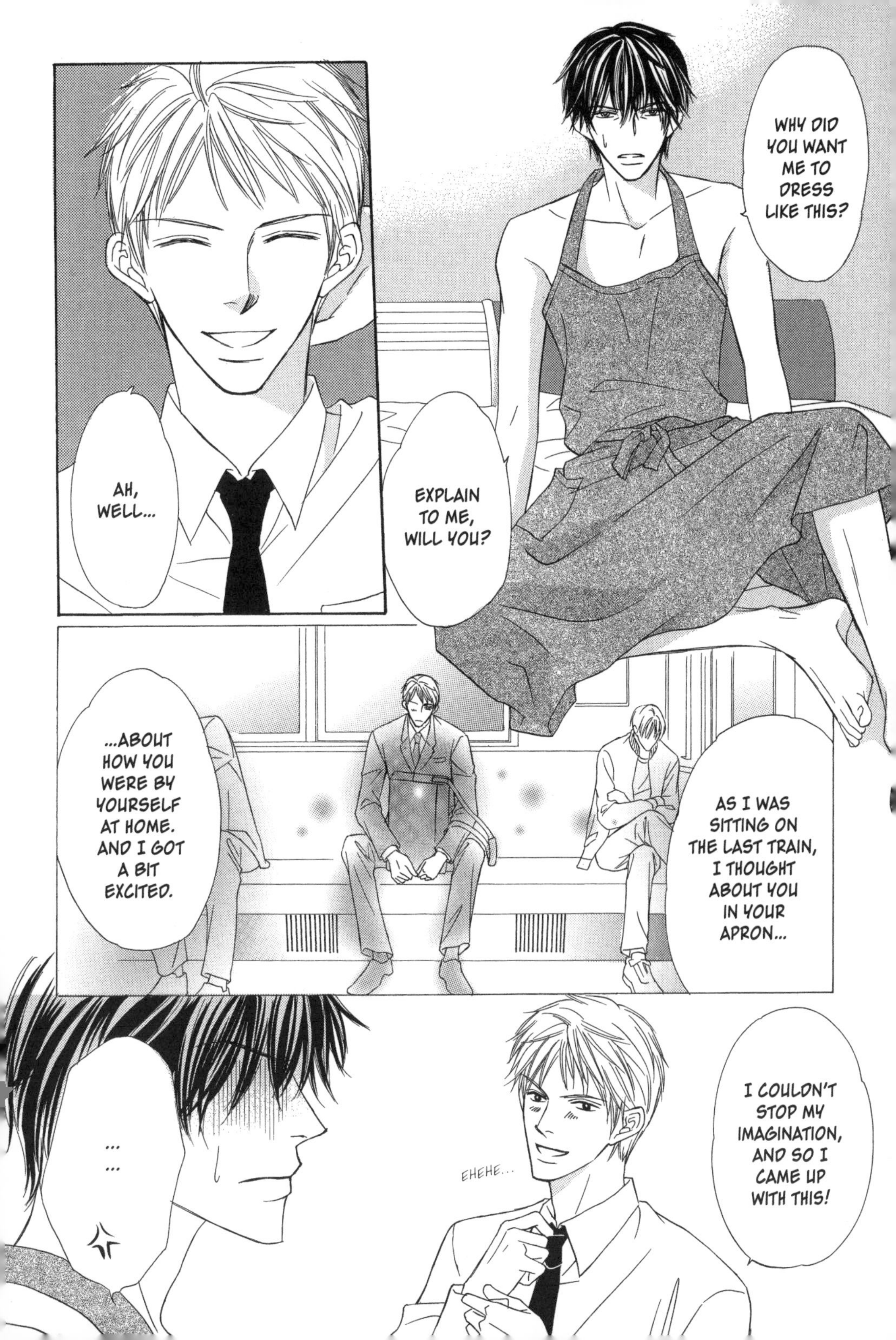
WHY DID YOU WANT ME TO DRESS LIKE THIS?
EXPLAIN TO ME, WILL YOU?
AH, WELL...
AS I WAS SITTING ON THE LAST TRAIN, I THOUGHT ABOUT YOU IN YOUR APRON...
...ABOUT HOW YOU WERE BY YOURSELF AT HOME. AND I GOT A BIT EXCITED.
I COULDN'T STOP MY IMAGINATION, AND SO I CAME UP WITH THIS!
EHEHE...
... ...

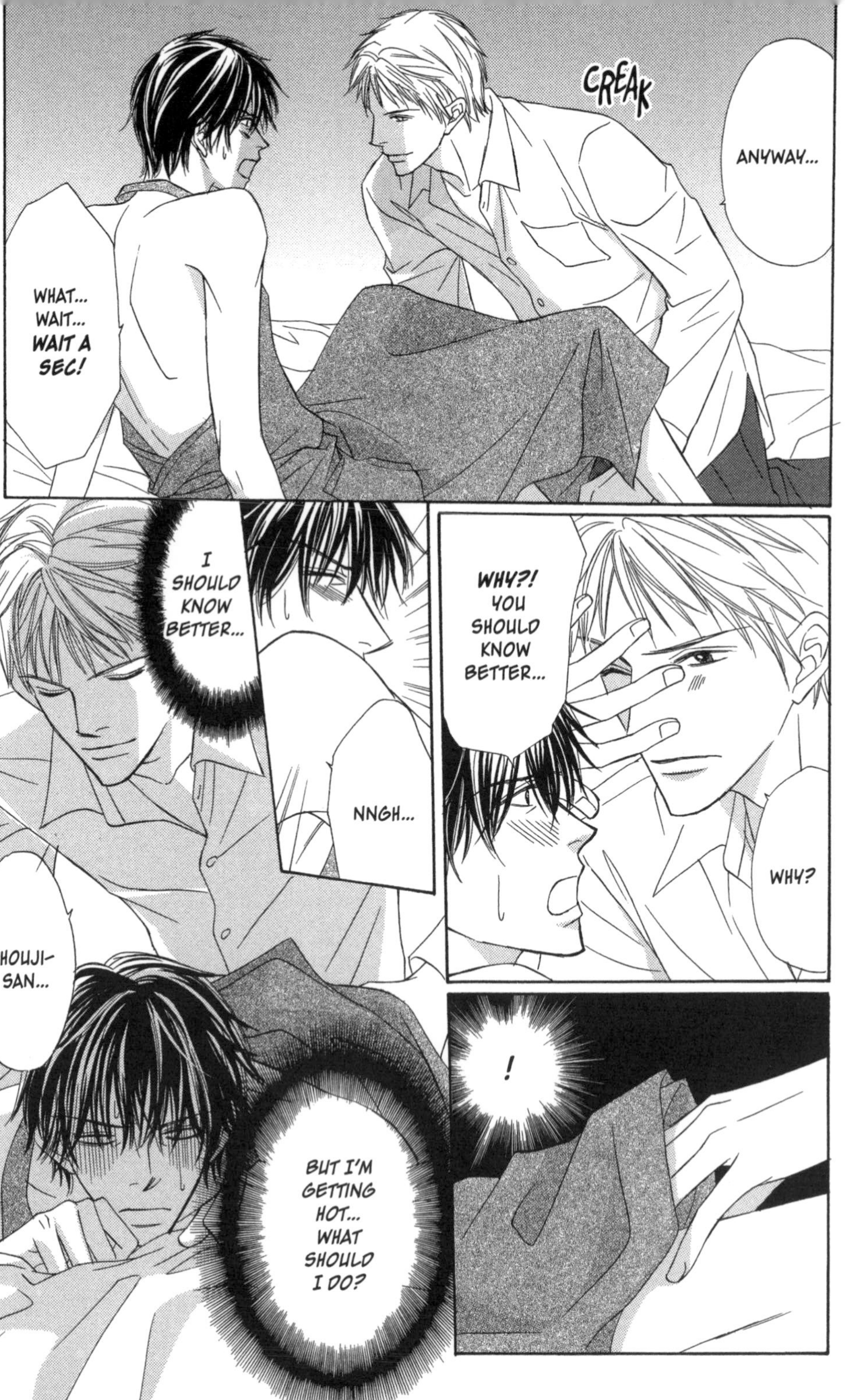
CREAK
ANYWAY...
WHAT... WAIT... WAIT A SEC!
WHY?! YOU SHOULD KNOW BETTER...
WHY?
!
I SHOULD KNOW BETTER...
NNGH...
SHOUJI-SAN...
BUT I'M GETTING HOT... WHAT SHOULD I DO?

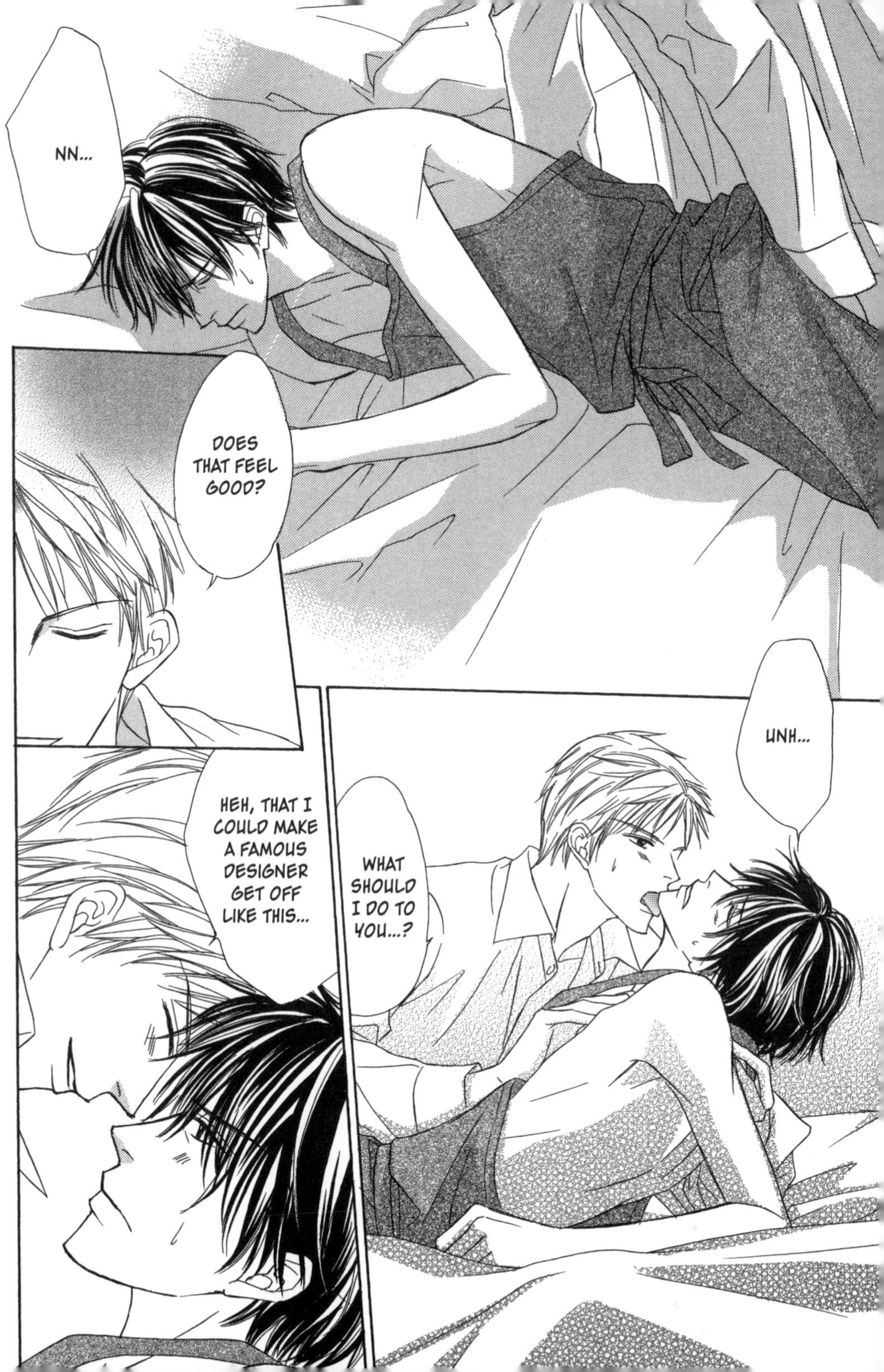
NN...
DOES THAT FEEL GOOD?
UNH...
WHAT SHOULD I DO TO YOU...?
HEH, THAT I COULD MAKE A FAMOUS DESIGNER GET OFF LIKE THIS...

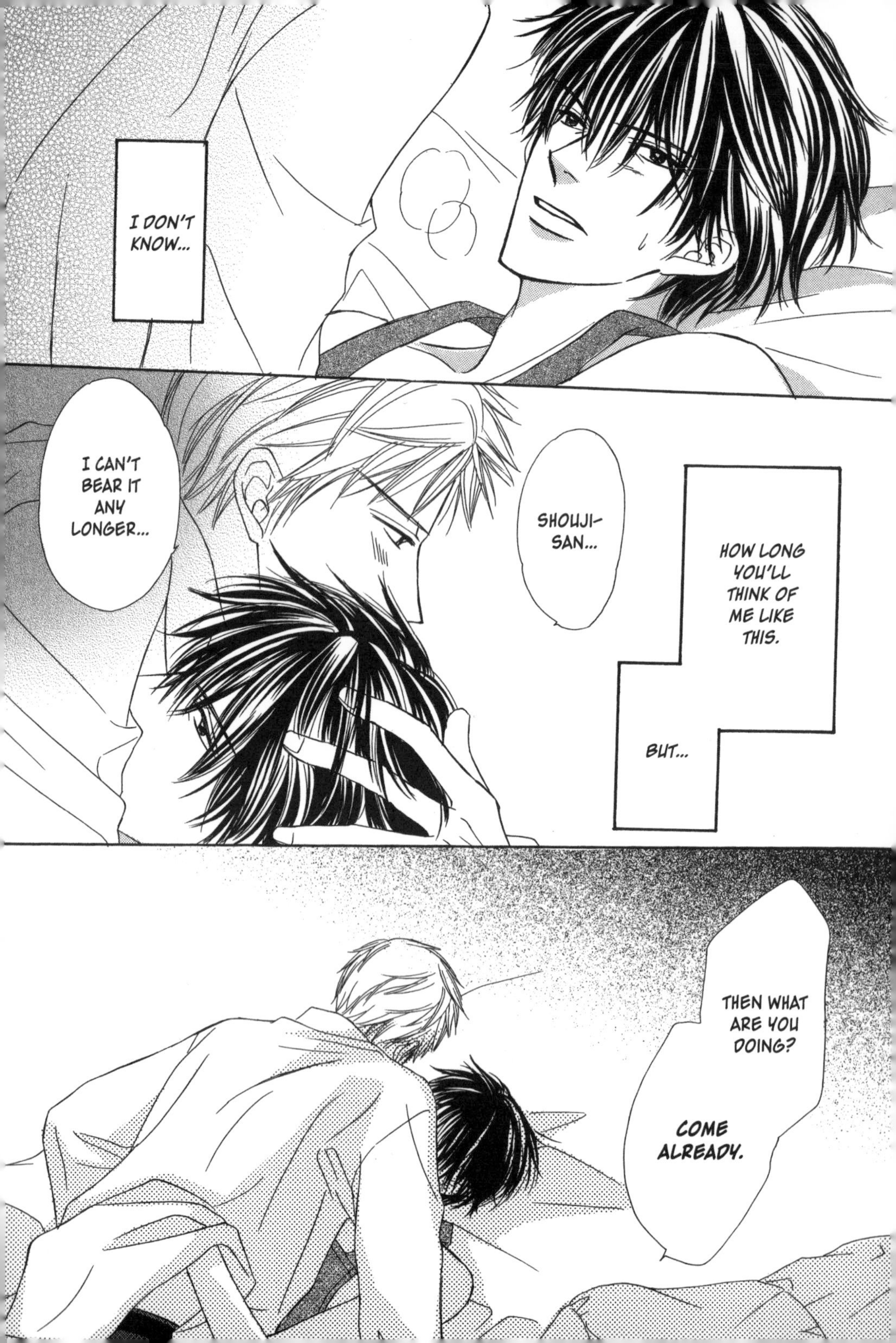
I DON'T KNOW...
HOW LONG YOU'LL THINK OF ME LIKE THIS.
BUT...
SHOUJI-SAN...
I CAN'T BEAR IT ANY LONGER...
THEN WHAT ARE YOU DOING?
COME ALREADY.

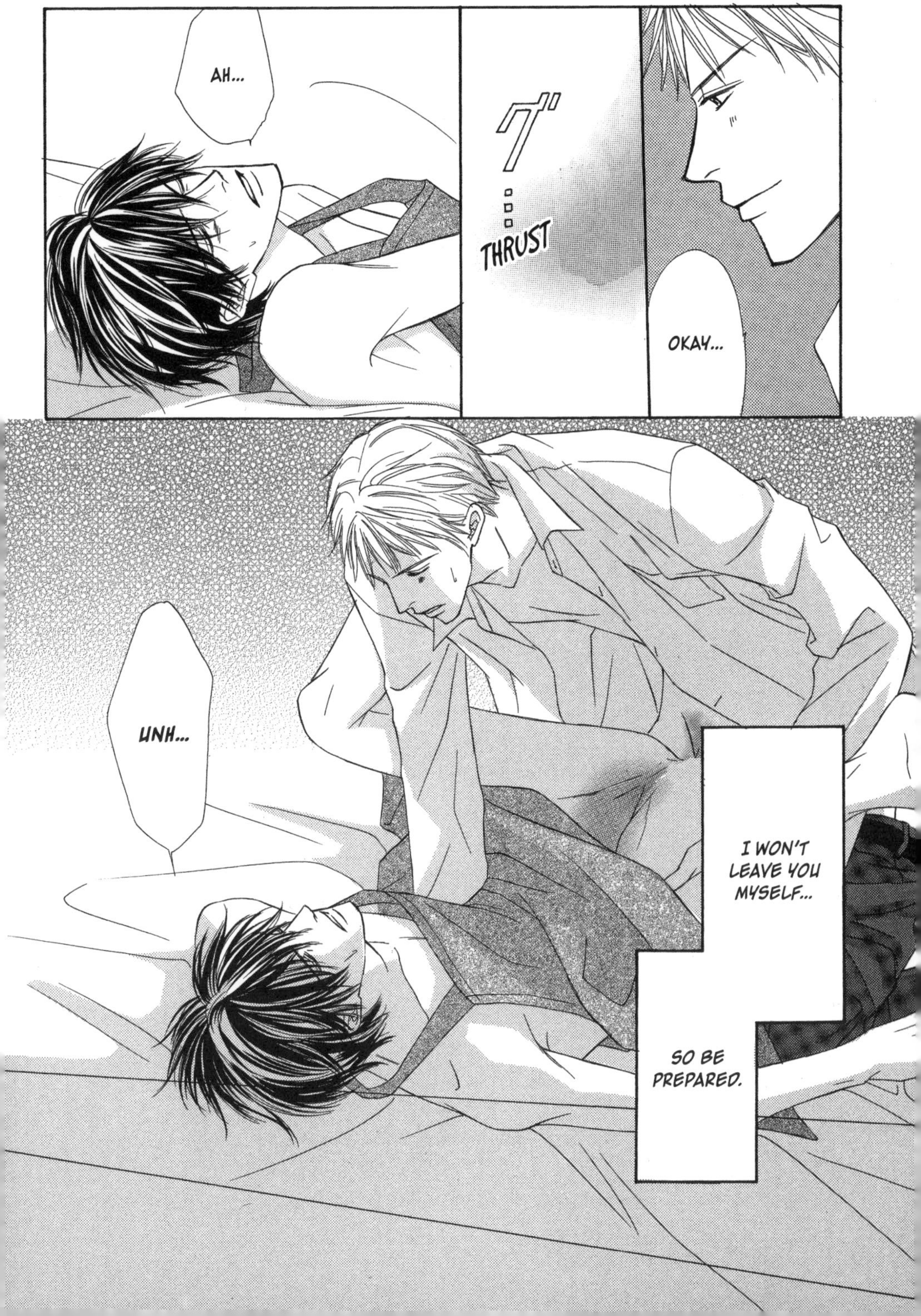
OKAY...
グ...
THRUST
AH...
I WON'T LEAVE YOU MYSELF...
SO BE PREPARED.
UNH...

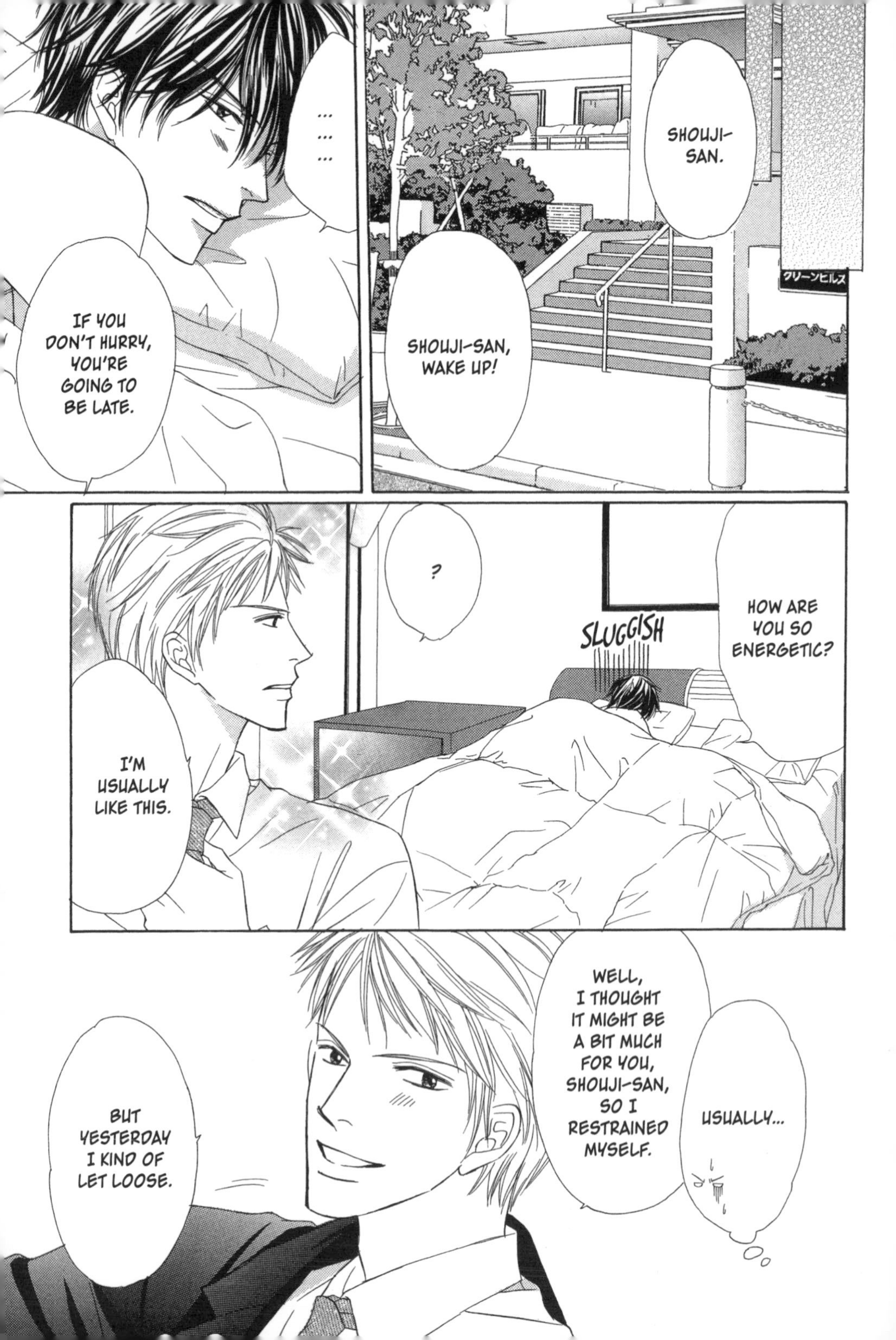
SHOUJI-SAN.
クリーンヒルズ
SHOUJI-SAN, WAKE UP!
...
...
...
IF YOU DON'T HURRY, YOU'RE GOING TO BE LATE.
HOW ARE YOU SO ENERGETIC?
SLUGGISH
?
I'M USUALLY LIKE THIS.
USUALLY...
WELL, I THOUGHT IT MIGHT BE A BIT MUCH FOR YOU, SHOUJI-SAN, SO I RESTRAINED MYSELF.
BUT YESTERDAY I KIND OF LET LOOSE.

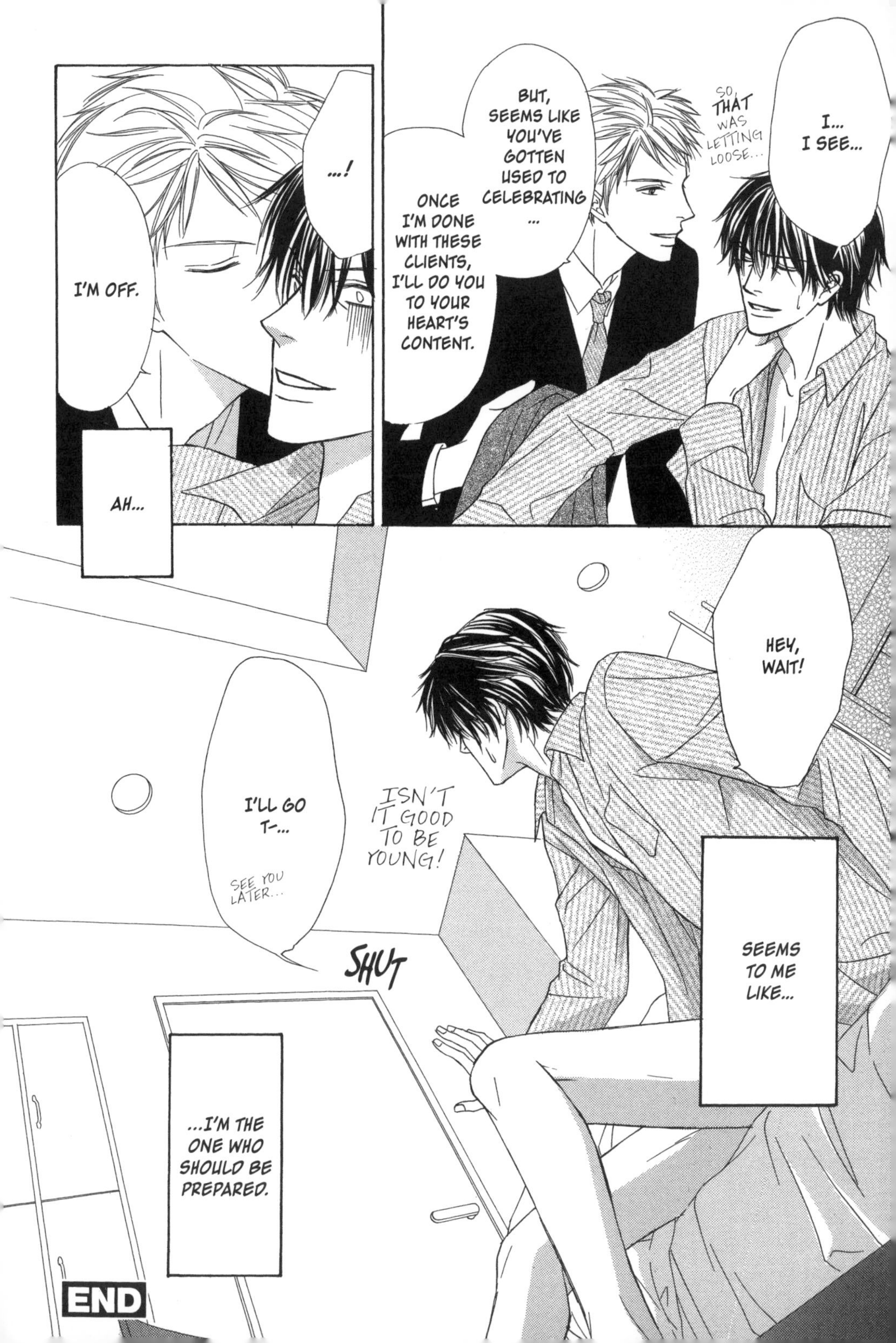
I... I SEE...
SO, THAT WAS LETTING LOOSE...
BUT, SEEMS LIKE YOU'VE GOTTEN USED TO CELEBRATING...
ONCE I'M DONE WITH THESE CLIENTS, I'LL DO YOU TO YOUR HEART'S CONTENT.
...!
I'M OFF.
AH...
HEY, WAIT!
SEEMS TO ME LIKE...
ISN'T IT GOOD TO BE YOUNG!
I'LL GO T-...
SEE YOU LATER...
SHUT
...I'M THE ONE WHO SHOULD BE PREPARED.
END

IN A BOX WITH YOU

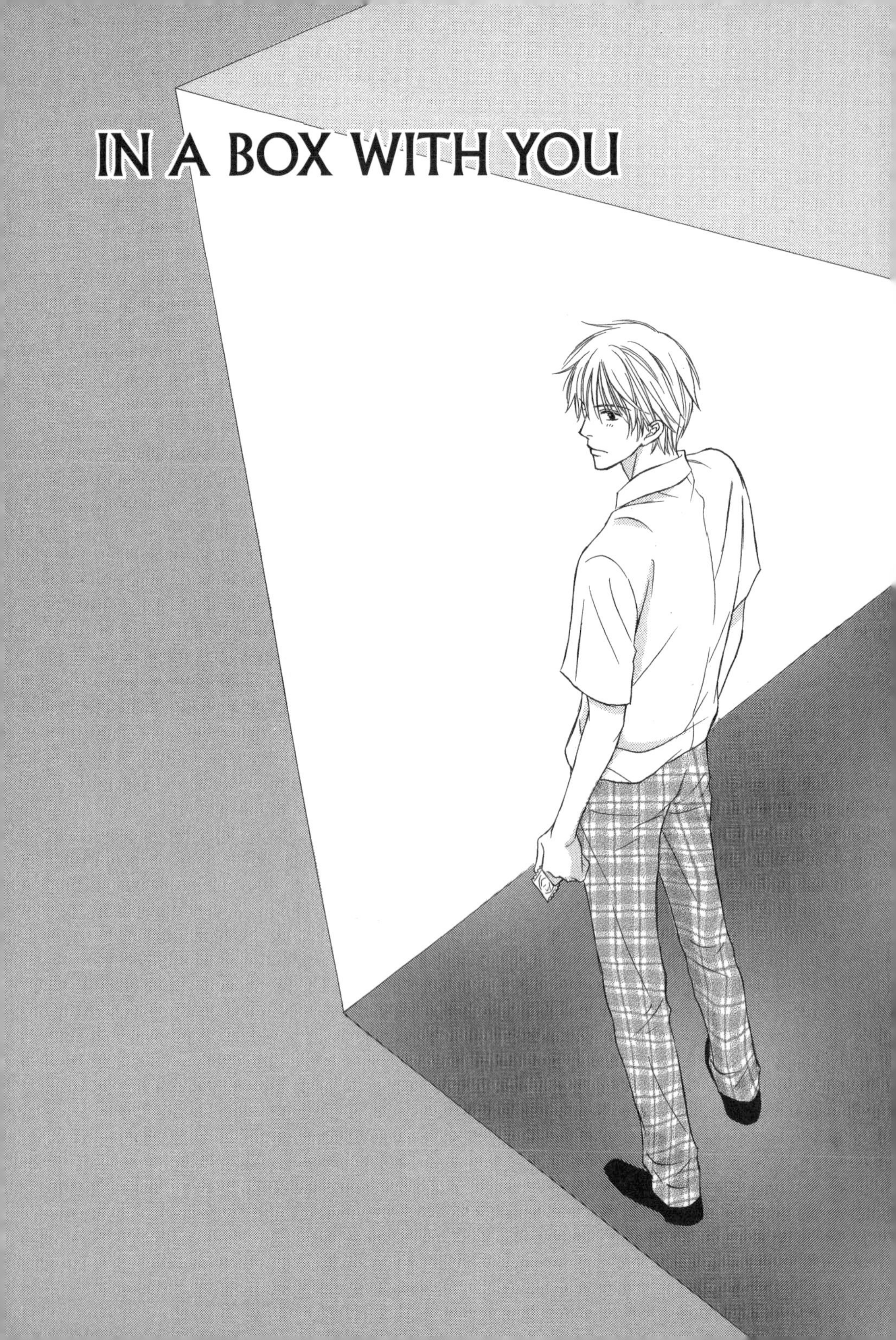

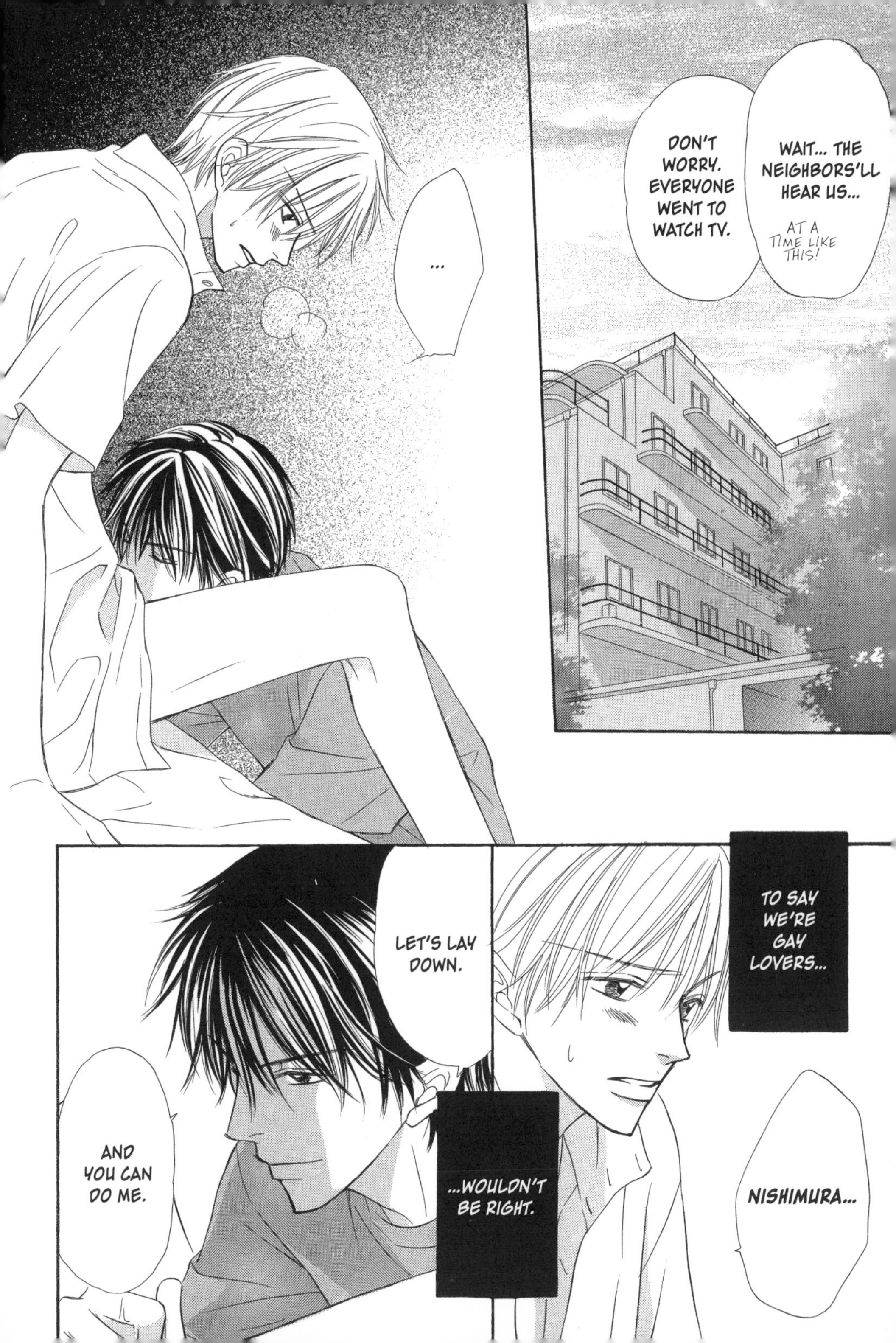
WAIT... THE NEIGHBORS'LL HEAR US...
AT A TIME LIKE THIS!
DON'T WORRY. EVERYONE WENT TO WATCH TV.
...
TO SAY WE'RE GAY LOVERS...
NISHIMURA...
LET'S LAY DOWN.
...WOULDN'T BE RIGHT.
AND YOU CAN DO ME.

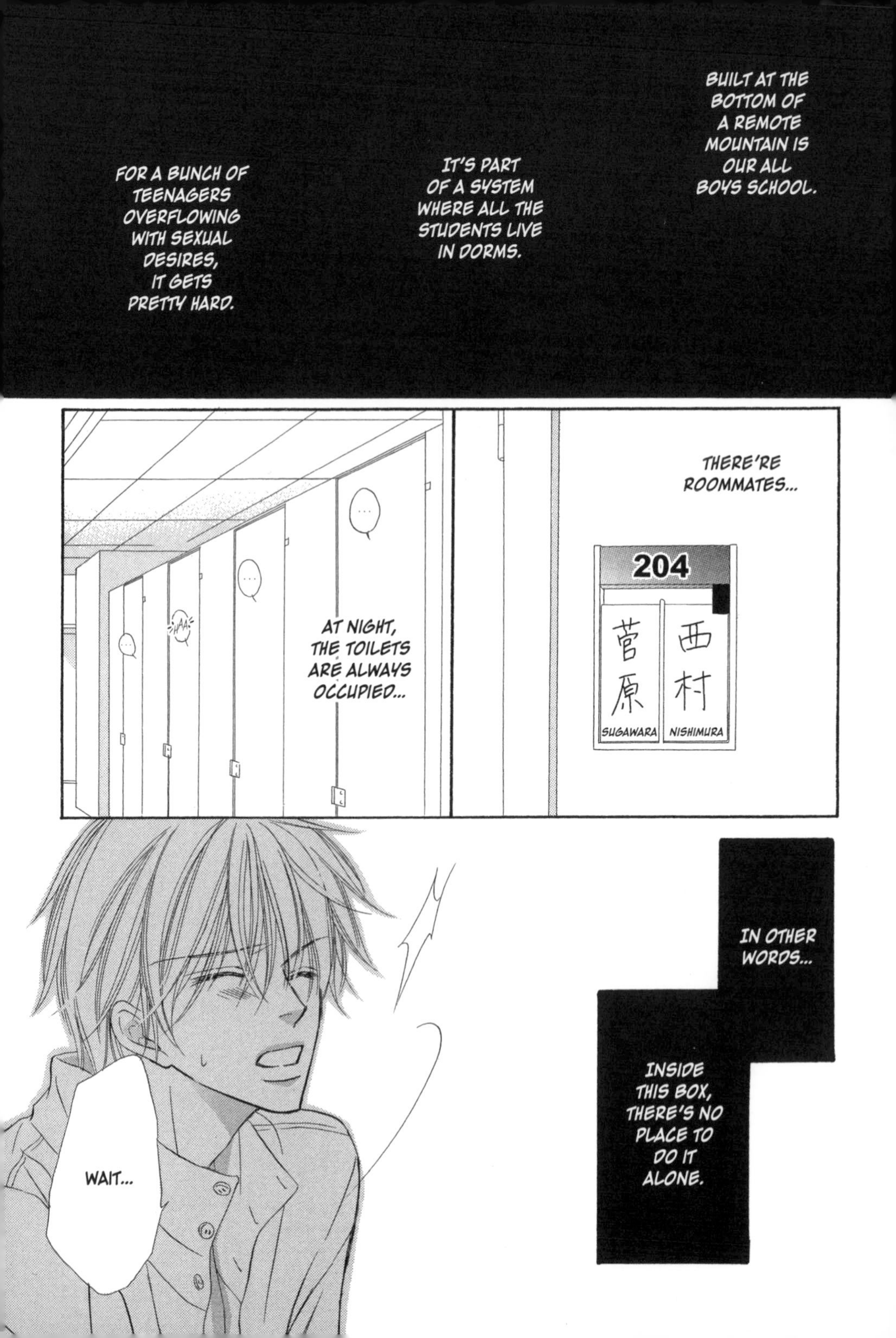
BUILT AT THE BOTTOM OF A REMOTE MOUNTAIN IS OUR ALL BOYS SCHOOL.
IT'S PART OF A SYSTEM WHERE ALL THE STUDENTS LIVE IN DORMS.
FOR A BUNCH OF TEENAGERS OVERFLOWING WITH SEXUAL DESIRES, IT GETS PRETTY HARD.
THERE'RE ROOMMATES...
204
菅原
SUGAWARA
西村
NISHIMURA
AT NIGHT, THE TOILETS ARE ALWAYS OCCUPIED...
HAA
IN OTHER WORDS...
INSIDE THIS BOX, THERE'S NO PLACE TO DO IT ALONE.
WAIT...

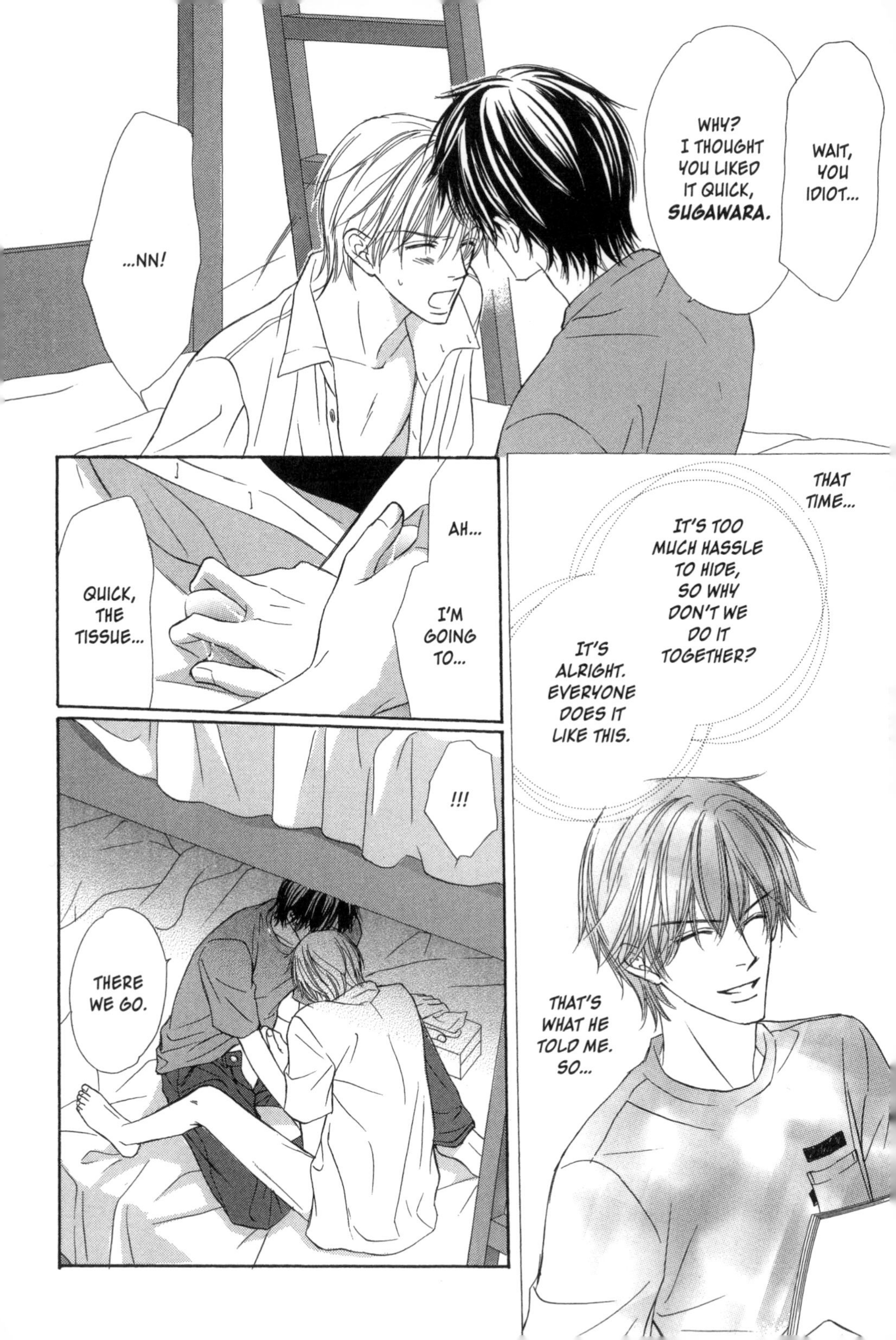
WAIT, YOU IDIOT...
WHY? I THOUGHT YOU LIKED IT QUICK, **SUGAWARA.**
...NN!
THAT TIME...
IT'S TOO MUCH HASSLE TO HIDE, SO WHY DON'T WE DO IT TOGETHER?
IT'S ALRIGHT. EVERYONE DOES IT LIKE THIS.
THAT'S WHAT HE TOLD ME. SO...
AH...
I'M GOING TO...
QUICK, THE TISSUE...
!!!
THERE WE GO.

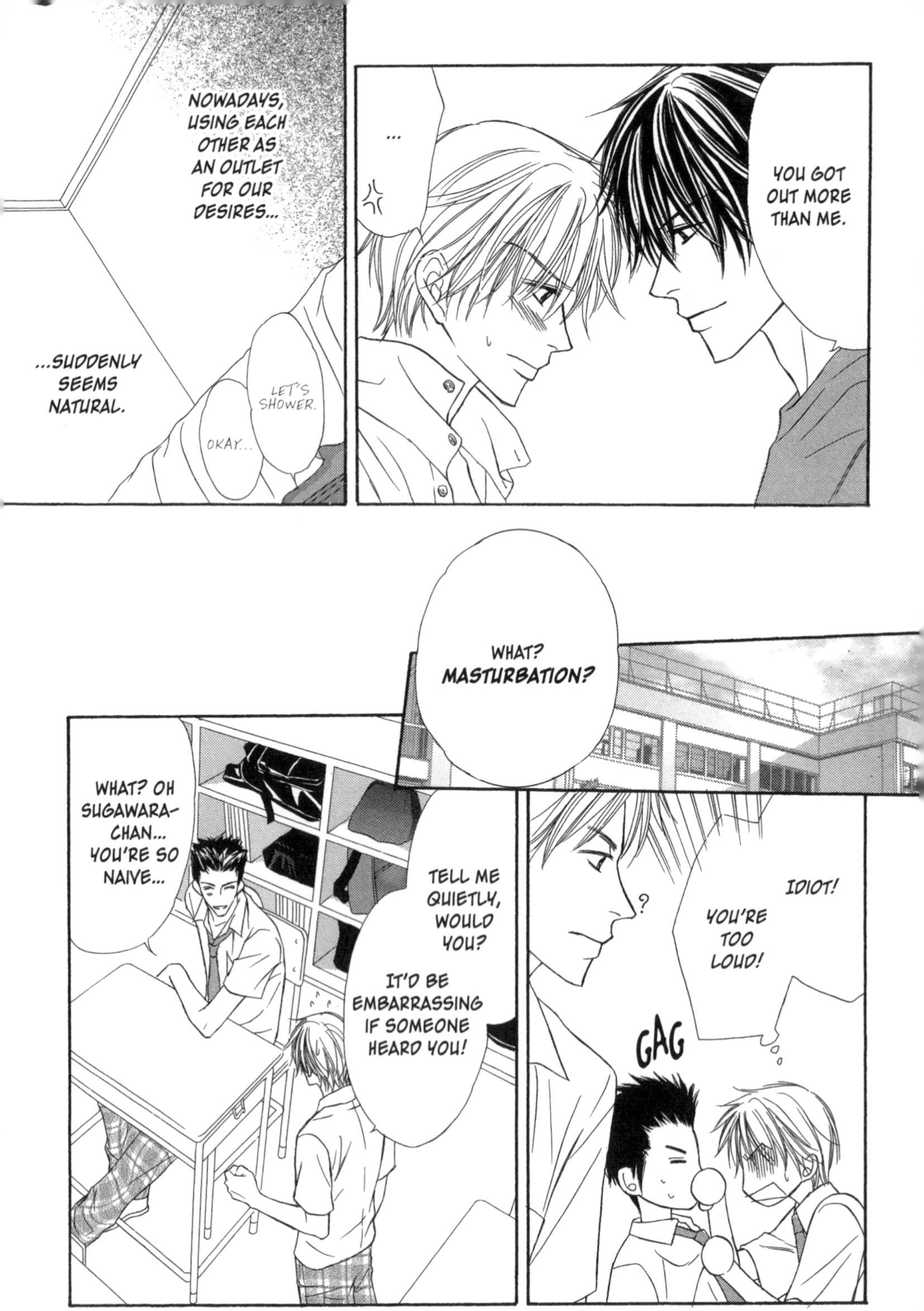
YOU GOT OUT MORE THAN ME.
...
NOWADAYS, USING EACH OTHER AS AN OUTLET FOR OUR DESIRES...
LET'S SHOWER.
OKAY...
...SUDDENLY SEEMS NATURAL.
WHAT? MASTURBATION?
IDIOT!
YOU'RE TOO LOUD!
GAG
TELL ME QUIETLY, WOULD YOU?
IT'D BE EMBARRASSING IF SOMEONE HEARD YOU!
WHAT? OH SUGAWARA-CHAN... YOU'RE SO NAIVE...

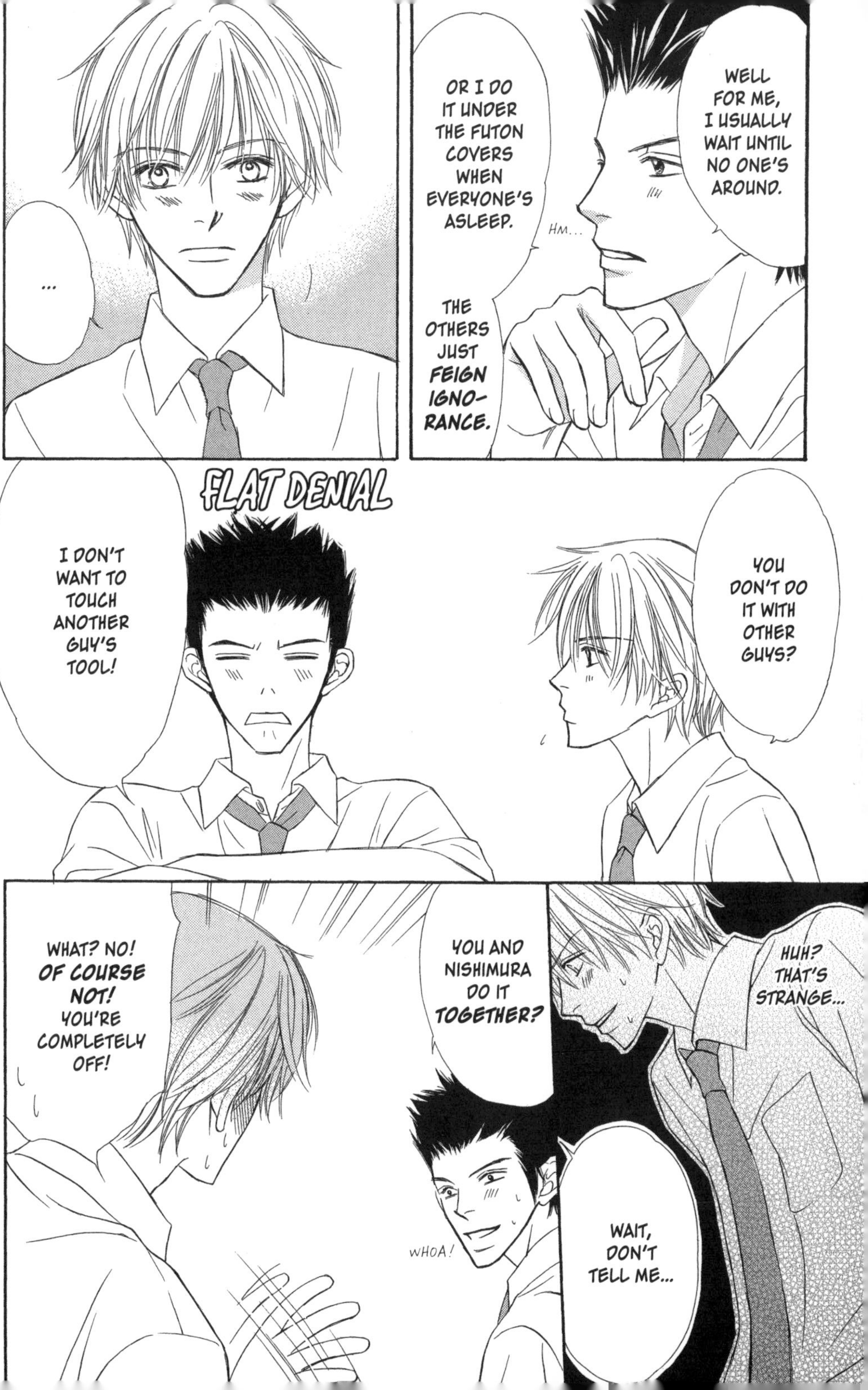
WELL FOR ME, I USUALLY WAIT UNTIL NO ONE'S AROUND.
HM...
OR I DO IT UNDER THE FUTON COVERS WHEN EVERYONE'S ASLEEP.
THE OTHERS JUST FEIGN IGNORANCE.
...
YOU DON'T DO IT WITH OTHER GUYS?
FLAT DENIAL
I DON'T WANT TO TOUCH ANOTHER GUY'S TOOL!
HUH? THAT'S STRANGE...
WAIT, DON'T TELL ME...
WHOA!
YOU AND NISHIMURA DO IT TOGETHER?
WHAT? NO! OF COURSE NOT! YOU'RE COMPLETELY OFF!

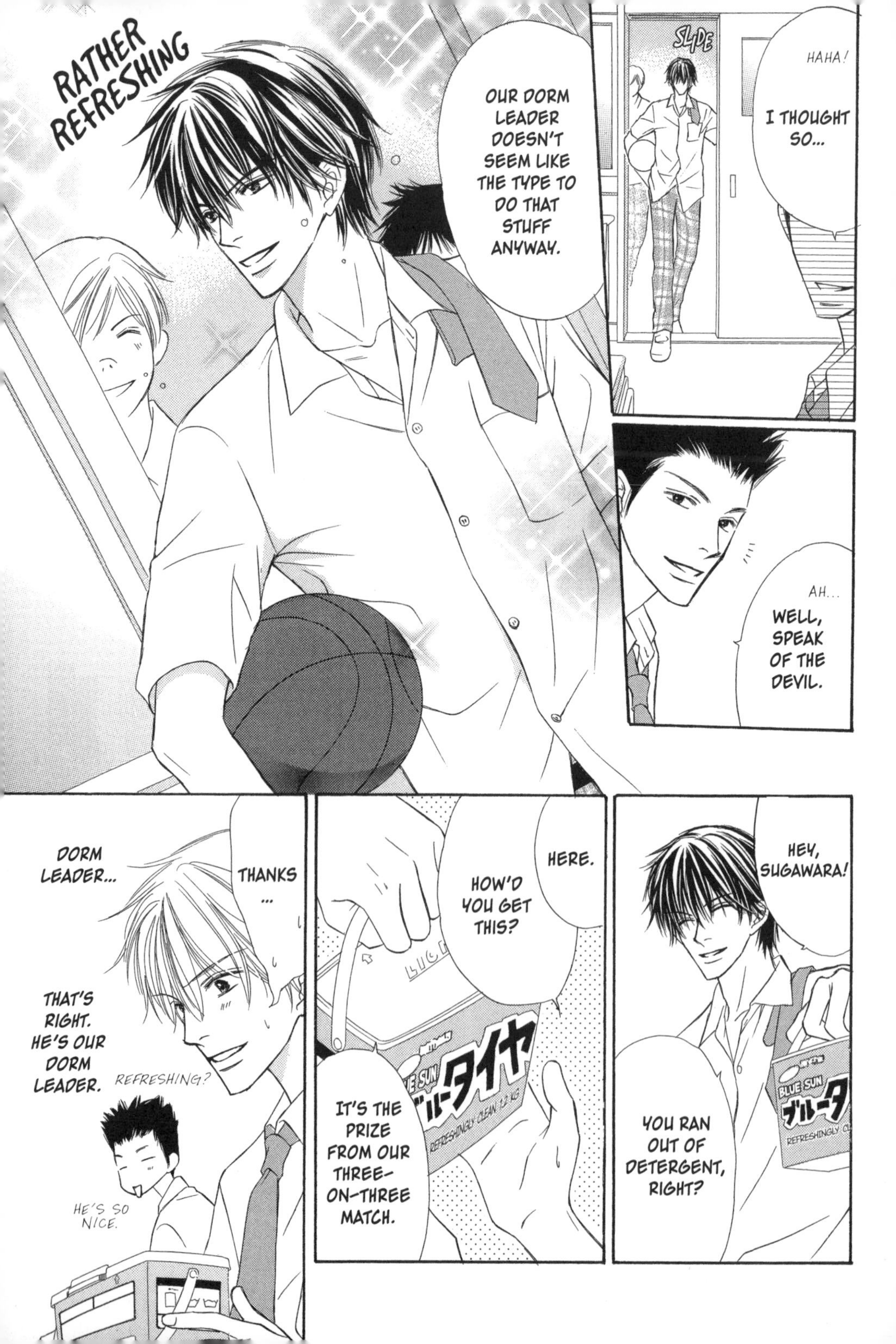
SLIDE
HAHA!
I THOUGHT SO...
AH...
WELL, SPEAK OF THE DEVIL.
OUR DORM LEADER DOESN'T SEEM LIKE THE TYPE TO DO THAT STUFF ANYWAY.
RATHER REFRESHING
HEY, SUGAWARA!
YOU RAN OUT OF DETERGENT, RIGHT?
HERE.
HOW'D YOU GET THIS?
BLUE SUN
ブルータイヤ
IT'S THE PRIZE FROM OUR THREE-ON-THREE MATCH.
THANKS ...
DORM LEADER...
THAT'S RIGHT. HE'S OUR DORM LEADER.
REFRESHING?
HE'S SO NICE.

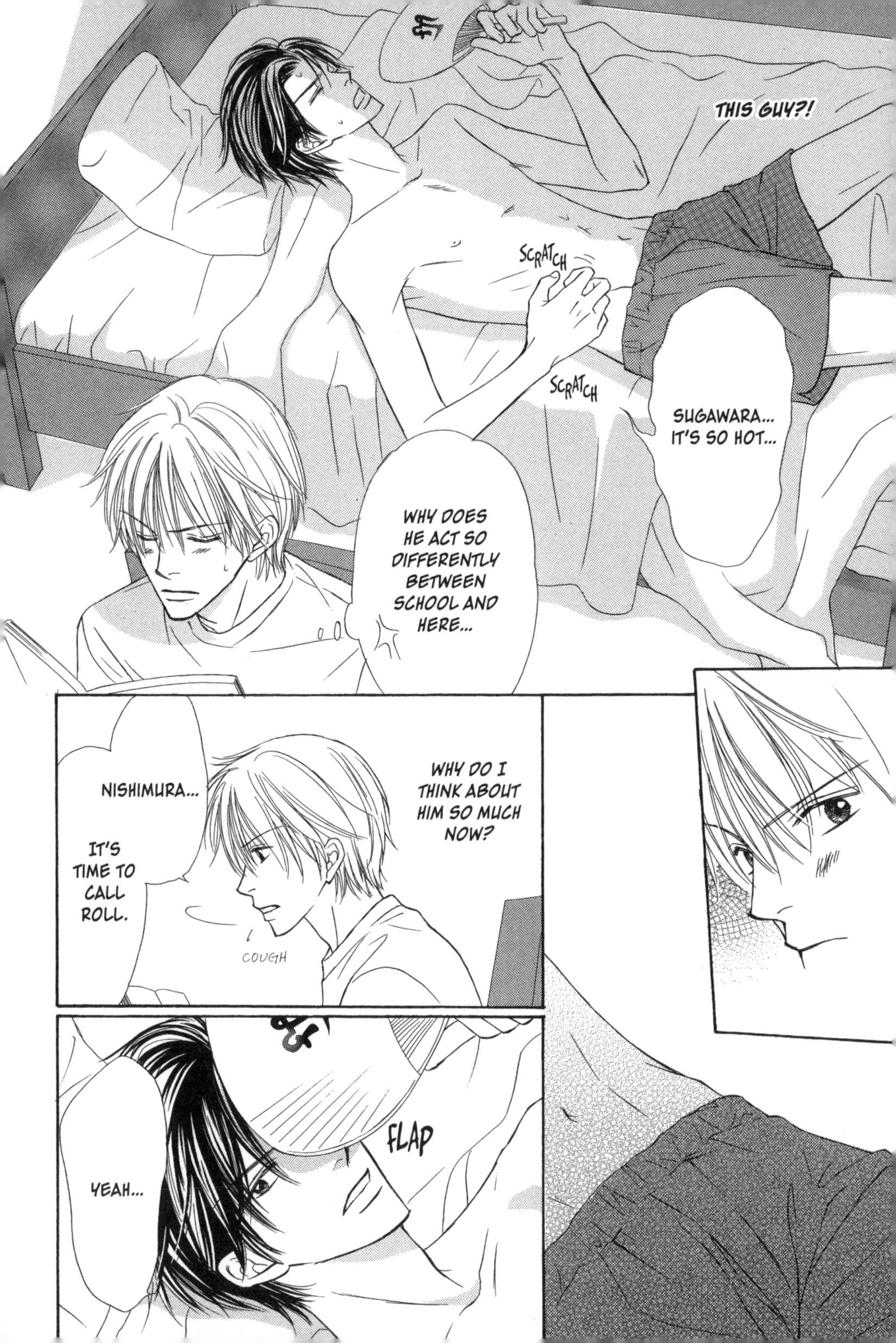
THIS GUY?!
SCRATCH
SUGAWARA... IT'S SO HOT...
SCRATCH
WHY DOES HE ACT SO DIFFERENTLY BETWEEN SCHOOL AND HERE...
WHY DO I THINK ABOUT HIM SO MUCH NOW?
NISHIMURA... IT'S TIME TO CALL ROLL.
COUGH
FLAP
YEAH...

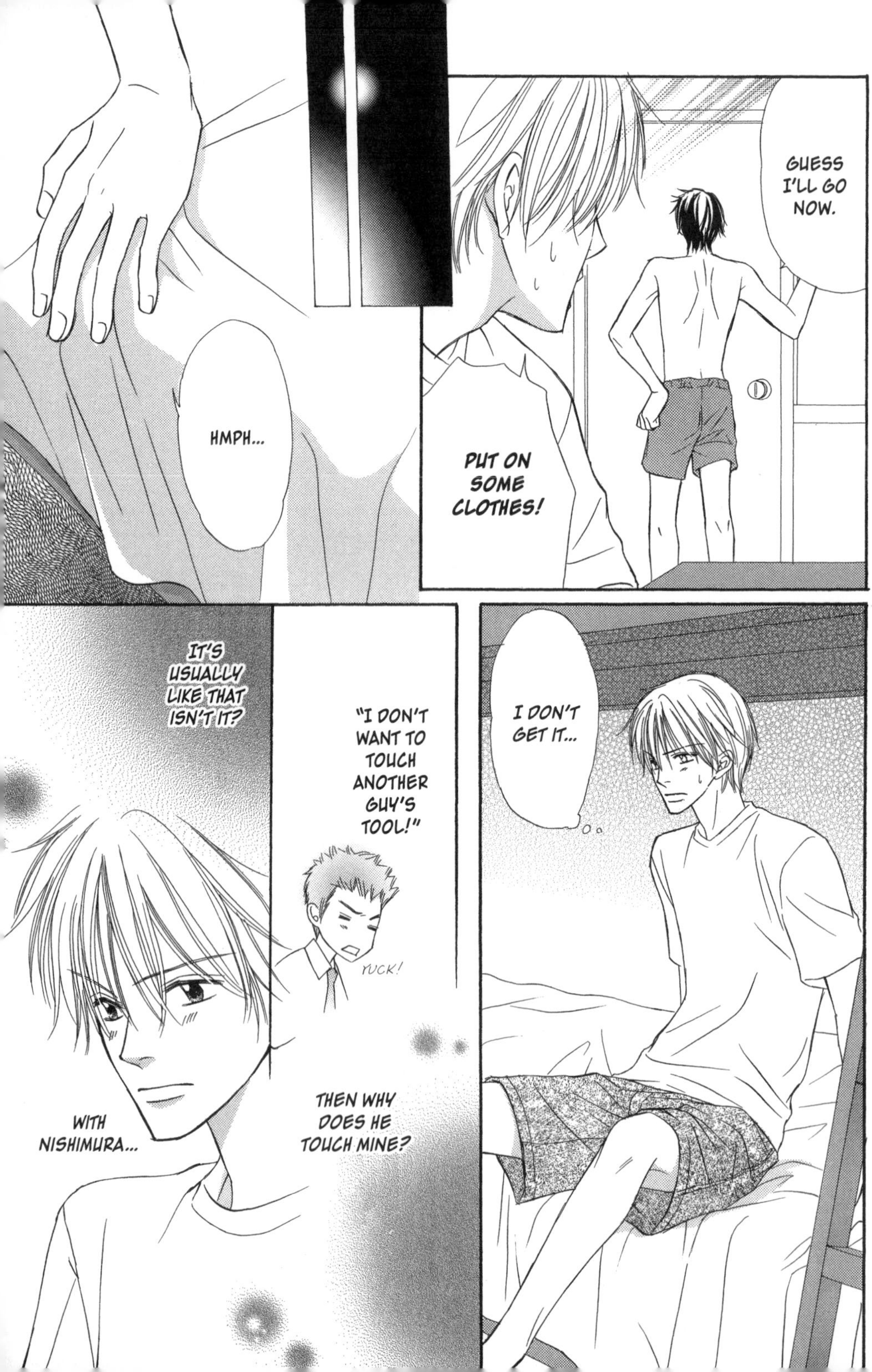
GUESS I'LL GO NOW.
PUT ON SOME CLOTHES!
HMPH...
I DON'T GET IT...
"I DON'T WANT TO TOUCH ANOTHER GUY'S TOOL!"
YUCK!
IT'S USUALLY LIKE THAT ISN'T IT?
WITH NISHIMURA...
THEN WHY DOES HE TOUCH MINE?

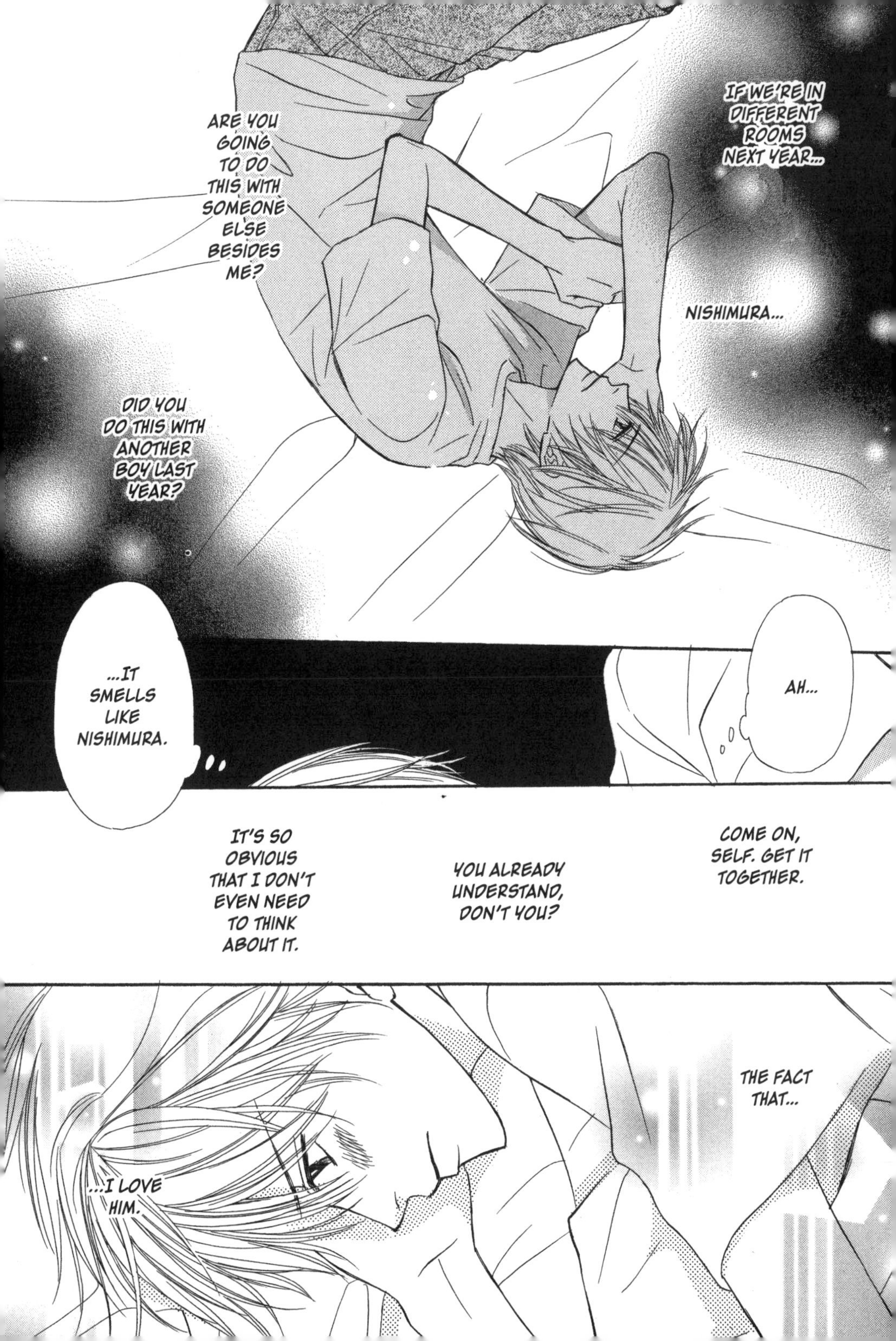
IF WE'RE IN DIFFERENT ROOMS NEXT YEAR...
NISHIMURA...
ARE YOU GOING TO DO THIS WITH SOMEONE ELSE BESIDES ME?
DID YOU DO THIS WITH ANOTHER BOY LAST YEAR?
AH...
...IT SMELLS LIKE NISHIMURA.
COME ON, SELF. GET IT TOGETHER.
YOU ALREADY UNDERSTAND, DON'T YOU?
IT'S SO OBVIOUS THAT I DON'T EVEN NEED TO THINK ABOUT IT.
THE FACT THAT...
...I LOVE HIM.

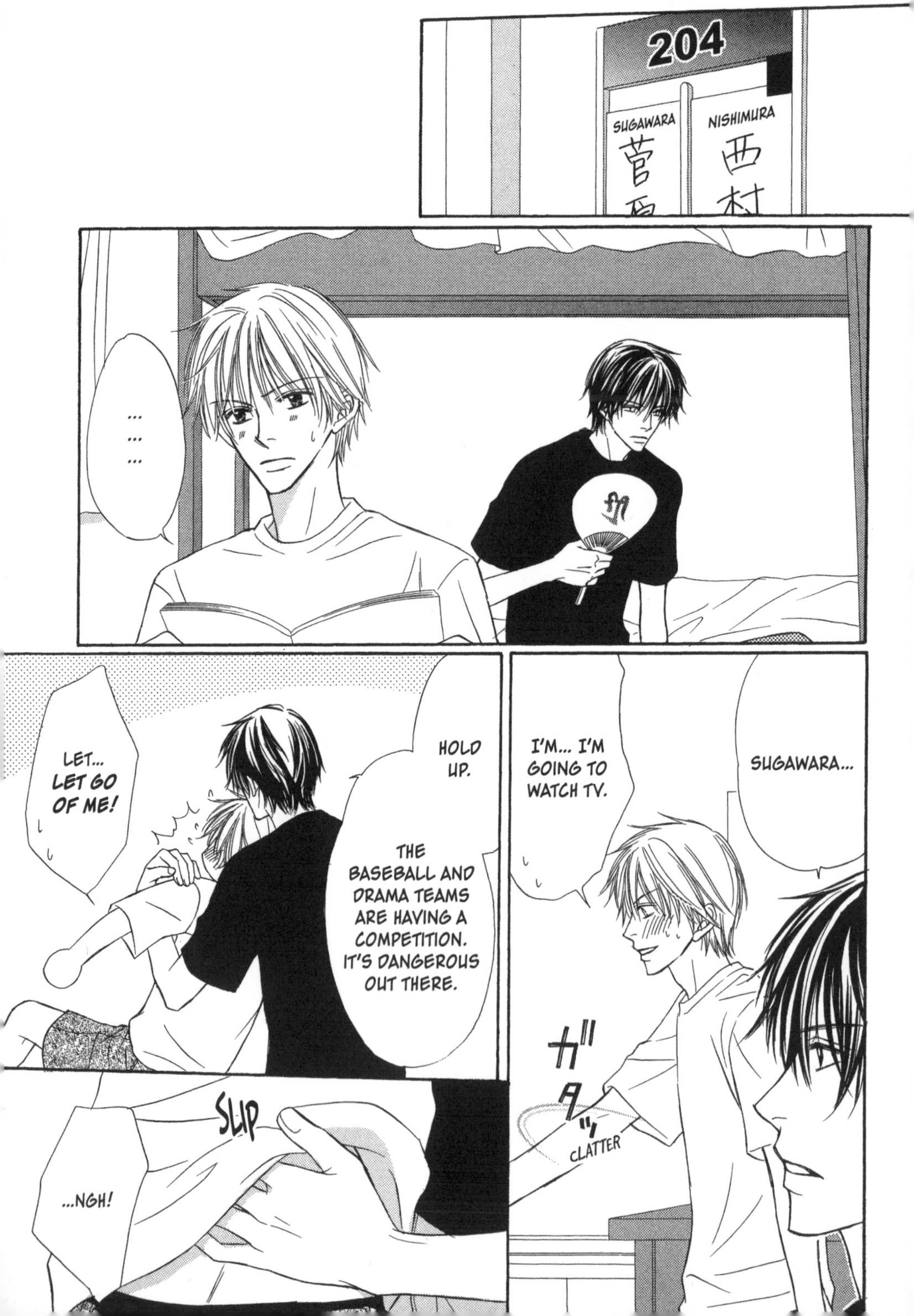
204
SUGAWARA
菅
NISHIMURA
西村
...
...
...
SUGAWARA...
I'M... I'M GOING TO WATCH TV.
ガタッ
CLATTER
HOLD UP.
THE BASEBALL AND DRAMA TEAMS ARE HAVING A COMPETITION. IT'S DANGEROUS OUT THERE.
LET... LET GO OF ME!
SLIP
...NGH!

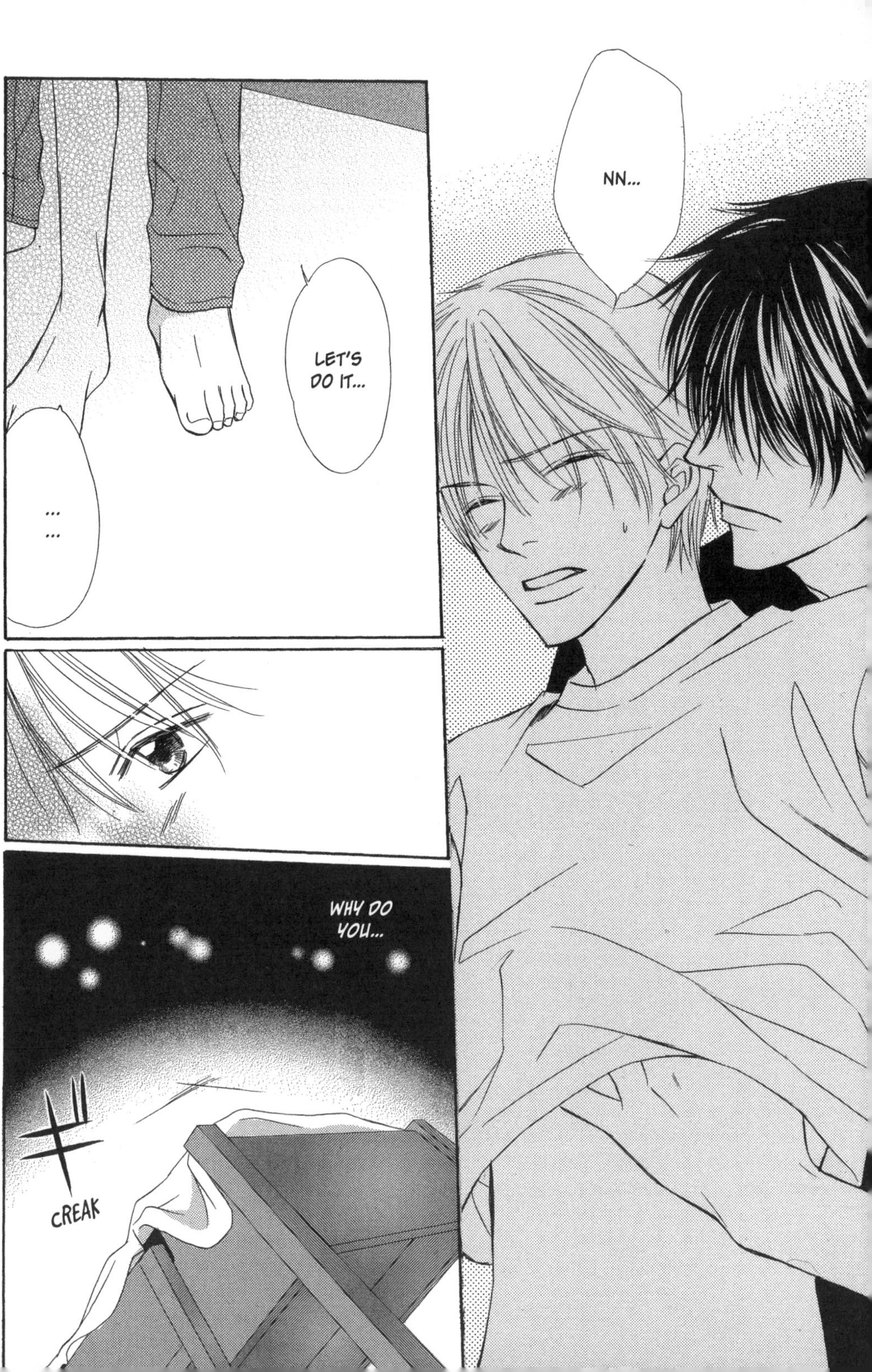
NN...
LET'S DO IT...
...
...
WHY DO YOU...
CREAK

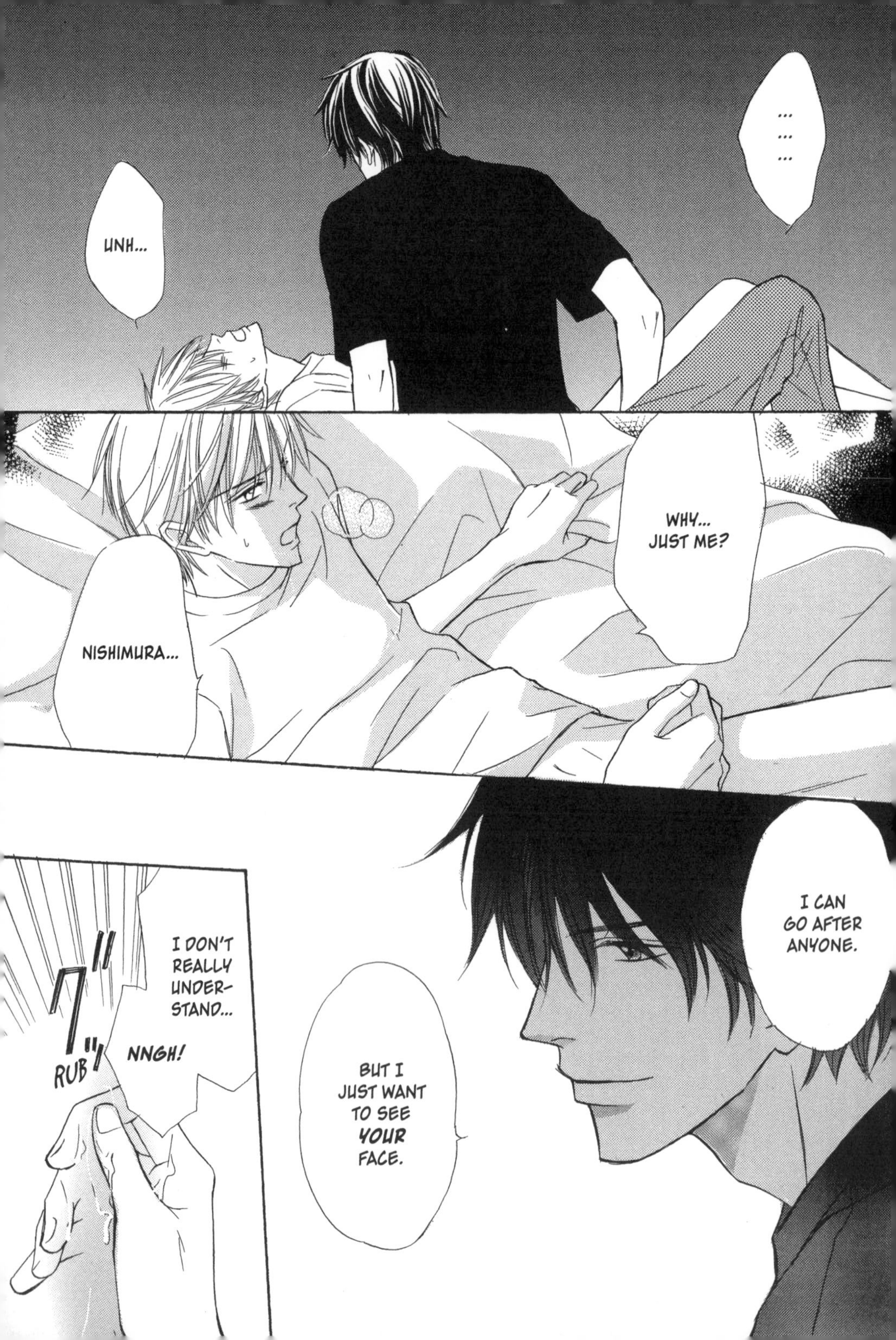
... ...
UNH...
WHY... JUST ME?
NISHIMURA...
I CAN GO AFTER ANYONE.
BUT I JUST WANT TO SEE *YOUR* FACE.
I DON'T REALLY UNDER-STAND...
NNGH!
RUB

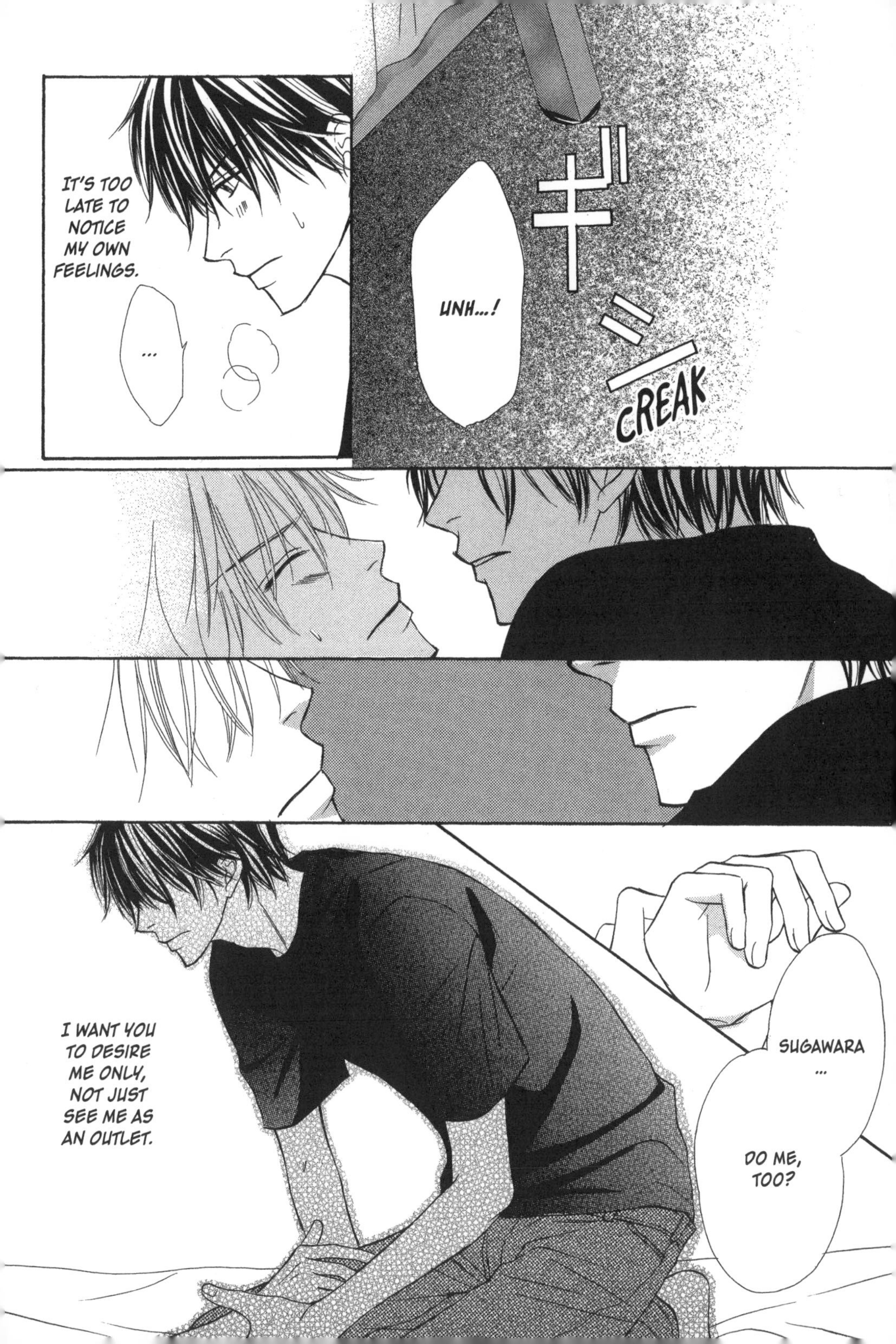
UNH...!
ギシ
CREAK
IT'S TOO LATE TO NOTICE MY OWN FEELINGS.
...
SUGAWARA ...
DO ME, TOO?
I WANT YOU TO DESIRE ME ONLY, NOT JUST SEE ME AS AN OUTLET.

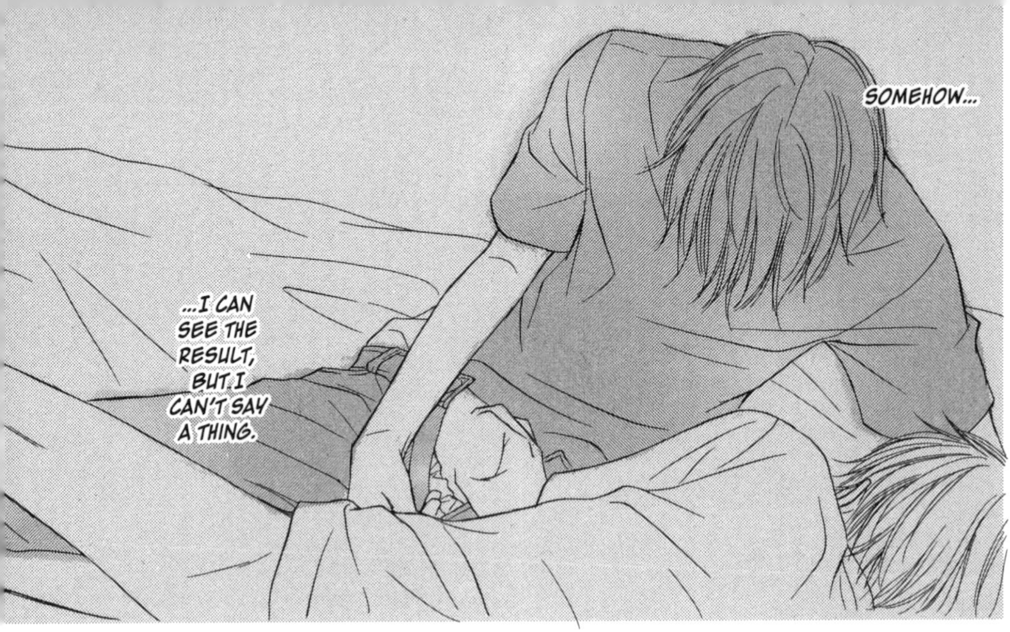
SOMEHOW...
...I CAN SEE THE RESULT, BUT I CAN'T SAY A THING.

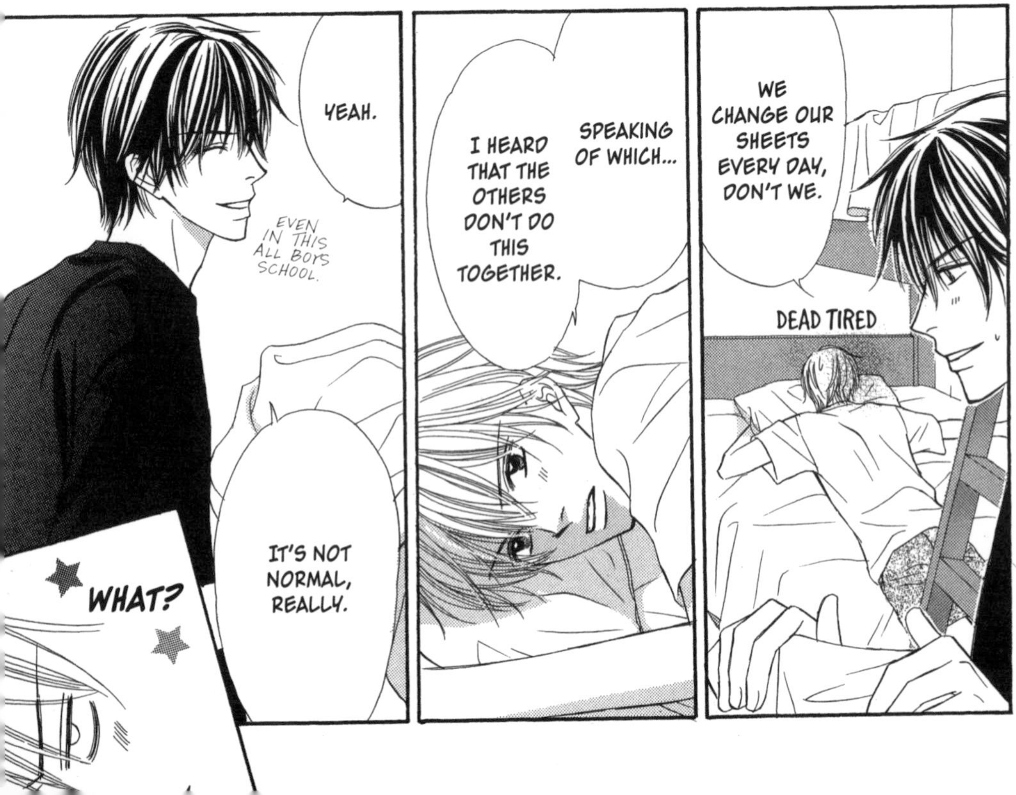
WE CHANGE OUR SHEETS EVERY DAY, DON'T WE.
DEAD TIRED
SPEAKING OF WHICH...
I HEARD THAT THE OTHERS DON'T DO THIS TOGETHER.
YEAH.
EVEN IN THIS ALL BOYS SCHOOL.
IT'S NOT NORMAL, REALLY.
WHAT?

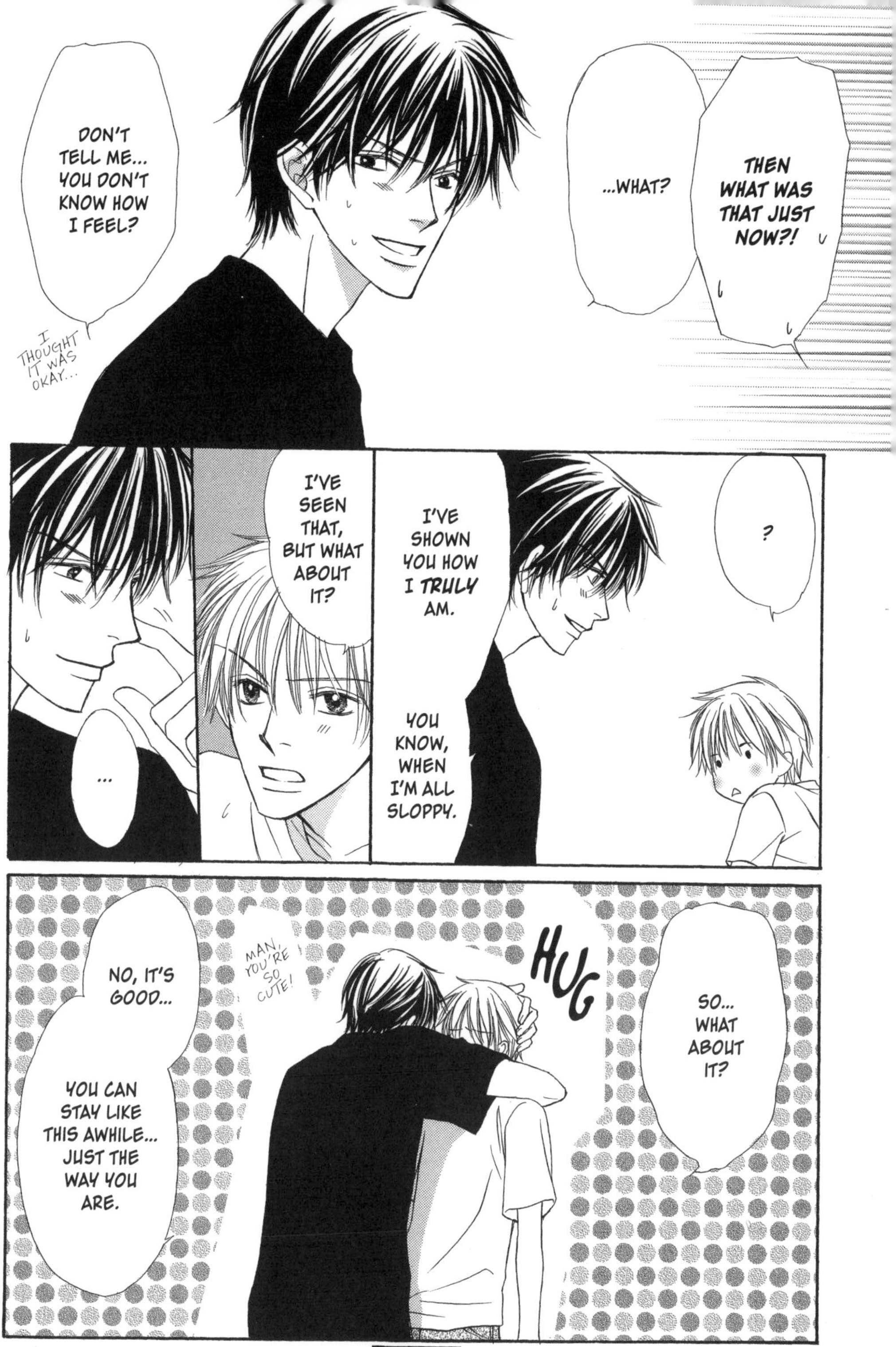
THEN WHAT WAS THAT JUST NOW?!
...WHAT?
DON'T TELL ME... YOU DON'T KNOW HOW I FEEL?
I THOUGHT IT WAS OKAY...
?
I'VE SHOWN YOU HOW I TRULY AM.
YOU KNOW, WHEN I'M ALL SLOPPY.
I'VE SEEN THAT, BUT WHAT ABOUT IT?
...
SO... WHAT ABOUT IT?
HUG
MAN, YOU'RE SO CUTE!
NO, IT'S GOOD...
YOU CAN STAY LIKE THIS AWHILE... JUST THE WAY YOU ARE.

END

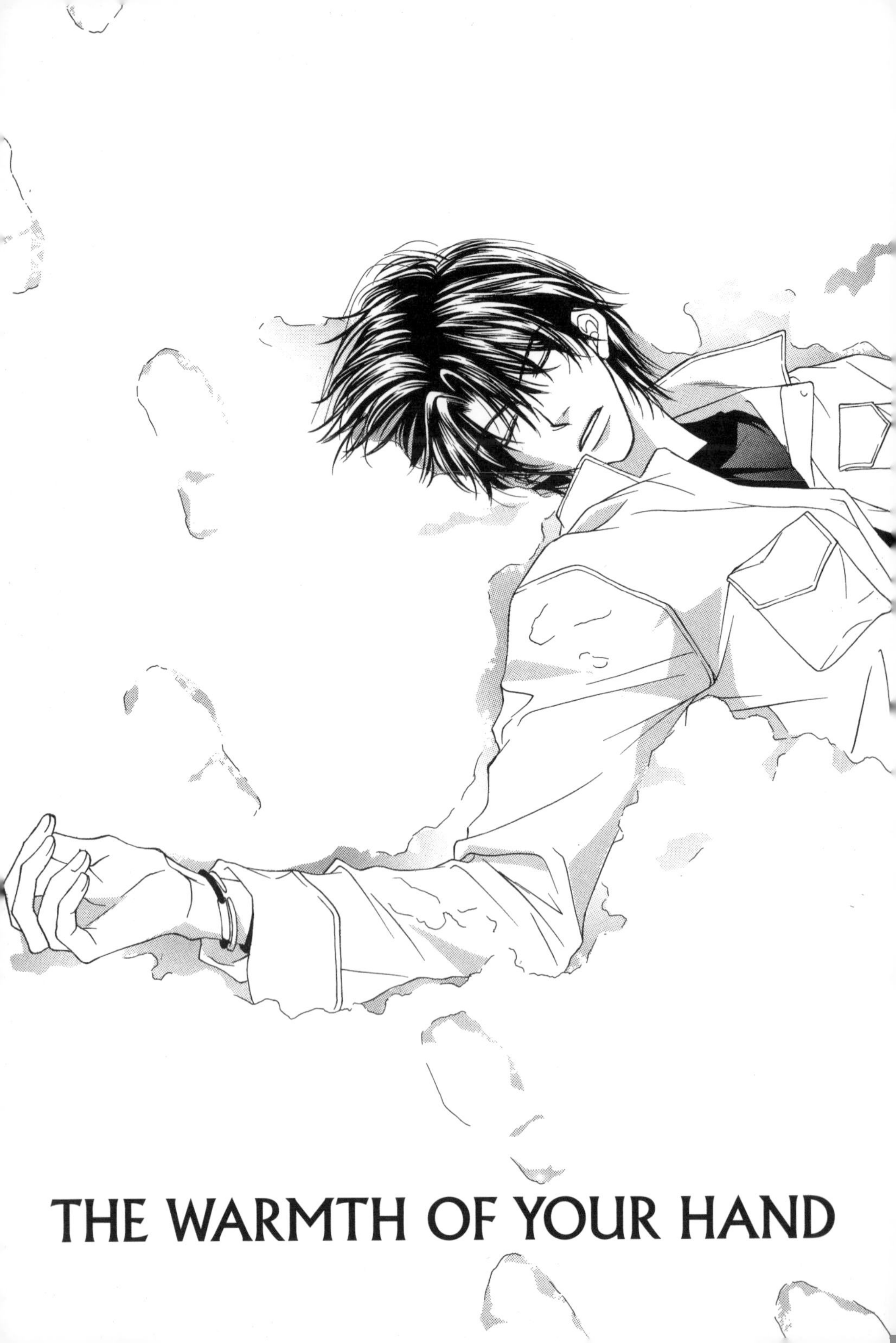

THE WARMTH OF YOUR HAND

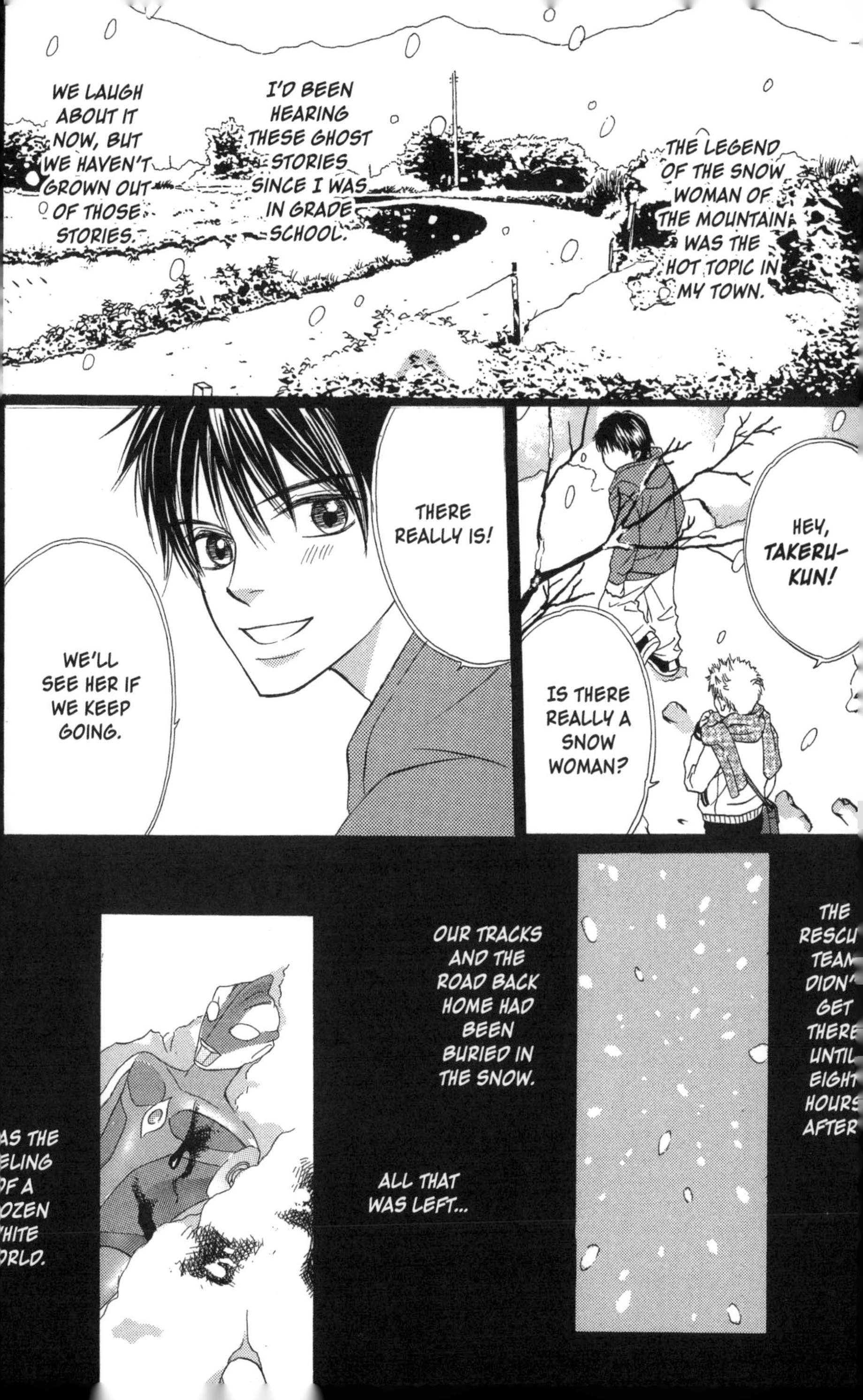
THE LEGEND OF THE SNOW WOMAN OF THE MOUNTAIN WAS THE HOT TOPIC IN MY TOWN.
I'D BEEN HEARING THESE GHOST STORIES SINCE I WAS IN GRADE SCHOOL.
WE LAUGH ABOUT IT NOW, BUT WE HAVEN'T GROWN OUT OF THOSE STORIES.
HEY, TAKERU-KUN!
IS THERE REALLY A SNOW WOMAN?
THERE REALLY IS!
WE'LL SEE HER IF WE KEEP GOING.
THE RESCU TEAM DIDN' GET THERE UNTIL EIGHT HOURS AFTER
OUR TRACKS AND THE ROAD BACK HOME HAD BEEN BURIED IN THE SNOW.
ALL THAT WAS LEFT...
AS THE ELING OF A OZEN HITE ORLD.

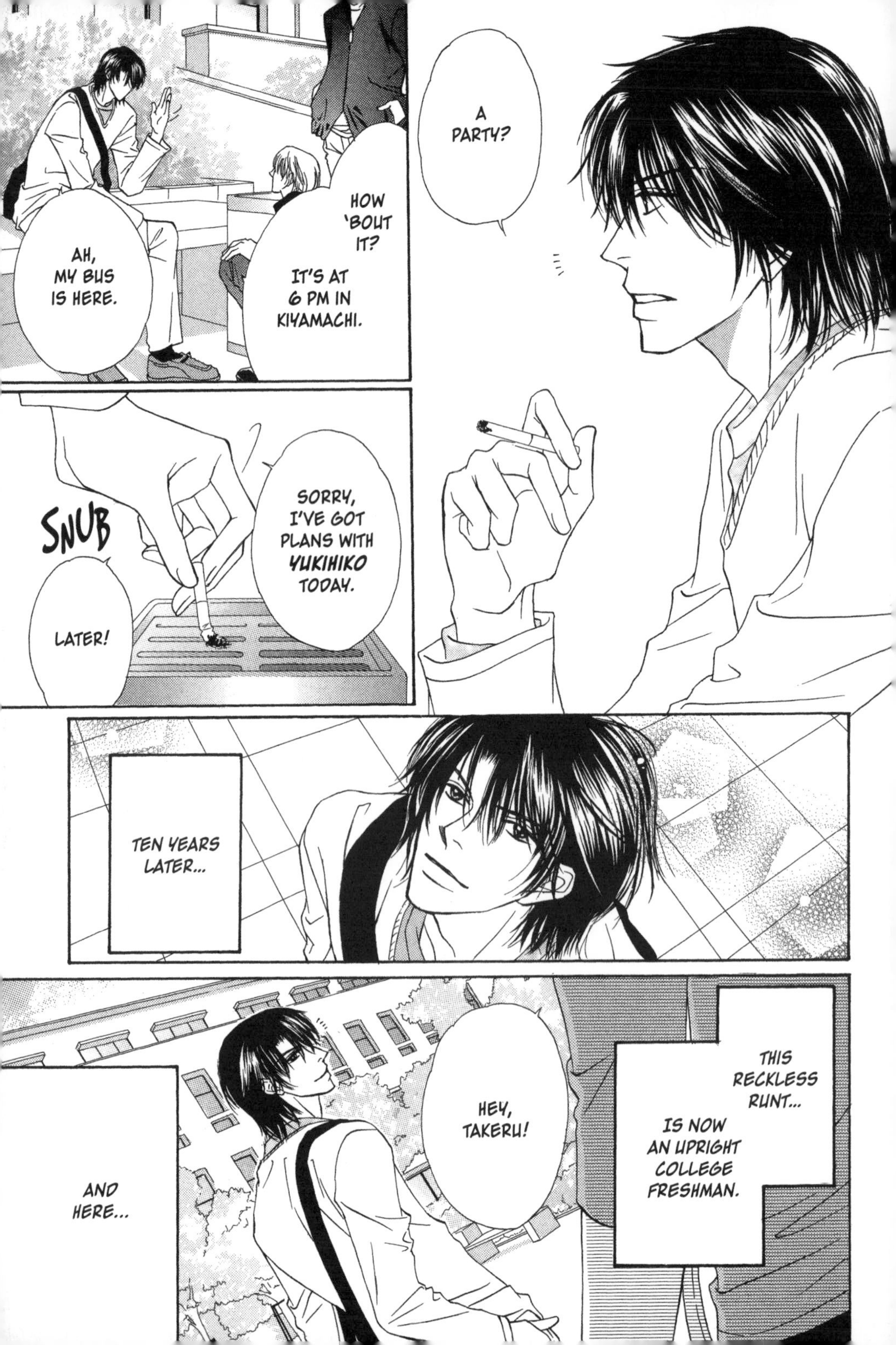
A PARTY?
HOW 'BOUT IT?
IT'S AT 6 PM IN KIYAMACHI.
AH, MY BUS IS HERE.
SORRY, I'VE GOT PLANS WITH YUKIHIKO TODAY.
SNUB
LATER!
TEN YEARS LATER...
THIS RECKLESS RUNT...
IS NOW AN UPRIGHT COLLEGE FRESHMAN.
HEY, TAKERU!
AND HERE...

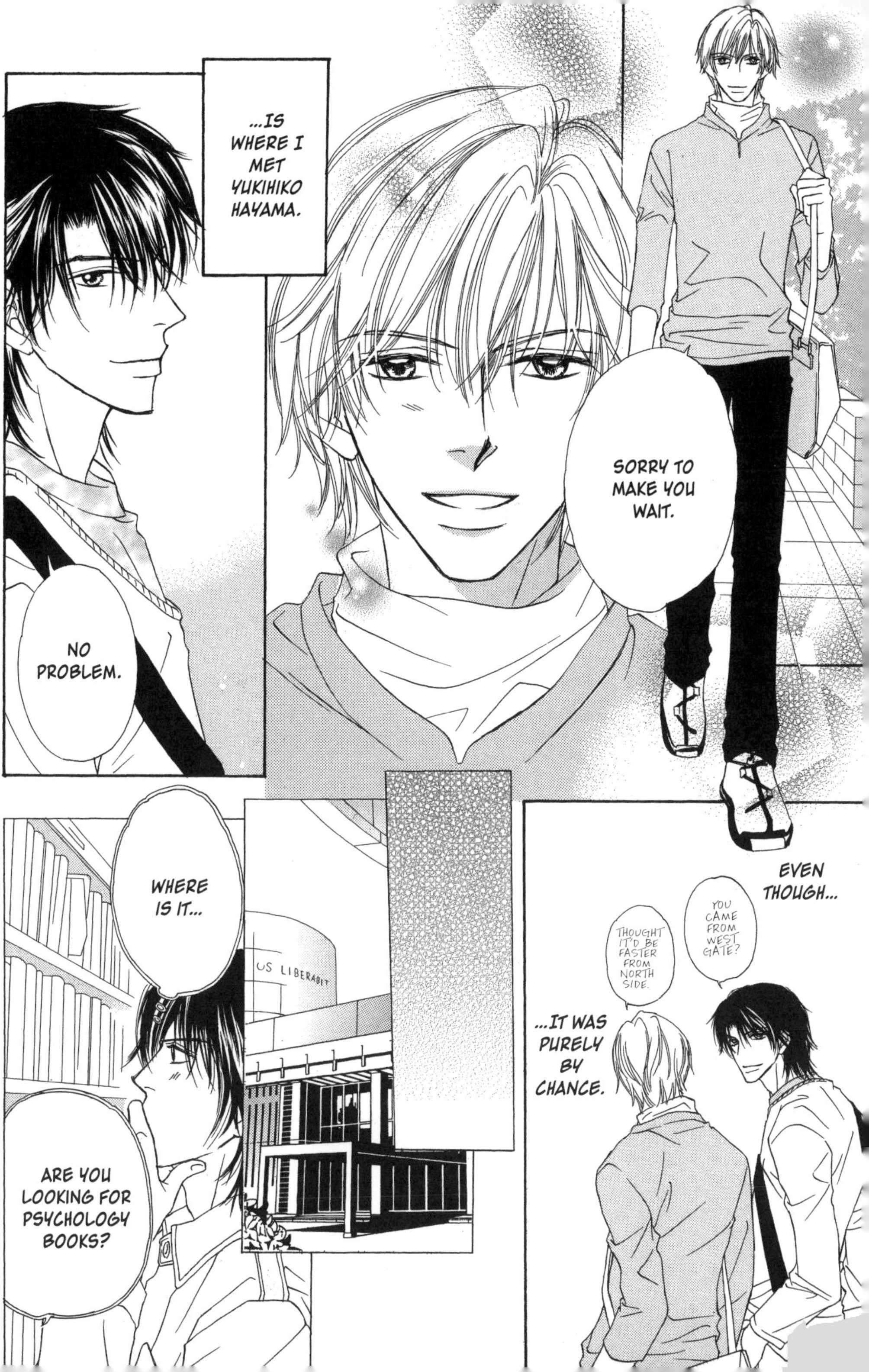
SORRY TO MAKE YOU WAIT.
...IS WHERE I MET YUKIHIKO HAYAMA.
NO PROBLEM.
EVEN THOUGH...
YOU CAME FROM WEST GATE?
THOUGHT IT'D BE FASTER FROM NORTH SIDE.
...IT WAS PURELY BY CHANCE.
US LIBERABIT
WHERE IS IT...
ARE YOU LOOKING FOR PSYCHOLOGY BOOKS?

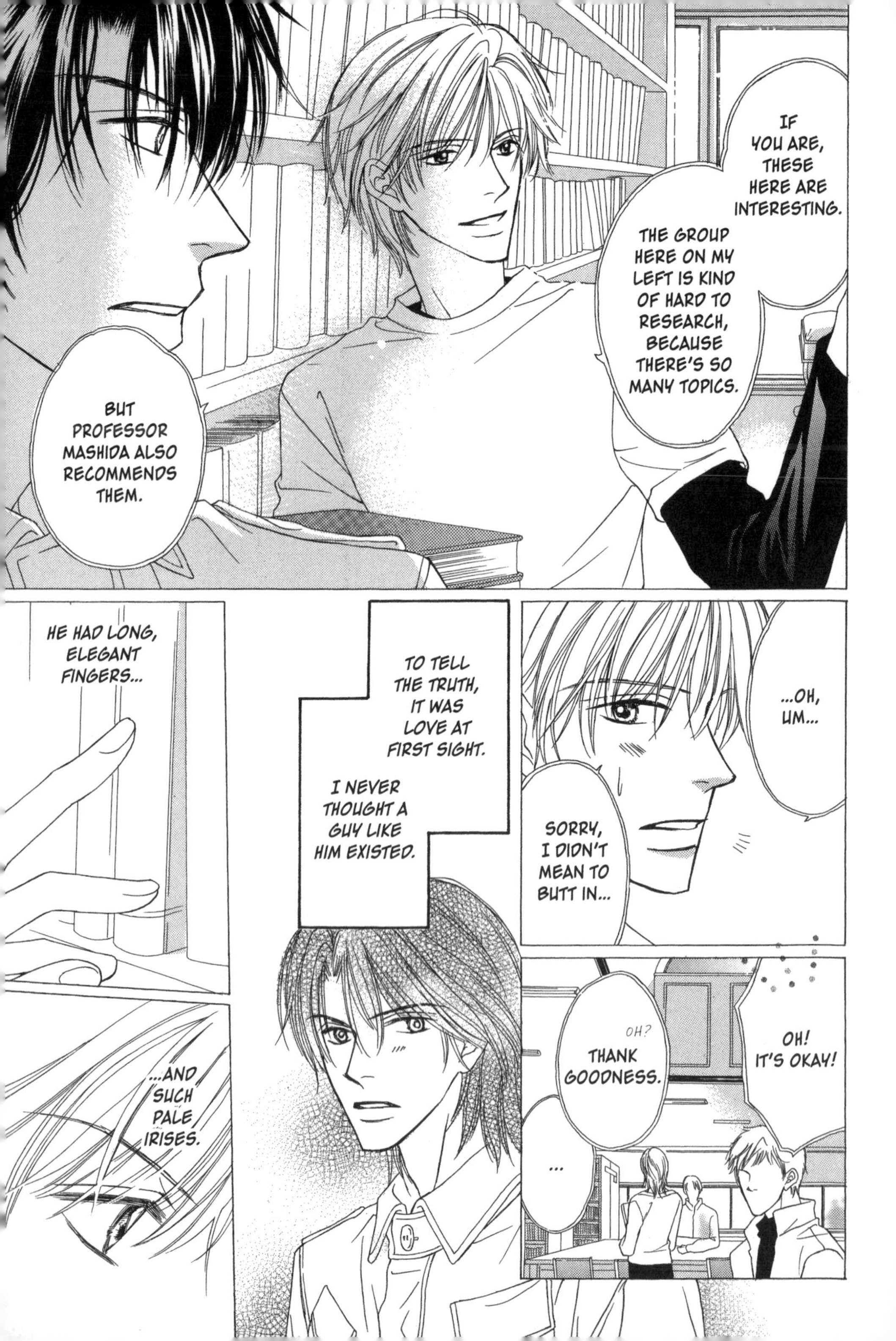
IF YOU ARE, THESE HERE ARE INTERESTING.
THE GROUP HERE ON MY LEFT IS KIND OF HARD TO RESEARCH, BECAUSE THERE'S SO MANY TOPICS.
BUT PROFESSOR MASHIDA ALSO RECOMMENDS THEM.
...OH, UM...
SORRY, I DIDN'T MEAN TO BUTT IN...
OH! IT'S OKAY!
OH? THANK GOODNESS.
...
TO TELL THE TRUTH, IT WAS LOVE AT FIRST SIGHT.
I NEVER THOUGHT A GUY LIKE HIM EXISTED.
HE HAD LONG, ELEGANT FINGERS...
...AND SUCH PALE IRISES.

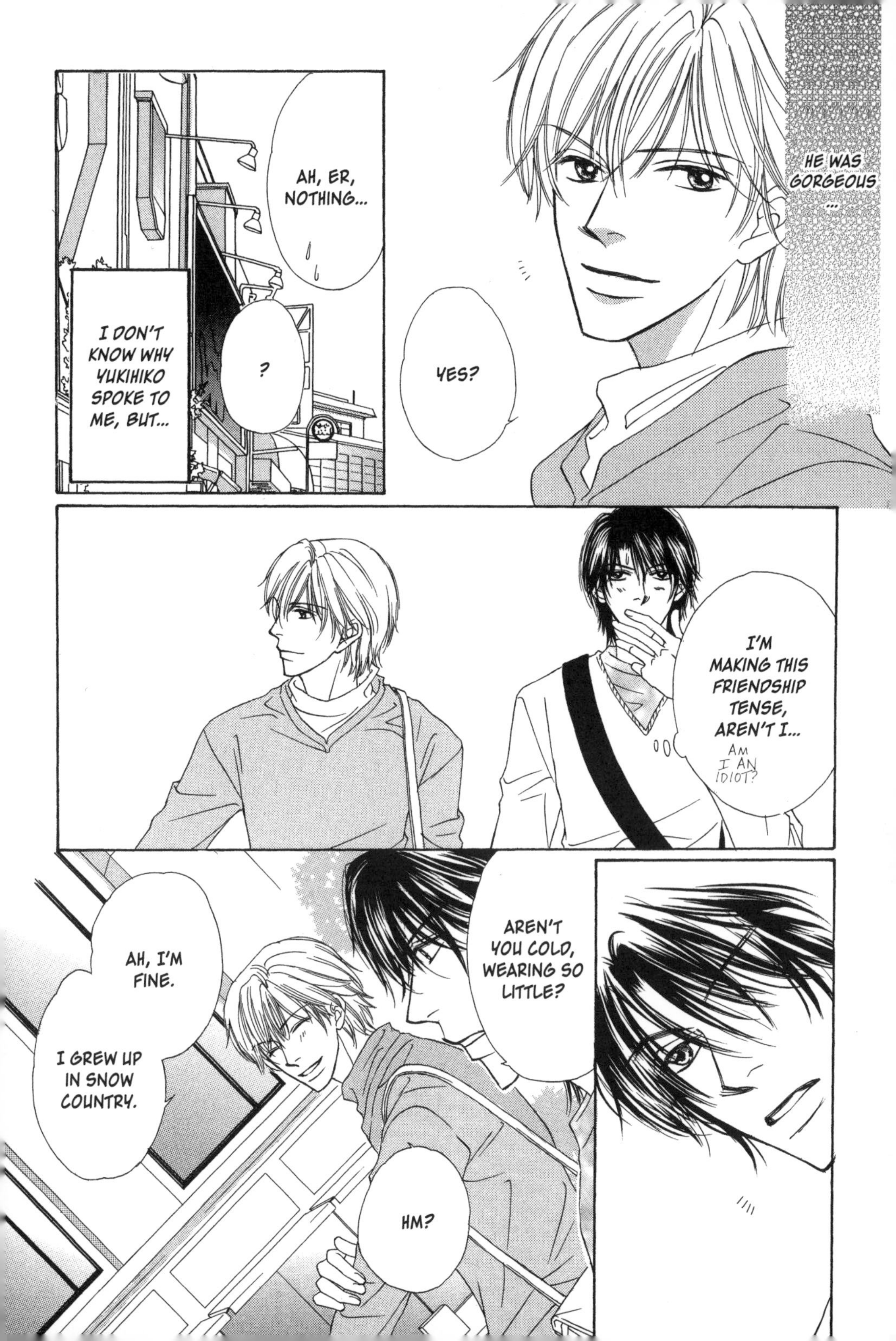
HE WAS GORGEOUS ...
YES?
AH, ER, NOTHING...
?
I DON'T KNOW WHY YUKIHIKO SPOKE TO ME, BUT...
I'M MAKING THIS FRIENDSHIP TENSE, AREN'T I...
AM I AN IDIOT?
AREN'T YOU COLD, WEARING SO LITTLE?
AH, I'M FINE.
I GREW UP IN SNOW COUNTRY.
HM?

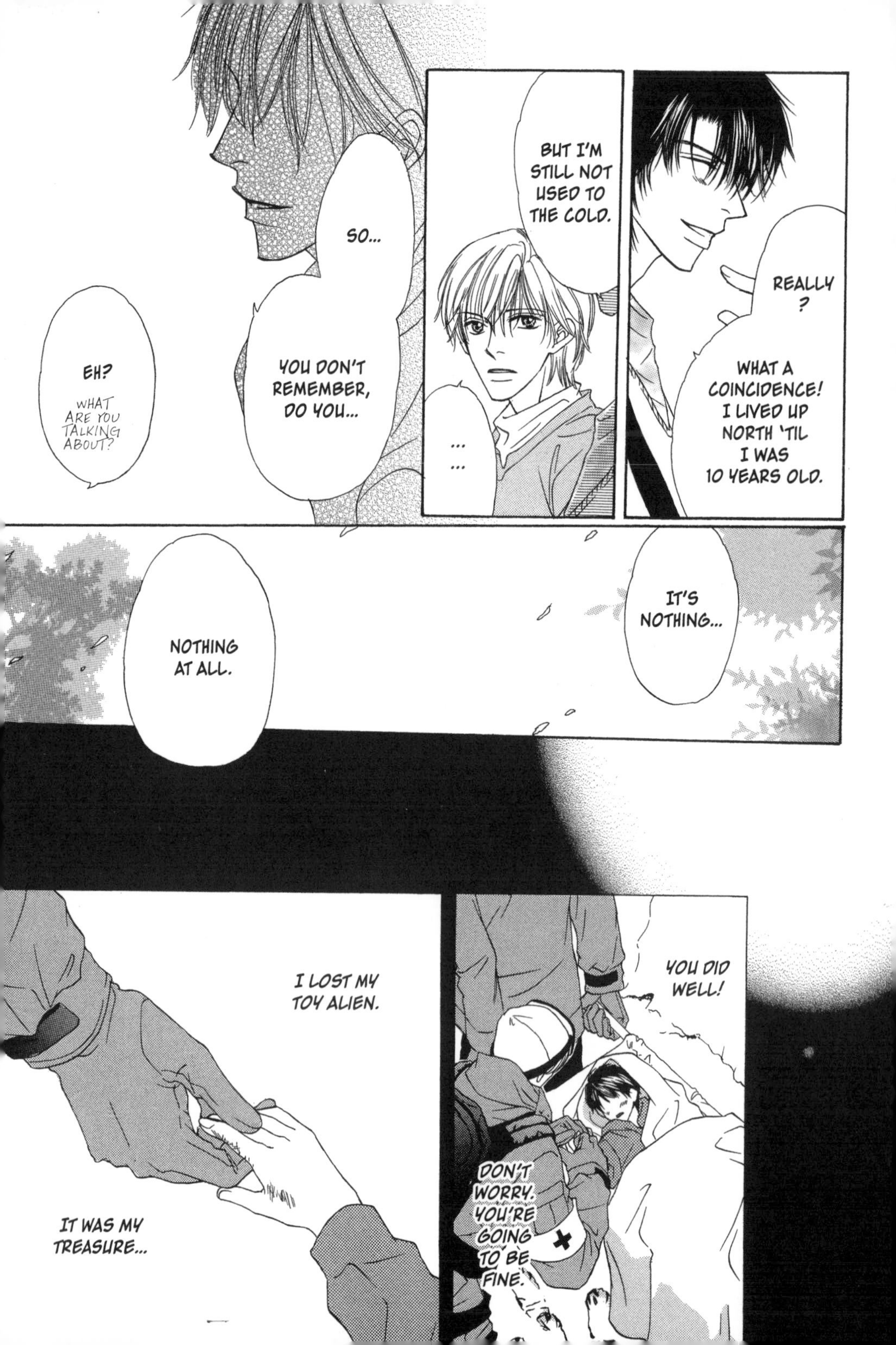
REALLY?
WHAT A COINCIDENCE! I LIVED UP NORTH 'TIL I WAS 10 YEARS OLD.
BUT I'M STILL NOT USED TO THE COLD.
......
SO...
YOU DON'T REMEMBER, DO YOU...
EH? WHAT ARE YOU TALKING ABOUT?
IT'S NOTHING...
NOTHING AT ALL.
YOU DID WELL!
DON'T WORRY. YOU'RE GOING TO BE FINE.
I LOST MY TOY ALIEN.
IT WAS MY TREASURE...

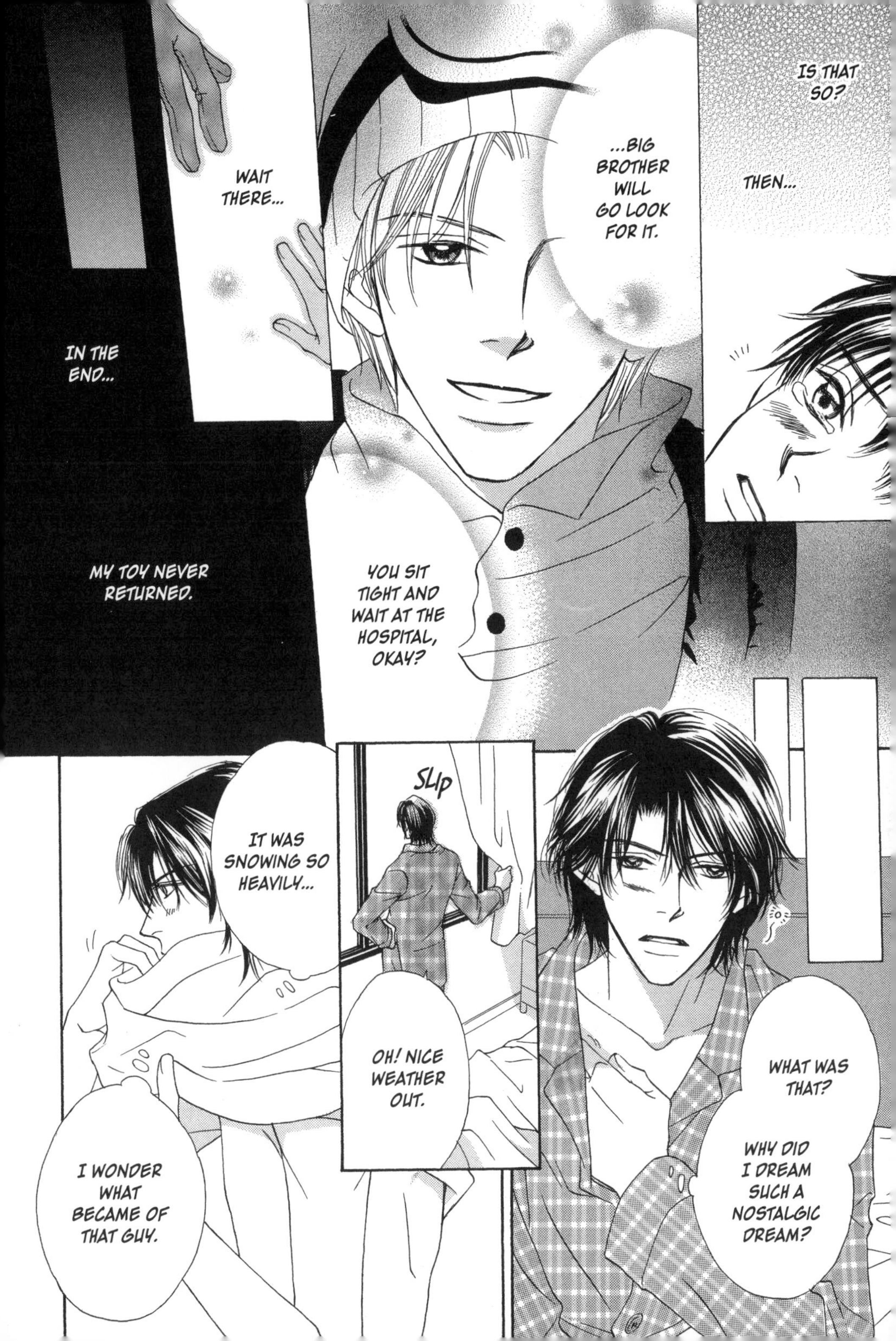
IS THAT SO?
THEN...
...BIG BROTHER WILL GO LOOK FOR IT.
WAIT THERE...
YOU SIT TIGHT AND WAIT AT THE HOSPITAL, OKAY?
IN THE END...
MY TOY NEVER RETURNED.
WHAT WAS THAT?
WHY DID I DREAM SUCH A NOSTALGIC DREAM?
SLIP
OH! NICE WEATHER OUT.
IT WAS SNOWING SO HEAVILY...
I WONDER WHAT BECAME OF THAT GUY.

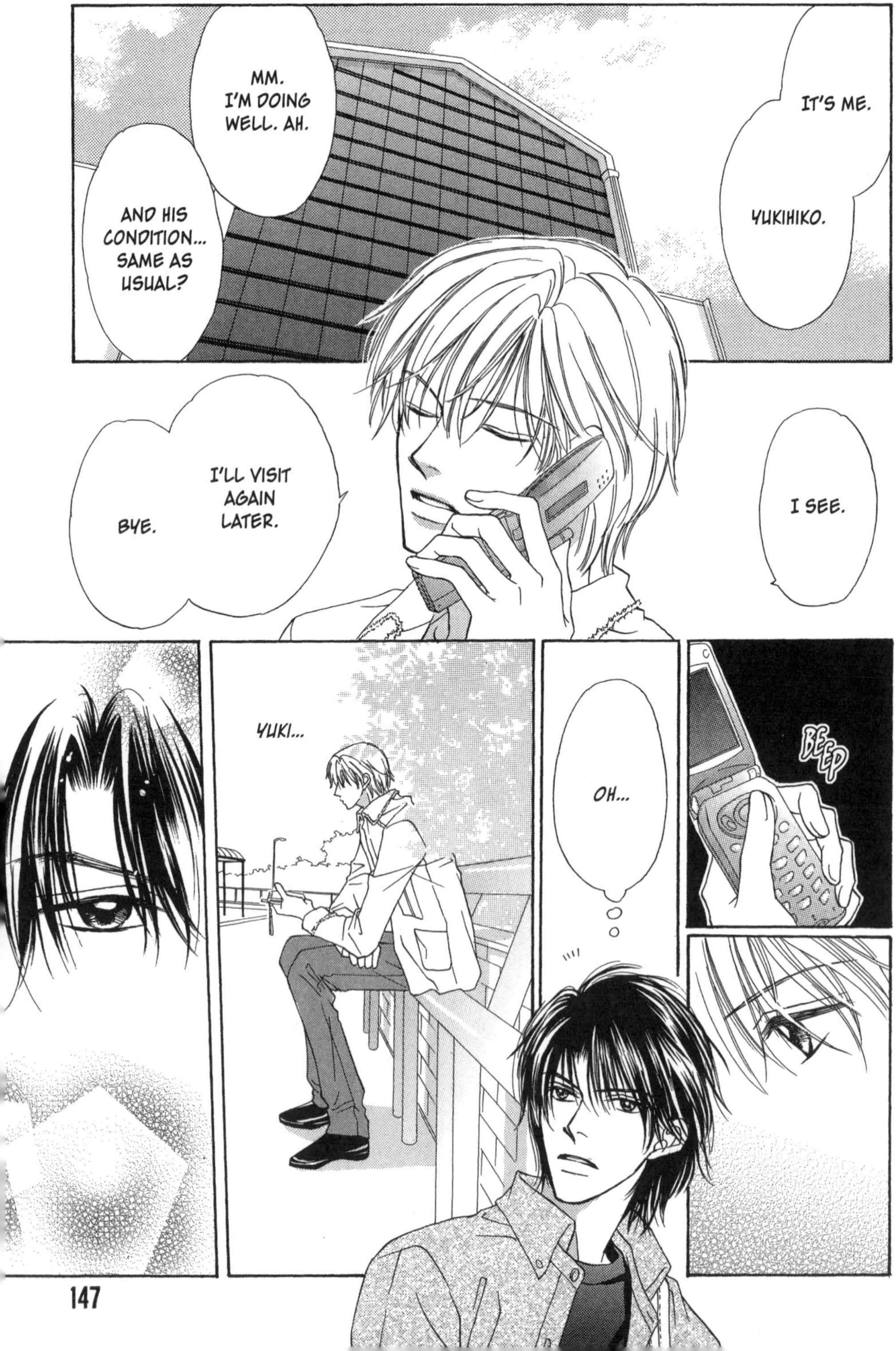
IT'S ME.
YUKIHIKO.
MM. I'M DOING WELL. AH.
AND HIS CONDITION... SAME AS USUAL?
I SEE.
I'LL VISIT AGAIN LATER.
BYE.
BEEP
OH...
YUKI...

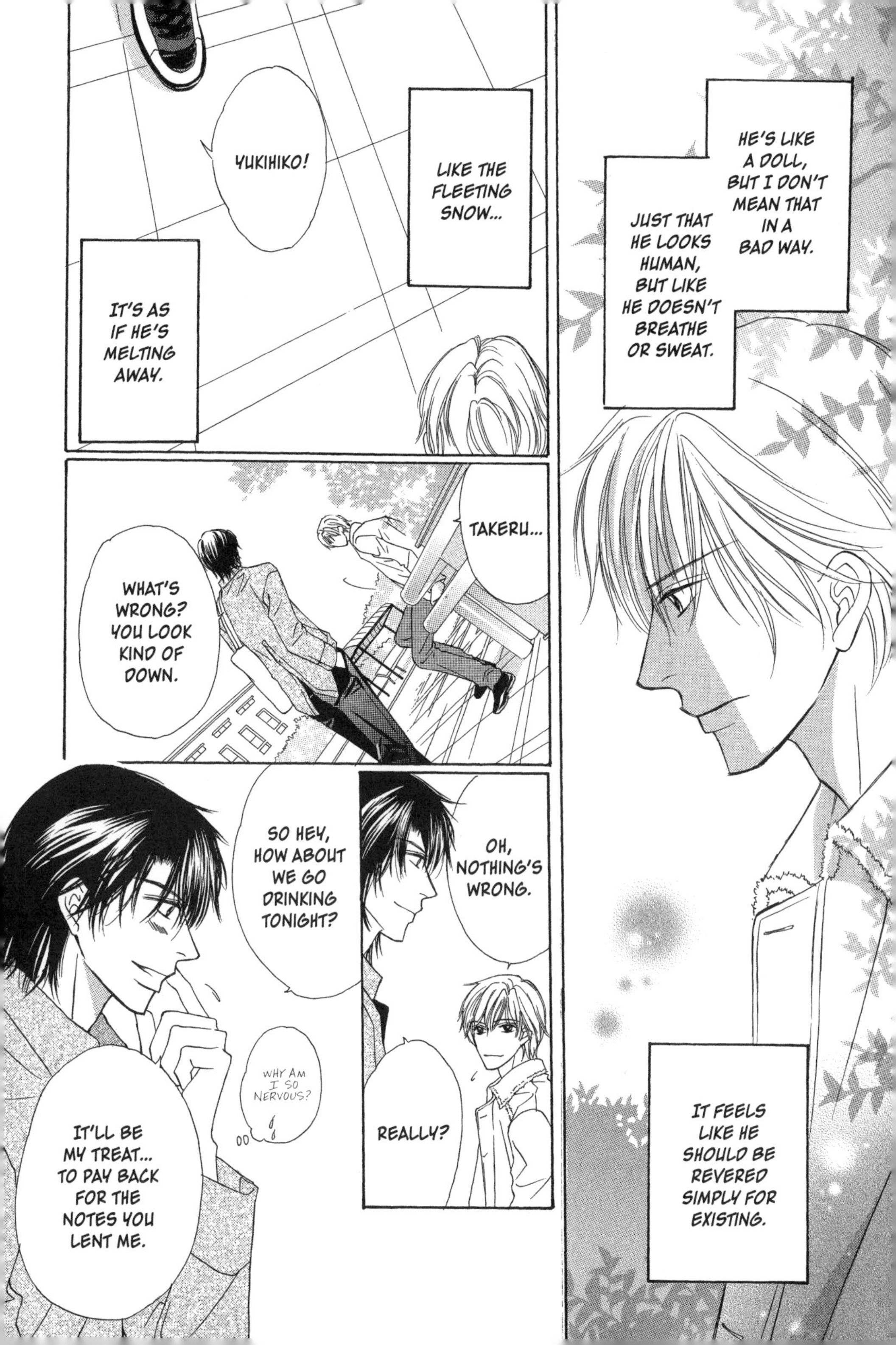
HE'S LIKE A DOLL, BUT I DON'T MEAN THAT IN A BAD WAY.
JUST THAT HE LOOKS HUMAN, BUT LIKE HE DOESN'T BREATHE OR SWEAT.
IT FEELS LIKE HE SHOULD BE REVERED SIMPLY FOR EXISTING.
LIKE THE FLEETING SNOW...
YUKIHIKO!
IT'S AS IF HE'S MELTING AWAY.
TAKERU...
WHAT'S WRONG? YOU LOOK KIND OF DOWN.
OH, NOTHING'S WRONG.
REALLY?
SO HEY, HOW ABOUT WE GO DRINKING TONIGHT?
WHY AM I SO NERVOUS?
IT'LL BE MY TREAT... TO PAY BACK FOR THE NOTES YOU LENT ME.

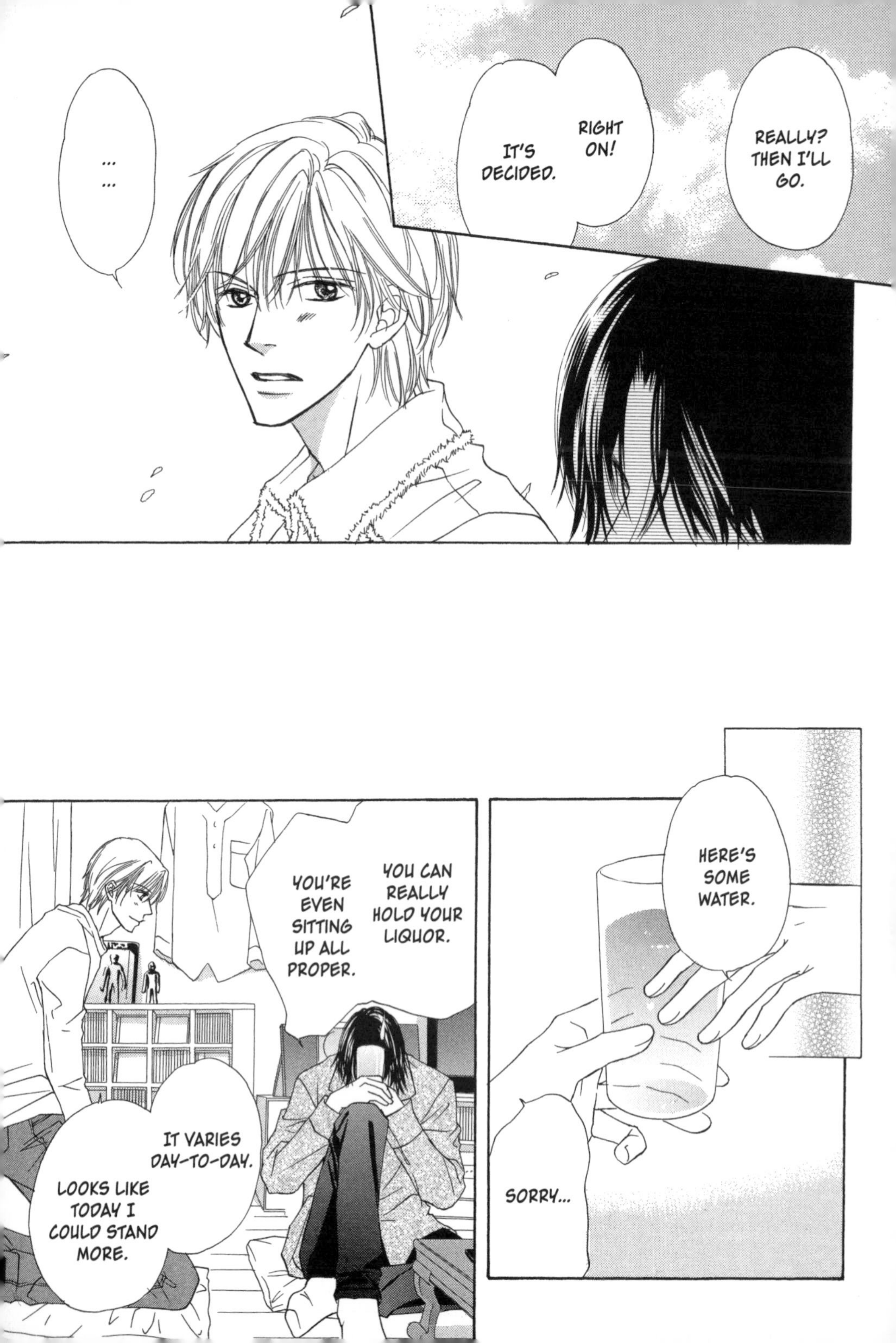
REALLY? THEN I'LL GO.
RIGHT ON!
IT'S DECIDED.
...
...
HERE'S SOME WATER.
SORRY...
YOU CAN REALLY HOLD YOUR LIQUOR.
YOU'RE EVEN SITTING UP ALL PROPER.
IT VARIES DAY-TO-DAY.
LOOKS LIKE TODAY I COULD STAND MORE.

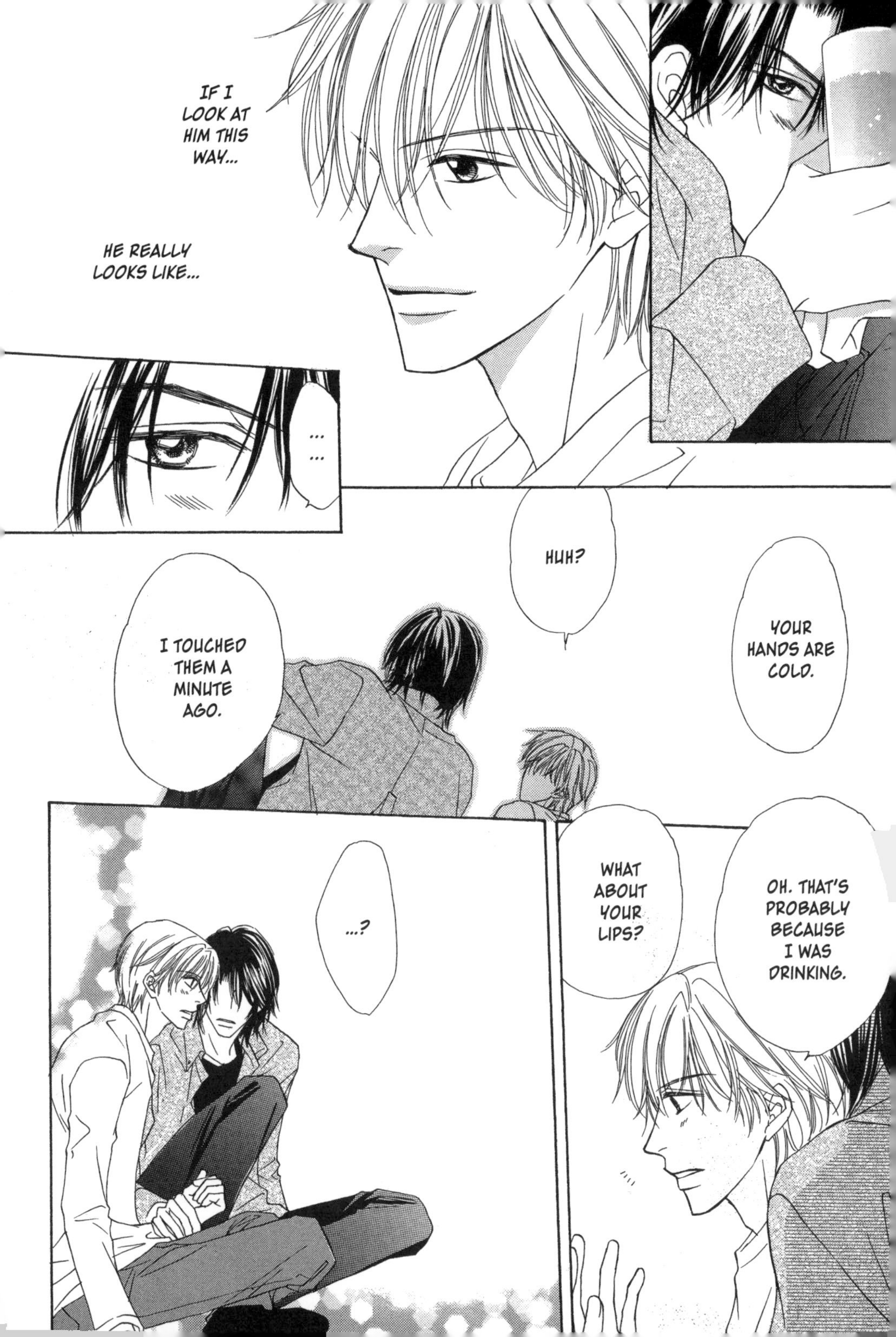
IF I LOOK AT HIM THIS WAY...
HE REALLY LOOKS LIKE...
... ...
YOUR HANDS ARE COLD.
HUH?
I TOUCHED THEM A MINUTE AGO.
OH. THAT'S PROBABLY BECAUSE I WAS DRINKING.
WHAT ABOUT YOUR LIPS?
...?

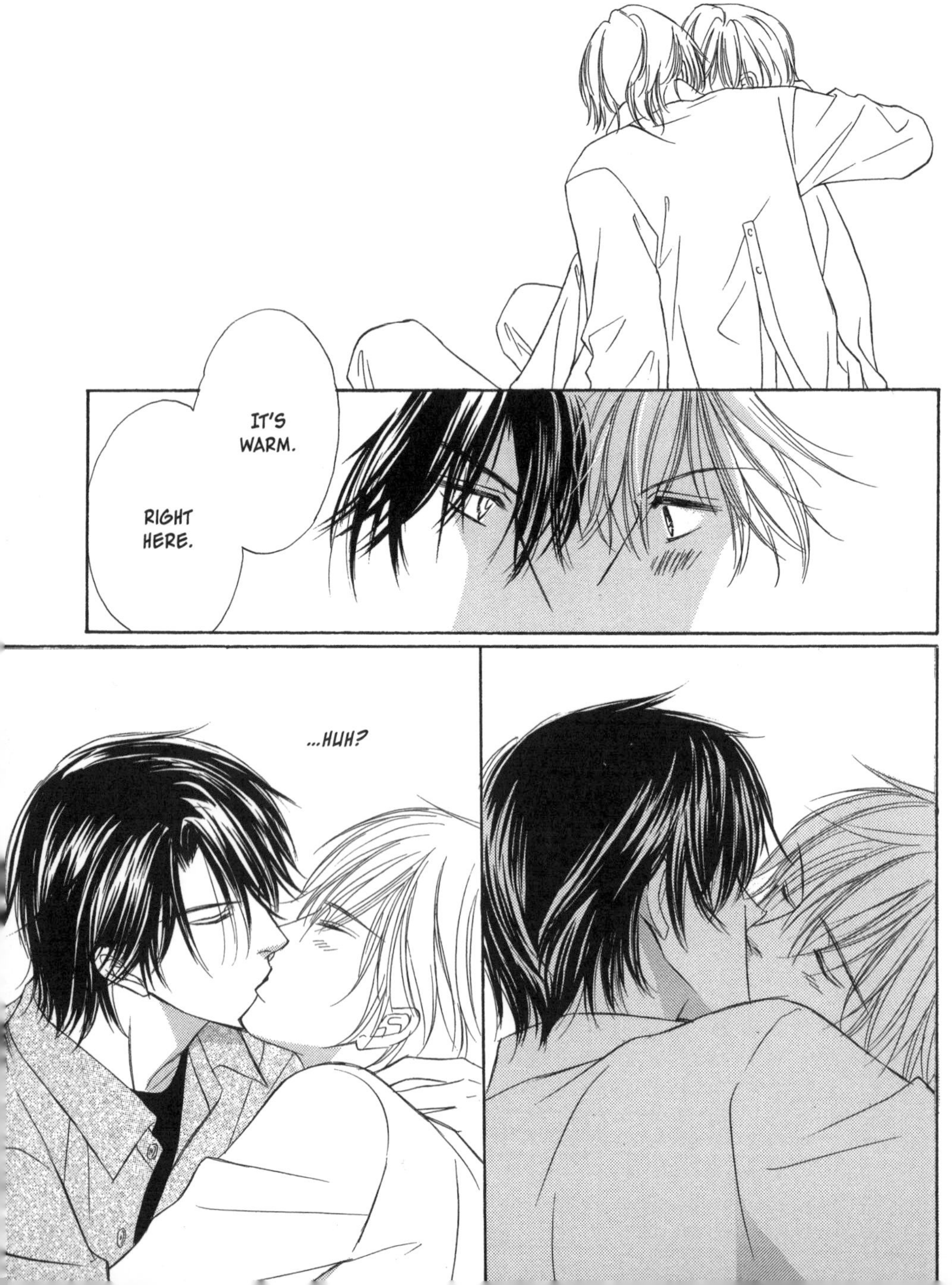
IT'S WARM.
RIGHT HERE.
...HUH?

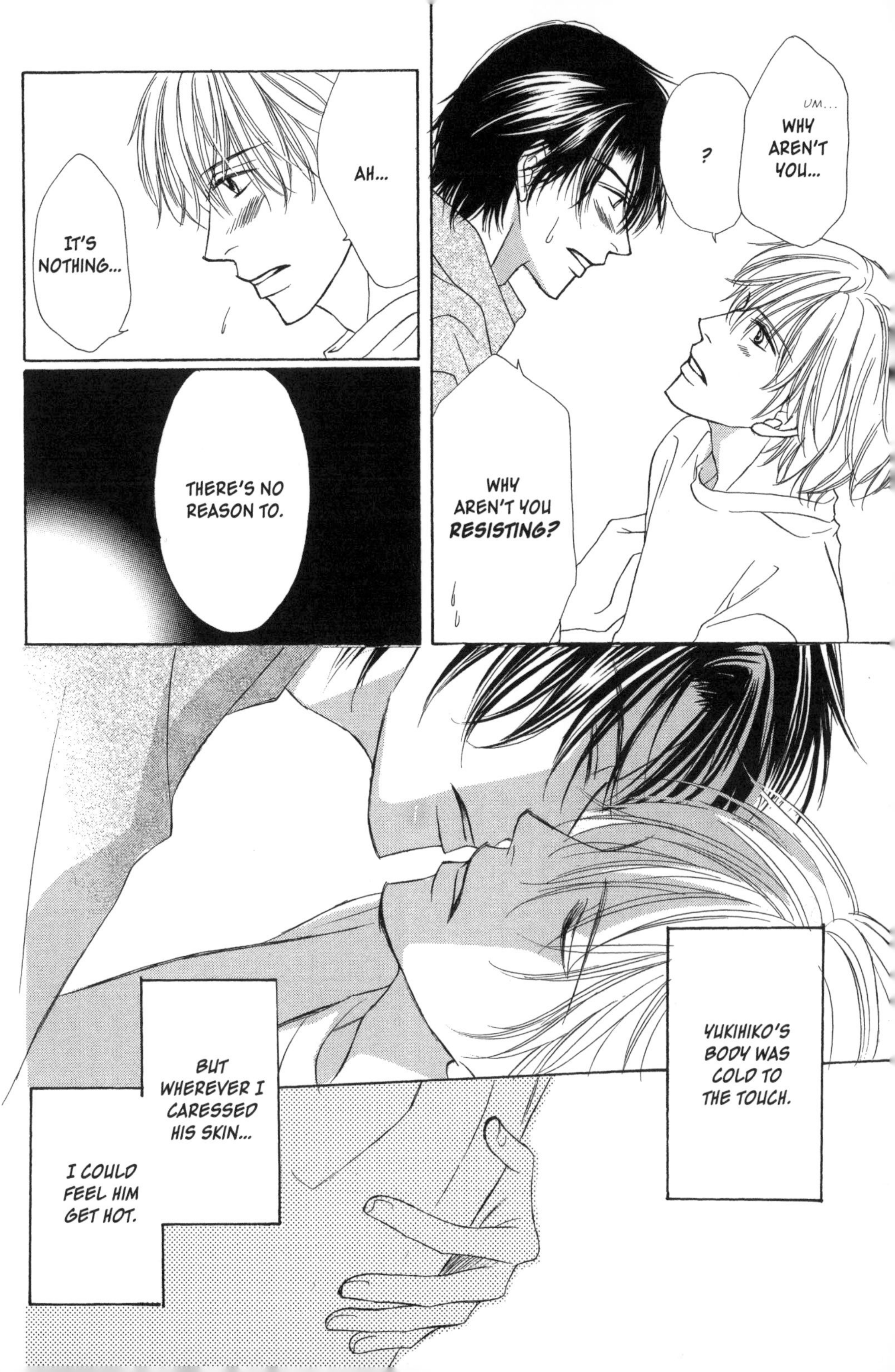
UM... WHY AREN'T YOU...
?
WHY AREN'T YOU RESISTING?
AH...
IT'S NOTHING...
THERE'S NO REASON TO.
YUKIHIKO'S BODY WAS COLD TO THE TOUCH.
BUT WHEREVER I CARESSED HIS SKIN...
I COULD FEEL HIM GET HOT.

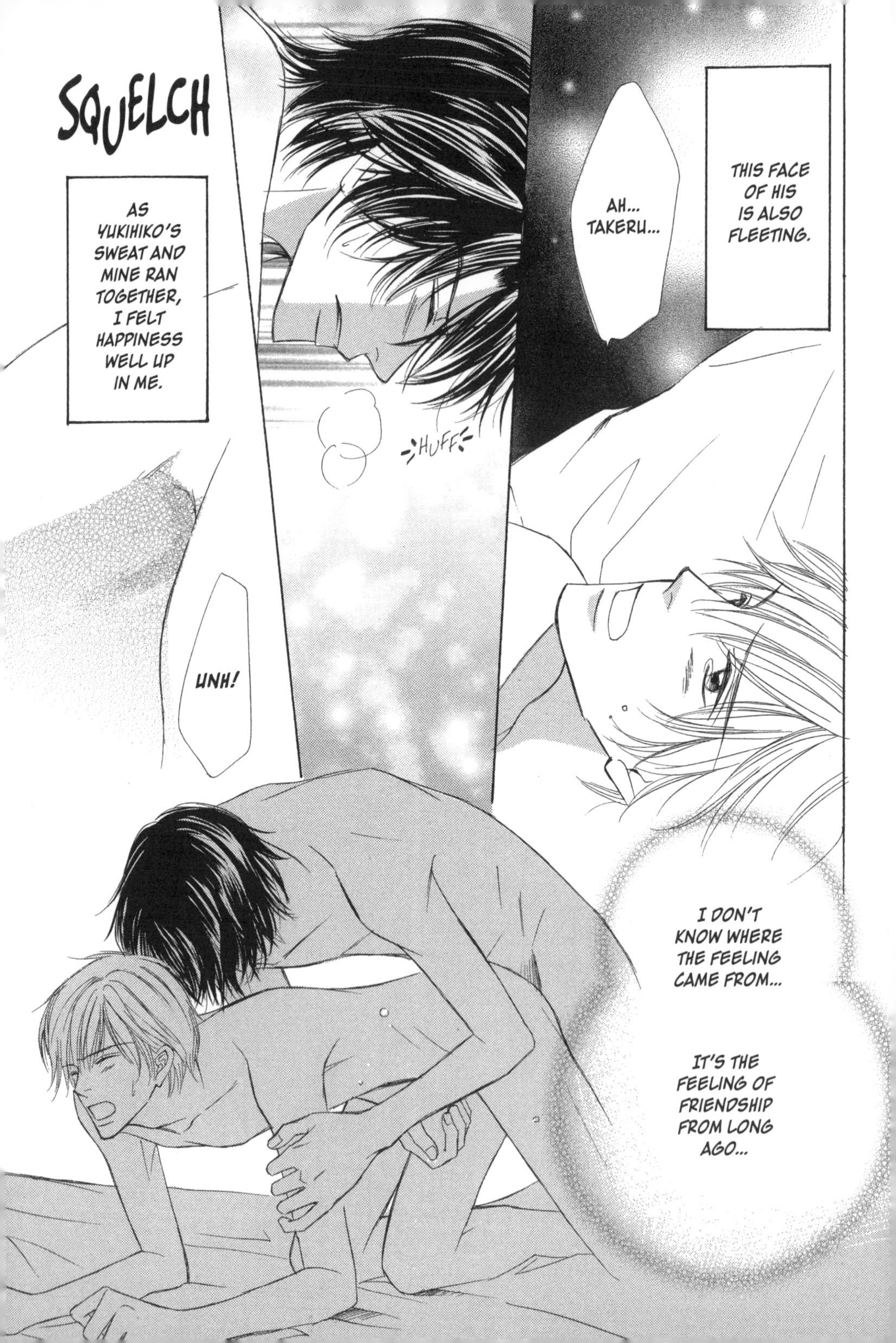
THIS FACE OF HIS IS ALSO FLEETING.
AH... TAKERU...
HUFF
SQUELCH
AS YUKIHIKO'S SWEAT AND MINE RAN TOGETHER, I FELT HAPPINESS WELL UP IN ME.
UNH!
I DON'T KNOW WHERE THE FEELING CAME FROM...
IT'S THE FEELING OF FRIENDSHIP FROM LONG AGO...

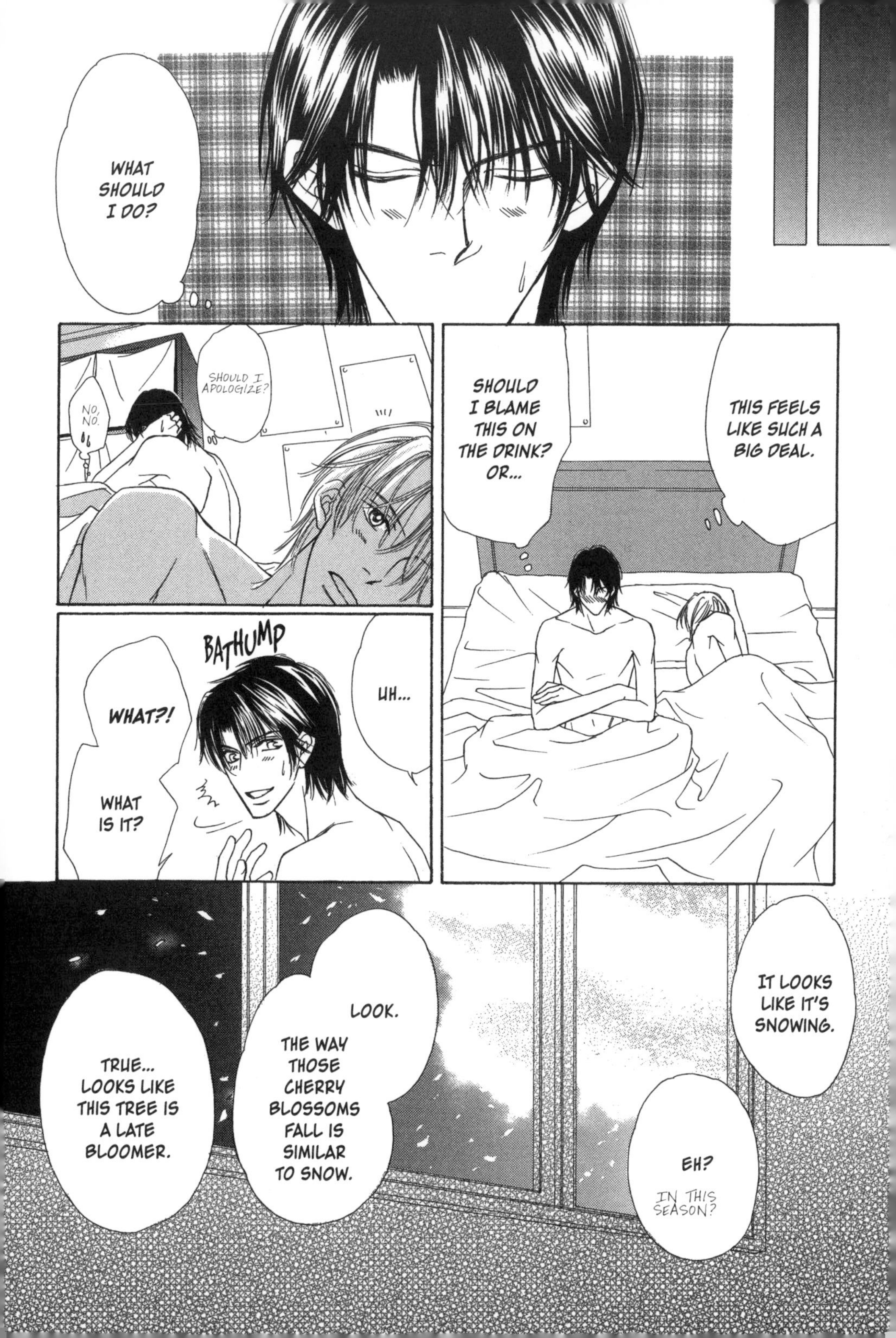
WHAT SHOULD I DO?
THIS FEELS LIKE SUCH A BIG DEAL.
SHOULD I BLAME THIS ON THE DRINK? OR...
SHOULD I APOLOGIZE?
NO, NO.
UH...
BATHUMP
WHAT?!
WHAT IS IT?
IT LOOKS LIKE IT'S SNOWING.
EH?
IN THIS SEASON?
LOOK.
THE WAY THOSE CHERRY BLOSSOMS FALL IS SIMILAR TO SNOW.
TRUE... LOOKS LIKE THIS TREE IS A LATE BLOOMER.

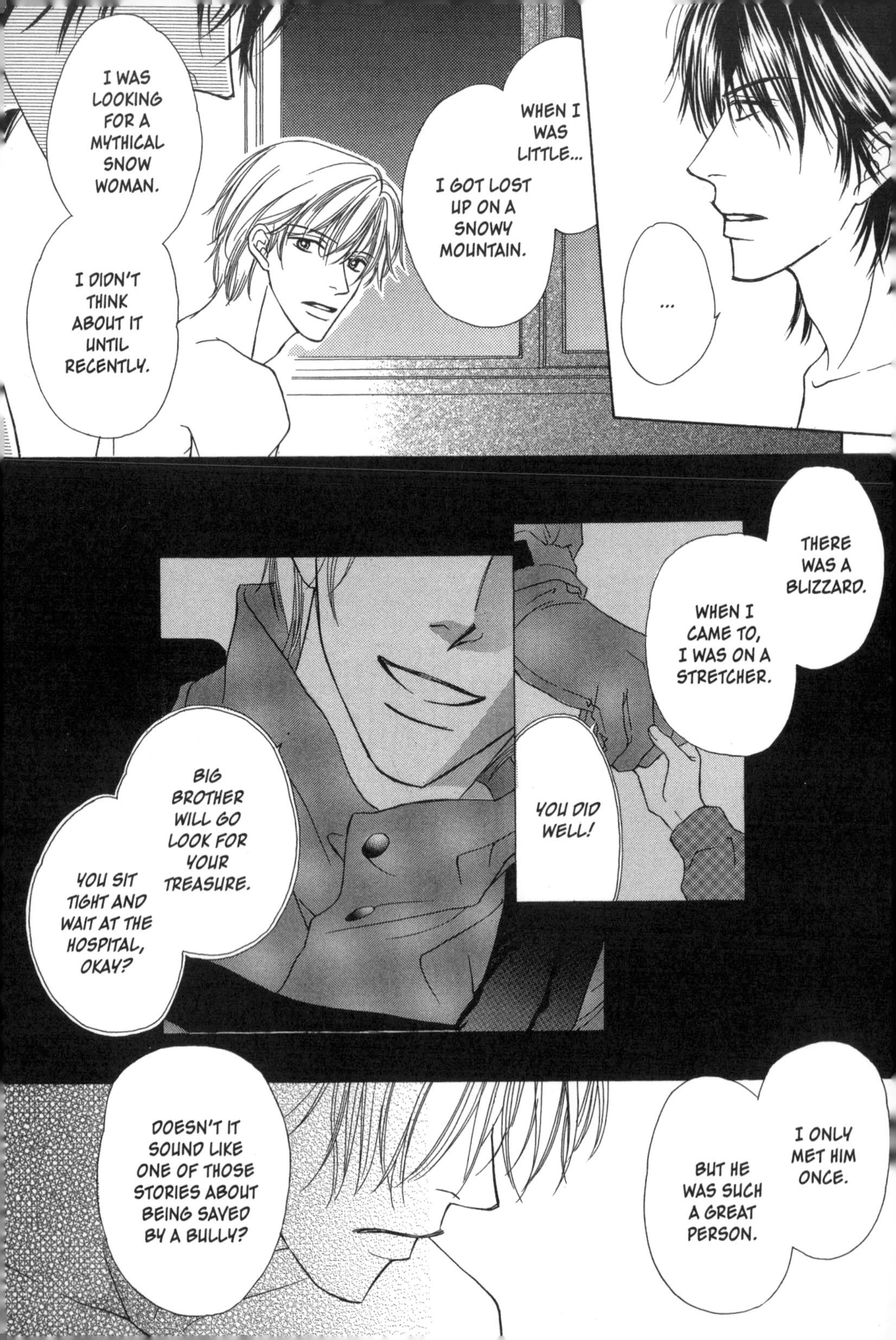
...
WHEN I WAS LITTLE...
I GOT LOST UP ON A SNOWY MOUNTAIN.
I WAS LOOKING FOR A MYTHICAL SNOW WOMAN.
I DIDN'T THINK ABOUT IT UNTIL RECENTLY.
THERE WAS A BLIZZARD.
WHEN I CAME TO, I WAS ON A STRETCHER.
YOU DID WELL!
BIG BROTHER WILL GO LOOK FOR YOUR TREASURE.
YOU SIT TIGHT AND WAIT AT THE HOSPITAL, OKAY?
I ONLY MET HIM ONCE.
BUT HE WAS SUCH A GREAT PERSON.
DOESN'T IT SOUND LIKE ONE OF THOSE STORIES ABOUT BEING SAVED BY A BULLY?

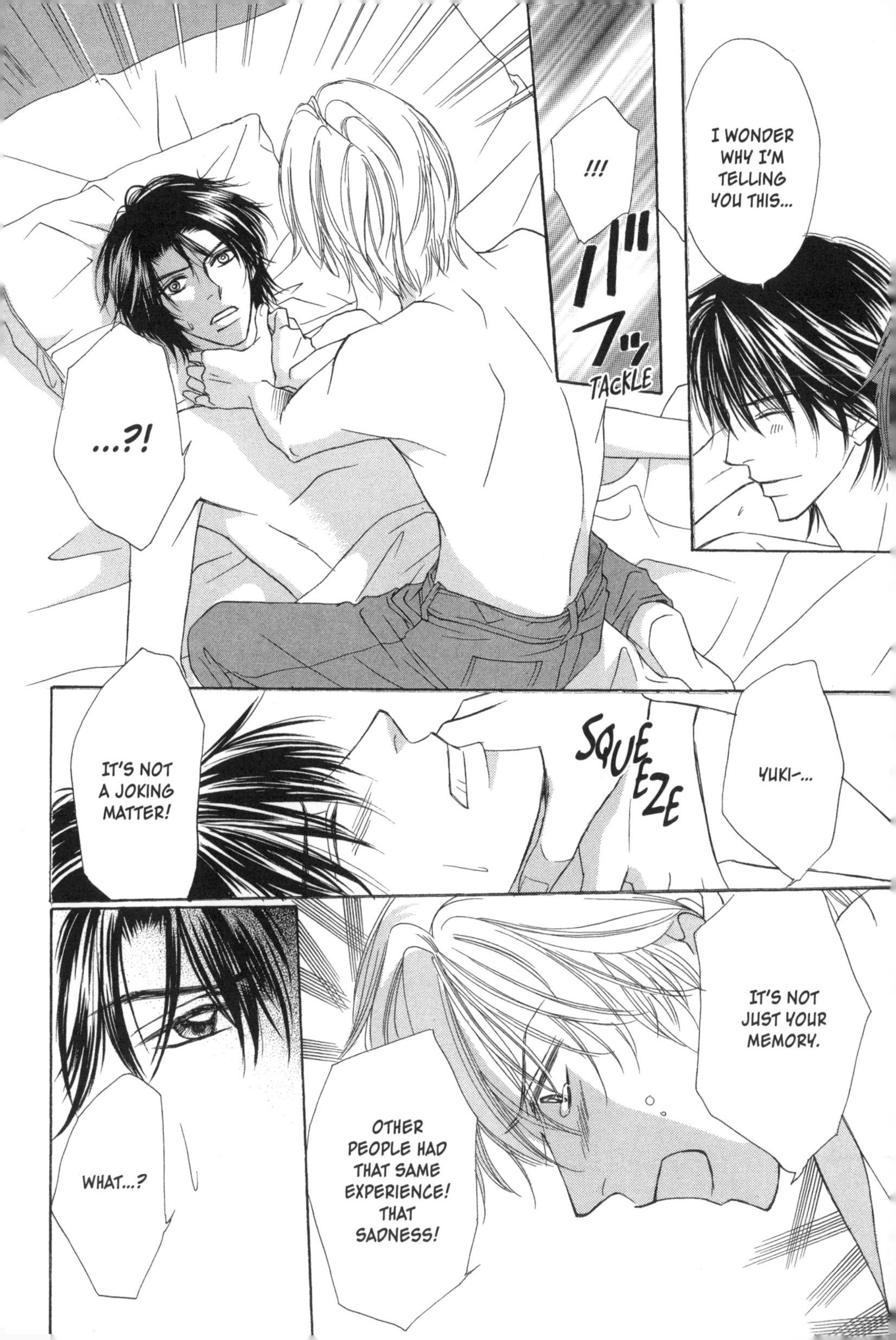
I WONDER WHY I'M TELLING YOU THIS...
!!!
TACKLE
...?!
YUKI-...
SQUEEZE
IT'S NOT A JOKING MATTER!
IT'S NOT JUST YOUR MEMORY.
OTHER PEOPLE HAD THAT SAME EXPERIENCE! THAT SADNESS!
WHAT...?

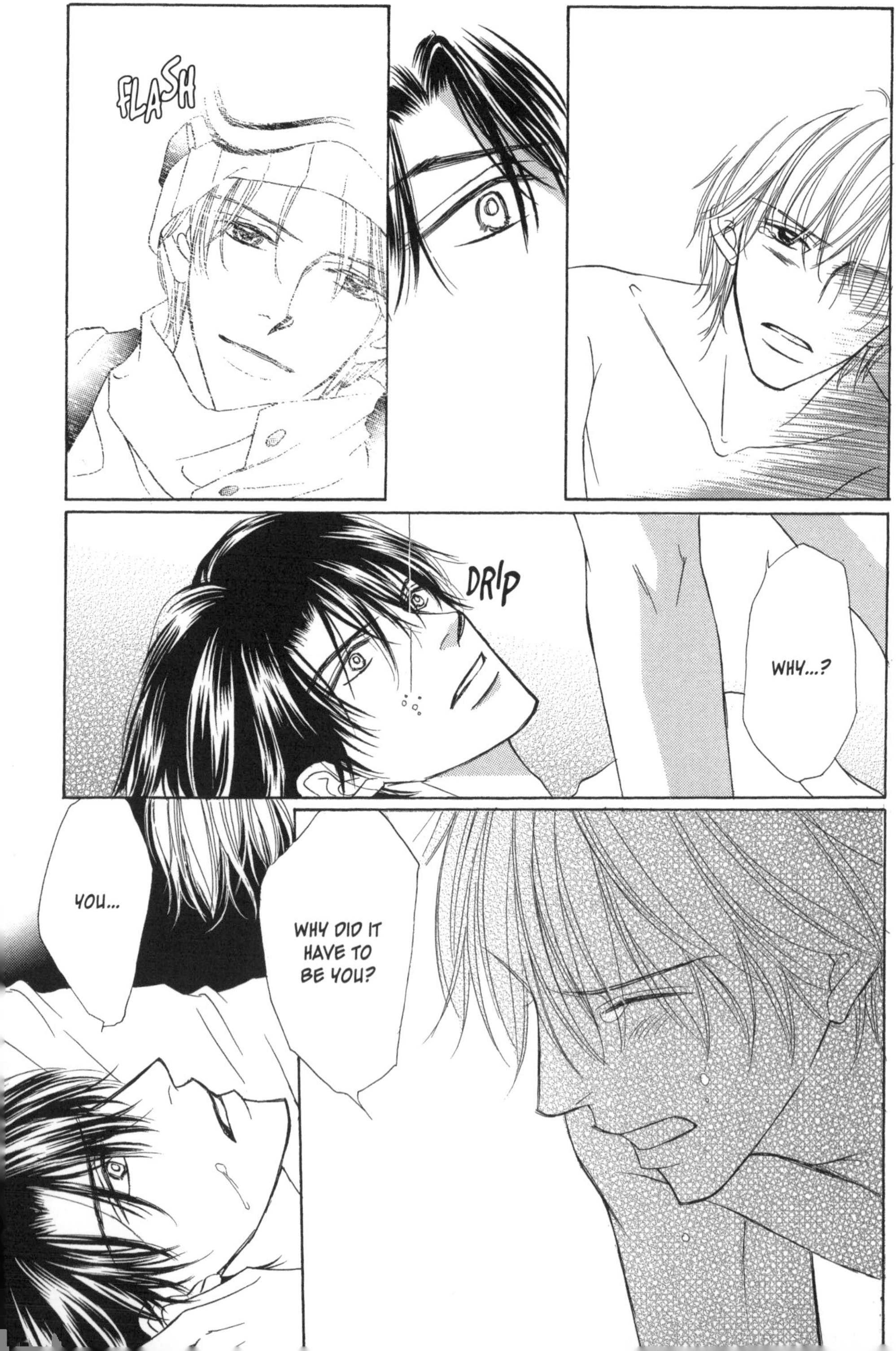
FLASH
DRIP
WHY...?
WHY DID IT HAVE TO BE YOU?
YOU...

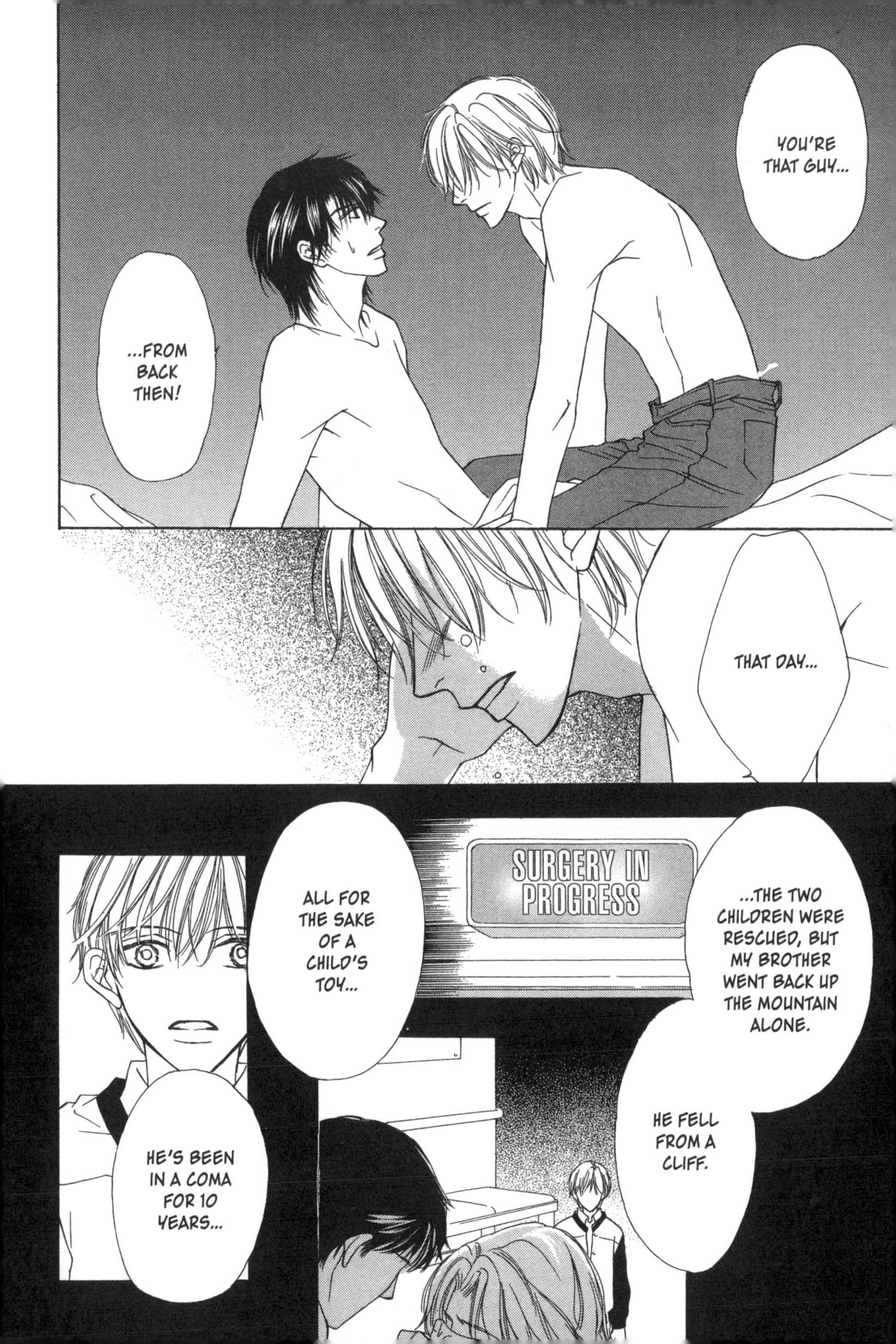
YOU'RE THAT GUY...
...FROM BACK THEN!
THAT DAY...
SURGERY IN PROGRESS
...THE TWO CHILDREN WERE RESCUED, BUT MY BROTHER WENT BACK UP THE MOUNTAIN ALONE.
HE FELL FROM A CLIFF.
ALL FOR THE SAKE OF A CHILD'S TOY...
HE'S BEEN IN A COMA FOR 10 YEARS...

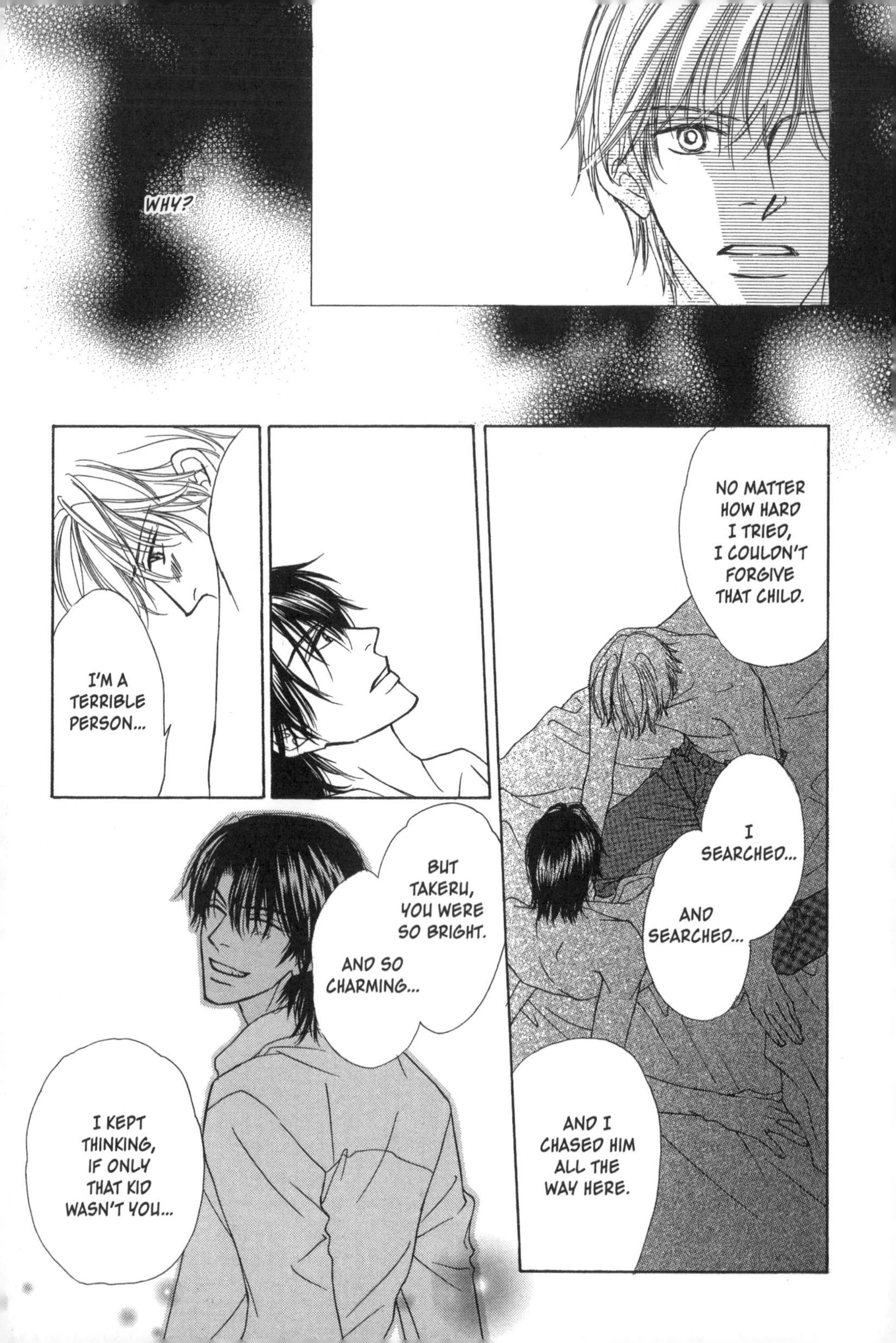
WHY?
NO MATTER HOW HARD I TRIED, I COULDN'T FORGIVE THAT CHILD.
I SEARCHED...
AND SEARCHED...
AND I CHASED HIM ALL THE WAY HERE.
I'M A TERRIBLE PERSON...
BUT TAKERU, YOU WERE SO BRIGHT.
AND SO CHARMING...
I KEPT THINKING, IF ONLY THAT KID WASN'T YOU...

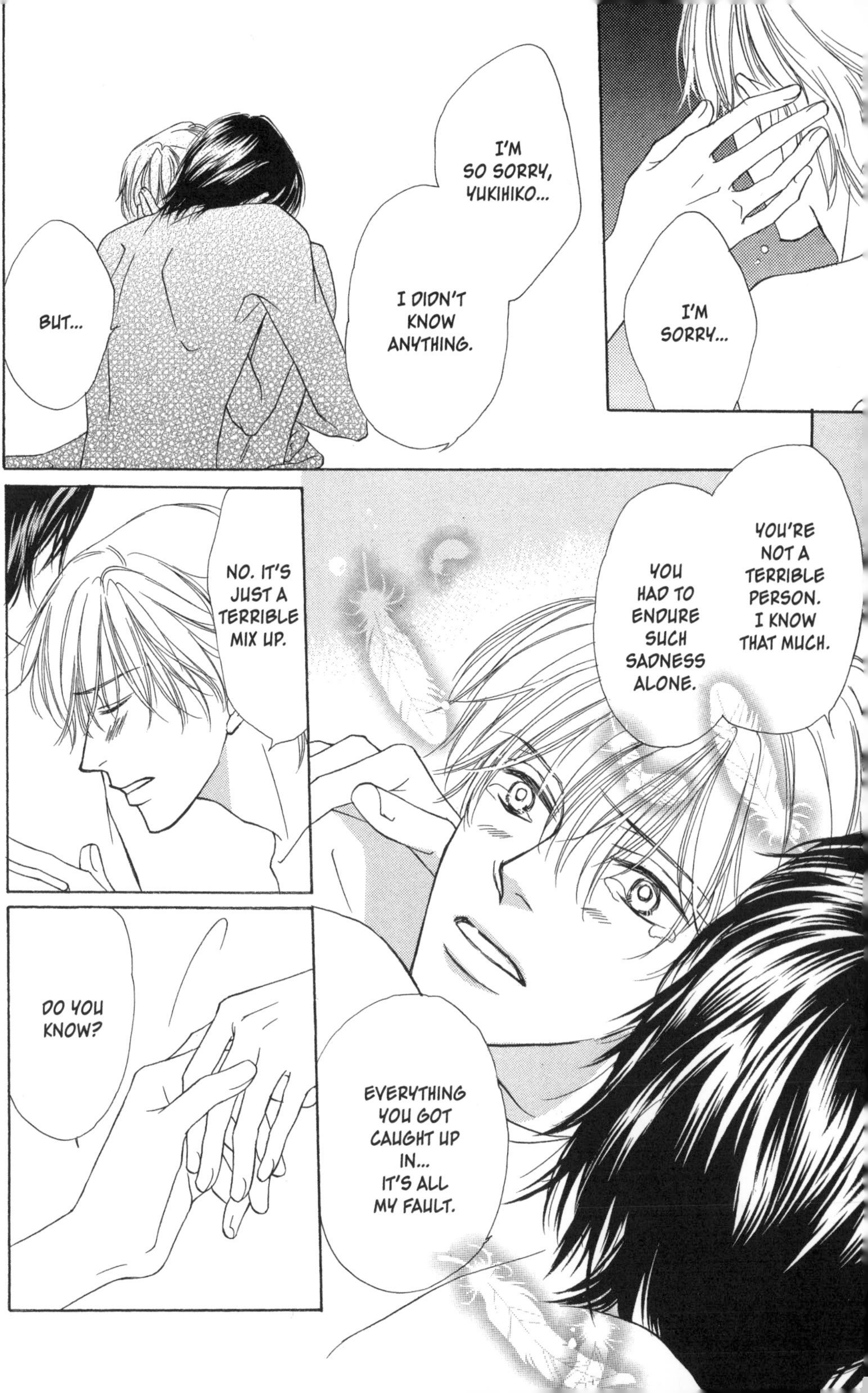
I'M SORRY...
I'M SO SORRY, YUKIHIKO...
I DIDN'T KNOW ANYTHING.
BUT...
YOU'RE NOT A TERRIBLE PERSON. I KNOW THAT MUCH.
YOU HAD TO ENDURE SUCH SADNESS ALONE.
EVERYTHING YOU GOT CAUGHT UP IN... IT'S ALL MY FAULT.
NO. IT'S JUST A TERRIBLE MIX UP.
DO YOU KNOW?

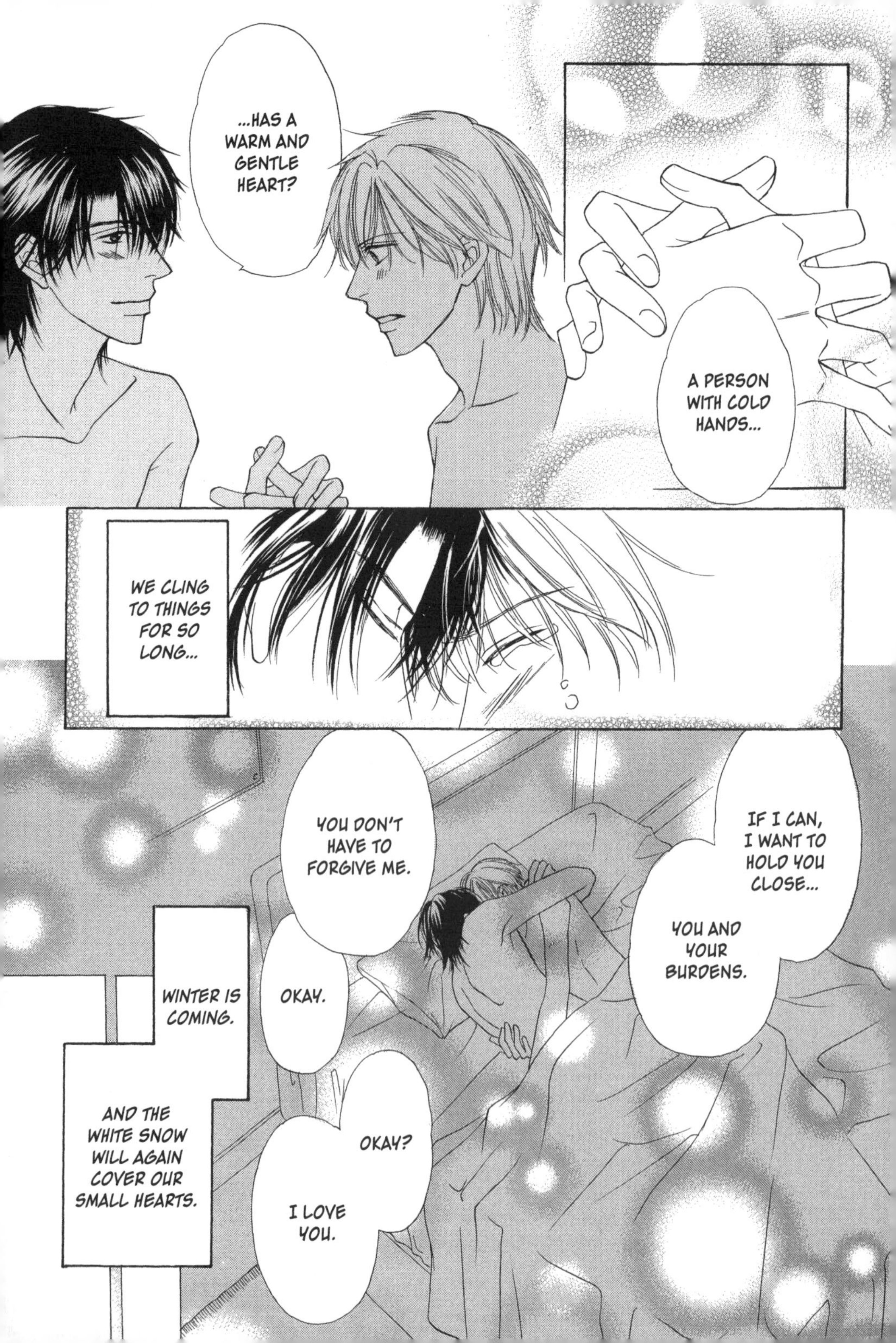
A PERSON WITH COLD HANDS...
...HAS A WARM AND GENTLE HEART?
WE CLING TO THINGS FOR SO LONG...
IF I CAN, I WANT TO HOLD YOU CLOSE...
YOU AND YOUR BURDENS.
YOU DON'T HAVE TO FORGIVE ME.
OKAY.
WINTER IS COMING.
OKAY?
I LOVE YOU.
AND THE WHITE SNOW WILL AGAIN COVER OUR SMALL HEARTS.

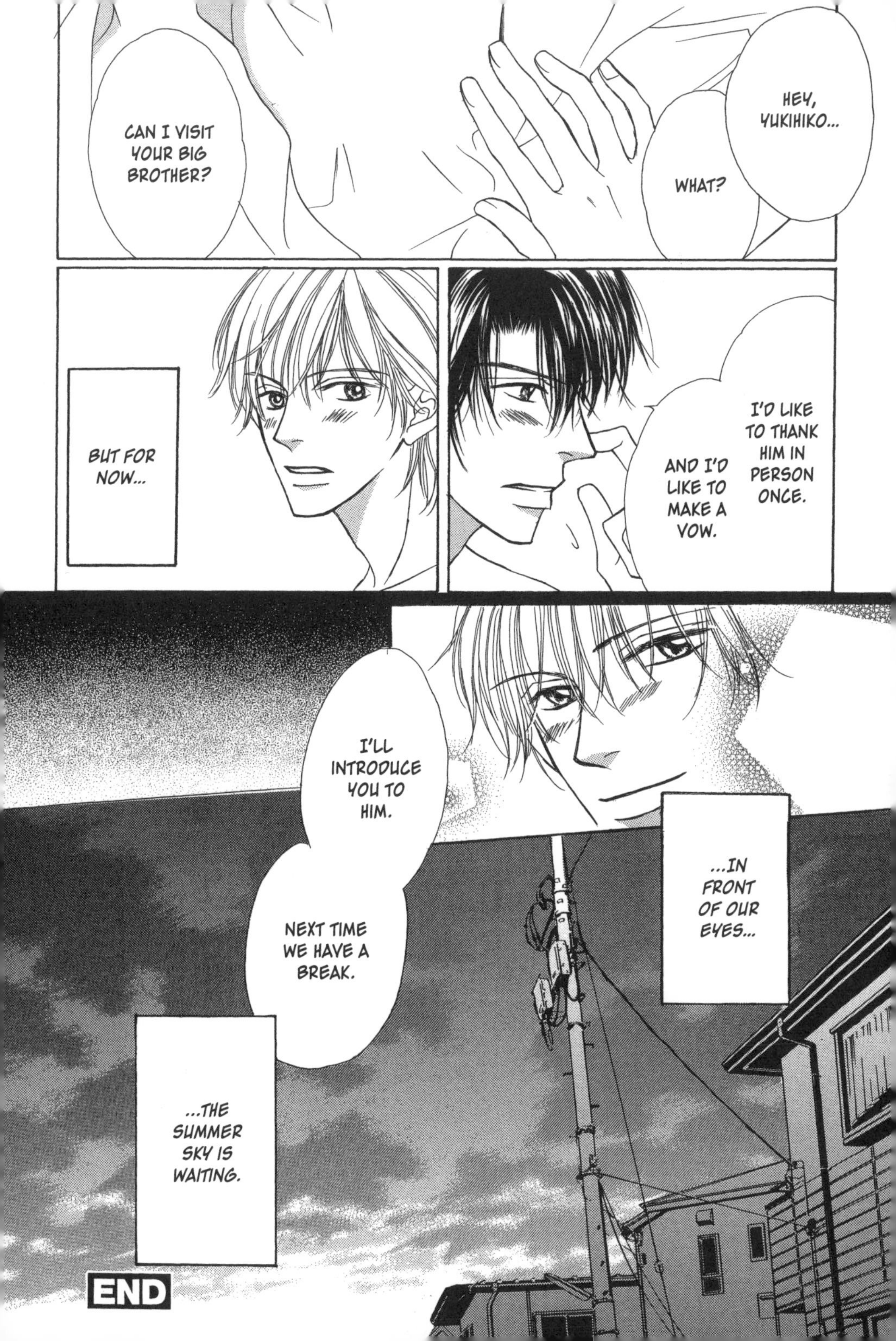
HEY, YUKIHIKO...
WHAT?
CAN I VISIT YOUR BIG BROTHER?
I'D LIKE TO THANK HIM IN PERSON ONCE.
AND I'D LIKE TO MAKE A VOW.
BUT FOR NOW...
I'LL INTRODUCE YOU TO HIM.
NEXT TIME WE HAVE A BREAK.
...IN FRONT OF OUR EYES...
...THE SUMMER SKY IS WAITING.
END

EXTRA TIME

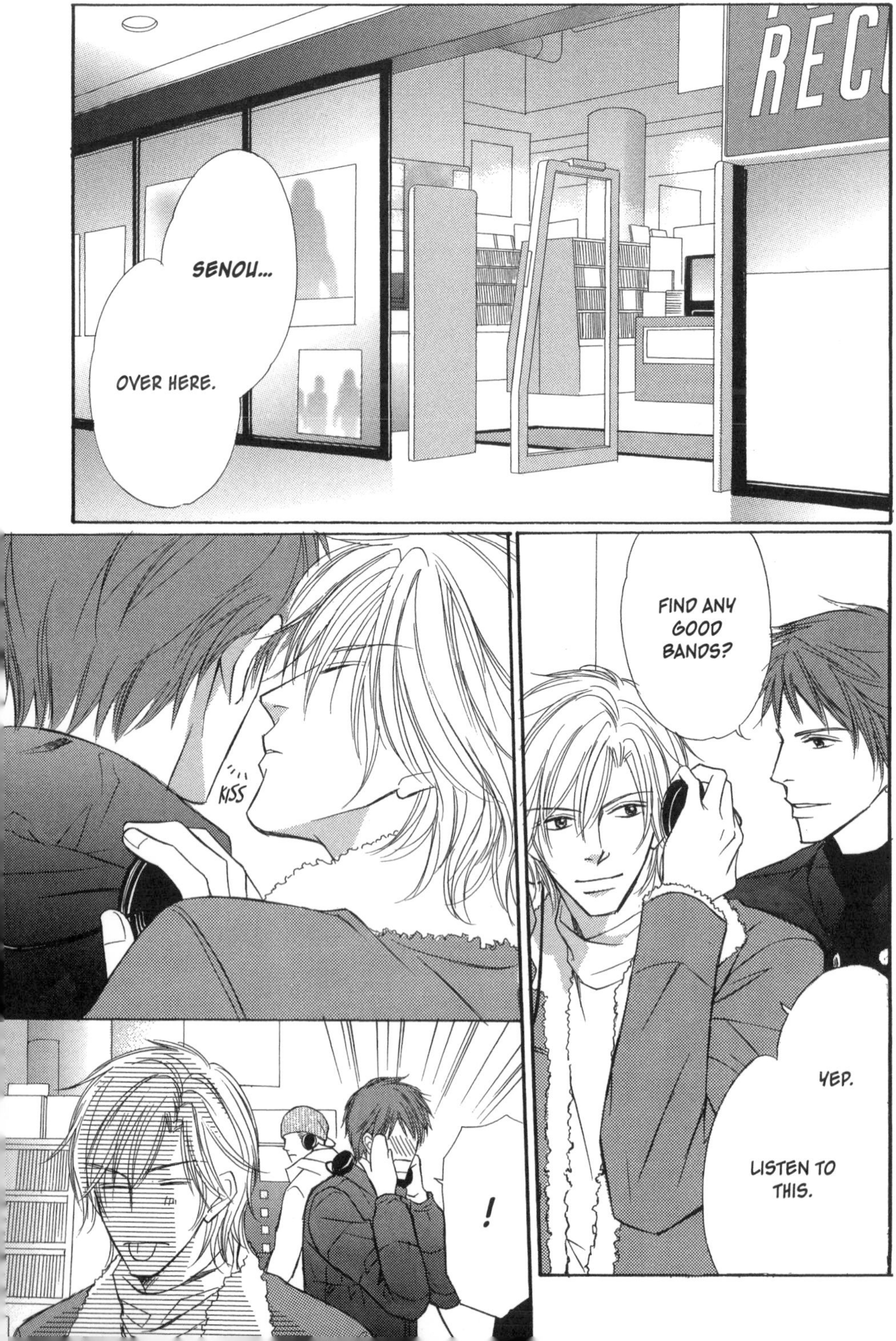
REC
SENOU...
OVER HERE.
FIND ANY GOOD BANDS?
YEP.
LISTEN TO THIS.
KISS
!

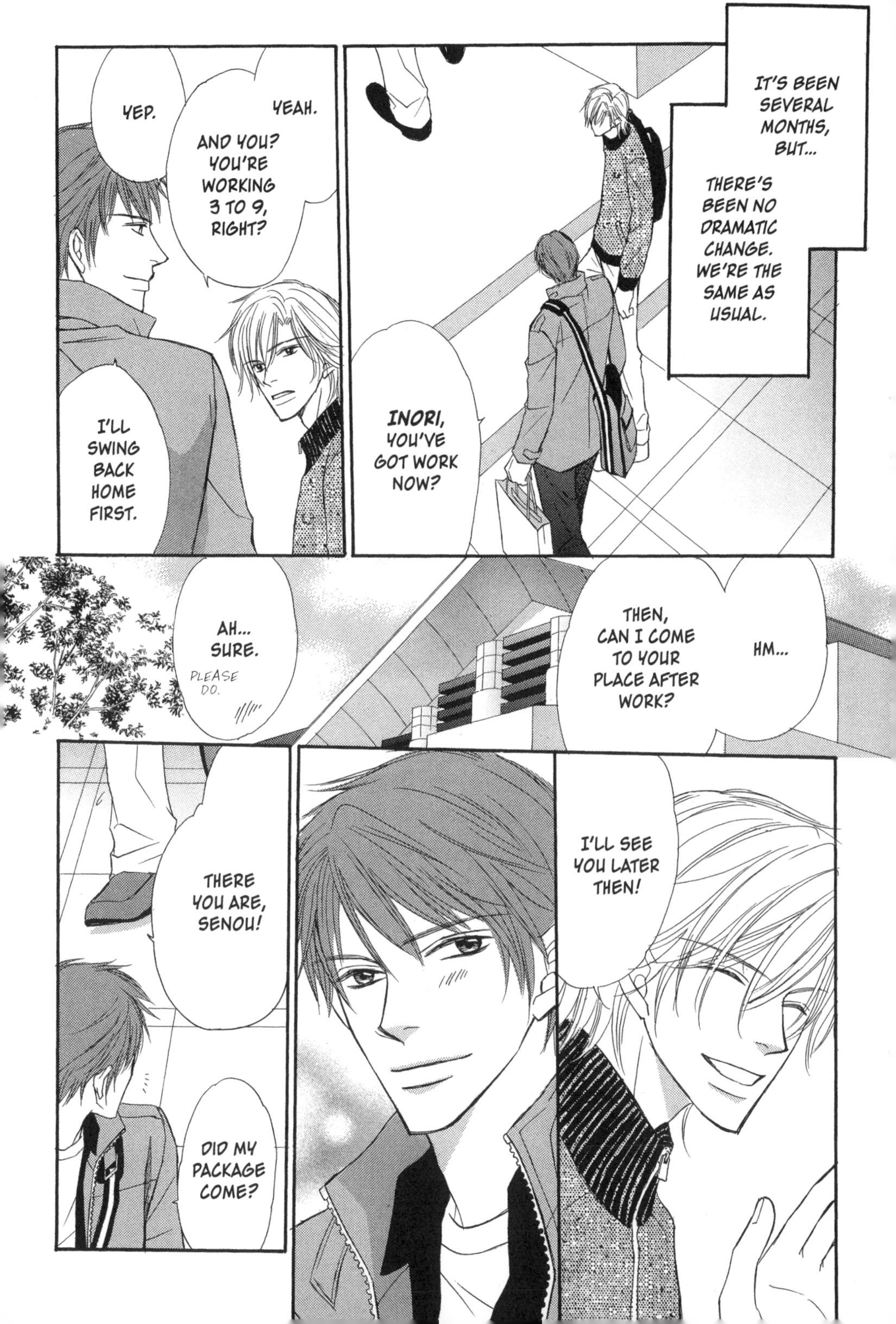
IT'S BEEN SEVERAL MONTHS, BUT...
THERE'S BEEN NO DRAMATIC CHANGE. WE'RE THE SAME AS USUAL.
INORI, YOU'VE GOT WORK NOW?
YEAH.
AND YOU? YOU'RE WORKING 3 TO 9, RIGHT?
YEP.
I'LL SWING BACK HOME FIRST.
HM...
THEN, CAN I COME TO YOUR PLACE AFTER WORK?
AH... SURE.
PLEASE DO.
I'LL SEE YOU LATER THEN!
THERE YOU ARE, SENOU!
DID MY PACKAGE COME?

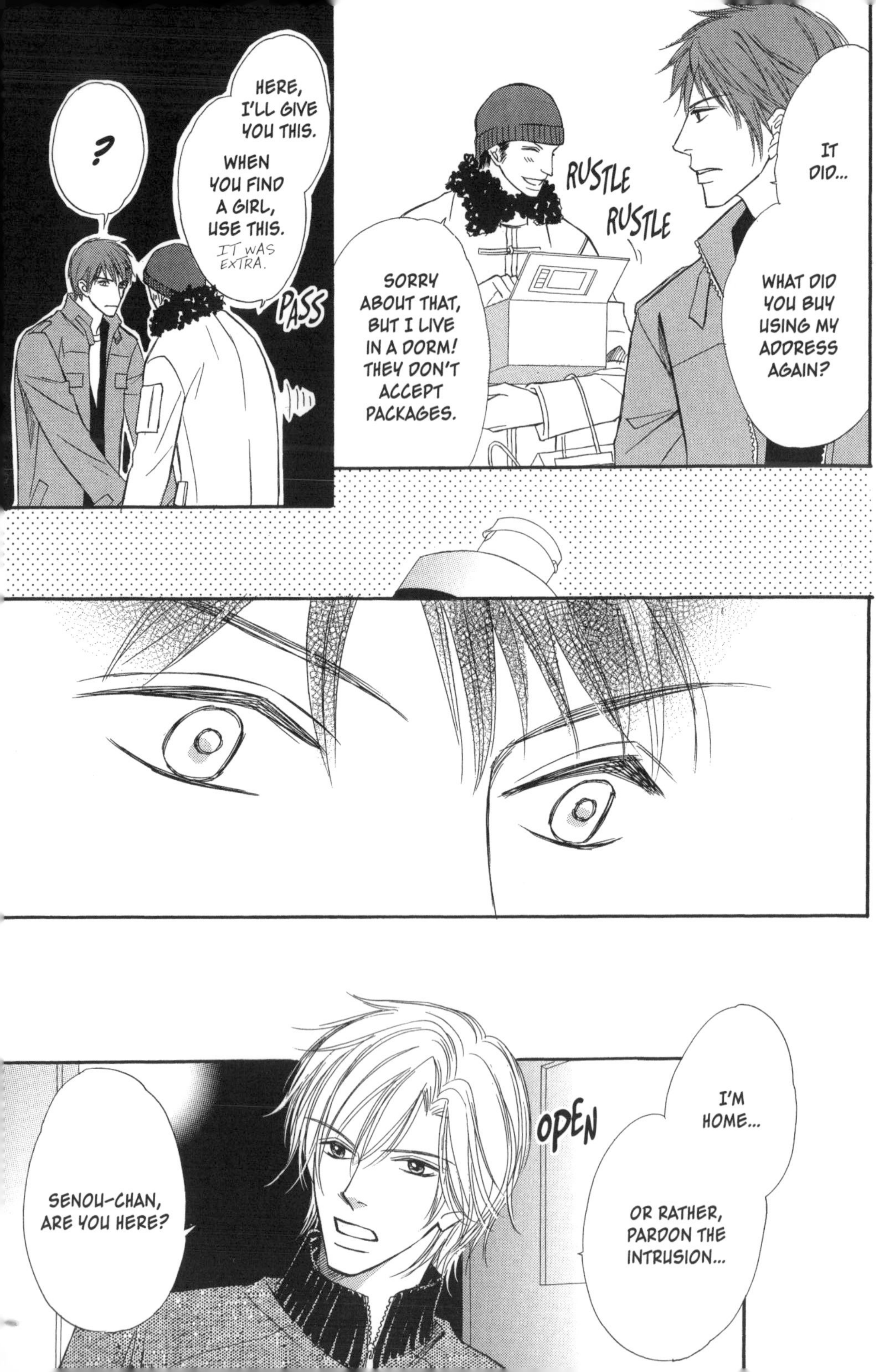
IT DID...
WHAT DID YOU BUY USING MY ADDRESS AGAIN?
RUSTLE RUSTLE
SORRY ABOUT THAT, BUT I LIVE IN A DORM! THEY DON'T ACCEPT PACKAGES.
HERE, I'LL GIVE YOU THIS.
WHEN YOU FIND A GIRL, USE THIS.
IT WAS EXTRA.
?
PASS
I'M HOME...
OR RATHER, PARDON THE INTRUSION...
OPEN
SENOU-CHAN, ARE YOU HERE?

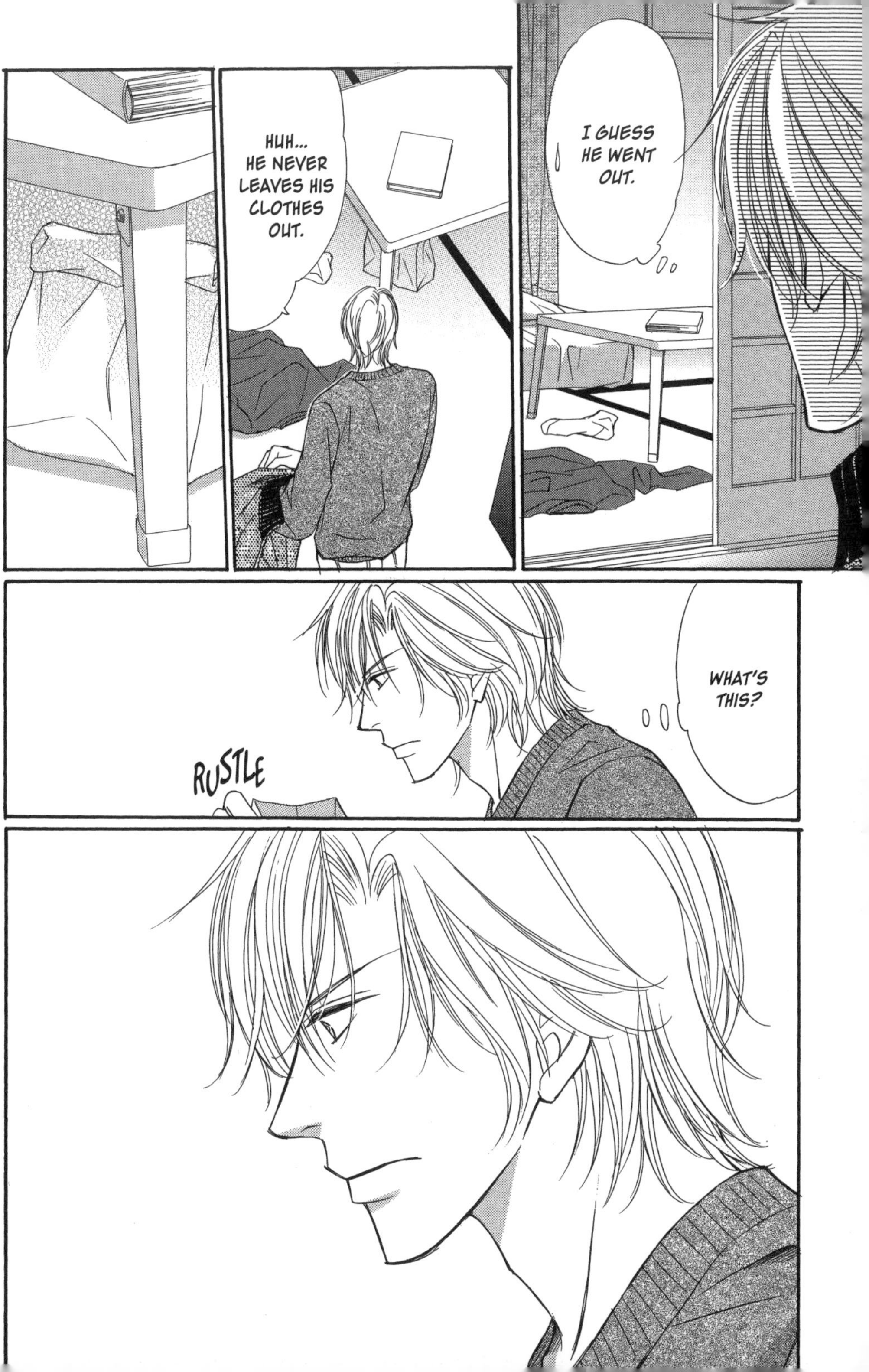
I GUESS HE WENT OUT.
HUH... HE NEVER LEAVES HIS CLOTHES OUT.
WHAT'S THIS?
RUSTLE

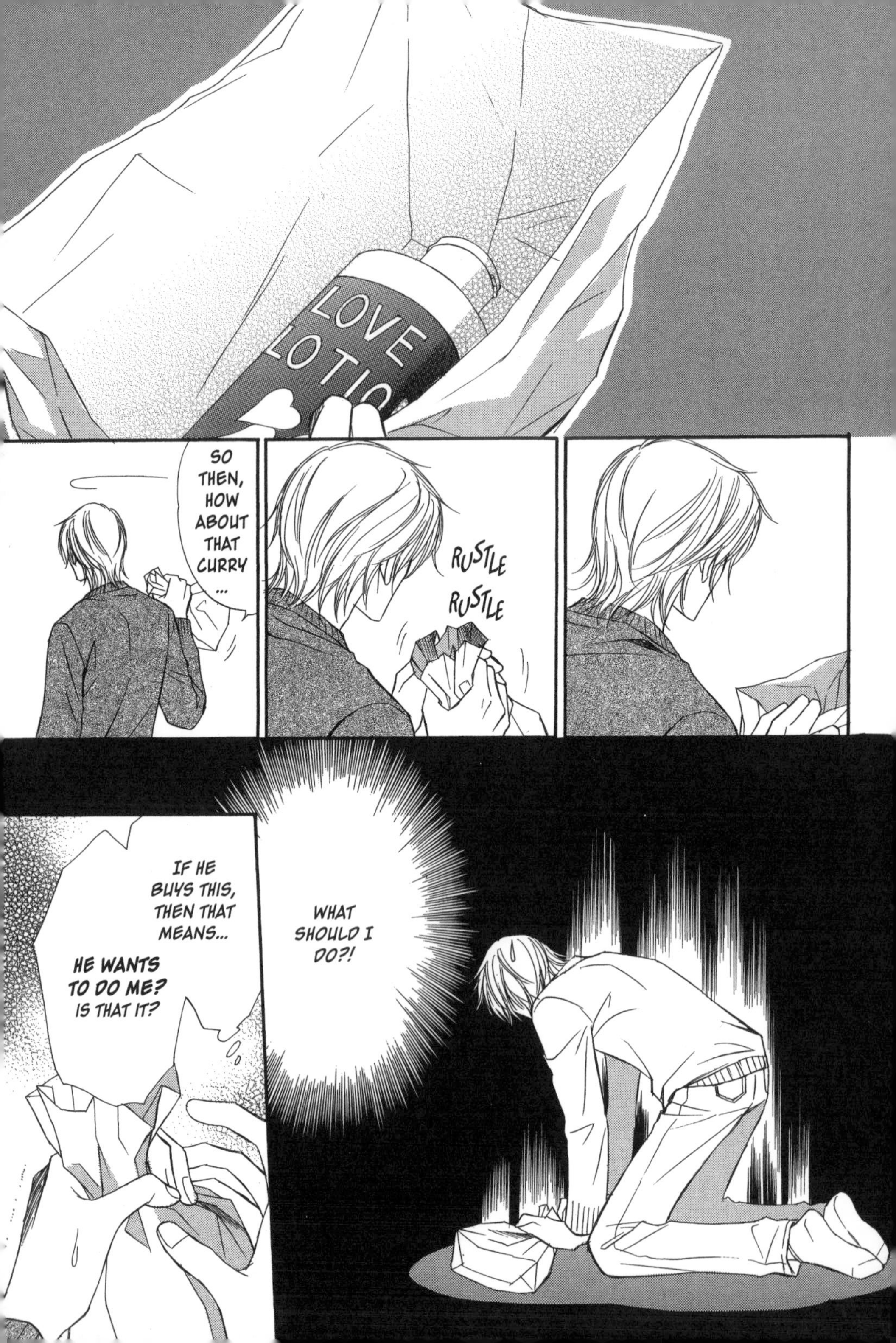
LOVE
LOTIO
RUSTLE
RUSTLE
SO THEN, HOW ABOUT THAT CURRY ...
WHAT SHOULD I DO?!
IF HE BUYS THIS, THEN THAT MEANS...
HE WANTS TO DO ME? IS THAT IT?

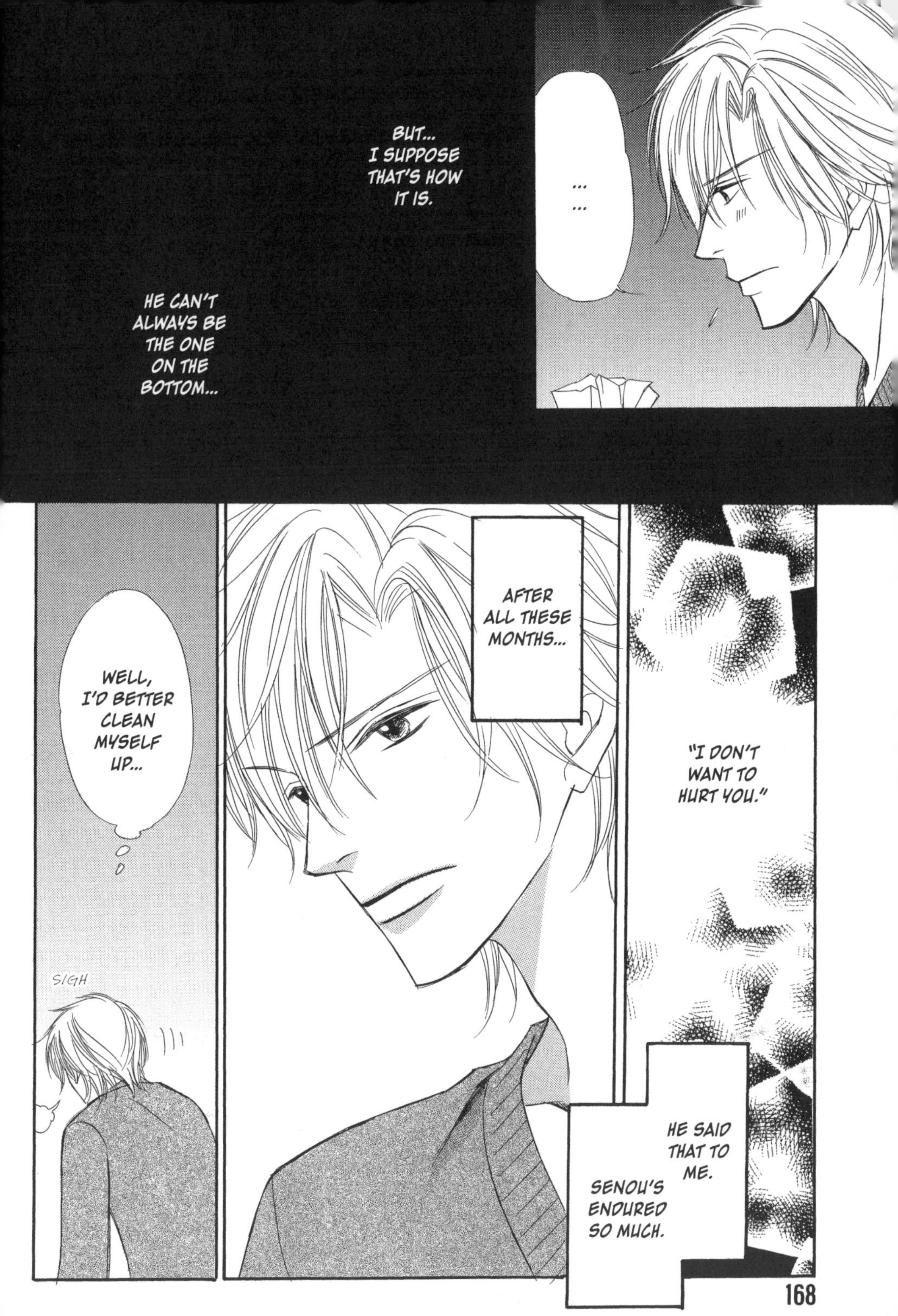

... ...
BUT... I SUPPOSE THAT'S HOW IT IS.
HE CAN'T ALWAYS BE THE ONE ON THE BOTTOM...
"I DON'T WANT TO HURT YOU."
HE SAID THAT TO ME.
SENOU'S ENDURED SO MUCH.
AFTER ALL THESE MONTHS...
WELL, I'D BETTER CLEAN MYSELF UP...
SIGH

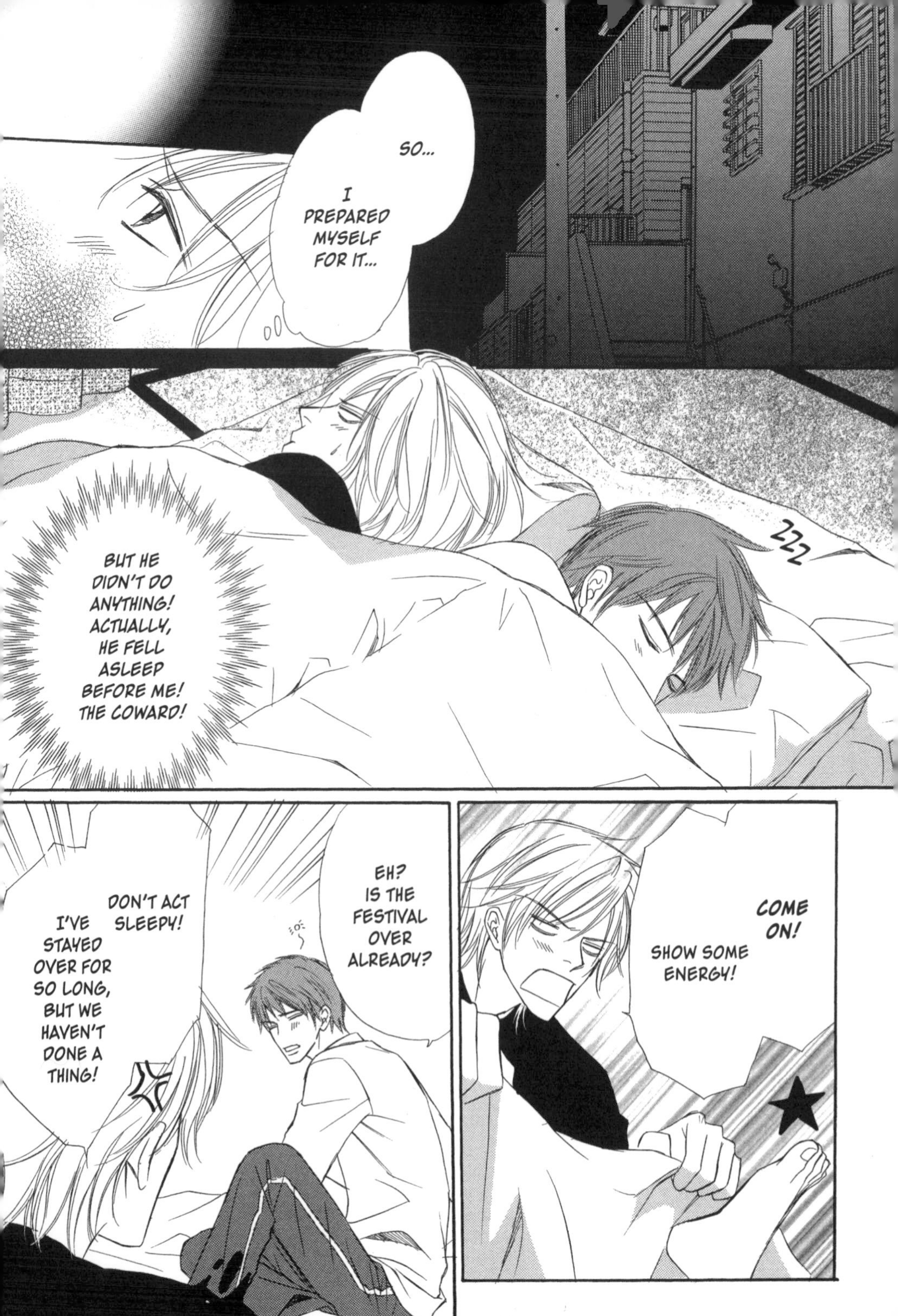
SO...
I PREPARED MYSELF FOR IT...
BUT HE DIDN'T DO ANYTHING! ACTUALLY, HE FELL ASLEEP BEFORE ME! THE COWARD!
ZZZ
COME ON!
SHOW SOME ENERGY!
EH? IS THE FESTIVAL OVER ALREADY?
DON'T ACT SLEEPY!
I'VE STAYED OVER FOR SO LONG, BUT WE HAVEN'T DONE A THING!

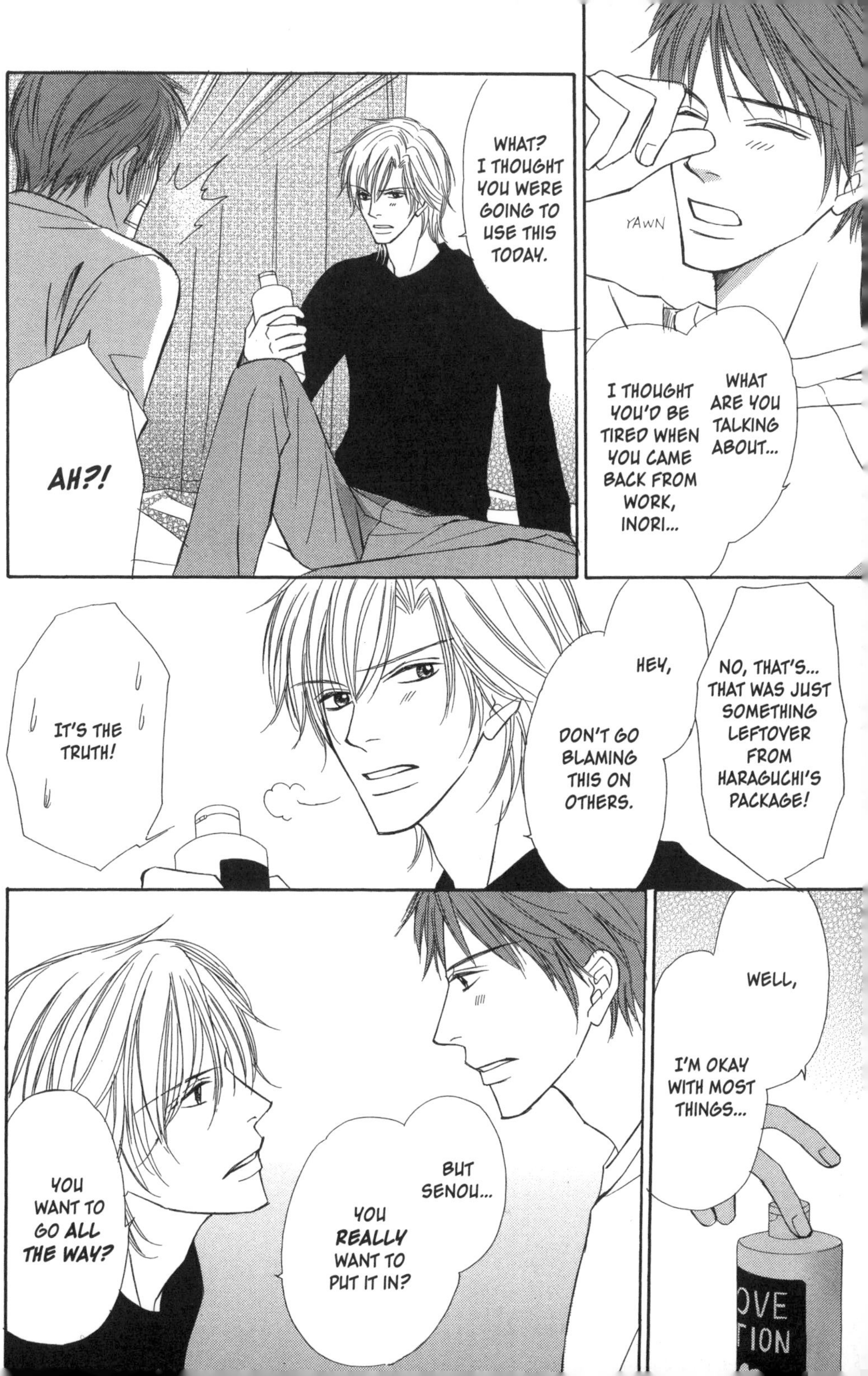
YAWN
WHAT ARE YOU TALKING ABOUT...
I THOUGHT YOU'D BE TIRED WHEN YOU CAME BACK FROM WORK, INORI...
WHAT? I THOUGHT YOU WERE GOING TO USE THIS TODAY.
AH?!
NO, THAT'S... THAT WAS JUST SOMETHING LEFTOVER FROM HARAGUCHI'S PACKAGE!
HEY, DON'T GO BLAMING THIS ON OTHERS.
IT'S THE TRUTH!
WELL, I'M OKAY WITH MOST THINGS...
BUT SENOU... YOU **REALLY** WANT TO PUT IT IN?
YOU WANT TO GO **ALL THE WAY?**

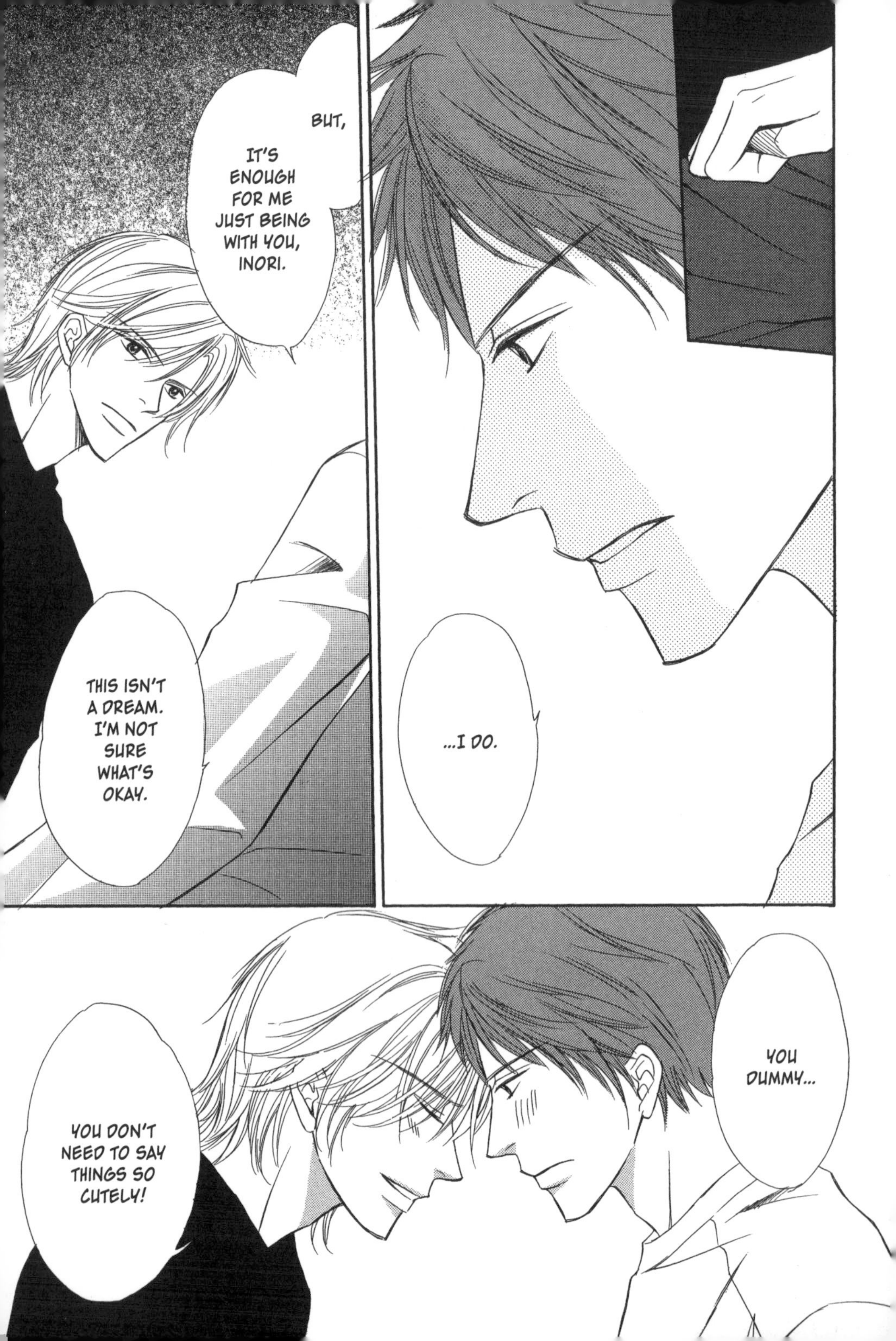
...I DO.
BUT,
IT'S ENOUGH FOR ME JUST BEING WITH YOU, INORI.
THIS ISN'T A DREAM. I'M NOT SURE WHAT'S OKAY.
YOU DUMMY...
YOU DON'T NEED TO SAY THINGS SO CUTELY!

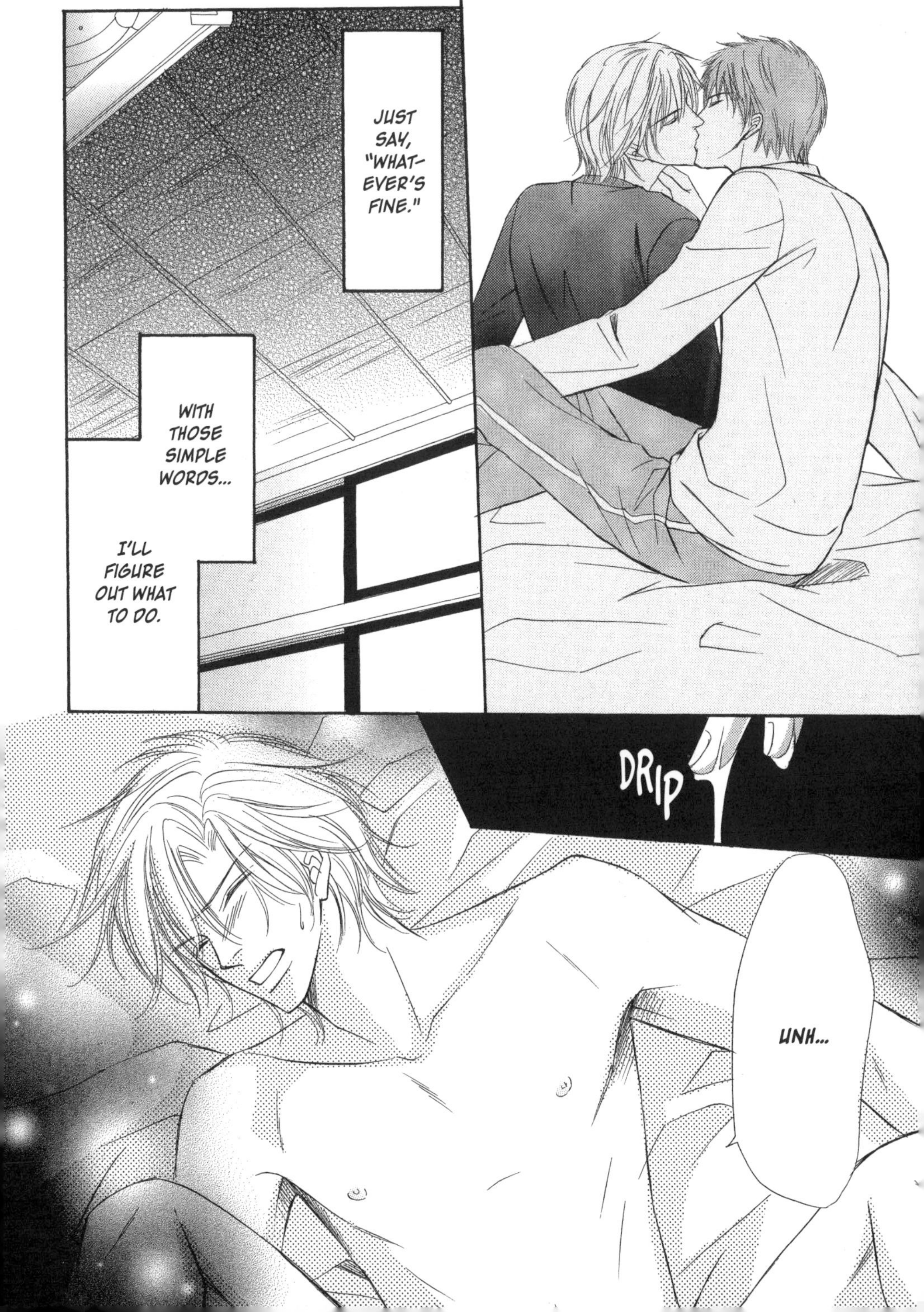
JUST SAY, "WHAT-EVER'S FINE."
WITH THOSE SIMPLE WORDS...
I'LL FIGURE OUT WHAT TO DO.
DRIP
UNH...

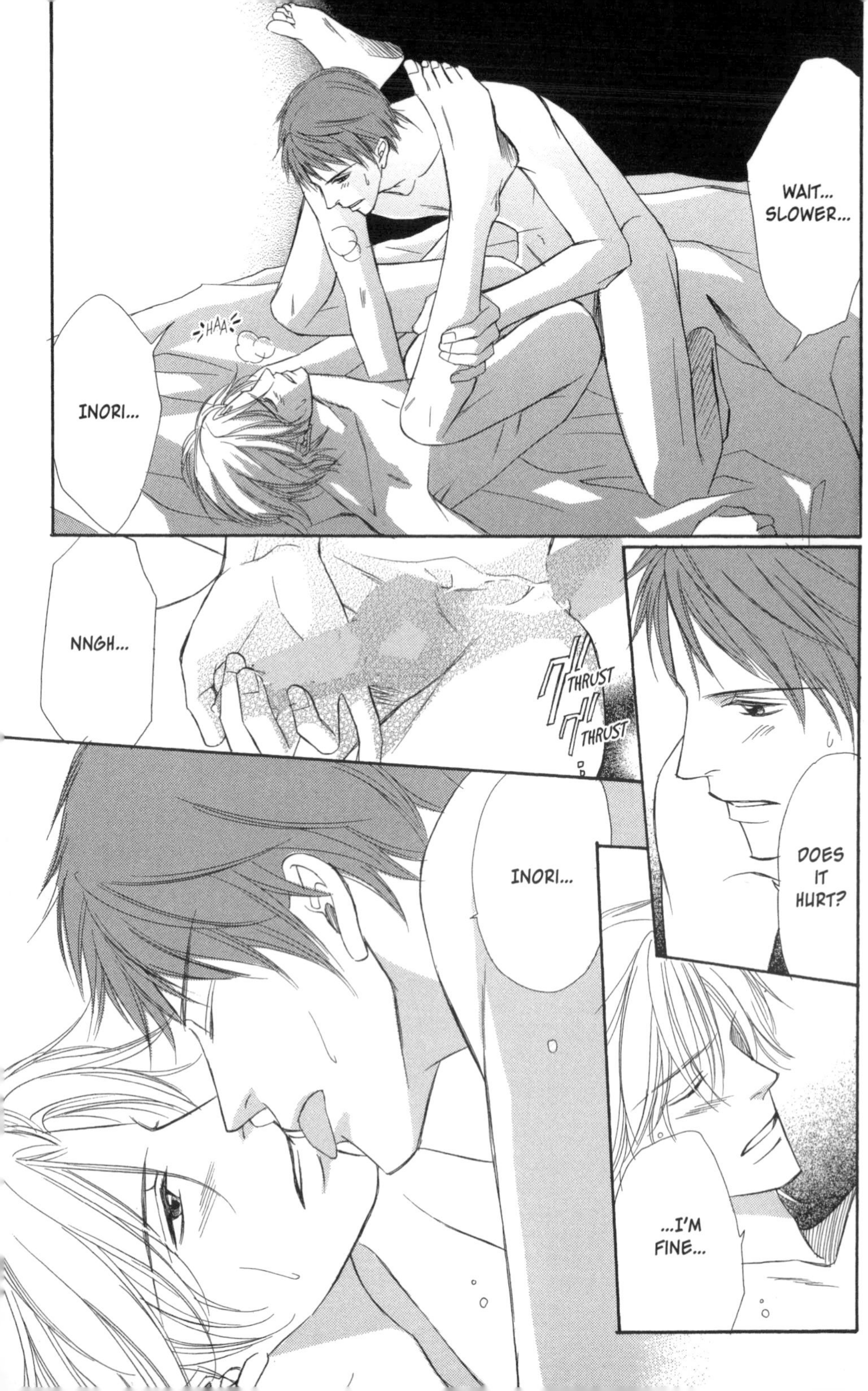
WAIT... SLOWER...
HAA
INORI...
DOES IT HURT?
NNGH...
THRUST
THRUST
INORI...
...I'M FINE...

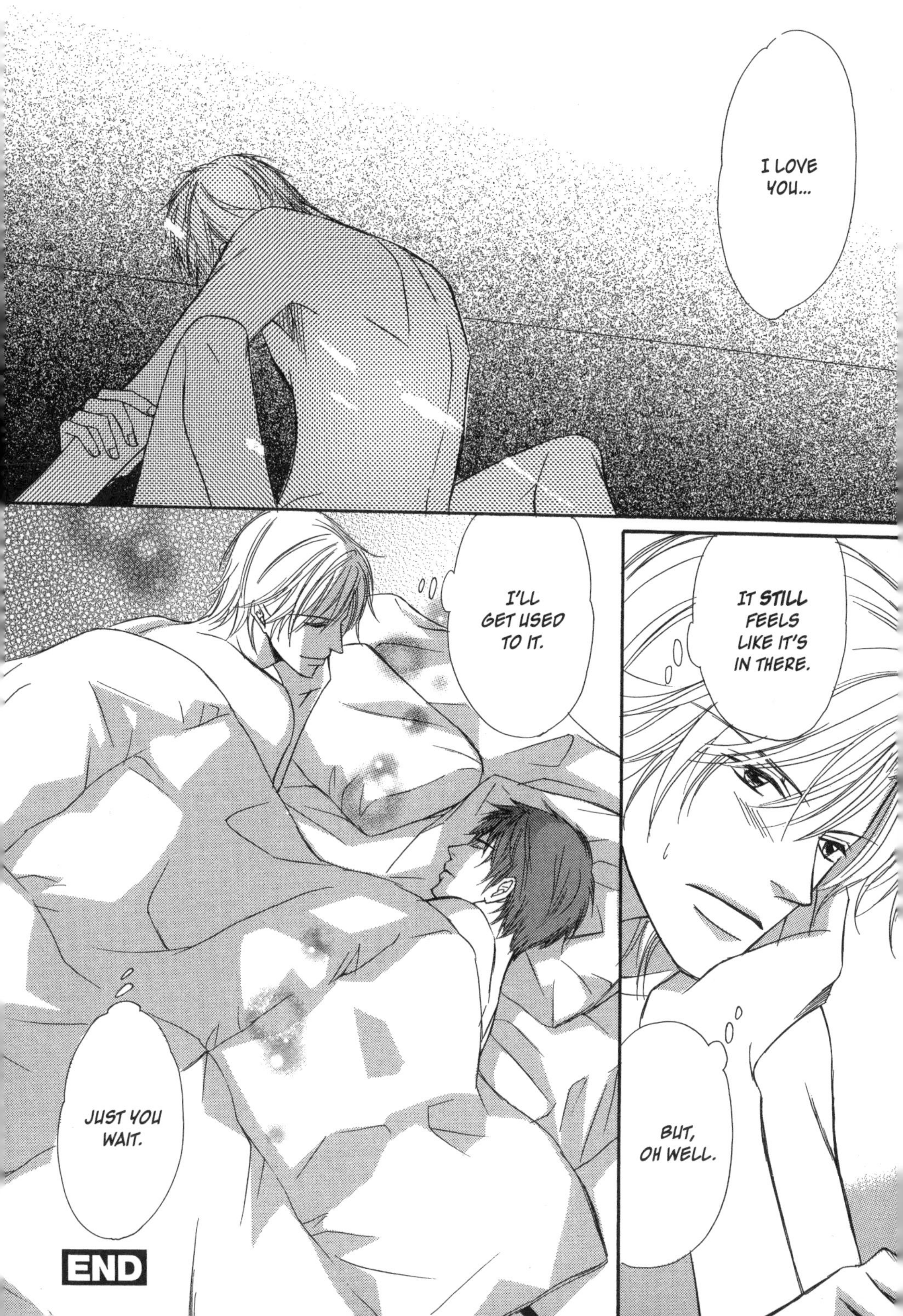
I LOVE YOU...
IT STILL FEELS LIKE IT'S IN THERE.
BUT, OH WELL.
I'LL GET USED TO IT.
JUST YOU WAIT.
END

EXTRA TIME PART 2

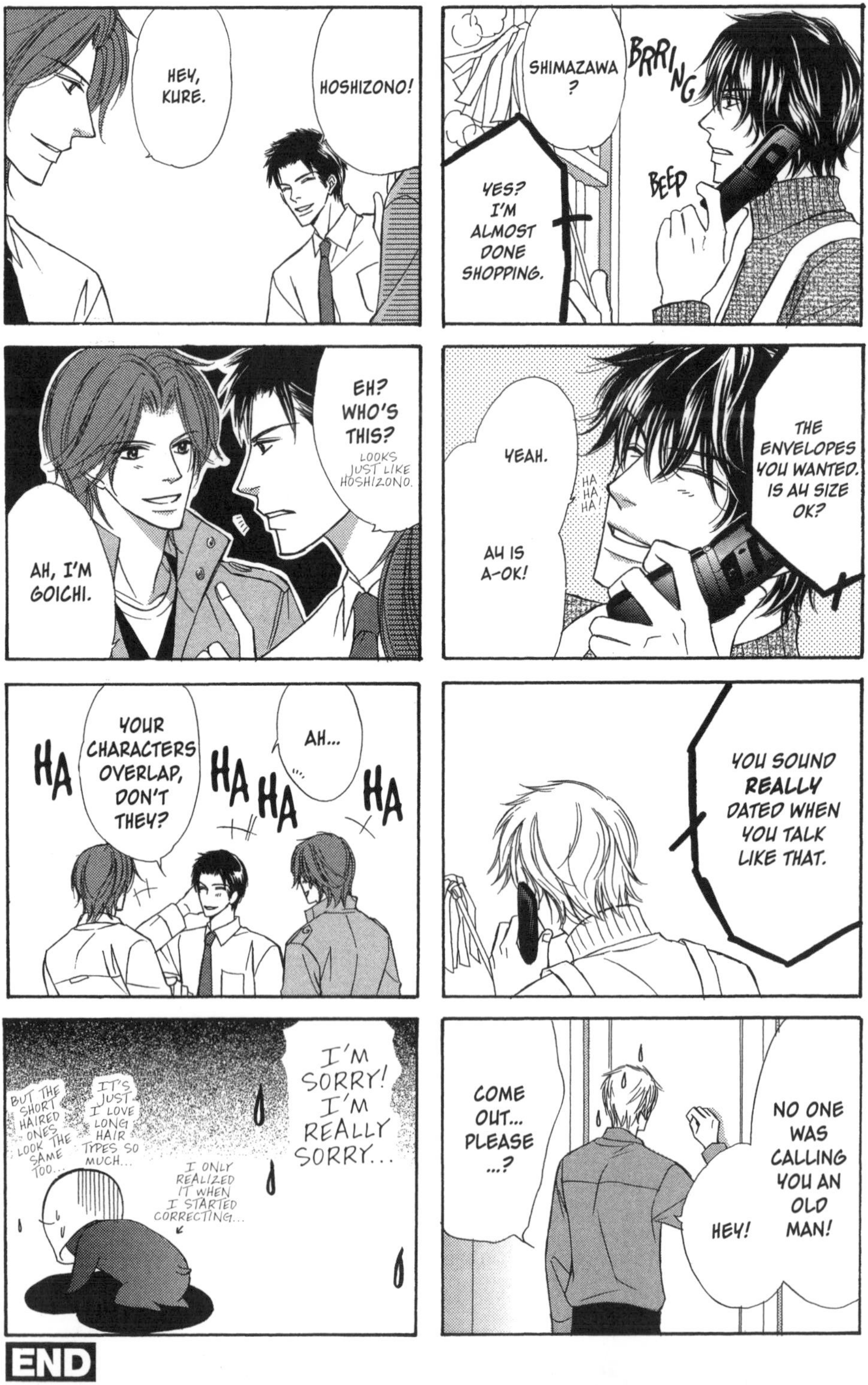
BRRRING
SHIMAZAWA ?
BEEP
YES? I'M ALMOST DONE SHOPPING.
THE ENVELOPES YOU WANTED. IS A4 SIZE OK?
YEAH.
HA HA HA!
A4 IS A-OK!
YOU SOUND REALLY DATED WHEN YOU TALK LIKE THAT.
NO ONE WAS CALLING YOU AN OLD MAN!
HEY!
COME OUT... PLEASE ...?
HOSHIZONO!
HEY, KURE.
EH? WHO'S THIS?
LOOKS JUST LIKE HOSHIZONO.
AH, I'M GOICHI.
HA
AH...
HA HA
YOUR CHARACTERS OVERLAP, DON'T THEY?
HA
I'M SORRY! I'M REALLY SORRY...
IT'S JUST I LOVE LONG HAIR TYPES SO MUCH...
BUT THE SHORT HAIRED ONES LOOK THE SAME TOO...
I ONLY REALIZED IT WHEN I STARTED CORRECTING...

END

AFTERWORD

GREAT JOB, EVERYBODY!

IN THIS LAST PART, I'D LIKE TO THANK MY EDITOR AND FRIENDS FOR ALL THEIR HELP AND EFFORT. AND ABOVE ALL, I SAY THANK YOU VERY, VERY MUCH TO ALL OF YOU WHO HAVE THIS BOOK IN YOUR HANDS AND READ IT.

I WILL DEFINITELY BE PUTTING OUT MORE WORKS SOON.

THE PICTURE YOU SEE AT THE END HERE BEARS NO CONNECTION TO THE BOOK WHATSOEVER. (THOUGH AT FIRST, I THOUGHT I'D BE DRAWING SOME S&M BONDAGE BETWEEN INORI AND SENOU).

THAT'S ALL...

RIE HONJYO

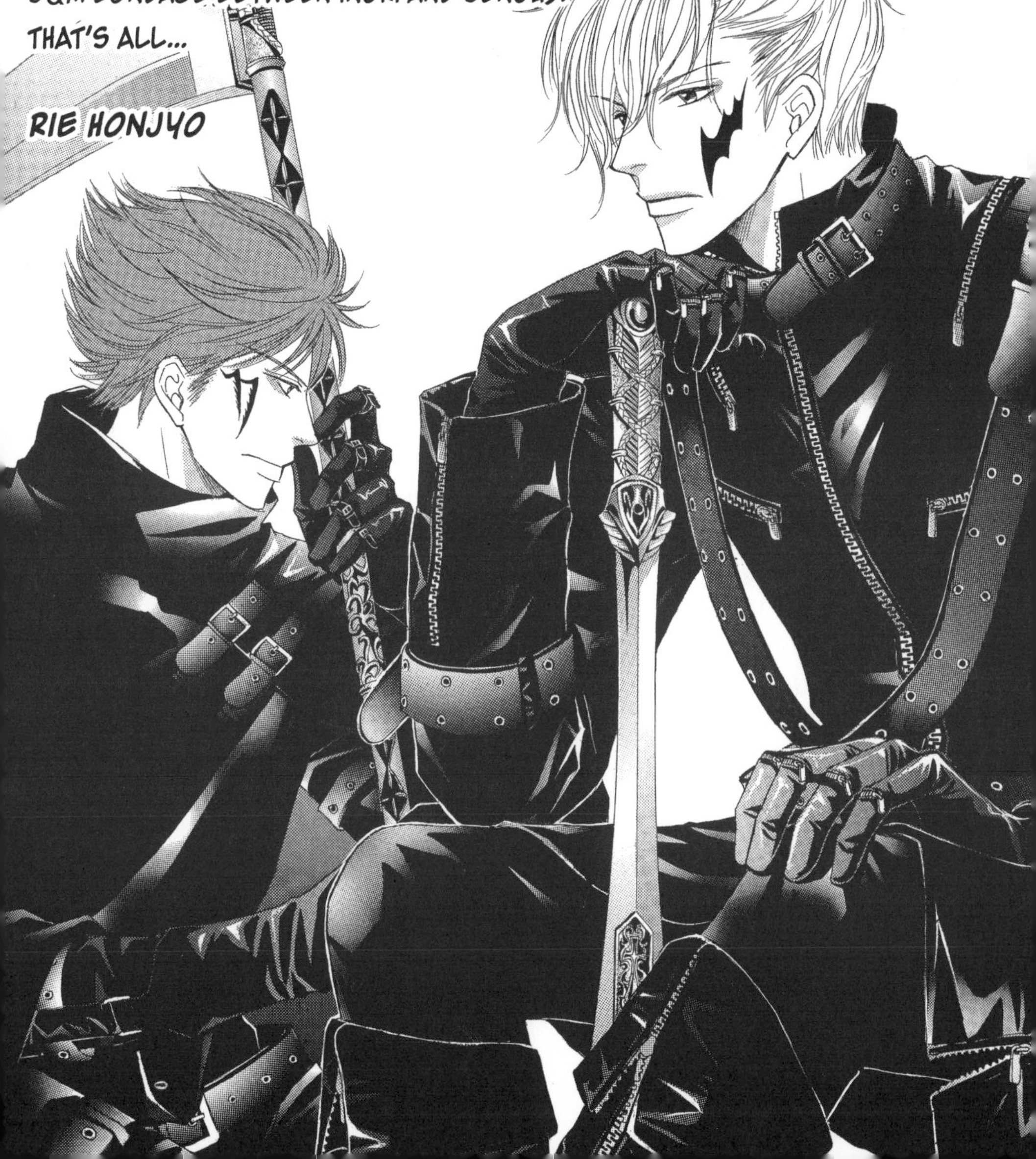

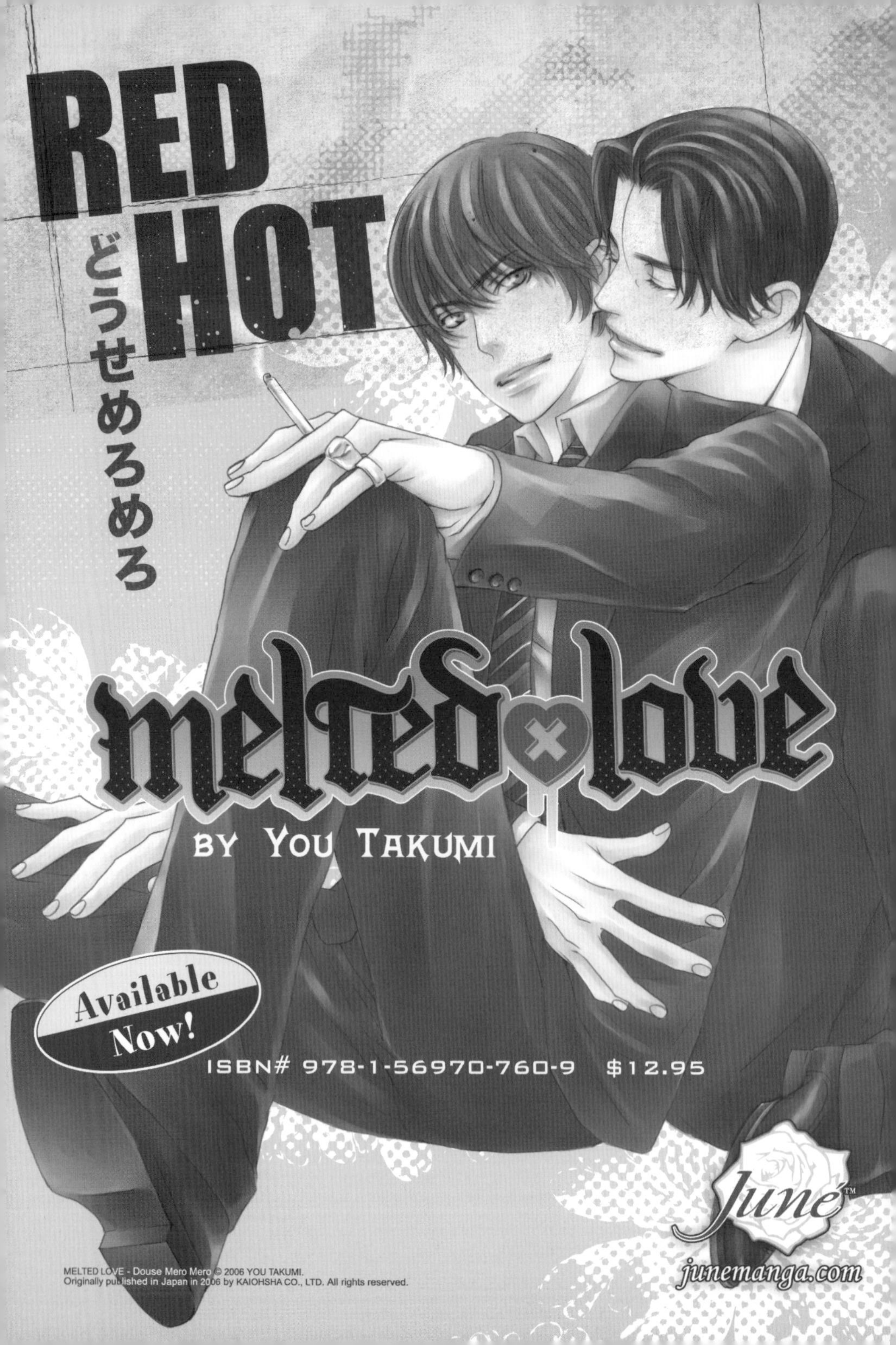
RED HOT
どうせめろめろ
melted×love
BY YOU TAKUMI
Available Now!
ISBN# 978-1-56970-760-9 $12.95
Juné™
junemanga.com
MELTED LOVE - Douse Mero Mero © 2006 YOU TAKUMI.
Originally published in Japan in 2006 by KAIOHSHA CO., LTD. All rights reserved.

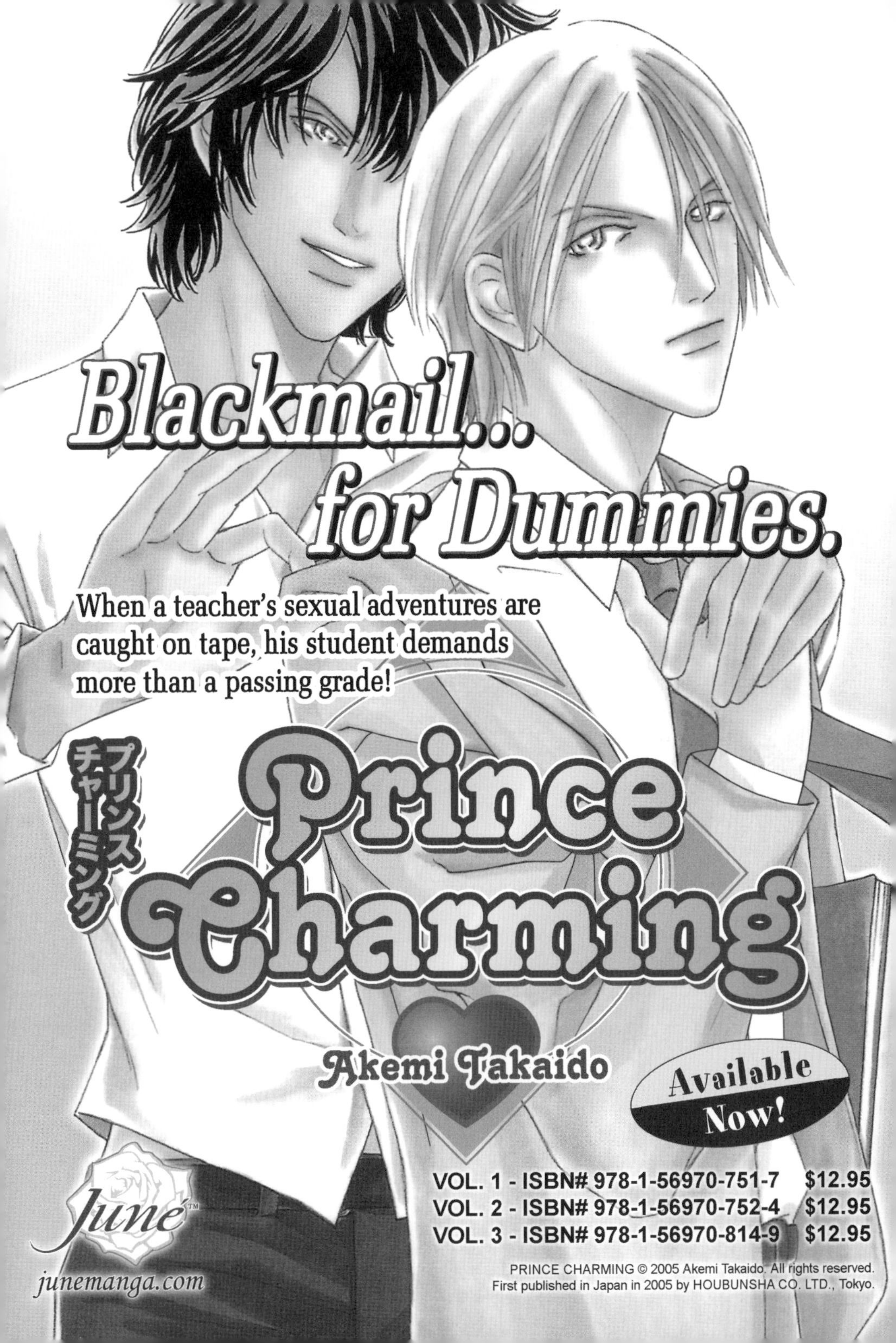
Blackmail... for Dummies.
When a teacher's sexual adventures are caught on tape, his student demands more than a passing grade!
プリンスチャーミング
Prince Charming
Akemi Takaido
Available Now!
VOL. 1 - ISBN# 978-1-56970-751-7 $12.95
VOL. 2 - ISBN# 978-1-56970-752-4 $12.95
VOL. 3 - ISBN# 978-1-56970-814-9 $12.95
PRINCE CHARMING © 2005 Akemi Takaido. All rights reserved.
First published in Japan in 2005 by HOUBUNSHA CO. LTD., Tokyo.
June™
junemanga.com

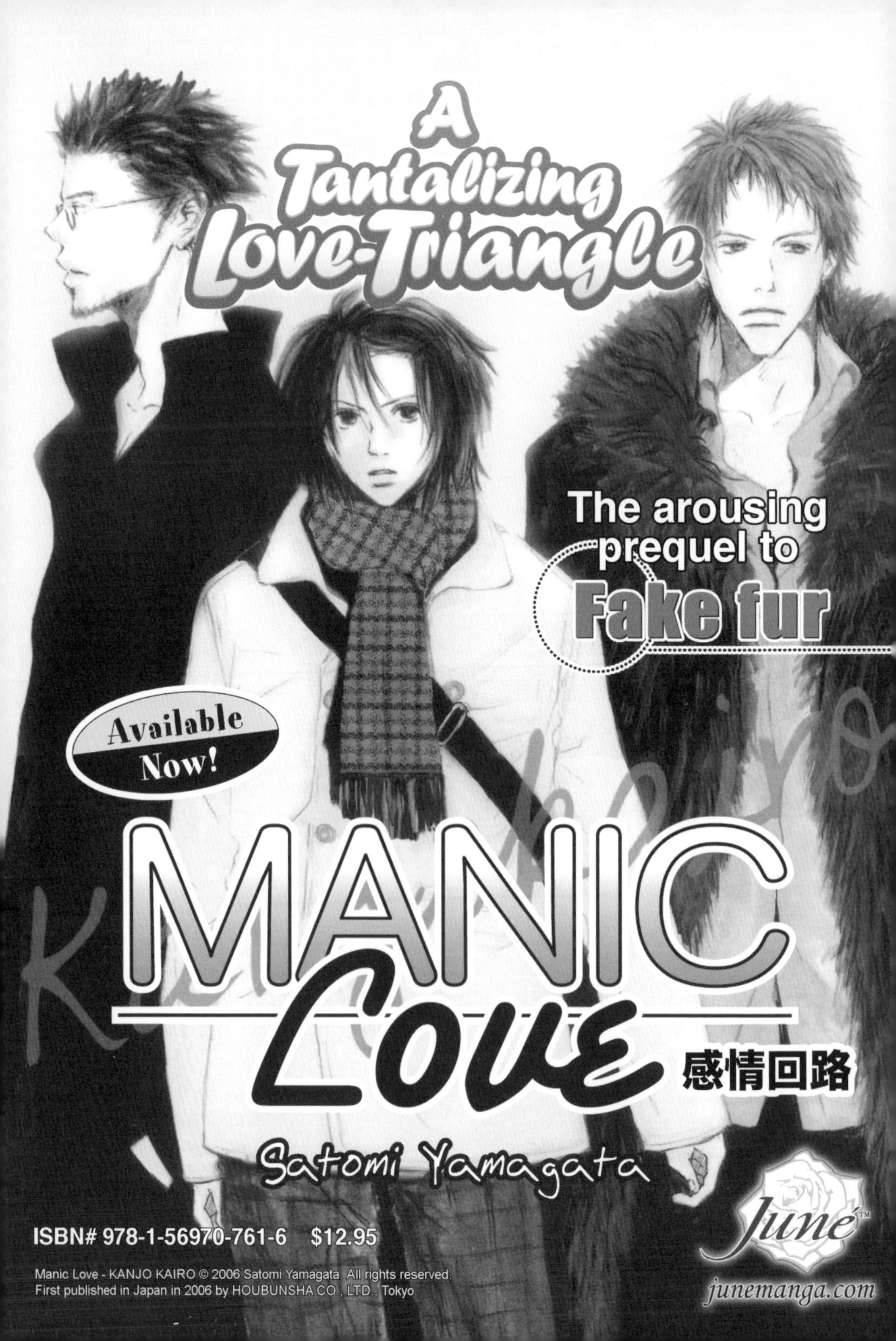
A Tantalizing Love-Triangle
The arousing prequel to Fake fur
Available Now!
MANIC Love
感情回路
Satomi Yamagata
ISBN# 978-1-56970-761-6 $12.95
Manic Love - KANJO KAIRO © 2006 Satomi Yamagata. All rights reserved.
First published in Japan in 2006 by HOUBUNSHA CO., LTD., Tokyo.
Juné™
junemanga.com

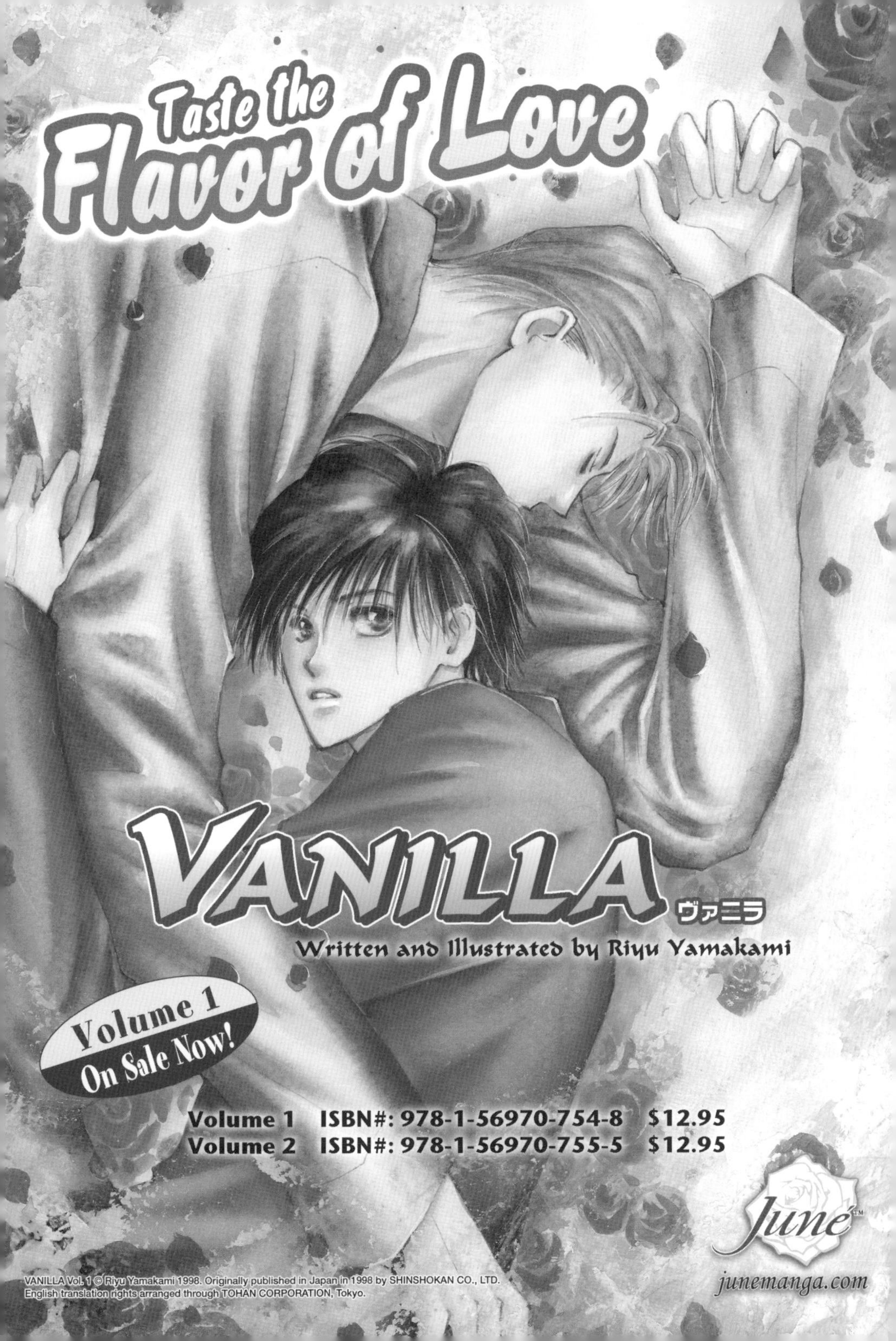
Taste the
Flavor of Love
VANILLA
ヴァニラ
Written and Illustrated by Riyu Yamakami
Volume 1
On Sale Now!
Volume 1 ISBN#: 978-1-56970-754-8 $12.95
Volume 2 ISBN#: 978-1-56970-755-5 $12.95
June™
junemanga.com
VANILLA Vol. 1 © Riyu Yamakami 1998. Originally published in Japan in 1998 by SHINSHOKAN CO., LTD.
English translation rights arranged through TOHAN CORPORATION, Tokyo.

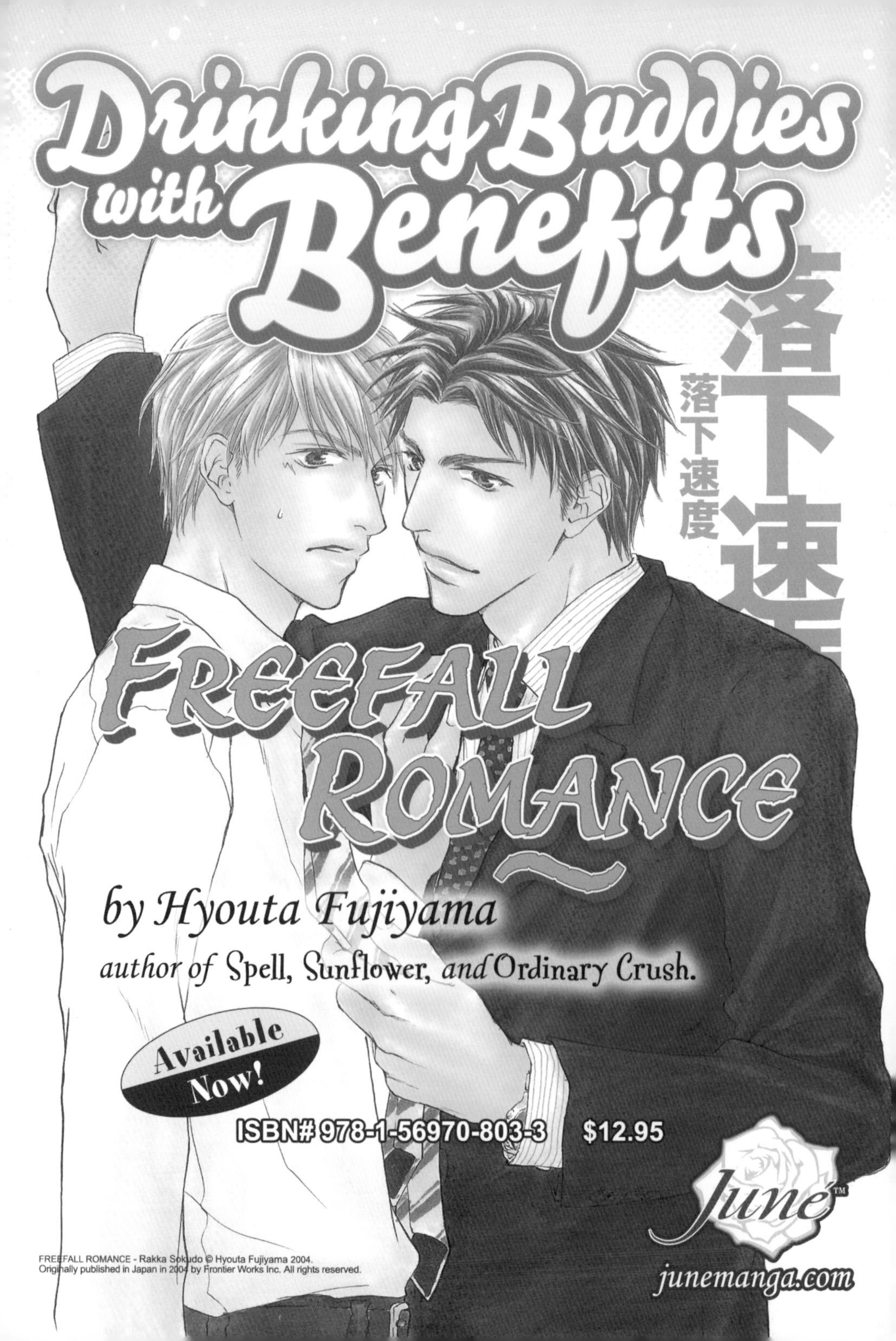
Drinking Buddies with Benefits
落下速度
落下速度
FREEFALL ROMANCE
by Hyouta Fujiyama
author of Spell, Sunflower, and Ordinary Crush.
Available Now!
ISBN# 978-1-56970-803-3 $12.95
Juné™
junemanga.com
FREEFALL ROMANCE - Rakka Sokudo © Hyouta Fujiyama 2004.
Originally published in Japan in 2004 by Frontier Works Inc. All rights reserved.

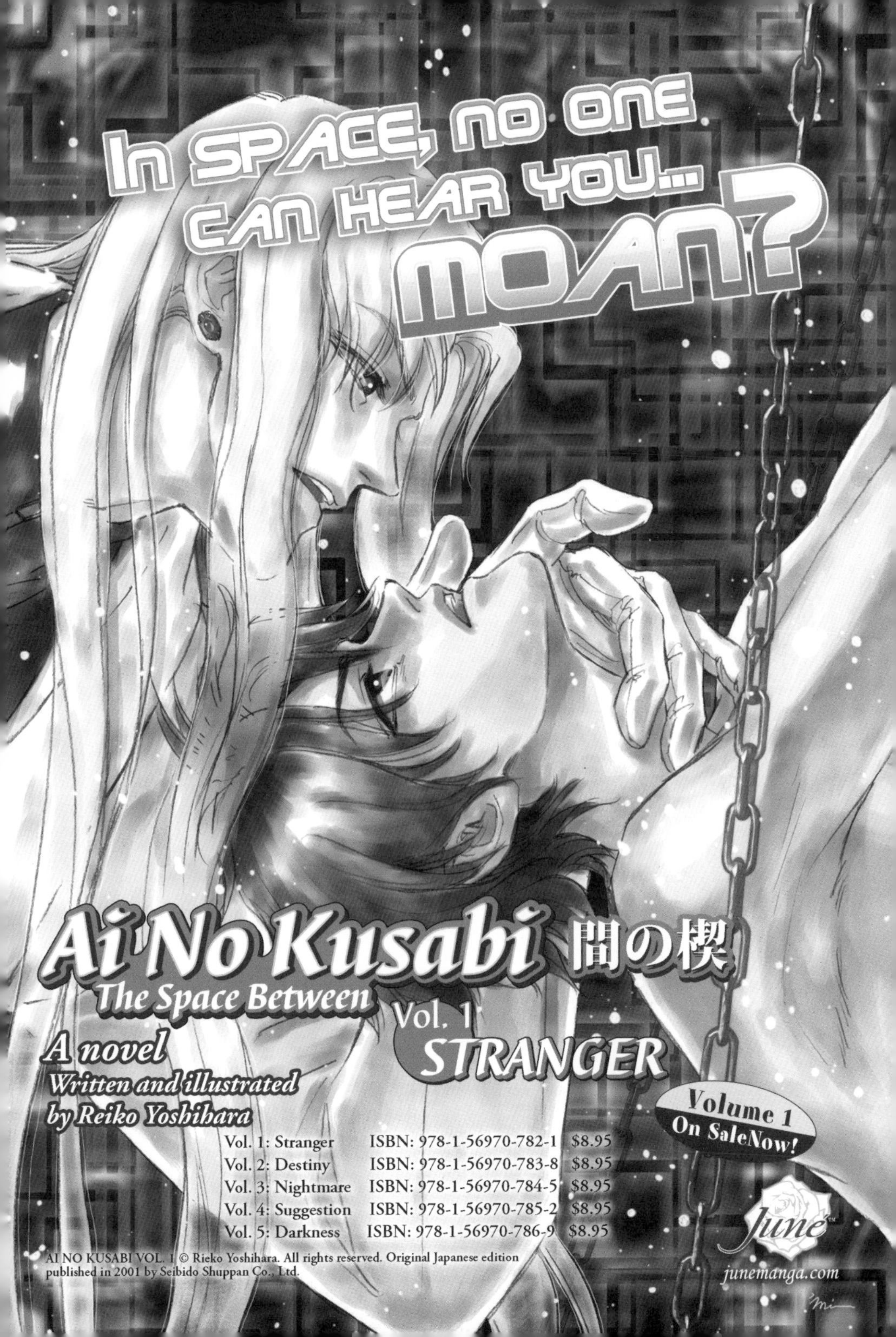
In SPACE, no one
can hear you...
MOAN?
Ai No Kusabi 間の楔
The Space Between
Vol. 1
STRANGER
A novel
Written and illustrated
by Reiko Yoshihara
Volume 1
On SaleNow!
Vol. 1: Stranger ISBN: 978-1-56970-782-1 $8.95
Vol. 2: Destiny ISBN: 978-1-56970-783-8 $8.95
Vol. 3: Nightmare ISBN: 978-1-56970-784-5 $8.95
Vol. 4: Suggestion ISBN: 978-1-56970-785-2 $8.95
Vol. 5: Darkness ISBN: 978-1-56970-786-9 $8.95
June
junemanga.com
AI NO KUSABI VOL. 1 © Rieko Yoshihara. All rights reserved. Original Japanese edition
published in 2001 by Seibido Shuppan Co., Ltd.

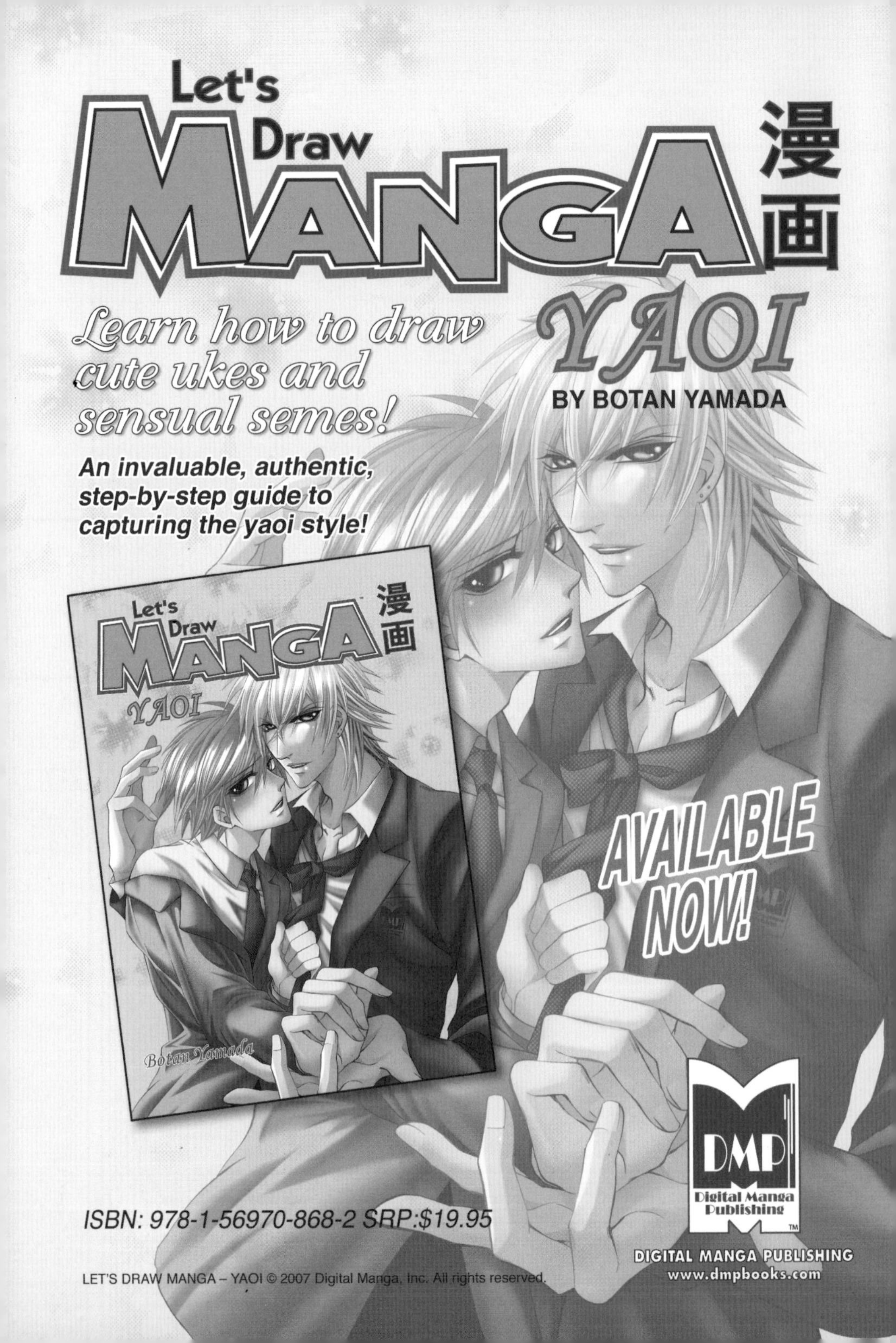
Let's Draw MANGA 漫画
YAOI
BY BOTAN YAMADA
Learn how to draw cute ukes and sensual semes!
An invaluable, authentic, step-by-step guide to capturing the yaoi style!
Let's Draw MANGA 漫画
YAOI
Botan Yamada
AVAILABLE NOW!
DMP
Digital Manga Publishing
ISBN: 978-1-56970-868-2 SRP:$19.95
DIGITAL MANGA PUBLISHING
www.dmpbooks.com
LET'S DRAW MANGA – YAOI © 2007 Digital Manga, Inc. All rights reserved.

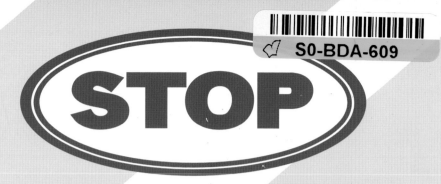

STOP

This is the back of the book!
Start from the other side.

NATIVE MANGA readers read manga from *right to left*.

1
1
2
2
3
3
4
4
5
5
6
6
7
8

If you run into our ***Native Manga*** *logo on any of our books... you'll know that this manga is published in it's true original native Japanese right to left reading format, as it was intended. Turn to the other side of the book and start reading from right to left, top to bottom.*

Follow the diagram to see how its done.
Surf's Up!

NATIVE MANGA
READ RIGHT TO LEFT

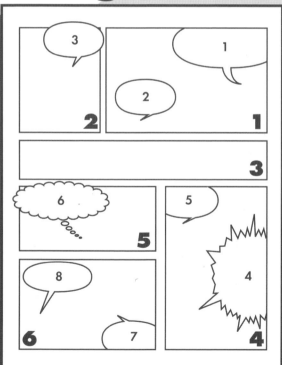

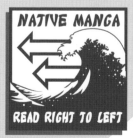